COMPLETE

MISSION

PRAISE

C O M P L E T E

MISSION

PRAISE

Compiled by
Peter Horrobin and Greg Leavers

WORDS EDITION

HarperCollins*Publishers*

HarperCollins*Publishers*
77–85 Fulham Palace Road, London W6 8JB
www.christian-publishing.com

First published in Great Britain in 1999 by Marshall Pickering

10 9 8 7 6

A catalogue record for this book is available from the British Library.

ISBN 0 551 04027 0

Music edition ISBN 0 551 04028 9
Easy-to-Read Words edition ISBN 0 551 04029 7
Large Print Words edition ISBN 0 551 04038 6

Text set by Barnes Music Engraving Ltd, East Sussex, England
Printed and bound in Great Britain by The Bath Press, Bath

PREFACE

Music has always been vital to the expression of Christian praise and worship, and a dynamic church will constantly find new ways of expressing Christian truth in hymns and songs. From the time of the psalmists to the present day, every age has left behind a heritage of words and music with which to bless succeeding generations.

The extraordinary success of *Mission Praise* owes much to its strategy of combining the best of the old with the best of the new. The old and the new together provide a rich tapestry of musical expression with which to enter the new millennium.

Mission Praise was first compiled for Mission England in 1984, but its wider potential was soon recognised by its users and in its expanded form it has been adopted in churches of many denominations, and in many countries, as one of the most popular and comprehensive hymn and song books there has ever been. As such, it has followed the pattern of Sankey's famous hymn book of a century earlier, born for the missions conducted by Moody and used by the church for at least a generation.

This latest edition of *Mission Praise*, now containing over a thousand items, includes every item that has appeared in former editions and also embraces many new songs (and new versions of older hymns) appearing in the collection for the first time.

The vision for *Mission Praise* has now extended far beyond our original expectations and we give thanks to God for the privilege of having been able to share with the publishers in compiling a new edition for the new millennium. Our prayer for this edition remains that God will use the hymns and songs in this volume to bring people into His presence through praise and worship and to enable them to express their relationship with Him through words and music. We pray that all who use this book will share in the rich blessings that come through giving their praise and worship to the living God.

Peter Horrobin and Greg Leavers

"Let us praise God's glory"

Ephesians 1:12

1
From John 13
© Roy Crabtree

A new commandment I give unto you,
that you love one another
    as I have loved you,
that you love one another
    as I have loved you.

By this shall all men know
    that you are My disciples,
if you have love one for another.
By this shall all men know
    that you are My disciples,
if you have love one for another.

2
Martin Luther (1483–1546)
tr. Thomas Carlyle (1795–1881)

1 **A safe stronghold our God is still,**
    a trusty shield and weapon;
    He'll help us clear from all the ill
    that has us now o'ertaken.
    The ancient prince of hell
    has risen with purpose fell;
    strong mail of craft and power
    he weareth in this hour;
    on earth is not his fellow.

2 With force of arms we nothing can,
    full soon were we down-ridden;
    but for us fights the proper Man
    whom God Himself has bidden.
    Ask ye: Who is this same?
    Christ Jesus is His name,
    the Lord Sabaoth's Son;
    He, and no other one,
    shall conquer in the battle.

3 And were this world all devils o'er,
    and watching to devour us,
    we lay it not to heart so sore;
    not they can overpower us.
    And let the prince of ill
    look grim as e'er he will,
    he harms us not a whit;
    for why? his doom is writ;
    a word shall quickly slay him.

4 God's word,
    for all their craft and force,
    one moment will not linger,
    but, spite of hell, shall have its course;
    'tis written by His finger.
    And though they take our life,
    goods, honour, children, wife,
    yet is their profit small;
    these things shall vanish all,
    the city of God remaineth.

3
Dave Bilbrough
© 1977 Kingsway's Thankyou Music

Abba Father, let me be
Yours and Yours alone.
May my will for ever be
evermore Your own.
Never let my heart grow cold,
never let me go,
Abba Father, let me be
Yours and Yours alone.

4
Henry Francis Lyte (1793–1847)

1 **Abide with me;**
    fast falls the eventide;
    the darkness deepens;
        Lord, with me abide;
    when other helpers fail,
        and comforts flee,
    help of the helpless, O abide with me.

2   Swift to its close
      ebbs out life's little day;
  earth's joys grown dim,
      its glories pass away;
  change and decay in all around I see:
  O Thou who changest not,
      abide with me!

3   I need Thy presence
      every passing hour;
  what but Thy grace
      can foil the tempter's power?
  Who like Thyself
      my guide and stay can be?
  Through cloud and sunshine,
      O abide with me.

4   I fear no foe
      with Thee at hand to bless;
  ills have no weight,
      and tears no bitterness.
  Where is death's sting?
      where, grave, thy victory?
  I triumph still, if Thou abide with me.

5   Hold Thou Thy cross
      before my closing eyes,
  shine through the gloom,
      and point me to the skies;
  heaven's morning breaks,
      and earth's vain shadows flee:
  in life, in death,
      O Lord, abide with me!

5   © Timothy Dudley-Smith

1 **Above the voices of the world
      around me,**
  my hopes and dreams,
      my cares and loves and fears,
  the long-awaited call of Christ
      has found me,
  the voice of Jesus echoes in my ears:
  'I gave My life to break the cords
      that bind you,
  I rose from death to set your spirit free;

turn from your sins
      and put the past behind you,
take up your cross
      and come and follow Me.'

2   What can I offer Him
      who calls me to Him?
  Only the wastes of sin and self
      and shame;
  a mind confused,
      a heart that never knew Him,
  a tongue unskilled
      at naming Jesus' name.
  Yet at Your call,
      and hungry for Your blessing,
  drawn by that cross
      which moves a heart of stone,
  now Lord I come,
      my tale of sin confessing,
  and in repentance turn to You alone.

3   Lord, I believe;
      help now my unbelieving;
  I come in faith
      because Your promise stands;
  Your word of pardon
      and of peace receiving,
  all that I am I place within Your hands.
  Let me become what You shall choose
      to make me,
  freed from the guilt and burden
      of my sins.
  Jesus is mine,
      who never shall forsake me,
  and in His love
      my new-born life begins.

6   © 1996 Kay Chance

Ah, Lord God,
Thou hast made the heavens and the earth
by Thy great power.
Ah, Lord God,
Thou hast made the heavens and the earth
by Thine outstretched arm.

Nothing is too difficult for Thee,
nothing is too difficult for Thee,
O great and mighty God;
great in counsel and mighty in deed,
nothing, nothing, absolutely nothing,
nothing is too difficult for Thee.

7 St Francis of Assisi (1182–1226)
tr. William Henry Draper (1855–1933)
reprinted by permission of J Curwen & Sons Ltd

1 **All creatures of our God and King,**
lift up your voice and with us sing:
hallelujah, hallelujah!
Thou burning sun with golden beam,
thou silver moon with softer gleam:
O praise Him, O praise Him,
hallelujah, hallelujah, hallelujah!

2 Thou rushing wind that art so strong,
ye clouds that sail in heaven along,
O praise Him, hallelujah!
Thou rising morn, in praise rejoice,
ye lights of evening, find a voice:
O praise Him ...

3 Thou flowing water, pure and clear,
make music for thy Lord to hear,
hallelujah, hallelujah!
Thou fire so masterful and bright,
that givest man both warmth and light:
O praise Him ...

4 And all ye men of tender heart,
forgiving others, take your part,
O sing ye, hallelujah!
Ye who long pain and sorrow bear,
praise God and on Him cast your care:
O praise Him ...

5 Let all things their Creator bless,
and worship Him in humbleness,
O praise Him, hallelujah!
Praise, praise the Father,
praise the Son,
and praise the Spirit, Three-in-One:
O praise Him ...

8 John Daniels and Phil Thomson
© 1986 HarperCollins*Religious*/CopyCare

1 **All earth was dark until You spoke,**
then all was light and all was peace.
Yet still, O God, so many wait,
to see the flame of love released.
Lights to the world, O Light of man,
kindle in us a mighty flame,
till every heart, consumed by love,
shall rise to praise Your holy name.

2 In Christ You gave Your gift of life
to save us from the depth of night.
O come and set our spirits free,
and draw us to Your perfect light.
Lights to the world ...

3 Where there is fear, may we bring joy,
and healing to a world in pain.
Lord, build Your kingdom
through our lives,
till Jesus walks this earth again.
Lights to the world ...

4 O burn in us, that we may burn
with love that triumphs in despair;
and touch our lives with such a fire,
that souls may search
and find You there.
Lights to the world ...

9 Theodulph of Orleans (c750–821)
tr. John Mason Neale (1818–66)

1 **All glory, laud and honour**
to Thee, Redeemer, King,
to whom the lips of children
made sweet hosannas ring.
Thou art the King of Israel,
Thou David's royal Son,
who in the Lord's name comest,
the King and blessèd one.

2 The company of angels
   are praising Thee on high,
   and mortal men and all things
   created make reply.
   The people of the Hebrews
   with psalms before Thee went;
   our praise and prayer and anthems
   before Thee we present.

3 To Thee before Thy passion
   they sang their hymns of praise;
   to Thee now high exalted
   our melody we raise.
   Thou didst accept their praises;
   accept the prayers we bring,
   who in all good delightest,
   Thou good and gracious King.

10 © 1986 Greg Leavers

All around me, Lord,
   I see Your goodness,
all creation sings Your praises,
all the world cries, 'God is love!'

11 Dave Moody
© 1981 Dayspring Music/Word Music/CopyCare

All hail King Jesus,
all hail Emmanuel;
King of kings,
Lord of lords, bright Morning Star,
every day You give me breath,
I'll sing Your praises
and I'll reign with You throughout eternity.

12 Dave Bilbrough
© 1987 Kingsway's Thankyou Music

All hail the Lamb enthroned on high,
His praise shall be our battle cry.
He reigns victorious, for ever glorious,
His name is Jesus, He is the Lord.

13 Edward Perronet (1726–92) and
John Rippon (1751–1836)

1 **All hail the power of Jesus' name!**
   let angels prostrate fall;
   bring forth the royal diadem,
   and crown Him Lord of all.

2 Crown Him, ye martyrs of our God,
   who from His altar call;
   extol the stem of Jesse's rod,
   and crown Him Lord of all.

3 Ye seed of Israel's chosen race,
   and ransomed from the fall,
   hail Him who saves you by His grace,
   and crown Him Lord of all.

4 Let every kindred, every tribe,
   on this terrestrial ball,
   to Him all majesty ascribe,
   and crown Him Lord of all.

5 O that with yonder sacred throng
   we at His feet may fall,
   join in the everlasting song,
   and crown Him Lord of all!

14 Noel and Tricia Richards
© 1987 Kingsway's Thankyou Music

1 **All heaven declares**
   the glory of the risen Lord;
   who can compare
   with the beauty of the Lord?
   For ever He will be
   the Lamb upon the throne;
   I gladly bow the knee,
   and worship Him alone.

2 I will proclaim
   the glory of the risen Lord,
   who once was slain
   to reconcile man to God.
   For ever You will be
   the Lamb upon the throne;
   I gladly bow the knee,
   and worship You alone.

15 Graham Kendrick and Chris Rolinson
© 1986 Kingsway's Thankyou Music

1 **All heaven waits with bated breath,**
for saints on earth to pray;
majestic angels ready stand
with swords of fiery blade.
Astounding power awaits a word
from God's resplendent throne;
but God awaits our prayer of faith
that cries, 'Your will be done.'

2 Awake, O Church, arise and pray,
complaining words discard;
the Spirit comes to fill your mouth
with truth, His mighty sword.
Go place your feet on Satan's ground,
and there proclaim Christ's name;
in step with heaven's armies march
to conquer and to reign!

WOMEN
3 Now in our hearts and on our lips
the word of faith is near;
let heaven's will on earth be done,
let heaven flow from here.
MEN
Come blend your prayers
with Jesus' own,
before the Father's throne;
and as the incense clouds ascend,
God's holy fire rains down.

4 Soon comes the day when,
with a shout,
King Jesus shall appear;
and with Him all the Church
from every age shall fill the air.
The brightness of His coming shall
consume the lawless one;
as with a word the breath of God
tears down his rebel throne.

5 One body here by heaven inspired,
we seek prophetic power;
in Christ agreed one heart and voice
to speak this day, this hour.

In every place where chaos rules,
and evil forces brood,
let Jesus' voice speak like the roar
of a great multitude.

16 after Joachim Neander (1650–80)
Robert Bridges (1844–1930)
by permission of Oxford University Press

1 **All my hope on God is founded,**
all my trust He shall renew;
He, my guide through changing order,
only good and only true.
God unknown,
He alone
calls my heart to be His own.

2 Pride of man and earthly glory,
sword and crown betray His trust;
all that human toil can fashion,
tower and temple, fall to dust.
But God's power,
hour by hour,
is my temple and my tower.

3 Day by day our mighty giver
grants to us His gifts of love;
in His will our souls find pleasure,
leading to our home above.
Love shall stand
at His hand,
joy shall wait for His command.

4 Still from man to God eternal
sacrifice of praise be done,
high above all praises praising
for the gift of Christ His Son.
Hear Christ's call
one and all:
we who follow shall not fall.

17 Andy and Becky Silver
© 1987 Andy Silver

All my life, Lord, to You I want to give;
this is my worship,
please show me how to live.
Take every part of me, make it Your own,
me on the cross, Lord, You on the throne.

18

Roy Turner
© 1984 Kingsway's Thankyou Music

1 **All over the world
   the Spirit is moving,**
   all over the world
       as the prophet said it would be;
   all over the world
       there's a mighty revelation
   of the glory of the Lord,
       as the waters cover the sea.

2 All over His Church
   God's Spirit is moving,
   all over His Church
       as the prophet said it would be;
   all over His Church
       there's a mighty revelation
   of the glory of the Lord,
       as the waters cover the sea.

3 Right here in this place
   the Spirit is moving,
   right here in this place
       as the prophet said it would be;
   right here in this place
       there's a mighty revelation
   of the glory of the Lord,
       as the waters cover the sea.

19

Charles Wesley (1707–88)

1 **All praise to our redeeming Lord,**
   who joins us by His grace,
   and bids us, each to each restored,
   together seek His face.

2 He bids us build each other up;
   and, gathered into one,
   to our high calling's glorious hope
   we hand in hand go on.

3 The gift which He on one bestows,
   we all delight to prove;
   the grace through every vessel flows,
   in purest streams of love.

4 Ev'n now we think and speak the same,
   and cordially agree;
   concentred all, through Jesu's name,
   in perfect harmony.

5 We all partake the joy of one,
   the common peace we feel,
   a peace to sensual minds unknown,
   a joy unspeakable.

6 And if our fellowship below
   in Jesus be so sweet,
   what heights of rapture shall we know
   when round His throne we meet!

20

William Kethe (1520–94)

1 **All people that on earth do dwell,**
   sing to the Lord with cheerful voice;
   Him serve with mirth,
       His praise forth tell;
   come ye before Him and rejoice.

2 The Lord, ye know, is God indeed:
   without our aid He did us make:
   we are His folk, He doth us feed;
   and for His sheep He doth us take.

3 O enter then His gates with praise,
   approach with joy His courts unto;
   praise, laud, and bless
       His name always,
   for it is seemly so to do.

4 For why? The Lord our God is good;
   His mercy is for ever sure;
   His truth at all times firmly stood,
   and shall from age to age endure.

21

Jan Harrington
© 1975 Celebration/Kingsway's Thankyou Music

All the riches of His grace,
all the fulness of His blessings,
all the sweetness of His love
He gives to you, He gives to me.

1 O the blood of Jesus, (*3 times*)
it washes white as snow.
All the riches . . .

2 O the word of Jesus, (*3 times*)
it cleanses white as snow.
All the riches . . .

3 O the love of Jesus, (*3 times*)
it makes His body whole.
All the riches . . .

4 O the blood of Jesus, (*3 times*)
it washes white as snow.
All the riches . . .

22 Frances van Alstyne (1820 –1915)
(Fanny J Crosby)

1 **All the way my Saviour leads me;**
what have I to ask beside?
Can I doubt His tender mercy,
who through life has been my guide?
Heavenly peace, divinest comfort,
here by faith in Him to dwell!
For I know whate'er befall me,
Jesus doeth all things well.

2 All the way my Saviour leads me,
cheers each winding path I tread,
gives me grace for every trial,
feeds me with the living bread.
Though my weary steps may falter,
and my soul a-thirst may be,
gushing from the rock before me,
Lo! a spring of joy I see.

3 All the way my Saviour leads me,
O the fulness of His love!
Perfect rest to me is promised
in my Father's house above.
When my spirit, clothed, immortal,
wings its flight to realms of day,
this, my song through endless ages:
Jesus led me all the way!

23 Cecil Frances Alexander (1818–95)

All things bright and beautiful,
all creatures great and small,
all things wise and wonderful,
the Lord God made them all.

1 Each little flower that opens,
each little bird that sings,
He made their glowing colours,
He made their tiny wings.
All things bright . . .

2 The purple-headed mountain,
the river running by,
the sunset, and the morning
that brightens up the sky;
All things bright . . .

3 The cold wind in the winter,
the pleasant summer sun,
the ripe fruits in the garden,
He made them every one.
All things bright . . .

4 He gave us eyes to see them,
and lips that we might tell
how great is God almighty,
who has made all things well.
All things bright . . .

24 George William Conder (1821–74)

1 **All things praise Thee,**
Lord most high,
heaven and earth and sea and sky,
all were for Thy glory made,
that Thy greatness, thus displayed,
should all worship bring to Thee;
all things praise Thee: Lord, may we.

2 All things praise Thee: night to night
  sings in silent hymns of light;
  all things praise Thee: day to day
  chants Thy power in burning ray;
  time and space are praising Thee;
  all things praise Thee: Lord, may we.

3 All things praise Thee, high and low,
  rain and dew, and seven-hued bow,
  crimson sunset, fleecy cloud,
  rippling stream, and tempest loud,
  summer, winter – all to Thee
  glory render: Lord, may we.

4 All things praise Thee,
      heaven's high shrine
  rings with melody divine;
  lowly bending at Thy feet,
  seraph and archangel meet;
  this their highest bliss, to be
  ever praising: Lord, may we.

5 All things praise Thee, gracious Lord,
  great Creator, powerful Word,
  omnipresent Spirit, now
  at Thy feet we humbly bow,
  lift our hearts in praise to Thee;
  all things praise Thee: Lord, may we.

25 Judson W Van de Venter (1855–1939)
   © HarperCollins*Religious*/CopyCare

1 **All to Jesus I surrender,**
  all to Him I freely give;
  I will ever love and trust Him,
  in His presence daily live.
      I surrender all,
      I surrender all,
      all to Thee, my blessèd Saviour,
      I surrender all.

2 All to Jesus I surrender,
  humbly at His feet I bow;
  worldly pleasures all forsaken,
  take me, Jesus, take me now.
      I surrender all . . .

3 All to Jesus I surrender,
  make me, Saviour, wholly Thine;
  let me feel the Holy Spirit,
  truly know that Thou art mine.
      I surrender all . . .

4 All to Jesus I surrender,
  Lord, I give myself to Thee;
  fill me with Thy love and power,
  let Thy blessing fall on me.
      I surrender all . . .

5 All to Jesus I surrender,
  now I feel the sacred flame;
  O the joy of full salvation!
  Glory, glory to His name!
      I surrender all . . .

26 Charles Wesley (1707–88) altd.

1 **All you that pass by,**
  to Jesus draw nigh;
  to you is it nothing
      that Jesus should die?
  Your ransom and peace,
  your surety He is,
  come, see if there ever
      was sorrow like His.

2 He dies to atone
  for sins not His own.
  Your debt He has paid
      and your work He has done:
  you all may receive
  the peace He did leave,
  who made intercession,
      'My Father, forgive.'

3 For you and for me
  He prayed on the tree:
  the prayer is accepted,
      the sinner is free.
  The sinner am I,
  who on Jesus rely,
  and come for the pardon
      God cannot deny.

4 His death is my plea;
   my advocate see,
   and hear the blood speak
      that has answered for me:
   He purchased the grace
   which now I embrace;
   O Father, You know
      Jesus died in my place!

27 Austin Martin
© 1983 Kingsway's Thankyou Music

Almighty God, we bring You praise
for Your Son, the Word of God;
by whose power the world was made,
by whose blood we are redeemed.
Morning Star, the Father's glory,
we now worship and adore You;
in our hearts Your light has risen;
Jesus, Lord, we worship You.

28 From *The Alternative Service Book 1980*
© 1980 The Archbishop's Council

Almighty God, our heavenly Father,
we have sinned against You
and against our fellow men,
in thought and word and deed,
through negligence, through weakness,
through our own deliberate fault.
We are truly sorry,
and repent of all our sins.
For the sake of Your Son Jesus Christ,
who died for us, who died for us,
      who died for us,
forgive us all that is past;
and grant that we may serve You
in newness of life
MEN   to the glory of Your name,
WOMEN   to the glory of Your name,
MEN   to the glory of Your name,
WOMEN   to the glory of Your name,
ALL   to the glory of Your name.
         Amen, amen.

29 Anon
Copyright control

1 **Alleluia** (*8 times*)

2 How I love Him . . .

3 Blessèd Jesus . . .

4 My Redeemer . . .

5 Jesus is Lord . . .

6 Alleluia . . .

30 Donald Fishel
© 1973 Word of God/CopyCare

Alleluia, alleluia,
   give thanks to the risen Lord;
   alleluia, alleluia,
   give praise to His name.

1 Jesus is Lord of all the earth,
   He is the King of creation.
   Alleluia, alleluia . . .

2 Spread the good news o'er all the
      earth,
   Jesus has died and has risen.
   Alleluia, alleluia . . .

3 We have been crucified with Christ;
   now we shall live for ever.
   Alleluia, alleluia . . .

4 God has proclaimed the just reward,
   life for all men, alleluia.
   Alleluia, alleluia . . .

5 Come let us praise the living God,
   joyfully sing to our Saviour:
   Alleluia, alleluia . . .

31 John Newton (1725–1807)

1 **Amazing grace –**
      how sweet the sound –
   that saved a wretch like me!
   I once was lost, but now am found,
   was blind, but now I see.

2 'Twas grace that taught my heart
          to fear,
  and grace my fears relieved;
  how precious did that grace appear
  the hour I first believed.

3 Through many dangers,
          toils and snares,
  I have already come;
  'tis grace hath brought me safe thus far,
  and grace will lead me home.

4 When we've been there
          ten thousand years
  bright shining as the sun,
  we've no less days to sing God's praise
  than when we've first begun.

32 Dave Bilbrough
       © 1983 Kingsway's Thankyou Music

1 **An army of ordinary people,**
  a kingdom where love is the key,
  a city, a light to the nations,
  heirs to the promise are we.
  A people whose life is in Jesus,
  a nation together we stand;
  only through grace are we worthy,
  inheritors of the land.
    A new day is dawning,
    a new age to come,
    when the children of promise
    shall flow together as one:
    a truth long neglected,
    but the time has now come,
    when the children of promise
    shall flow together as one.

2 A people without recognition,
  but with Him a destiny sealed,
  called to a heavenly vision:
  His purpose shall be fulfilled.

Come, let us stand strong together,
abandon ourselves to the King;
His love shall be ours for ever,
this victory song we shall sing.
  A new day . . .

33 Charles Wesley (1707–88)

1 **And can it be that I should gain**
  an interest in the Saviour's blood?
  Died He for me, who caused His pain?
  For me, who Him to death pursued?
  Amazing love! how can it be
  that Thou, my God,
          shouldst die for me!

2 'Tis mystery all! The Immortal dies:
  who can explore His strange design?
  In vain the first-born seraph tries
  to sound the depths of love divine.
  'Tis mercy all! let earth adore,
  let angel minds inquire no more.

3 He left His Father's throne above –
  so free, so infinite His grace –
  emptied Himself of all but love,
  and bled for Adam's helpless race.
  'Tis mercy all, immense and free;
  for, O my God, it found out me!

4 Long my imprisoned spirit lay
  fast bound in sin and nature's night;
  Thine eye diffused a quickening ray –
  I woke, the dungeon flamed with light;
  my chains fell off, my heart was free.
  I rose, went forth, and followed Thee.

5 No condemnation now I dread;
  Jesus, and all in Him, is mine!
  Alive in Him, my living Head,
  and clothed in righteousness divine,
  bold I approach the eternal throne,
  and claim the crown,
          through Christ, my own.

34 Francis Pott (1832–1909)

1 **Angel voices ever singing**
round Thy throne of light,
angel harps for ever ringing,
rest not day nor night;
thousands only live to bless Thee,
and confess Thee Lord of might.

2 Thou who art beyond the farthest
mortal eye can scan,
can it be that Thou regardest
songs of sinful man?
Can we know that Thou art near us
and wilt hear us? Yes, we can.

3 Yes, we know that Thou rejoicest
o'er each work of Thine;
Thou didst ears and hands and voices
for Thy praise design;
craftsman's art and music's measure
for Thy pleasure all combine.

4 In Thy house, great God, we offer
of Thine own to Thee;
and for Thine acceptance proffer,
all unworthily,
hearts and minds and hands and voices
in our choicest psalmody.

5 Honour, glory, might, and merit
Thine shall ever be:
Father, Son, and Holy Spirit,
Blessèd Trinity:
of the best that Thou hast given,
earth and heaven render Thee.

35 James Montgomery (1771–1854)
© in this version Jubilate Hymns

1 **Angels from the realms of glory,**
wing your flight through all the earth;
heralds of creation's story
now proclaim Messiah's birth!

Come and worship
Christ, the new-born King;
come and worship,
worship Christ the new-born King.

2 Shepherds in the fields abiding,
watching by your flocks at night,
God with man is now residing:
see, there shines the infant light!
Come and worship ...

3 Wise men, leave your contemplations!
brighter visions shine afar;
seek in Him the hope of nations,
you have seen His rising star:
Come and worship ...

4 Though an infant now we view Him,
He will share His Father's throne,
gather all the nations to Him;
every knee shall then bow down:
Come and worship ...

36 Eric Glass
© 1992 Gordon V Thompson and
Warner/Chappell Music Canada Ltd

1 **Behold, the darkness shall cover**
the earth,
and gross darkness the people;
but the Lord shall arise upon thee,
and His glory shall be seen upon thee.
Arise, shine; for thy light is come,
and the glory of the Lord is risen.
O arise, shine; for thy light is come,
and the glory of the Lord is upon thee.

2 The Gentiles shall come to thy light,
and kings to the brightness
of thy rising:
and they shall call thee
the city of the Lord,
the Zion of the Holy One of Israel.
Arise, shine ...

3 Lift up thine eyes round about and see,
they gather themselves together;
and they shall come,
thy sons from afar,
and thy daughters shall be nursed
at thy side.
Arise, shine; for thy light is come,
and the glory of the Lord is risen.
O arise, shine; for thy light is come,
and the glory of the Lord is upon thee.

4 Then shalt thou see and flow together,
and thy heart shall be enlarged;
the abundance of the sea
is converted unto thee,
and the nations shall come unto thee.
Arise, shine . . .

5 The sun shall no more go down,
neither shall the moon withdraw itself;
but the Lord shall be
thine everlasting light,
and the days of thy mourning
shall be ended.
Arise, shine . . .

37 Martin Nystrom
© 1983 Restoration Music Ltd/Sovereign Music UK

1 **As the deer pants for the water,**
so my soul longs after You.
You alone are my heart's desire
and I long to worship You.
You alone are my strength, my shield,
to You alone may my spirit yield.
You alone are my heart's desire
and I long to worship You.

2 I want You more than gold or silver,
only You can satisfy.
You alone are the real joy-giver
and the apple of my eye.
You alone are . . .

3 You're my friend
and You're my brother,
even though You are a king.
I love You more than any other,
so much more than anything.
You alone are . . .

38 John Daniels
© 1979 Word's Spirit of Praise Music/
CopyCare

As we are gathered, Jesus is here,
one with each other, Jesus is here;
joined by the Spirit, washed in His blood,
part of the body, the Church of God.
As we are gathered, Jesus is here,
one with each other, Jesus is here.

39 William Chatterton Dix (1837–98)
altered © 1986 Horrobin/Leavers

1 **As with gladness men of old**
did the guiding star behold;
as with joy they hailed its light,
leading onward, beaming bright,
so, most gracious God, may we
led by You for ever be.

2 As with joyful steps they sped,
Saviour, to Your lowly bed,
there to bend the knee before
You whom heaven and earth adore,
so may we with one accord,
seek forgiveness from our Lord.

3 As they offered gifts most rare,
gold and frankincense and myrrh,
so may we, cleansed from our sin,
lives of service now begin,
as in love our treasures bring,
Christ, to You our heavenly King.

4 Holy Jesus, every day
keep us in the narrow way;
and when earthly things are past,
bring our ransomed souls at last
where they need no star to guide,
where no clouds Your glory hide.

5 In the heavenly country bright
need they no created light;
You its light, its joy, its crown,
You its sun which goes not down.
There for ever may we sing
hallelujahs to our King.

40 Mary Kirkbridge Barthow, Mary Lou King
© 1979 Peter West/Integrity's Hosanna! Music/
Kingsway's Thankyou Music

Ascribe greatness to our God the rock,
His work is perfect
     and all His ways are just.
Ascribe greatness to our God the rock,
His work is perfect
     and all His ways are just.
A God of faithfulness
     and without injustice;
good and upright is He.
A God of faithfulness
     and without injustice;
good and upright is He.

41 Caroline Maria Noel (1817–77)

1 **At the name of Jesus**
every knee shall bow,
every tongue confess Him
King of glory now.
'Tis the Father's pleasure
we should call Him Lord,
who from the beginning
was the mighty Word.

2 Mighty and mysterious
in the highest height,
God from everlasting,
very Light of light.
In the Father's bosom,
with the spirits blest,
love, in love eternal,
rest, in perfect rest.

3 Humbled for a season,
to receive a name
from the lips of sinners
unto whom He came;
faithfully He bore it
spotless to the last,
brought it back victorious,
when from death He passed.

4 Bore it up triumphant
with its human light,
through all ranks of creatures,
to the central height;
to the throne of Godhead,
to the Father's breast,
filled it with the glory
of that perfect rest.

5 In your hearts enthrone Him;
there let Him subdue
all that is not holy,
all that is not true;
crown Him as your captain
in temptation's hour,
let His will enfold you
in its light and power.

6 Brothers, this Lord Jesus
shall return again,
with His Father's glory,
with His angel-train;
for all wreaths of empire
meet upon His brow,
and our hearts confess Him
King of glory now.

42
Graham Kendrick
© 1988 Make Way Music

At this time of giving,
gladly now we bring
gifts of goodness and mercy
from a heavenly King.

1 Earth could not contain the treasures
heaven holds for you,
perfect joy and lasting pleasures,
love so strong and true.
At this time of giving . . .

2 May His tender love surround you
at this Christmastime;
may you see His smiling face
that in the darkness shines.
At this time of giving . . .

3 But the many gifts He gives
are all poured out from one;
come receive the greatest gift,
the gift of God's own Son.
At this time of giving . . .

Last two choruses and verses:
Lai, lai, lai . . . (etc.)

43
Henry Twells (1823–1900)

1 **At even, ere the sun was set,**
the sick, O Lord, around Thee lay;
O in what divers pains they met!
O with what joy they went away!

2 Once more 'tis eventide, and we,
oppressed with various ills, draw near;
what if Thy form we cannot see?
we know and feel that Thou art here.

3 O Saviour Christ, our woes dispel:
for some are sick, and some are sad,
and some have never loved Thee well,
and some have lost the love they had;

4 And some have found the world is vain,
yet from the world they break not free;
and some have friends
who give them pain,
yet have not sought a friend in Thee;

5 And none, O Lord, have perfect rest,
for none are wholly free from sin;
and they who fain would serve Thee
best
are conscious most of wrong within.

6 O Saviour Christ, Thou too art man;
Thou hast been troubled,
tempted, tried;
Thy kind but searching glance can scan
the very wounds
that shame would hide.

7 Thy touch has still its ancient power,
no word from Thee can fruitless fall;
hear, in this solemn evening hour,
and in Thy mercy heal us all.

44
Janis Miller
© 1983 Christian Fellowship of Columbia

At Your feet, O Lord, we wait for You,
yearning, Lord, hungry, Lord,
for more of You.
Bowed before You, Lord,
we desire only You:
fill us, Lord, revive us, Lord,
with more of You.

45
David Fellingham
© 1982 Kingsway's Thankyou Music

1 **At Your feet we fall,**
mighty risen Lord,
as we come before Your throne
to worship You.
By Your Spirit's power
You now draw our hearts,
and we hear Your voice
in triumph ringing clear:

'I am He that liveth,
that liveth and was dead.
Behold, I am alive
for evermore.'

2 There we see You stand,
    mighty risen Lord,
clothed in garments pure and holy,
    shining bright;
eyes of flashing fire,
    feet like burnished bronze,
and the sound of many waters
    is Your voice.
    'I am He that liveth . . . '

3 Like the shining sun
    in its noon-day strength,
we now see the glory
    of Your wondrous face:
once that face was marred,
    but now You're glorified;
and Your words,
    like a two-edged sword,
    have mighty power.
    'I am He that liveth . . . '

47 verses 1 and 2: Anon
verse 3: J T McFarland (c1906)

1 **Away in a manger,**
    no crib for a bed,
the little Lord Jesus
    laid down His sweet head;
the stars in the bright sky
    looked down where He lay;
the little Lord Jesus asleep in the hay.

2 The cattle are lowing, the baby awakes,
but little Lord Jesus,
    no crying He makes:
I love You, Lord Jesus!
    look down from the sky
and stay by my side
    until morning is nigh.

3 Be near me, Lord Jesus;
    I ask You to stay
close by me for ever
    and love me, I pray;
bless all the dear children
    in Your tender care,
and fit us for heaven
    to live with You there.

46 David Hadden
© 1981 Word's Spirit of Praise Music/
CopyCare

Awake, awake, O Zion,
come clothe yourself with strength.
Awake, awake, O Zion,
come clothe yourself with strength.

1 Put on your garments of splendour,
    O Jerusalem;
come sing your songs
    of joy and triumph,
see that your God reigns.
    Awake, awake . . .

2 Burst into songs of joy together,
    O Jerusalem;
the Lord has comforted His people,
    the redeemed Jerusalem.
    Awake, awake . . .

48 Anon
Copyright control

1 **Be still and know that I am God.**
Be still and know that I am God.
Be still and know that I am God.

2 I am the Lord that healeth thee.
I am the Lord that healeth thee.
I am the Lord that healeth thee.

3 In Thee, O Lord, I put my trust.
In Thee, O Lord, I put my trust.
In Thee, O Lord, I put my trust.

49 Morris Chapman
© 1983 Word Music/CopyCare

Be bold, be strong,
for the Lord your God is with you;
be bold, be strong,
for the Lord your God is with you!
I am not afraid, (No! No! No!)
I am not dismayed, (Not me!)
for I'm walking in faith and victory:
come on and walk in faith and victory,
for the Lord your God is with you.

50 David J Evans
© 1986 Kingsway's Thankyou Music

1 **Be still,**
for the presence of the Lord,
the Holy One, is here;
come bow before Him now
with reverence and fear:
in Him no sin is found –
we stand on holy ground.
Be still,
for the presence of the Lord,
the Holy One, is here.

2 Be still,
for the glory of the Lord
is shining all around;
He burns with holy fire,
with splendour He is crowned:
how awesome is the sight –
our radiant King of light!
Be still,
for the glory of the Lord
is shining all around.

3 Be still,
for the power of the Lord
is moving in this place:
He comes to cleanse and heal,
to minister His grace –
no work too hard for Him.
In faith receive from Him.
Be still,
for the power of the Lord
is moving in this place.

51 From *The Poem Book of the Gael*
selected and edited by Eleanor Hull
originally published by Chatto & Windus
© Estate of the late Eleanor Hull

1 **Be Thou my vision,**
O Lord of my heart;
naught be all else to me,
save that Thou art –
Thou my best thought,
by day or by night,
waking or sleeping,
Thy presence my light.

2 Be Thou my wisdom,
Thou my true Word;
I ever with Thee, Thou with me, Lord;
Thou my great Father, I Thy true son;
Thou in me dwelling,
and I with Thee one.

3 Be Thou my battle-shield,
sword for the fight,
be Thou my dignity, Thou my delight.
Thou my soul's shelter,
Thou my high tower:
raise Thou me heavenward,
O Power of my power.

4 Riches I heed not,
nor man's empty praise,
Thou mine inheritance,
now and always:
Thou and Thou only, first in my heart,
High King of heaven,
my treasure Thou art.

5 High King of heaven, after victory won,
  may I reach heaven's joys,
    O bright heaven's Sun!
  Heart of my own heart,
    whatever befall,
  still be my vision, O ruler of all.

52 Gloria and William J Gaither
© 1971 Gaither Music Publishing/WJG Inc/
Kingsway's Thankyou Music

1 **God sent His Son,**
    they called Him Jesus;
  He came to love, heal, and forgive;
  He lived and died to buy my pardon,
  an empty grave is there
      to prove my Saviour lives.
  Because He lives I can face tomorrow;
  because He lives all fear is gone;
  because I know He holds the future,
  and life is worth the living
      just because He lives.

2 How sweet to hold a new-born baby,
  and feel the pride and joy he gives;
  but greater still the calm assurance,
  this child can face uncertain days
      because He lives.
  Because He lives . . .

3 And then one day I'll cross the river;
  I'll fight life's final war with pain;
  and then as death gives way to victory,
  I'll see the lights of glory
      and I'll know He lives.
  Because He lives . . .

53 Phil Potter
© 1981 Kingsway's Thankyou Music

1 **Because Your love**
    is better than life,
  with my lips I will glorify You;
  I will praise You as long as I live,
  in Your name I lift my hands.

2 Because Your Son has given me life,
  with my lips I will glorify You,
  I will praise You as long as I live,
  in Your name I lift my hands.

3 Because Your Spirit is filling my life,
  with my lips I will glorify You,
  I will praise You as long as I live,
  in Your name I lift my hands.

4 Because Your love is better than life,
  with my lips I will glorify You,
  I will praise You as long as I live,
  in Your name I lift my hands.

54 Bob Gillman
© 1977 Kingsway's Thankyou Music

  Bind us together, Lord,
  bind us together
  with cords that cannot be broken;
  bind us together, Lord,
  bind us together,
  O bind us together with love.

1 There is only one God,
  there is only one King,
  there is only one body –
  that is why we sing:
  Bind us together . . .

2 Made for the glory of God,
  purchased by His precious Son.
  Born with the right to be clean,
  for Jesus the victory has won.
  Bind us together . . .

3 You are the family of God,
  You are the promise divine,
  You are God's chosen desire,
  You are the glorious new wine.
  Bind us together . . .

55 Elizabeth Cecilia Clephane (1830–69)

1 **Beneath the cross of Jesus**
I fain would take my stand –
the shadow of a mighty rock
within a weary land;
a home within a wilderness,
a rest upon the way,
from the burning of the noontide heat
and the burden of the day.

2 Upon that cross of Jesus
mine eye at times can see
the very dying form of One
who suffered there for me;
and from my stricken heart, with tears,
two wonders I confess –
the wonders of redeeming love,
and my own worthlessness.

3 I take, O cross, thy shadow,
for my abiding-place!
I ask no other sunshine than
the sunshine of His face;
content to let the world go by,
to know no gain or loss –
my sinful self my only shame,
my glory all – the cross.

56 Andrae Crouch
© 1973 Bud John Songs/EMI Christian
Music Publishing/CopyCare

Bless the Lord, O my soul,
and all that is within me
bless His holy name.
He has done great things,
He has done great things,
He has done great things,
bless His holy name.
Bless the Lord, O my soul,
and all that is within me
bless His holy name.

57 From Psalm 103
Copyright control

Bless the Lord, O my soul,
bless the Lord, O my soul,
and all that is within me
bless His holy name.
Bless the Lord, O my soul,
bless the Lord, O my soul,
and all that is within me
bless His holy name.
King of kings (for ever and ever),
Lord of lords (for ever and ever),
King of kings (for ever and ever),
King of kings and Lord of lords!
Bless the Lord, O my soul,
Bless the Lord, O my soul,
and all that is within me
bless His holy name.
Bless the Lord, O my soul,
Bless the Lord, O my soul,
and all that is within me
bless His holy name.

58 Betty Lou Mills
© 1979 Kingsway's Thankyou Music

Blessèd are the pure in heart,
for they shall see God;
blessèd are the pure in heart,
for they shall see God.

1 To see God, the Alpha and Omega,
to see God, Creator, Life-sustainer,
to see God,
to think that this is possibility.
Blessèd are . . .

2 To see God, the everlasting Father,
to see God,
whose love endures for ever,
to see God,
how wonderful to think
that this could be.
Blessèd are . . .

3 To see God,
    the God who talked with Moses,
to see God,
    whose mercies are so endless,
to see God,
    what better incentive for purity.
    Blessèd are . . .

4 To see God,
    the One I've loved
    and longed for,
to see God, the Father of my Saviour,
to see God,
    a dream come true,
    at last His face I'll see.
    Blessèd are . . .

59 Frances van Alstyne (1820–1915)
(Fanny J Crosby)

1 **Blessèd assurance, Jesus is mine:**
O what a foretaste of glory divine!
Heir of salvation, purchase of God;
born of His Spirit,
    washed in His blood.
    This is my story, this is my song,
    praising my Saviour all the day long;
    this is my story, this is my song,
    praising my Saviour all the day long.

2 Perfect submission, perfect delight,
visions of rapture burst on my sight;
angels descending, bring from above
echoes of mercy, whispers of love.
    This is my story . . .

3 Perfect submission, all is at rest,
I in my Saviour am happy and blest;
watching and waiting, looking above,
filled with His goodness,
    lost in His love.
    This is my story . . .

60 John Fawcett (1740–1817) altd.

1 **Blest be the tie that binds**
our hearts in Christian love;
the fellowship of kindred minds
is like to that above.

2 Before our Father's throne
we pour our ardent prayers;
our fears, our hopes, our aims are one,
our comforts and our cares.

3 We share our mutual woes,
our mutual burdens bear,
and often for each other flows
the sympathizing tear.

4 When for awhile we part,
this thought will soothe our pain,
that we shall still be joined in heart,
and hope to meet again.

5 This glorious hope revives
our courage by the way,
while each in expectation lives,
and longs to see the day.

6 From sorrow, toil, and pain,
and sin we shall be free;
and perfect love and friendship reign
through all eternity.

61 From Romans 8
© Timothy Dudley-Smith

1 **Born by the Holy Spirit's breath,**
loosed from the law of sin and death,
now cleared in Christ from every claim
no judgement stands against our name.

2 In us the Spirit makes His home
that we in Him may overcome;
Christ's risen life, in all its powers,
its all-prevailing strength, is ours.

3 Sons, then, and heirs
    of God most high,
  we by His Spirit, 'Father' cry;
  that Spirit with our spirit shares
  to frame and breathe
    our wordless prayers.

4 One is His love, His purpose one:
  to form the likeness of His Son
  in all who, called and justified,
  shall reign in glory at His side.

5 Nor death nor life, nor powers unseen,
  nor height nor depth
    can come between;
  we know through peril, pain and sword,
  the love of God in Christ our Lord.

4 Hope of the world,
    Mary's child,
  You're coming soon to reign:
  King of the earth,
    Mary's child,
  walk in our streets again.

63 Anon
Copyright control

Break forth into joy, O my soul;
break forth into joy, O my soul.
In the presence of the Lord
there is joy for evermore;
break forth, break forth into joy.

62 Geoffrey Ainger
© 1964 Stainer & Bell Ltd

1 **Born in the night,**
    Mary's child,
  a long way from Your home;
  coming in need,
    Mary's child,
  born in a borrowed room.

2 Clear shining light,
    Mary's child,
  Your face lights up our way:
  light of the world,
    Mary's child,
  dawn on our darkened day.

3 Truth of our life,
    Mary's child,
  You tell us God is good:
  prove it is true,
    Mary's child,
  go to Your cross of wood.

64 Mary Artemisia Lathbury (1841–1913)
and Alexander Groves (1843–1909)

1 **Break Thou the bread of life,**
    dear Lord to me,
  as Thou didst break the bread
    beside the sea;
  beyond the sacred page
    I seek Thee, Lord;
  my spirit longs for Thee,
    Thou living Word!

2 Thou art the bread of life,
    O Lord, to me,
  Thy holy word the truth
    that saveth me;
  give me to eat and live
    with Thee above,
  teach me to love Thy truth,
    for Thou art love.

3 O send Thy Spirit, Lord,
    now unto me,
that He may touch my eyes,
    and make me see;
show me the truth concealed
    within Thy word,
and in Thy book revealed
    I see Thee, Lord.

4 Bless Thou the bread of life
    to me, to me,
as Thou didst bless the loaves
    by Galilee;
then shall all bondage cease,
    all fetters fall,
and I shall find my peace,
    my all-in-all!

65 Reginald Heber (1783–1826)

1 **Brightest and best**
    of the sons of the morning,
dawn on our darkness
    and lend us Thine aid;
star of the east, the horizon adorning,
guide where our infant Redeemer
    is laid.

2 Cold on His cradle
    the dew-drops are shining;
low lies His head
    with the beasts of the stall:
angels adore Him, in slumber reclining,
maker and monarch,
    and Saviour of all.

3 Say, shall we yield Him,
    in costly devotion,
odours of Edom, and offerings divine;
gems of the mountain,
    and pearls of the ocean,
myrrh from the forest,
    or gold from the mine?

4 Vainly we offer each ample oblation;
vainly with gifts
    would His favour secure;
richer by far is the heart's adoration;
dearer to God
    are the prayers of the poor.

5 Brightest and best
    of the sons of the morning,
dawn on our darkness
    and lend us Thine aid;
star of the east, the horizon adorning,
guide where our infant Redeemer
    is laid.

66 Janet Lunt
© 1978 Sovereign Music UK

Broken for me, broken for you,
the body of Jesus broken for you.

1 He offered His body,
    He poured out His soul,
Jesus was broken
    that we might be whole:
    Broken for me . . .

2 Come to My table and with Me dine,
eat of My bread and drink of My wine:
    Broken for me . . .

3 This is My body given for you,
eat it remembering I died for you:
    Broken for me . . .

4 This is My blood I shed for you,
for your forgiveness, making you new:
    Broken for me . . .

67 Edwin Hatch (1835–89)

1 **Breathe on me, breath of God,**
fill me with life anew,
that I may love what Thou dost love,
and do what Thou wouldst do.

2 Breathe on me, breath of God,
until my heart is pure,
until with Thee I will one will,
to do and to endure.

3 Breathe on me, breath of God,
till I am wholly Thine,
until this earthly part of me
glows with Thy fire divine.

4 Breathe on me, breath of God,
so shall I never die,
but live with Thee the perfect life
of Thine eternity.

68 Edward R Miller
© 1974 Maranatha! Music/CopyCare

1 **Cause me to come to Thy river,
O Lord,** (*3 times*)
cause me to come, cause me to drink,
cause me to live.

2 Cause me to drink from Thy river,
O Lord, (*3 times*)
cause me to come, cause me to drink,
cause me to live.

3 Cause me to live by Thy river,
O Lord, (*3 times*)
cause me to come, cause me to drink,
cause me to live.

69 Eddie Espinosa
© 1982 Mercy/Vineyard Publishing/
CopyCare

Change my heart, O God,
make it ever true;
change my heart, O God,
may I be like You.

You are the potter,
I am the clay;
mould me and make me,
this is what I pray.

Change my heart, O God,
make it ever true;
change my heart, O God,
may I be like You.

70 John Henley (1800–42)

1 **Children of Jerusalem**
sang the praise of Jesus' name;
children, too, of modern days,
join to sing the Saviour's praise:
Hark, hark, hark!
while children's voices sing,
hark, hark, hark!
while children's voices sing
loud hosannas, loud hosannas,
loud hosannas to our King.

2 We are taught to love the Lord,
we are taught to read His word,
we are taught the way to heaven;
praise for all to God be given:
Hark, hark, hark . . .

3 Parents, teachers, old and young,
all unite to swell the song;
higher and yet higher rise,
till hosannas reach the skies:
Hark, hark, hark . . .

71 after Mary MacDonald (1789–1872)
Lachlan Macbean (1853–1931)
Copyright control

1 **Child in the manger,
infant of Mary,**
outcast and stranger, Lord of all!
Child who inherits
all our transgressions,
all our demerits on Him fall.

2 Once the most holy child of salvation
gentle and lowly lived below:
now as our glorious mighty Redeemer,
see Him victorious over each foe.

3 Prophets foretold Him,
     infant of wonder;
angels behold Him on His throne:
worthy our Saviour of all their praises;
happy for ever are His own.

4 Here entrust to all Your servants
what we long from You to gain –
that on earth and in the heavens
we one people shall remain,
till united in Your glory
evermore with You we reign.

5 Praise and honour to the Father,
praise and honour to the Son,
praise and honour to the Spirit,
ever Three and ever One:
one in power and one in glory
while eternal ages run.

72 Major T W Maltby
© 1943 Salvationist Publishing & Supplies/
CopyCare

Christ is the answer to my every need;
Christ is the answer,
     He is my friend indeed.
Problems of life my spirit may assail,
with Christ my Saviour I need never fail,
for Christ is the answer to my need.

73 From the Latin, John Mason Neale (1818–66)
© in this version Jubilate Hymns

1 **Christ is made the sure foundation,**
Christ the head and corner-stone
chosen of the Lord and precious,
binding all the Church in one;
holy Zion's help for ever,
and her confidence alone.

2 All within that holy city
dearly loved of God on high,
in exultant jubilation
sing, in perfect harmony;
God the One-in-Three adoring
in glad hymns eternally.

3 We as living stones invoke you:
Come among us, Lord, today!
with Your gracious loving-kindness
hear Your children as we pray;
and the fulness of Your blessing
in our fellowship display.

74 John Samuel Bewley Monsell (1811–75)

1 **Christ is risen! hallelujah!**
risen our victorious Head;
sing His praises; hallelujah!
Christ is risen from the dead.
Gratefully our hearts adore Him,
as His light once more appears;
bowing down in joy before Him,
rising up from grief and tears.
     Christ is risen! hallelujah!
     risen our victorious Head;
     sing His praises; hallelujah!
     Christ is risen from the dead.

2 Christ is risen! all the sadness
of His earthly life is o'er;
through the open gates of gladness
He returns to life once more.
Death and hell before Him bending,
He doth rise the victor now,
angels on His steps attending,
glory round His wounded brow.
     Christ is risen . . .

3 Christ is risen! henceforth never
death or hell shall us enthral;
we are Christ's, in Him for ever
we have triumphed over all;

all the doubting and dejection
of our trembling hearts have ceased.
'Tis His day of resurrection;
let us rise and keep the feast.
Christ is risen! hallelujah!
risen our victorious Head;
sing His praises; hallelujah!
Christ is risen from the dead.

75 From Revelation 22
© Christopher Idle / Jubilate Hymns

1 **Christ is surely coming,**
   bringing His reward,
Alpha and Omega,
   First and Last and Lord:
root and stem of David,
   brilliant Morning Star –
Meet your Judge and Saviour,
   nations near and far;
meet your Judge and Saviour,
   nations near and far!

2 See the holy city! There they enter in,
all by Christ made holy,
   washed from every sin:
thirsty ones, desiring
   all He loves to give,
Come for living water,
   freely drink, and live;
come for living water,
   freely drink, and live!

3 Grace be with God's people!
   Praise His holy name!
Father, Son, and Spirit,
   evermore the same:
hear the certain promise
   from the eternal home:
'Surely I come quickly!' –
   Come, Lord Jesus, come;
'Surely I come quickly!' –
   Come, Lord Jesus, come!

76 Charles Wesley (1707–88)

1 **Christ the Lord is risen today;**
   hallelujah!
sons of men and angels say:
raise your joys and triumphs high;
sing, ye heavens; thou earth, reply:

2 Love's redeeming work is done,
fought the fight, the battle won;
Lo! our sun's eclipse is o'er,
Lo! He sets in blood no more:

3 Vain the stone, the watch, the seal;
Christ hath burst the gates of hell;
death in vain forbids Him rise;
Christ hath opened paradise;

4 Lives again our glorious King;
where, O death, is now thy sting?
Once He died our souls to save;
where thy victory, O grave?

5 Soar we now where Christ hath led,
following our exalted Head;
made like Him, like Him we rise;
ours the cross, the grave, the skies:

6 Hail the Lord of earth and heaven,
praise to Thee by both be given:
Thee we greet, in triumph sing
Hail, our resurrected King:

77 © Michael Saward / Jubilate Hymns

1 **Christ triumphant, ever reigning,**
Saviour, Master, King,
Lord of heaven, our lives sustaining,
hear us as we sing:
   Yours the glory and the crown,
   the high renown, the eternal name.

2 Word incarnate, truth revealing,
    Son of Man on earth!
    power and majesty concealing
    by Your humble birth:
        Yours the glory . . .

3 Suffering servant, scorned, ill-treated,
    victim crucified!
    death is through the cross defeated,
    sinners justified:
        Yours the glory . . .

4 Priestly King, enthroned for ever
    high in heaven above!
    sin and death and hell shall never
    stifle hymns of love:
        Yours the glory . . .

5 So, our hearts and voices raising
    through the ages long,
    ceaselessly upon You gazing,
    this shall be our song:
        Yours the glory . . .

78 From the Book of Proverbs
    © Timothy Dudley-Smith

1 **Christ the Way of life possess me,**
    lift my heart to love and praise;
    guide and keep, sustain and bless me,
    all my days, all my days.

2 Well of life, for ever flowing,
    make my barren soul and bare
    like a watered garden growing
    fresh and fair, fresh and fair.

3 May the Tree of life in splendour
    from its leafy boughs impart
    grace divine and healing tender,
    strength of heart, strength of heart.

4 Path of life before me shining,
    let me come when earth is past,
    sorrow, self and sin resigning,
    home at last, home at last.

79 Charles Wesley (1707–88)

1 **Christ, whose glory fills the skies,**
    Christ, the true, the only light,
    Sun of righteousness, arise,
    triumph o'er the shades of night:
    Day-spring from on high, be near;
    Day-star, in my heart appear.

2 Dark and cheerless is the morn
    unaccompanied by Thee;
    joyless is the day's return,
    till Thy mercy's beams I see;
    till they inward light impart,
    glad my eyes, and warm my heart.

3 Visit then this soul of mine;
    pierce the gloom of sin and grief;
    fill me, radiancy divine;
    scatter all my unbelief;
    more and more Thyself display,
    shining to the perfect day.

80 John Byrom (1692–1763) altd.

1 **Christians, awake!**
        salute the happy morn,
    whereon the Saviour of mankind
        was born;
    rise to adore the mystery of love
    which hosts of angels
        chanted from above;
    with them the joyful tidings first begun
    of God incarnate, and the Virgin's Son.

2 Then to the watchful shepherds
        it was told,
    who heard the angelic herald's voice,
        'Behold,
    I bring good tidings of a Saviour's birth
    to you and all the nations upon earth:
    this day hath God fulfilled
        His promised word,
    this day is born a Saviour,
        Christ the Lord.'

3 He spake; and straightway
    the celestial choir,
in hymns of joy unknown before
    conspire;
the praises of redeeming love
    they sang,
and heaven's whole orb
    with hallelujahs rang:
God's highest glory
    was their anthem still,
'On earth be peace,
    and unto men goodwill.'

4 To Bethlehem straight
    the enlightened shepherds ran,
to see the wonder
    God had wrought for man;
then to their flocks,
    still praising God, return,
and their glad hearts
    with holy rapture burn;
amazed, the wondrous tidings
    they proclaim,
the first apostles of His infant fame.

5 Then may we hope,
    the angelic hosts among,
to sing, redeemed,
    a glad triumphal song:
He that was born upon this joyful day
around us all His glory shall display;
saved by His love,
    incessant we shall sing
eternal praise to heaven's
    almighty King.

2 Glorious is the Lord most high,
terrible in majesty;
He His sovereign sway maintains,
King o'er all the earth He reigns.

3 Jesus is gone up on high,
takes His seat above the sky:
shout the angel-choirs aloud,
echoing to the trump of God.

4 Sons of earth, the triumph join,
praise Him with the host divine;
emulate the heavenly powers,
their victorious Lord is ours.

5 Shout the God enthroned above,
trumpet forth His conquering love;
praises to our Jesus sing,
praises to our glorious King!

6 Power is all to Jesus given,
power o'er hell, and earth, and heaven!
Power He now to us imparts;
praise Him with believing hearts.

7 Wonderful in saving power,
Him let all our hearts adore;
earth and heaven repeat the cry,
'Glory be to God most high!'

82 R Hudson Pope (1879–1967)
© SGM International

Cleanse me from my sin, Lord,
put Thy power within, Lord,
take me as I am, Lord,
and make me all Thine own.
Keep me day by day, Lord,
underneath Thy sway, Lord,
make my heart Thy palace,
and Thy royal throne.

81 Charles Wesley (1707–88)

1 **Clap your hands, you people all,**
praise the God on whom you call;
lift your voice, and shout His praise,
triumph in His sovereign grace!

83 Valerie Collison
© 1972 High-Fye Music Ltd

Come and join the celebration,
it's a very special day;
come and share our jubilation,
there's a new King born today!

1 See the shepherds
hurry down to Bethlehem;
gaze in wonder
at the Son of God who lay before them.
   Come and join . . .

2 Wise men journey,
led to worship by a star,
kneel in homage,
bringing precious gifts
      from lands afar, so
   Come and join . . .

3 'God is with us,'
'round the world the message bring;
He is with us,
'Welcome!' all the bells on earth
      are pealing.
   Come and join . . .

84 Mike Kerry
© 1982 Kingsway's Thankyou Music

Come and praise the living God,
come and worship, come and worship.
He has made you priest and king,
come and worship the living God.

1 We come not to a mountain
      of fire and smoke,
not to gloom and darkness
      or trumpet sound;
we come to the new Jerusalem,
the holy city of God.
   Come and praise . . .

2 By His voice He shakes the earth,
His judgements known
      throughout the world.
But we have a city that for ever stands,
the holy city of God.
   Come and praise . . .

85 Graham Kendrick
© 1989 Make Way Music

1 **Come and see, come and see,**
come and see the King of love;
see the purple robe
      and crown of thorns He wears.
Soldiers mock, rulers sneer
as He lifts the cruel cross;
lone and friendless now,
      He climbs towards the hill.
   We worship at Your feet,
   where wrath and mercy meet,
   and a guilty world is washed
      by love's pure stream.
   For us He was made sin –
   oh, help me take it in.
   Deep wounds of love cry out,
   'Father, forgive.'
   I worship, I worship
   the Lamb who was slain.

2 Come and weep, come and mourn
for your sin that pierced Him there;
so much deeper than the wounds
      of thorn and nail.
All our pride, all our greed,
all our fallenness and shame;
and the Lord has laid the punishment
      on Him.
   We worship at Your feet . . .

3 Man of heaven, born to earth
to restore us to Your heaven.
Here we bow in awe
      beneath Your searching eyes.
From Your tears comes our joy,
from Your death our life shall spring;
by Your resurrection power
      we shall rise.
   We worship at Your feet . . .

86
From Revelation 4 and 5
© Christopher Idle/Jubilate Hymns

1 **Come and see the shining hope**
   that Christ's apostle saw:
   on the earth, confusion,
      but in heaven an open door,
   where the living creatures
      praise the Lamb for evermore;
   Love has the victory for ever!
   Amen, He comes!
   to bring His own reward;
   amen, praise God!
   for justice now restored.
   Kingdoms of the world
   become the kingdoms of the Lord:
   love has the victory for ever!

2 All the gifts You send us, Lord,
      are faithful, good, and true;
   holiness and righteousness
      are shown in all You do:
   who can see Your greatest gift
      and fail to worship You?
   Love has the victory for ever!
   Amen, He comes . . .

3 Power and salvation
      all belong to God on high:
   So the mighty multitudes of heaven
      make their cry,
   singing, 'Alleluia!'
      where the echoes never die;
   love has the victory for ever!
   Amen, He comes . . .

87
A Carter
© 1977 Kingsway's Thankyou Music

Come and praise Him,
   royal priesthood,
come and worship, holy nation,
worship Jesus, our Redeemer,
He is precious, King of glory.

88
From Psalm 134
Copyright control

Come, bless the Lord,
all ye servants of the Lord,
who stand by night
in the house of the Lord;
lift up your hands
in the holy place,
come, bless the Lord,
come, bless the Lord.

89
after Bianco da Siena (d1434)
Richard F Littledale (1833–90)

1 **Come down, O Love divine,**
   seek Thou this soul of mine
   and visit it
      with Thine own ardour glowing;
   O Comforter, draw near,
   within my heart appear,
   and kindle it,
      Thy holy flame bestowing.

2 O let it freely burn,
   till earthly passions turn
   to dust and ashes,
      in its heat consuming;
   and let Thy glorious light
   shine ever on my sight,
   and clothe me round,
      the while my path illuming.

3 Let holy charity
   mine outward vesture be,
   and lowliness become
      mine inner clothing;
   true lowliness of heart,
   which takes the humbler part,
   and o'er its own shortcomings
      weeps with loathing.

4 And so the yearning strong,
with which the soul will long,
    shall far outpass
        the power of human telling;
for none can guess its grace,
till he become the place
    wherein the Holy Spirit
        makes His dwelling.

90

after R Maurus (c776–856)
J Cosin (1594–1672)

1 **Come, Holy Ghost,
    our souls inspire,**
and lighten with celestial fire:
Thou the anointing Spirit art,
who dost Thy sevenfold gifts impart.

2 Thy blessèd unction from above
is comfort, life, and fire of love:
enable with perpetual light
the dullness of our blinded sight.

3 Anoint and cheer our soilèd face
with the abundance of Thy grace:
keep far our foes, give peace at home –
where Thou art guide no ill can come.

4 Teach us to know the Father, Son,
and Thee, of both, to be but One;
that, through the ages all along,
this, this may be our endless song:

Praise to Thy eternal merit,
Father, Son, and Holy Spirit! Amen.

91

© 1985 Andy Silver

Come, let us bow down in worship,
let us kneel before the Lord our maker.
Come, let us bow down in worship,
for He is our God and we are His people,

for He is our God,
    the people of His pasture,
the flock under His care.
Come, let us bow down in worship,
let us kneel before the Lord.

92

From Psalm 95
© Timothy Dudley-Smith

1 **Come, let us praise the Lord,**
with joy our God acclaim,
His greatness tell abroad
and bless His saving name.
    Lift high your songs
    before His throne
    to Whom alone
    all praise belongs.

2 Our God of matchless worth,
our King beyond compare,
the deepest bounds of earth,
the hills, are in His care.
    He all decrees,
    Who by His hand
    prepared the land
    and formed the seas.

3 In worship bow the knee,
our glorious God confess;
the great Creator, He,
the Lord our righteousness.
    He reigns unseen:
    His flock He feeds
    and gently leads
    in pastures green.

4 Come, hear His voice today,
receive what love imparts;
His holy will obey
and harden not your hearts.
    His ways are best;
    and lead at last,
    all troubles past,
    to perfect rest.

93 Isaac Watts (1674–1748)

1 **Come, let us join**
   our cheerful songs
   with angels round the throne;
   ten thousand thousand
   are their tongues,
   but all their joys are one.

2 'Worthy the Lamb that died!' they cry,
   'to be exalted thus';
   'Worthy the Lamb!' our lips reply,
   'for He was slain for us.'

3 Jesus is worthy to receive
   honour and power divine;
   and blessings more than we can give
   be, Lord, for ever Thine.

4 The whole creation join in one,
   to bless the sacred name
   of Him that sits upon the throne,
   and to adore the Lamb.

94 Robert Walmsley (1831–1905)

1 **Come, let us sing**
   of a wonderful love,
   tender and true;
   out of the heart of the Father above,
   streaming to me and to you:
   wonderful love
   dwells in the heart of the Father above.

2 Jesus, the Saviour, this gospel to tell,
   joyfully came;
   came with the helpless
      and hopeless to dwell,
   sharing their sorrow and shame;
   seeking the lost,
   saving, redeeming at measureless cost.

3 Jesus is seeking the wanderers yet;
   Why do they roam?
   Love only waits to forgive and forget;
   Home! weary wanderers, home!
   Wonderful love
   dwells in the heart of the Father above.

4 Come to my heart,
      O Thou wonderful Love,
   come and abide,
   lifting my life till it rises above
   envy and falsehood and pride;
   seeking to be
   lowly and humble, a learner of Thee.

95 © 1987 Ruth Hooke

MEN	**Come, let us sing** **for joy to the Lord.**
WOMEN	Come, let us sing for joy to the Lord.
MEN	We will sing, we will sing, we will sing.
WOMEN	We will sing, we will sing, we will sing.
MEN	Let us shout aloud to the rock of our salvation.
WOMEN	Let us shout aloud to the rock of our salvation.
MEN	We will shout! We will shout! We will shout!
WOMEN	We will shout! We will shout! We will shout!
ALL	For the Lord is the great God, the great King above all gods.
MEN	Splendour and majesty,
WOMEN	splendour and majesty,
MEN	are before Him,
WOMEN	are before Him.
MEN	Strength and glory,
WOMEN	strength and glory,
ALL	are in His sanctuary.

96

after S Suzanne Toolan
© Michael Baughen/Jubilate Hymns

1 **Come, let us worship Christ**
to the glory of God the Father,
for He is worthy of all our love;
He died and rose for us!
praise Him as Lord and Saviour.
And when the trumpet shall sound,
and Jesus comes in great power,
then He will raise us to be with Him
for evermore.

2 'I am the bread of life;
he who comes to Me shall not hunger:
and all who trust in Me
      shall not thirst' –
this is what Jesus said:
praise Him as Lord and Saviour.
And when the trumpet . . .

3 'I am the door to life;
he who enters by Me is saved,
abundant life he will then receive' –
this is what Jesus said:
praise Him as Lord and Saviour.
And when the trumpet . . .

4 'I am the Light of the world;
if you follow Me, darkness ceases,
and in its place
      comes the light of life' –
this is what Jesus said:
praise Him as Lord and Saviour.
And when the trumpet . . .

5 Lord, we are one with You;
we rejoice in Your new creation:
our hearts are fired
      by Your saving love –
take up our lives, O Lord,
and use us for Your glory.
And when the trumpet . . .

97

From Psalm 95, Sarah Turner-Smith
© HarperCollins*Religious*/CopyCare

Come, let us worship
our Redeemer,
let us bow down before His throne;
come, let us kneel before our maker:
holy is His name.

1 Come into His presence
      with thanksgiving,
make a joyful noise;
for the Lord is a great God:
King above all gods.
Come, let us worship . . .

2 We are the people of His pasture,
the sheep of His hand:
for Christ the Lord is our shepherd,
He will lead us home.
Come, let us worship . . .

3 All praises be to God the Father,
praise to Christ His Son;
praise be to God the Holy Spirit:
bless the Three-in-One!
Come, let us worship . . .

98

© Timothy Dudley-Smith

1 **Come now with awe,**
      earth's ancient vigil keeping:
cold under starlight lies the stony way.
Down from the hillside
      see the shepherds creeping,
hear in our hearts
      the whispered news they say:
'Laid in a manger
      lies an infant sleeping,
Christ our Redeemer,
      born for us today.'

2 Come now with joy
      to worship and adore Him;
hushed in the stillness,
      wonder and behold,

Christ in the stable
    where His mother bore Him,
Christ whom the prophets
    faithfully foretold:
High King of ages,
    low we kneel before Him,
starlight for silver,
    lantern-light for gold.

3 Come now with faith,
    the age-long secret guessing,
hearts rapt in wonder,
    soul and spirit stirred;
see in our likeness
    love beyond expressing,
All God has spoken,
    all the prophets heard;
born for us sinners,
    bearer of all blessing,
flesh of our flesh,
    behold the eternal Word!

4 Come now with love:
    beyond our comprehending
Love in its fulness lies in mortal span!
How should we love,
    whom Love is so befriending?
Love rich in mercy
    since our race began
now stoops to save us,
    sighs and sorrows ending,
Jesus our Saviour,
    Son of God made man.

99 Trish Morgan
© 1984 Kingsway's Thankyou Music

Come on and celebrate!
His gift of love we will celebrate –
the Son of God, who loved us
and gave us life.

We'll shout Your praise, O King:
You give us joy nothing else can bring;
we'll give to You our offering
in celebration praise.

Come on and celebrate, celebrate,
celebrate and sing,
celebrate and sing to the King:
Come on and celebrate, celebrate,
celebrate and sing,
celebrate and sing to the King!

100 Graham Kendrick
© 1985 Kingsway's Thankyou Music

Come, see the beauty of the Lord,
come, see the beauty of His face.
See the Lamb that once was slain,
see on His palms is carved your name.
See how our pain has pierced His heart,
and on His brow He bears our pride;
a crown of thorns.

But only love pours from His heart,
as silently He takes the blame.
He has my name upon His lips,
my condemnation falls on Him.
This love is marvellous to me,
His sacrifice has set me free,
and now I live.

Come, see the beauty of the Lord,
come, see the beauty of His face.

101 Jack C Winslow (1882–1974)
© Mrs J Tyrrell

1 **Come, sing the praise of Jesus,**
sing His love with hearts aflame,
sing His wondrous birth of Mary,
when to save the world He came;
tell the life He lived for others,
and His mighty deeds proclaim,
for Jesus Christ is King.
    Praise and glory be to Jesus,
    praise and glory be to Jesus,
    praise and glory be to Jesus,
    for Jesus Christ is King!

2 When foes arose and slew Him,
He was victor in the fight;
over death and hell He triumphed
in His resurrection-might;
He has raised our fallen manhood
and enthroned it in the height,
for Jesus Christ is King.
  Praise and glory . . .

3 There's joy for all who serve Him,
more than human tongue can say;
there is pardon for the sinner,
and the night is turned to day;
there is healing for our sorrows,
there is music all the way,
for Jesus Christ is King.
  Praise and glory . . .

4 We witness to His beauty,
and we spread His love abroad;
and we cleave the host of darkness,
with the Spirit's piercing sword;
we will lead the souls in prison
to the freedom of the Lord,
for Jesus Christ is King.
  Praise and glory . . .

5 To Jesus be the glory,
the dominion, and the praise;
He is Lord of all creation,
He is guide of all our ways;
and the world shall be His empire
in the fulness of the days,
for Jesus Christ is King.
  Praise and glory . . .

102 Charles Wesley (1707–88)

1 **Come, Thou long-expected Jesus,**
born to set Thy people free;
from our fears and sins release us;
let us find our rest in Thee.

2 Israel's strength and consolation,
hope of all the earth Thou art;
dear desire of every nation,
joy of every longing heart.

3 Born Thy people to deliver;
born a child, and yet a King;
born to reign in us for ever;
now Thy gracious kingdom bring.

4 By Thine own eternal Spirit
rule in all our hearts alone:
by Thine all-sufficient merit
raise us to Thy glorious throne.

103 Job Hupton (1762–1849)
and John Mason Neale (1818–66)

1 **Come, ye faithful,**
    raise the anthem,
cleave the skies with shouts of praise;
sing to Him who found the ransom,
Ancient of eternal days,
God eternal, Word incarnate,
whom the heaven of heaven obeys.

2 Ere He raised the lofty mountains,
formed the sea, or built the sky,
love eternal, free, and boundless,
forced the Lord of life to die,
lifted up the Prince of princes
on the throne of Calvary.

3 Now on those eternal mountains
stands the sapphire throne, all bright,
with the ceaseless alleluias
which they raise, the sons of light;
Sion's people tell His praises,
victor after hard-won fight.

4 Laud and honour to the Father,
laud and honour to the Son,
laud and honour to the Spirit,
ever Three and ever One,
One in love, and One in splendour,
while unending ages run.

104

Jodi Page Clark
© 1975 Celebration/Kingsway's Thankyou Music

Come to the waters
and I will give you rest;
come to the waters
and you will be refreshed.

1 Jesus said, 'Come unto Me
all ye weary, heavy-laden.'
Come to the waters . . .

2 Jesus said, of the waters that He gave,
'He who drinks shall never thirst again.'
Come to the waters . . .

3 Jesus said, 'He who believes in Me,
out of him shall flow living waters.'
Come to the waters . . .

4 So with joy we shall draw water
out of wells of salvation.
Come to the waters . . .

3 Who would not journey far to share
the wisdom of the wise,
and gaze with them in wonder where
the world's Redeemer lies?
The Lord of all the lords that are
is born at Bethlehem,
and kings shall kneel beneath His star
and we will bow with them.

4 Lift every heart the hymn of praise
that all creation sings;
the angel host its homage pays,
the shepherds and the kings.
For earth and sky with one accord,
O Child of Bethlehem,
are come to worship Christ the Lord
and we will come with them.

105

© Timothy Dudley-Smith

1 **Come, watch with us**
 this Christmas night;
our hearts must travel far
to darkened hills and heavens bright
with star on shining star;
to where in shadowy silence sleep
the fields of Bethlehem,
as shepherds wake their watch to keep
and we will watch with them.

2 Who would not join the angel-songs
that tell the Saviour's birth?
The Lord for whom creation longs
has come at last to earth;
the fulness of the Father's love
is ours at Bethlehem,
while angels throng the skies above
and we will sing with them.

106

Henry Alford (1810–71)
© in this version Jubilate Hymns

1 **Come, you thankful people, come,**
raise the song of harvest home!
fruit and crops are gathered in
safe before the storms begin:
God our maker will provide
for our needs to be supplied;
come, with all His people, come,
raise the song of harvest home!

2 All the world is God's own field,
harvests for His praise to yield;
wheat and weeds together sown
here for joy or sorrow grown:
first the blade and then the ear,
then the full corn shall appear –
Lord of harvest, grant that we
wholesome grain and pure may be.

3 For the Lord our God shall come
and shall bring His harvest home;
He Himself on that great day,
worthless things shall take away,
give His angels charge at last
in the fire the weeds to cast,
but the fruitful ears to store
in His care for evermore.

4 Even so, Lord, quickly come –
bring Your final harvest home!
gather all Your people in
free from sorrow, free from sin,
there together purified,
ever thankful at Your side –
come, with all Your angels, come,
bring that glorious harvest home!

3 Evil things are there before Thee;
in the heart, where they have fed,
wilt Thou pitifully enter,
Son of Man, and lay Thy head?
Enter, then, O Christ most holy;
make a Christmas in my heart;
make a heaven on my manger:
It is heaven where Thou art.

4 And to those who never listened
to the message of Thy birth,
who have winter, but no Christmas
bringing them Thy peace on earth,
send to these the joyful tidings;
by all people, in each home,
be there heard the Christmas anthem:
Praise to God, the Christ has come!

108
David Fellingham
© 1983 Kingsway's Thankyou Music

Create in me a clean heart, O God,
and renew a right spirit in me.
Create in me a clean heart, O God,
and renew a right spirit in me.

Wash me, cleanse me, purify me,
make my heart as white as snow.
Create in me a clean heart, O God,
and renew a right spirit in me.

107
George Stringer Rowe (1830–1913)

1 **Cradled in a manger, meanly**
laid the Son of Man His head;
sleeping His first earthly slumber
where the oxen had been fed.
Happy were those shepherds listening
to the holy angel's word;
happy they within that stable,
worshipping their infant Lord.

2 Happy all who hear the message
of His coming from above;
happier still who hail His coming,
and with praises greet His love.
Blessèd Saviour, Christ most holy,
in a manger Thou didst rest;
canst Thou stoop again, yet lower
and abide within my breast?

109
Matthew Bridges (1800–94)
and Godfrey Thring (1823–1903)

1 **Crown Him with many crowns,**
the Lamb upon His throne;
Hark! how the heavenly anthem
drowns
all music but its own:
awake, my soul, and sing
of Him who died for thee,
and hail Him as thy chosen King
through all eternity.

2 Crown Him the Son of God
before the worlds began;
and ye who tread where He hath trod,
crown Him the Son of Man,
who every grief hath known
that wrings the human breast,
and takes and bears them for His own,
that all in Him may rest.

3 Crown Him the Lord of life,
who triumphed o'er the grave,
and rose victorious in the strife,
for those He came to save:
His glories now we sing,
who died and rose on high,
who died eternal life to bring,
and lives that death may die.

4 Crown Him the Lord of heaven,
enthroned in worlds above;
crown Him the King to whom is given
the wondrous name of Love:
all hail, Redeemer, hail!
for Thou hast died for me;
Thy praise shall never, never fail
throughout eternity.

110 Graham Kendrick
© 1985 Kingsway's Thankyou Music

1 **Darkness like a shroud**
covers the earth,
evil like a cloud
covers the people;
but the Lord will rise upon you,
and His glory will appear on you,
nations will come to your light.
*Arise, shine, your light has come,
the glory of the Lord has risen on you;
arise, shine, your light has come –
Jesus the Light of the world has come.*

2 Children of the light,
be clean and pure;
rise, you sleepers,
Christ will shine on you:

take the Spirit's
flashing two-edged sword
and with faith
declare God's mighty word;
stand up, and in His strength be strong!
Arise, shine . . .

3 Here among us now,
Christ the Light
kindles brighter flames
in our trembling hearts:
Living Word, our lamp,
come guide our feet –
as we walk as one in light and peace,
justice and truth shine like the sun.
Arise, shine . . .

4 Like a city bright,
so let us blaze;
lights in every street
turning night to day:
and the darkness shall not overcome,
till the fulness
of Christ's kingdom comes,
dawning to God's eternal day.
*Arise, shine, your light has come,
the glory of the Lord has risen on you;
arise, shine, your light has come –
Jesus the Light of the world,
Jesus the Light of the world,
Jesus the Light of the world has come.*

111 John Greenleaf Whittier (1807–82)

1 **Dear Lord and Father of mankind,**
forgive our foolish ways;
re-clothe us in our rightful mind;
in purer lives Thy service find,
in deeper reverence, praise.

2 In simple trust like theirs who heard,
beside the Syrian sea,
the gracious calling of the Lord,
let us, like them, without a word
rise up and follow Thee.

3 O Sabbath rest by Galilee!
  O calm of hills above,
  where Jesus knelt to share with Thee
  the silence of eternity,
  interpreted by love!

4 With that deep hush subduing all
  our words and works that drown
  the tender whisper of Thy call,
  as noiseless let Thy blessing fall
  as fell Thy manna down.

5 Drop Thy still dews of quietness,
  till all our strivings cease;
  take from our souls
        the strain and stress,
  and let our ordered lives confess
  the beauty of Thy peace.

6 Breathe through the heats of our desire
  Thy coolness and Thy balm;
  let sense be dumb, let flesh retire;
  speak through the earthquake,
        wind, and fire,
  O still small voice of calm!

112 © 1985 Andy Silver

Delight yourself in the Lord,
and He will give you
        the desires of your heart.
Commit your way to the Lord;
trust in Him and He will make your
        righteousness shine,
shining like the dawn and like the
        noon-day sun.

The righteous will dwell
        in the land for ever,
to share His inheritance.

Delight yourself in the Lord,
and He will give you
        the desires of your heart.
Commit your way to the Lord,
commit your way to the Lord.

113 David Bolton
© 1978 Word's Spirit of Praise Music/ CopyCare

Delight yourselves in the Lord,
delight yourselves in the Lord;
for He delights in the praises
of His own people;
for He delights in the praises
of His own people.

Let your well spring up within
and overflow to one another;
let your well spring up within
and overflow to the Lord.

114 George Ratcliffe Woodward (1848–1934)
© SPCK

1 **Ding dong! Merrily on high**
  in heaven the bells are ringing.
  Ding dong! Verily the sky
  is riven with angels singing:
      Gloria, hosanna in excelsis;
      gloria, hosanna in excelsis!

2 E'en so, here below, below,
  let steeple bells be swungen;
  and i-o, i-o, i-o,
  by priest and people sungen!
      Gloria . . .

3 Pray you, dutifully prime
  your matin chime, ye ringers;
  may you beautifully rime
  your eve-time song, ye singers:
      Gloria . . .

115 Gerald Markland
© 1978 Kevin Mayhew Ltd

Do not be afraid,
for I have redeemed you.
I have called you by your name;
you are Mine.

1 When you walk through the waters
    I'll be with you;
  you will never sink beneath the waves.
    Do not be afraid,
    for I have redeemed you.
    I have called you by your name;
    you are Mine.

2 When the fire is burning
    all around you,
  you will never be consumed
    by the flames.
    Do not be afraid . . .

3 When the fear of loneliness is looming,
  then remember I am at your side.
    Do not be afraid . . .

4 When you dwell in the exile
    of the stranger,
  remember you are precious in My eyes.
    Do not be afraid . . .

5 You are Mine, O My child;
    I am your Father,
  and I love you with a perfect love.
    Do not be afraid . . .

116 William E Booth-Clibborn (1893–1969)
© 1921 Zondervan Corporation/Brentwood
Benson Music Publishing/CopyCare

1 **Down from His glory,**
    ever-living story,
  my God and Saviour came,
    and Jesus was His name;
  born in a manger
    to His own a stranger,
  a man of sorrows, tears and agony!
    O how I love Him! how I adore Him!
    My breath, my sunshine, my all-in-all!
    The great Creator became my Saviour,
    and all God's fulness dwelleth in Him!

2 What condescension,
    bringing us redemption,
  that in the dead of night,
    not one faint hope in sight;
  God, gracious, tender,
    laid aside His splendour,
  stooping to woo, to win,
    to save my soul.
    O how I love Him . . .

3 Without reluctance, flesh and blood,
    His substance,
  He took the form of man,
    revealed the hidden plan;
  O glorious mystery,
    sacrifice of Calvary!
  And now I know He is the great 'I AM'!
    O how I love Him . . .

117 From John 14:1–6
© 1980 Bible Society

1 **Do not be worried and upset.**
  Believe in God, believe also in Me,
  there are many rooms
    in My Father's house,
  and I'm going to prepare a place,
  prepare a place for you.
    I am the way, the truth and the life;
    no-one goes to the Father except by Me.
    I am the way, the truth and the life,
    and I'm going to prepare a place,
    prepare a place for you.

2 After I go and prepare a place for you,
  I will come back
    and take you to Myself,
  so that you may come
    and be where I am:
  and I'm going to prepare a place,
  prepare a place for you.

I am the way, the truth and the life;
no-one goes to the Father except by Me.
I am the way, the truth and the life,
and I'm going to prepare a place,
prepare a place for you;
and I'm going to prepare a place,
prepare a place for you.

118
Achor
© 1980 Word's Spirit of Praise Music/
CopyCare

Draw near to God
    and He'll draw near to you;
draw near to God
    and He'll draw near to you.
Lift up holy hands to Him
    and sing of what He's done;
open up your hearts to Him
    and praise Him for His Son.

119
Michael Card
© 1981 Whole Armor Publishing/
Windswept Pacific Music Ltd

El-Shaddai, El-Shaddai
    (God almighty, God almighty),
El-Elyon na Adonai
    (God in the highest, O Lord),
age to age You're still the same
by the power of the name.
El-Shaddai, El-Shaddai
    (God almighty, God almighty),
Erkamka na Adonai
    (We will love You, O Lord),
we will praise and lift You high,
El-Shaddai.

1 Through Your love
      and through the ram
  You saved the son of Abraham.
  Through the power of Your hand,
  turned the sea into dry land.

To the outcast on her knees
You were the God who really sees,
and by Your might
    You set Your children free.
    El-Shaddai, El-Shaddai . . .

2 Through the years You made it clear,
  that the time of Christ was near.
  Though the people couldn't see
  what Messiah ought to be.
  Though Your word contained the plan
  they just could not understand.
  Your most awesome work was done
  through the frailty of Your Son.
    El-Shaddai, El-Shaddai . . .

120
© 1987 Greg Leavers

MEN AND WOMEN IN CANON
Emmanuel, (Emmanuel,)
God with us, (God with us,)
Wonderful (Wonderful)
Counsellor, (Counsellor,)
ALL
Prince of peace –
a Saviour is born to redeem the world,
and His name is Jesus.
MEN AND WOMEN IN CANON
King of kings, (King of kings,)
Lord of lords (Lord of lords) is He.

1 God Himself will give a sign;
  a virgin shall bear a son
  who shall be called Emmanuel.
    Emmanuel . . .

2 People who now walk in darkness
  soon will see the light of Jesus,
  He is the Light of the world.
    Emmanuel . . .

3 Hear a voice cry in the desert,
  clear a way for the Messiah,
  make straight a highway for God.
    Emmanuel . . .

4 Bringing good news,
      healing heartaches,
   preaching freedom, releasing captives,
   giving a mantle of praise.
   Emmanuel, (Emmanuel,)
   God with us, (God with us,)
   Wonderful (Wonderful)
   Counsellor, (Counsellor,)
   Prince of peace –
   a Saviour is born to redeem the world,
   and His name is Jesus.
   King of kings, (King of kings,)
   Lord of lords (Lord of lords) is He.

3 O Holy Spirit, who didst brood
   upon the waters dark and rude,
   and bid their angry tumult cease,
   and give, for wild confusion, peace:
   O hear us when we cry to Thee
   for those in peril on the sea.

4 O Trinity of love and power,
   our brethren shield in danger's hour;
   from rock and tempest, fire and foe,
   protect them wheresoe'er they go:
   thus evermore shall rise to Thee
   glad hymns of praise
      from land and sea.

121 Bob McGee
© 1976 CA Music/Word Music Services/
CopyCare

Emmanuel, Emmanuel,
His name is called Emmanuel –
   God with us,
      revealed in us –
His name is called Emmanuel.

122 William Whiting (1825–78)

1 **Eternal Father, strong to save,**
   whose arm hath bound
      the restless wave,
   who bidd'st the mighty ocean deep
   its own appointed limits keep:
   O hear us when we cry to Thee
   for those in peril on the sea.

2 O Christ, whose voice the waters heard,
   and hushed their raging at Thy word,
   who walkedst on the foaming deep,
   and calm amid the storm didst sleep:
   O hear us when we cry to Thee
   for those in peril on the sea.

123 David Fellingham
© 1983 Kingsway's Thankyou Music

Eternal God, we come to You,
we come before Your throne;
we enter by a new and living way,
with confidence we come.
We declare Your faithfulness,
Your promises are true;
we will now draw near to worship You.

MEN
O holy God, we come to You,
O holy God,
      we see Your faithfulness and love,
Your mighty power, Your majesty,
are now revealed to us in Jesus
      who has died,
Jesus who was raised,
Jesus now exalted on high.

WOMEN
O holy God, full of justice,
wisdom and righteousness,
faithfulness and love;
Your mighty power and Your majesty
are now revealed to us
in Jesus who has died for our sin,
Jesus who was raised from the dead,
Jesus now exalted on high.

124

Rick Ridings
© 1977, 1980 Scripture in Song/
Integrity Music/Kingsway's Thankyou Music

Exalt the Lord our God,
exalt the Lord our God,
and worship at His footstool,
worship at His footstool;
holy is He, holy is He.

125

From Luke 2
© Timothy Dudley-Smith

1 **Faithful vigil ended,**
watching, waiting cease:
Master, grant Your servant
his discharge in peace.

2 All the Spirit promised,
all the Father willed,
now these eyes behold it
perfectly fulfilled.

3 This Your great deliverance
sets Your people free;
Christ their light uplifted
all the nations see.

4 Christ, Your people's glory!
Watching, doubting cease:
grant to us Your servants
our discharge in peace.

126

Frank Houghton (1894–1972)
© OMF

1 **Facing a task unfinished,**
that drives us to our knees,
a need that, undiminished,
rebukes our slothful ease,
we who rejoice to know Thee,
renew before Thy throne
the solemn pledge we owe Thee,
to go and make Thee known.

2 Where other lords beside Thee
hold their unhindered sway,
where forces that defied Thee
defy Thee still today,
with none to heed their crying
for life, and love, and light,
unnumbered souls are dying,
and pass into the night.

3 We bear the torch that, flaming,
fell from the hands of those
who gave their lives, proclaiming
that Jesus died and rose.
Ours is the same commission,
the same glad message ours;
fired by the same ambition,
to Thee we yield our powers.

4 O Father who sustained them,
O Spirit who inspired,
Saviour, whose love constrained them
to toil with zeal untired,
from cowardice defend us,
from lethargy awake!
Forth on Thine errands send us,
to labour for Thy sake.

127

John Eddison
© Scripture Union

1 **Father, although I cannot see**
the future You have planned,
and though the path is sometimes dark
and hard to understand:
yet give me faith, through joy and pain,
to trace Your loving hand.

2 When I recall that in the past
Your promises have stood
through each perplexing circumstance
and every changing mood,
I rest content that all things work
together for my good.

3 Whatever, then, the future brings
of good or seeming ill,
I ask for strength to follow You
and grace to trust You still;
and I would look for no reward,
except to do Your will.

4 Alleluia,
alleluia,
alleluia,
alleluia.

(repeat last verse)

128
Ian Smale
© 1984 Kingsway's Thankyou Music

Father God, I wonder
how I managed to exist
without the knowledge
of Your parenthood
and Your loving care.
But now I am Your son,
I am adopted in Your family,
and I can never be alone
'cause, Father God,
You're there beside me.

I will sing Your praises,
I will sing Your praises,
I will sing Your praises for evermore.
I will sing Your praises,
I will sing Your praises,
I will sing Your praises for evermore.

129
© Joan Robinson

1 **Father God, I love You,**
Father God, I love You,
Father God, I love You,
come into my life.

2 Jesus, I love You,
Jesus, I love You,
Jesus, I love You,
come into my life.

3 Spirit, I love You,
Spirit, I love You,
Spirit, I love You,
come into my life.

130
© John Richards/Renewal Servicing

1 **Father God, the Lord, Creator,**
by whose hand we all are fed,
in Your mercy re-create us
at the breaking of the bread.

2 Christ our Lord, be present with us,
risen victorious from the dead!
In Your mercy may we know You,
in the breaking of the bread.

3 Holy Spirit, God's empowering,
by whose life the Church is led;
in Your mercy, send us strengthened
from the breaking of the bread.

4 Father, Son, and Holy Spirit,
hear our praises – sung and said.
From our hearts
comes our thanksgiving
for the breaking of the bread.

131
Graham Kendrick
© 1981 Kingsway's Thankyou Music

1 **Father God, we worship You,**
make us part of all You do.
As You move among us now
we worship You.

2 Jesus, King, we worship You,
help us listen now to You.
As You move among us now
we worship You.

3 Spirit pure, we worship You,
with Your fire our zeal renew.
As You move among us now
we worship You.

132 Love Maria Willis (1824–1908)

1 **Father, hear the prayer we offer:**
not for ease that prayer shall be,
but for strength, that we may ever
live our lives courageously.

2 Not for ever in green pastures
do we ask our way to be:
but by steep and rugged pathways
would we strive to climb to Thee.

3 Not for ever by still waters
would we idly quiet stay;
but would smite the living fountains
from the rocks along our way.

4 Be our strength in hours of weakness,
in our wanderings be our guide;
through endeavour, failure, danger,
Father, be Thou at our side.

5 Let our path be bright or dreary,
storm or sunshine be our share;
may our souls, in hope unweary,
make Thy work our ceaseless prayer.

133 Jenny Hewer
© 1975 Kingsway's Thankyou Music

1 **Father, I place into Your hands**
the things that I can't do.
Father, I place into Your hands
the times that I've been through.
Father, I place into Your hands
the way that I should go,
for I know I always can trust You.

2 Father, I place into Your hands
my friends and family.
Father, I place into Your hands
the things that trouble me.
Father, I place into Your hands
the person I would be,
for I know I always can trust You.

3 Father, we love to seek Your face,
we love to hear Your voice.
Father, we love to sing Your praise,
and in Your name rejoice.
Father, we love to walk with You
and in Your presence rest,
for we know we always can trust You.

4 Father, I want to be with You
and do the things You do.
Father, I want to speak the words
that You are speaking too.
Father, I want to love the ones
that You will draw to You,
for I know that I am one with You.

134 Dave Bilbrough
© 1985 Kingsway's Thankyou Music

1 **Father in heaven,**
our voices we raise:
receive our devotion,
receive now our praise
as we sing of the glory
of all that You've done –
the greatest love-story
that's ever been sung.
*And we will crown You Lord of all,
yes, we will crown You Lord of all,
for You have won the victory:
yes, we will crown You Lord of all.*

2 Father in heaven,
   our lives are Your own;
   we've been caught by a vision
   of Jesus alone –
   who came as a servant
   to free us from sin:
   Father in heaven,
   our worship we bring.
   And we will crown You Lord of all,
   yes, we will crown You Lord of all,
   for You have won the victory:
   yes, we will crown You Lord of all.

3 We will sing, 'Alleluia',
   we will sing to the King,
   to our mighty deliverer
   our alleluias will ring.
   Yes, our praise is resounding
   to the Lamb on the throne:
   He alone is exalted
   through the love He has shown.
   And we will crown . . .

135 Bob Fitts
© 1985 Scripture in Song/Integrity Music/
Kingsway's Thankyou Music

Father in heaven, how we love You,
we lift Your name in all the earth.
May Your kingdom be established
   in our praises
as Your people declare Your mighty works.
Blessèd be the Lord God almighty,
who was and is and is to come,
blessèd be the Lord God almighty,
who reigns for evermore.

136 © 1985 John Richards/Renewal Servicing

1 **Father, sending Your anointed**
   Son to save, forgive, and heal;
   and, through Him, Your Holy Spirit,
   to make our salvation real;

2 Look upon our ills and trouble,
   and on those who suffer much.
   Send Your Church the Spirit's unction
   in Christ's name to heal and touch.

3 Grant forgiveness to the faithful;
   bring to unity their prayer;
   use it for Your work unhindered,
   through both sacrament and care.

OPTIONAL VERSE
FOR WHEN ANOINTING TAKES PLACE
4 May the *one/ones* to be anointed
   outwardly with oil this hour,
   know Christ's fullest restoration
   through the Holy Spirit's power.

5 Heal Your Church! Anoint and send us
   out into the world to tell
   of Your love and blessings to us;
   how, in Christ, 'All will be well.'

137 Rick Ridings
© 1976, 1983 Scripture in Song/
Integrity Music/Kingsway's Thankyou Music

1 **Father, make us one,**
   Father, make us one,
   that the world may know
      Thou hast sent the Son,
   Father, make us one.

2 Behold how pleasant
      and how good it is
   for brethren to dwell in unity,
   for there the Lord
      commands the blessing,
   life for evermore.

138 Graham Kendrick
© 1988 Make Way Music

1 **Father, never was love so near;**
   tender, my deepest wounds to heal.
   Precious to me,
   Your gift of love;
   for me You gave
   Your only Son.

And now thanks be to God
for His gift beyond words,
the Son whom He loved;
no, He did not withhold Him,
but with Him gave everything;
now He's everything to me.

2   Jesus, the heart of God revealed,
with us, feeling the pain we feel.
Cut to the heart,
wounded for me,
taking the blame,
making me clean.
    And now thanks be to God . . .

2   Jesus, we love You,
because You first loved us;
You reached out and healed us
with Your mighty touch.
    All the earth . . .

3   Spirit, we need You,
to lift us from this mire;
consume and empower us
with Your holy fire.
    All the earth . . .

Holy is He; blessèd is He;
worthy is He; gracious is He;
faithful is He; awesome is He;
Saviour is He; Master is He;
mighty is He:
have mercy on me.

139   Terrye Coelho
© 1972 Maranatha! Music/CopyCare

1   **Father, we adore You,**
lay our lives before You:
how we love You!

2   Jesus, we adore You,
lay our lives before You:
how we love You!

3   Spirit, we adore You,
lay our lives before You:
how we love You!

141   Everett Perry
© 1983 Kingsway's Thankyou Music

Father, Your love is precious
    beyond all loves,
Father, Your love overwhelms me.
Father, Your love is precious
    beyond all loves,
Father, Your love overwhelms me.
So I lift up my hands,
an expression of my love,
and I give You my heart
in joyful obedience.
Father, Your love is precious
    beyond all loves,
Father, Your love overwhelms me.

140   Carl Tuttle
© 1982 Mercy/Vineyard Publishing/
CopyCare

1   **Father, we adore You,**
You've drawn us to this place;
we bow down before You,
humbly on our face.
    All the earth shall worship
    at the throne of the King;
    of His great and awesome power,
    we shall sing!

142   Donna Adkins
© 1976, 1981 Maranatha! Music/
CopyCare

1   **Father, we love You,**
we worship and adore You:
glorify Your name
in all the earth.
Glorify Your name, (*3 times*)
in all the earth.

2 Jesus, we love You,
   we worship and adore You:
   glorify Your name
   in all the earth.
   Glorify Your name, (*3 times*)
   in all the earth.

3 Spirit, we love You,
   we worship and adore You:
   glorify Your name
   in all the earth.
   Glorify Your name, (*3 times*)
   in all the earth.

143 John Samuel Bewley Monsell (1811–75)

1 **Fight the good fight
   with all thy might;**
   Christ is thy strength,
       and Christ thy right.
   Lay hold on life, and it shall be
   thy joy and crown eternally.

2 Run the straight race
       through God's good grace,
   lift up thine eyes, and seek His face;
   life with its path before thee lies;
   Christ is the way, and Christ the prize.

3 Cast care aside, lean on thy guide,
   His boundless mercy will provide;
   lean, and thy trusting soul shall prove
   Christ is thy life, and Christ thy love.

4 Faint not, nor fear, His arm is near,
   He changeth not, and thou art dear;
   only believe, and thou shalt see
   that Christ is all-in-all to thee.

144 Priscilla Wright Porter © 1971, 1975 Celebration/ Kingsway's Thankyou Music

Fear not, rejoice and be glad,
the Lord hath done a great thing;
hath poured out His Spirit
    on all mankind,
on those who confess His name.

1 The fig tree is budding,
       the vine beareth fruit,
   the wheat fields are golden with grain.
   Thrust in the sickle, the harvest is ripe,
   the Lord has given us rain.
       Fear not, rejoice . . .

2 Ye shall eat in plenty and be satisfied,
   the mountains will drip
       with sweet wine.
   My children shall drink
       of the fountain of life,
   My children will know they are Mine.
       Fear not, rejoice . . .

3 My people shall know
       that I am the Lord,
   their shame I have taken away.
   My Spirit will lead them
       together again,
   My Spirit will show them the way.
       Fear not, rejoice . . .

4 My children shall dwell
       in a body of love,
   a light to the world they will be.
   Life shall come forth
       from the Father above,
   My body will set mankind free.
       Fear not, rejoice . . .

145 Chris Bowater © 1983 Sovereign Lifestyle Music

Fill the place, Lord, with Your glory,
at this gathering of Your own;
reign in sovereign grace and power
from Your praise-surrounded throne.

Fill the place, Lord, with Your glory,
at this gathering of Your own;
we exalt You, we adore You,
thankful hearts now join as one.

You're the Christ, the King of glory,
Father's well-belovèd Son.
Fill the place, Lord, with Your glory,
at this gathering of Your own.

146 Horatius Bonar (1808–82)

1 **Fill Thou my life, O Lord my God,**
in every part with praise,
that my whole being may proclaim
Thy being and Thy ways.

2 Not for the lip of praise alone,
nor e'en the praising heart,
I ask, but for a life made up
of praise in every part:

3 Praise in the common things of life,
its goings out and in;
praise in each duty and each deed,
however small and mean.

4 Fill every part of me with praise:
let all my being speak
of Thee and of Thy love, O Lord,
poor though I be and weak.

5 So shalt Thou, Lord, from me,
e'en me,
receive Thy glory due;
and so shall I begin on earth
the song for ever new.

6 So shall no part of day or night
from sacredness be free;
but all my life, in every step,
be fellowship with Thee.

147 From Psalm 147
© Timothy Dudley-Smith

1 **Fill your hearts**
with joy and gladness,
sing and praise your God and mine!
Great the Lord in love and wisdom,
might and majesty divine!
He who framed the starry heavens
knows and names them as they shine.

2 Praise the Lord, His people,
praise Him!
wounded souls His comfort know;
those who fear Him find His mercies,
peace for pain and joy for woe;
humble hearts are high exalted,
human pride and power laid low.

3 Praise the Lord for times and seasons,
cloud and sunshine, wind and rain;
spring to melt the snows of winter
till the waters flow again;
grass upon the mountain pastures,
golden valleys thick with grain.

4 Fill your hearts with joy and gladness,
peace and plenty crown your days;
love His laws, declare His judgements,
walk in all His words and ways;
He the Lord and we His children –
praise the Lord, all people, praise!

148 William Walsham How (1823–97)

1 **For all the saints**
who from their labours rest,
who Thee by faith
before the world confessed,
Thy name, O Jesu, be for ever blest.
Alleluia!

2 Thou wast their rock,
their fortress, and their might;
Thou, Lord, their Captain
in the well-fought fight;
Thou in the darkness drear
their one true light.
Alleluia!

3 O may Thy soldiers,
faithful, true and bold,
fight as the saints
who nobly fought of old,
and win, with them,
the victor's crown of gold!
Alleluia!

4 O blest communion, fellowship divine!
  We feebly struggle, they in glory shine;
  yet all are one in Thee,
      for all are Thine.
  Alleluia!

5 And when the strife is fierce,
      the warfare long,
  steals on the ear
      the distant triumph-song,
  and hearts are brave again,
      and arms are strong.
  Alleluia!

6 The golden evening
      brightens in the west;
  soon, soon to faithful warriors
      cometh rest;
  sweet is the calm of paradise the blest.
  Alleluia!

7 But lo! there breaks
      a yet more glorious day:
  the saints triumphant
      rise in bright array;
  the King of glory passes on His way.
  Alleluia!

8 From earth's wide bounds,
      from ocean's farthest coast,
  through gates of pearl
      streams in the countless host,
  singing to Father, Son and Holy Ghost.
  Alleluia!

149 Graham Kendrick
© 1988 Make Way Music

WOMEN
1 **For God so loved the world**
  that He gave His only Son;
  and all who believe in Him
  shall not die,
  but have eternal life;
  no, they shall not die,
  but have eternal life.

ALL
2 And God showed His love for you,
  when He gave His only Son;
  and you, if you trust in Him,
  shall not die,
  but have eternal life;
  no, you shall not die,
  but have eternal life.

150 Dale Garratt
© 1972 Scripture in Song/Integrity Music/
Kingsway's Thankyou Music

For His name is exalted,
His glory above heaven and earth.
Holy is the Lord God almighty,
who was and who is and who is to come.

For His name is exalted,
His glory above heaven and earth.
Holy is the Lord God almighty,
who sitteth on the throne
      and who lives for evermore.

151 Dave Richards
© 1977 Kingsway's Thankyou Music

For I'm building a people of power
and I'm making a people of praise,
that will move through this land
      by My Spirit,
and will glorify My precious name.
Build Your Church, Lord,
make us strong, Lord,
join our hearts, Lord, through Your Son;
make us one, Lord, in Your body,
in the kingdom of Your Son.

152
Folliott Pierpoint (1835–1917)
altered © 1986 Horrobin/Leavers

1 **For the beauty of the earth,**
   for the beauty of the skies,
   for the love which from our birth
   over and around us lies;
   Father, unto You we raise
   this our sacrifice of praise.

2 For the beauty of each hour
   of the day and of the night,
   hill and vale, and tree and flower,
   sun and moon, and stars of light;
   Father, unto You we raise
   this our sacrifice of praise.

3 For the joy of love from God,
   that we share on earth below;
   for our friends and family,
   and the love that they can show;
   Father, unto You we raise
   this our sacrifice of praise.

4 For each perfect gift divine
   to our race so freely given,
   thank You Lord that they are mine,
   here on earth as gifts from heaven;
   Father, unto You we raise
   this our sacrifice of praise.

153
Fred Pratt Green
© Stainer & Bell Ltd

1 **For the fruits of His creation,**
   thanks be to God!
   For His gifts to every nation,
   thanks be to God!
   For the ploughing, sowing, reaping,
   silent growth while we are sleeping;
   future needs in earth's safe keeping,
   thanks be to God!

2 In the just reward of labour,
   God's will is done;
   in the help we give our neighbour,
   God's will is done;

in our world-wide task of caring
for the hungry and despairing;
in the harvests we are sharing,
God's will is done.

3 For the harvests of the Spirit,
   thanks be to God!
   For the good we all inherit,
   thanks be to God!
   For the wonders that astound us,
   for the truths that still confound us;
   most of all, that love has found us,
   thanks be to God!

154
Charles Silvester Horne (1865–1914)

1 **For the might of Your arm**
     we bless You,
   our God, our fathers' God;
   You have kept Your pilgrim people
   by the strength of Your staff and rod;
   You have called us to the journey
   which faithless feet ne'er trod;
     For the might of Your arm we bless You,
     our God, our fathers' God.

2 For the love of Christ constraining,
   that bound their hearts as one;
   for the faith in truth and freedom
   in which their work was done;
   for the peace of God's evangel
   wherewith their feet were shod;
     For the might . . .

3 We are watchers of a beacon
   whose light must never die;
   we are guardians of an altar
   that shows You ever nigh;
   we are children of Your freemen
   who sleep beneath the sod;
     For the might . . .

4 May the shadow of Your presence
around our camp be spread;
baptize us with the courage
You gave unto our dead;
O keep us in the pathway
their saintly feet have trod;
For the might of Your arm we bless You,
our God, our fathers' God.

155 Graham Kendrick
© 1985 Kingsway's Thankyou Music

1 **For this purpose**
   Christ was revealed,
to destroy all the works of the evil one.
Christ in us has overcome,
so with gladness we sing
and welcome His kingdom in.
MEN *Over sin He has conquered:*
WOMEN *hallelujah! He has conquered.*
MEN *Over death victorious:*
WOMEN *hallelujah! victorious.*
MEN *Over sickness He has triumphed:*
WOMEN *hallelujah! He has triumphed.*
ALL *Jesus reigns over all!*

2 In the name of Jesus we stand;
by the power of His blood
we now claim this ground:
Satan has no authority here,
powers of darkness must flee,
for Christ has the victory.
Over sin . . .

156 From Isaiah 9
Copyright control

For unto us a child is born,
unto us a son is given;
and the government
shall be upon His shoulders.

And His name shall be called
wonderful, counsellor,
the mighty God,
the everlasting Father,
and the Prince of peace is He.

157 David Hadden
© 1984 Restoration Music Ltd/
Sovereign Music UK

1 **For unto us a child is born,**
unto us a son is given,
and the government
   shall be upon His shoulder;
for unto us a child is born,
unto us a son is given,
and the government
   shall be upon His shoulder.
And He will be called wonderful,
wonderful counsellor, mighty God,
the everlasting Father, Prince of peace,
Mighty God.

2 And there shall be no end
to the increase of His rule,
to the increase of His government
   and peace;
for He shall sit on David's throne
upholding righteousness,
our God shall accomplish this.
And He will be called . . .

3 For He is the mighty God,
He is the Prince of peace,
the King of kings and Lord of lords:
all honour to the King,
all glory to His name,
for now and for evermore!
And He will be called . . .

158

© 1977 Pete Sanchez Jr, ASCAP/ Gabriel Music Inc.

For Thou, O Lord,
art high above all the earth;
Thou art exalted far above all gods.
For Thou, O Lord,
art high above all the earth;
Thou art exalted far above all gods.
I exalt Thee, I exalt Thee,
I exalt Thee, O Lord;
I exalt Thee, I exalt Thee,
I exalt Thee, O Lord.

159

Charles Wesley (1707–88)

1 **Forth in Thy name, O Lord, I go,**
my daily labour to pursue,
Thee, only Thee, resolved to know
in all I think, or speak, or do.

2 The task Thy wisdom hath assigned
O let me cheerfully fulfil;
in all my works Thy presence find,
and prove Thy acceptable will.

3 Thee may I set at my right hand,
whose eyes my inmost substance see;
and labour on at Thy command,
and offer all my works to Thee.

4 Give me to bear Thy easy yoke,
and every moment watch and pray,
and still to things eternal look,
and hasten to Thy glorious day.

5 For Thee delightfully employ
whate'er Thy bounteous grace
    hath given,
and run my course with even joy,
and closely walk with Thee to heaven.

160

George Hunt Smyttan (1822–70) altd.

1 **Forty days and forty nights**
Thou wast fasting in the wild;
forty days and forty nights
tempted and yet undefiled.

2 Sunbeams scorching all the day,
chilly dew-drops nightly shed,
prowling beasts about Thy way,
stones Thy pillow, earth Thy bed.

3 Let us Thy endurance share
and from earthly greed abstain,
with Thee watching unto prayer,
with Thee strong to suffer pain.

4 Then if evil on us press,
flesh or spirit to assail,
victor in the wilderness,
may we never faint or fail!

5 So shall peace divine be ours;
holier gladness ours shall be;
come to us angelic powers,
such as ministered to Thee.

161

© Timothy Dudley-Smith

1 **Freely, for the love He bears us,**
God has made His purpose plain:
Christ has died and Christ is risen,
Christ will come again.

2 Christ has died, the world's Redeemer,
Lamb of God for sinners slain:
Christ has died . . .

3 Christ is risen, high-ascended,
Lord of all to rule and reign:
Christ has died . . .

4 Christ is coming, King of glory,
firmly then the faith maintain:
Christ has died . . .

162

Graham Kendrick
© 1983 Kingsway's Thankyou Music

1 **From heaven You came,**
    helpless babe,
entered our world, Your glory veiled,
not to be served but to serve,
and give Your life that we might live.

This is our God, the Servant King,
He calls us now to follow Him,
to bring our lives as a daily offering
of worship to the Servant King.

2 There in the garden of tears
   my heavy load He chose to bear;
   His heart with sorrow was torn,
   'Yet not my will but yours,' He said.
   This is our God . . .

3 Come see His hands and His feet,
   the scars that speak of sacrifice,
   hands that flung stars into space
   to cruel nails surrendered.
   This is our God . . .

4 So let us learn how to serve
   and in our lives enthrone Him,
   each other's needs to prefer,
   for it is Christ we're serving.
   This is our God . . .

163 From Psalm 113
         © Paul S Deming/Integrity Music/
         Kingsway's Thankyou Music

From the rising of the sun
to the going down of the same,
the Lord's name is to be praised.
From the rising of the sun
to the going down of the same,
the Lord's name is to be praised.
Praise ye the Lord,
praise Him, O ye servants of the Lord,
praise the name of the Lord;
blessèd be the name of the Lord
from this time forth,
and for evermore.

164 Graham Kendrick
         © 1988 Make Way Music

1 **From the sun's rising**
      unto the sun's setting,
   Jesus our Lord
      shall be great in the earth;
   and all earth's kingdoms
      shall be His dominion –
   all of creation shall sing of His worth.
      Let every heart, every voice,
      every tongue join with spirits ablaze;
      one in His love,
      we will circle the world
      with the song of His praise.
      O let all His people rejoice,
      and let all the earth hear His voice!

2 To every tongue, tribe
      and nation He sends us,
   to make disciples, to teach and baptize;
   for all authority to Him is given;
   now as His witnesses we shall arise.
      Let every heart . . .

3 Come let us join with
      the Church from all nations,
   cross every border,
      throw wide every door;
   workers with Him
      as He gathers His harvest,
   till earth's far corners
      our Saviour adore.
      Let every heart . . .

      Let all His people rejoice,
      and let all the earth hear His voice!

165 © 1988 Gillian Hutchinson

1 **Give me a heart**
      that will love the unlovely,
   open my eyes to the needy and lost,
   help me, O Lord,
      to show Your love in action,
   give, without counting the cost,
   give, without counting the cost.

2   Help me remember
        I'm empty without You,
    help me to find my strength
        only in You.
    I can give nothing
        unless You first fill me,
    Your love alone must shine through,
    Your love alone must shine through.

3   Make me be willing
        to go where You send me,
    make me be ready to answer Your call.
    Give me a heart
        that rejoices to serve You,
    sharing the best love of all,
    sharing the best love of all.

166 Katherine Agnes May Kelly (1869–1942)
         © National Young Life Campaign

1   **Give me a sight, O Saviour,**
    of Thy wondrous love to me,
    of the love that brought Thee
        down to earth,
    to die on Calvary.
      O make me understand it,
      help me to take it in;
      what it meant to Thee,
      the Holy One,
      to bear away my sin.

2   Was it the nails, O Saviour,
    that bound Thee to the tree?
    Nay, 'twas Thine everlasting love,
    Thy love for me, for me.
      O make me understand . . .

3   O wonder of all wonders,
    that through Thy death for me
    my open sins, my secret sins,
    can all forgiven be!
      O make me understand . . .

4   Then melt my heart, O Saviour,
    bend me, yes, break me down,
    until I own Thee Conqueror,
    and Lord, and Sovereign crown.
      O make me understand . . .

167 A Sevison
         Copyright control

1   **Give me oil in my lamp,**
      keep me burning,
    give me oil in my lamp, I pray;
    give me oil in my lamp,
      keep me burning,
    keep me burning till the break of day.
      Sing hosanna, sing hosanna,
      sing hosanna to the King of kings!
      Sing hosanna, sing hosanna,
      sing hosanna to the King!

2   Make me a fisher of men,
      keep me seeking,
    make me a fisher of men, I pray;
    make me a fisher of men,
      keep me seeking,
    keep me seeking till the break of day.
      Sing hosanna . . .

3   Give me joy in my heart,
      keep me singing,
    give me joy in my heart, I pray;
    give me joy in my heart,
      keep me singing,
    keep me singing till the break of day.
      Sing hosanna . . .

4   Give me love in my heart,
      keep me serving,
    give me love in my heart, I pray;
    give me love in my heart,
      keep me serving,
    keep me serving till the break of day.
      Sing hosanna . . .

168
Charles Wesley (1707–88)

1 **Give me the faith
which can remove**
and sink the mountain to a plain;
give me the childlike, praying love,
which longs to build Thy house again;
Thy love let it my heart o'erpower,
let it my ransomed soul devour.

2 I would the precious time redeem,
and longer live for this alone –
to spend and to be spent for them
who have not yet my Saviour known;
fully on these my mission prove,
and only breathe to breathe Thy love.

3 My talents, gifts, and graces, Lord,
into Thy blessèd hands receive;
and let me live to preach Thy word,
and let me to Thy glory live;
my every sacred moment spend
in publishing the sinners' friend.

4 Enlarge, inflame, and fill my heart
with boundless charity divine;
so shall I all my strength exert,
and love them with a zeal like Thine;
and lead them to Thine open side,
the sheep for whom their shepherd
died.

169
Mark Hayes
© 1995 Lorenz Publishing Co/
MCA Music Publishing/CopyCare

1 **Give thanks to the Lord
for He is good,**
His love endures for ever.
Give thanks to the God of gods,
His love endures for ever.
O give thanks to the Lord of lords,
His love endures for ever.
To Him alone who does great works,
His love endures for ever.

2 By His understanding
made the heavens,
His love endures for ever.
Who made the great and shining lights,
His love endures for ever.
The mighty sun to rule the day,
His love endures for ever.
And the moon and the stars
to rule at night,
His love endures for ever.
*Hallelujah, hallelu,
the Lord Jehovah reigns.
He is the same from age to age;
His love will never change.*

3 God led His children
through the wilderness,
His love endures for ever.
And struck down many mighty kings,
His love endures for ever.
And gave to them an inheritance,
His love endures for ever.
A promised land for Israel,
His love endures for ever.
Hallelujah . . .

4 He remembered us in our low estate,
His love endures for ever.
And freed us from our enemies,
His love endures for ever.
To every creature He gives food,
His love endures for ever.
Give thanks to the God of heaven,
His love endures for ever,
His love endures for ever,
His love endures for ever.

170
Henry Smith
© 1978 Integrity's Hosanna! Music/
Kingsway's Thankyou Music

Give thanks with a grateful heart,
give thanks to the Holy One;
give thanks because He's given
Jesus Christ, His Son.
Give thanks . . .

And now let the weak say, 'I am strong',
let the poor say, 'I am rich',
because of what the Lord has done for us;
and now let the weak say, 'I am strong',
let the poor say, 'I am rich',
because of what the Lord has done for us.
    Give thanks . . .

And now . . .

172
Danny Reed
© 1987 Kingsway's Thankyou Music

Glorious Father, we exalt You;
we worship, honour and adore You;
we delight to be in Your presence, O Lord.
We magnify Your holy name,
and we sing, 'Come, Lord Jesus,
glorify Your name!'
and we sing, 'Come, Lord Jesus,
glorify Your name!'

171
Isaac Watts (1674–1748) altd.

1 **Give to our God immortal praise;**
   mercy and truth are all His ways:
   wonders of grace to God belong,
   repeat His mercies in your song.

2 Give to the Lord of lords renown;
   the King of kings with glory crown:
   His mercies ever shall endure,
   when lords and kings
        are known no more.

3 He built the earth, He spread the sky,
   and fixed the starry lights on high:
   wonders of grace to God belong,
   repeat His mercies in your song.

4 He fills the sun with morning light,
   He bids the moon direct the night:
   His mercies ever shall endure,
   when suns and moons
        shall shine no more.

5 He sent His Son with power to save
   from guilt and darkness and the grave:
   wonders of grace to God belong,
   repeat His mercies in your song.

173
John Newton (1725–1807)

1 **Glorious things of thee are spoken,**
   Zion, city of our God;
   He, whose word cannot be broken,
   formed thee for His own abode:
   on the rock of ages founded,
   what can shake thy sure repose?
   With salvation's walls surrounded,
   thou may'st smile at all thy foes.

2 See, the streams of living waters,
   springing from eternal love,
   well supply thy sons and daughters
   and all fear of want remove:
   who can faint, while such a river
   ever flows their thirst to assuage?
   Grace which, like the Lord, the giver,
   never fails from age to age.

3 Saviour, if of Zion's city
   I, through grace, a member am,
   let the world deride or pity,
   I will glory in Thy name:
   fading is the worldling's pleasure,
   all his boasted pomp and show;
   solid joys and lasting treasure
   none but Zion's children know.

174

Danny Daniels
© 1987 Mercy/Vineyard Publishing/
CopyCare

Glory, glory in the highest,
glory, to the Almighty;
glory to the Lamb of God,
and glory to the living Word;
glory to the Lamb!
Glory, glory . . .

MEN	I give glory,
WOMEN	glory,
MEN	glory,
WOMEN	glory,
MEN	glory,
ALL	glory to the Lamb!
MEN	I give glory . . .
ALL	I give glory to the Lamb!

175

© 1984 John Richards/Renewal Servicing

1 **Glory be to God in heaven,**
   and to all on earth, His peace;
   Lord and Father, King in glory,
   gifts of praise in us release,
   so our worship and thanksgiving
   from our hearts will never cease.

2 Christ incarnate, sent by Father
   to redeem, renew, restore;
   risen Lamb, in glory seated,
   hear our prayers, Lord, we implore.
   Now to Father, Son, and Spirit
   be all glory evermore.

176

Thomas Ken (1637–1710)
© in this version Jubilate Hymns

1 **Glory to You, my God, this night**
   for all the blessings of the light;
   keep me, O keep me, King of kings,
   beneath Your own almighty wings.

2 Forgive me, Lord,
        through Your dear Son,
   the wrong that I this day have done,
   that peace with God and man may be,
   before I sleep, restored to me.

3 Teach me to live, that I may dread
   the grave as little as my bed;
   teach me to die, that so I may
   rise glorious at the awesome day.

4 O may my soul on You repose
   and restful sleep my eyelids close;
   sleep that shall me more vigorous make
   to serve my God when I awake.

5 If in the night I sleepless lie,
   my mind with peaceful thoughts
        supply;
   let no dark dreams disturb my rest,
   no powers of evil me molest.

6 Praise God
        from whom all blessings flow
   in heaven above and earth below;
   one God, three persons, we adore –
   to Him be praise for evermore!

177

© 1986 Greg Leavers

Glory to God in the highest,
peace upon earth,
Jesus Christ has come to earth;
that's why we sing,
Jesus the King,
Jesus has come for you.

1 The shepherds who were sitting there
   were suddenly filled with fear;
   the dark night was filled with light,
   angels singing everywhere.
   Glory to God . . .

2 The next time we hear a song
   of worship from a heavenly throng,
   will be when Jesus comes again,
   then with triumph we'll all sing:
   Glory to God . . .

5 Go forth and tell!
      O Church of God, arise!
   Go in the strength
      which Christ your Lord supplies;
   go till all nations His great name adore
   and serve Him, Lord and King
      for evermore.

178 James E Seddon (1915–83)
© Mavis Seddon/Jubilate Hymns

1 **Go forth and tell!**
      O Church of God, awake!
   God's saving news
      to all the nations take:
   proclaim Christ Jesus,
      Saviour, Lord and King,
   that all the world
      His worthy praise may sing.

2 Go forth and tell!
      God's love embraces all;
   He will in grace
      respond to all who call:
   how shall they call
      if they have never heard
   the gracious invitation of His word?

3 Go forth and tell!
      men still in darkness lie;
   in wealth or want,
      in sin they live and die:
   give us, O Lord,
      concern of heart and mind,
   a love like Yours
      which cares for all mankind.

4 Go forth and tell!
      the doors are open wide:
   share God's good gifts –
      let no-one be denied;
   live out your life
      as Christ your Lord shall choose,
   your ransomed powers
      for His sole glory use.

179 © Geoffrey Marshall-Taylor/
Jubilate Hymns

Go, tell it on the mountain,
over the hills and everywhere;
go, tell it on the mountain
that Jesus is His name.

1 He possessed no riches,
      no home to lay His head;
   He saw the needs of others
      and cared for them instead.
   Go tell it on the mountain . . .

2 He reached out and touched them,
      the blind, the deaf, the lame;
   He spoke and listened gladly
      to anyone who came.
   Go tell it on the mountain . . .

3 Some turned away in anger,
      with hatred in the eye;
   they tried Him and condemned Him,
      then led Him out to die.
   Go tell it on the mountain . . .

4 'Father, now forgive them' –
      those were the words He said;
   in three more days He was alive
      and risen from the dead.
   Go tell it on the mountain . . .

5 He still comes to people,
      His life moves through the lands;
   He uses us for speaking,
      He touches with our hands.
   Go tell it on the mountain . . .

180
Marilyn Baker
© 1982 Word's Spirit of Praise Music/
CopyCare

1 **God came among us,**
   He became a man,
   became a baby, though through Him
      the world began.
   He came to earth to bring us peace,
   but where is that peace today?
   It can be found by those
      who will let Him
      direct their way.

2 He came to serve, to show us
      how much He cared;
   our joys and sorrows
      He so willingly shared.
   He came to earth to bring us joy,
   but where is that joy today?
   It can be found by those
      who let Him
      wash their guilt away.

3 Death tried to hold Him,
      but it could not succeed;
   He rose again,
      and now we can be freed.
   He longs to give eternal life
   to all who will simply receive,
   yes, to all who will open their hearts
      and just believe.

181
Carol Owens
© 1972 Bud John Songs/EMI Christian
Music Publishing/CopyCare

1 **God forgave my sin in Jesus' name;**
   I've been born again in Jesus' name,
   and in Jesus' name I come to you
   to share His love as He told me to.
      He said:
      'Freely, freely you have received,
      freely, freely give;
      go in My name
         and because you believe,
      others will know that I live.'

2 All power is given in Jesus' name
   in earth and heaven in Jesus' name;
   and in Jesus' name I come to you
   to share His power as He told me to.
      He said . . .

182
© 1966, 1984 Willard F Jabusch/
OCP Publications

God has spoken to His people,
alleluia,
   and His words are words of wisdom,
   alleluia!

1 Open your ears, O Christian people,
   open your ears and hear good news;
   open your hearts, O royal priesthood,
   God has come to you.
      God has spoken . . .

2 They who have ears
      to hear His message,
   they who have ears, then let them hear;
   they who would learn
      the way of wisdom,
   let them hear God's word!
      God has spoken . . .

3 Israel comes to greet the Saviour,
   Judah is glad to see His day;
   from east and west the peoples travel,
   He will show the way.
      God has spoken . . .

183
Joseph Parker (1830–1902)

1 **God holds the key of all unknown,**
   and I am glad:
   if other hands should hold the key,
   or if He trusted it to me,
   I might be sad, I might be sad.

2 What if tomorrow's cares were here
  without its rest?
  I'd rather He unlocked the day,
  and, as the hours swing open, say,
  'My will is best, My will is best.'

3 The very dimness of my sight
  makes me secure;
  for, groping in my misty way,
  I feel His hand; I hear Him say,
  'My help is sure, My help is sure.'

4 I cannot read His future plans;
  but this I know:
  I have the smiling of His face,
  and all the refuge of His grace,
  while here below, while here below.

5 Enough: this covers all my wants;
  and so I rest!
  for what I cannot, He can see,
  and in His care I saved shall be,
  for ever blest, for ever blest.

184 Anon
Copyright control

1 **God is building a house,**
  God is building a house,
  God is building a house that will stand.
  He is building by His plan
  with the living stones of man,
  God is building a house that will stand.

2 God is building a house,
  God is building a house,
  God is building a house that will stand.
  With apostles, prophets, pastors,
  with evangelists and teachers,
  God is building a house that will stand.

3 Christ is head of this house,
  Christ is head of this house,
  Christ is head of this house
    that will stand.
  He abideth in its praise,
  will perfect it in its ways,
  Christ is head of this house
    that will stand.

4 We are part of this house,
  we are part of this house,
  we are part of this house
    that will stand.
  We are called from every nation
  to enjoy His full salvation,
  we are part of this house
    that will stand.

185 Graham Kendrick
© 1985 Kingsway's Thankyou Music

God is good – we sing and shout it,
God is good – we celebrate;
God is good – no more we doubt it,
God is good – we know it's true!

And when I think of His love for me,
my heart fills with praise
and I feel like dancing;
for in His heart there is room for me,
and I run with arms opened wide.

God is good – we sing and shout it,
God is good – we celebrate;
God is good – no more we doubt it,
God is good – we know it's true! *Hey!*

186
William Tidd Matson (1833–99)

1 **God is in His temple,**
the almighty Father,
round His footstool let us gather:
Him with adoration
serve, the Lord most holy,
who has mercy on the lowly:
let us raise
hymns of praise,
for His great salvation:
God is in His temple!

2 Christ comes to His temple:
we, His word receiving,
are made happy in believing.
Lo! from sin delivered,
He has turned our sadness,
our deep gloom, to light and gladness!
let us raise
hymns of praise,
for our bonds are severed:
Christ comes to His temple!

3 Come and claim Your temple,
gracious Holy Spirit!
In our hearts Your home inherit:
make in us Your dwelling,
Your high work fulfilling,
into ours Your will instilling,
till we raise
hymns of praise
beyond mortal telling,
in the eternal temple.

187
Timothy Rees (1874–1939) altd.
© A R Mowbray & Co Ltd,
a division of Cassell Publishers Ltd

1 **God is love: let heaven adore Him;**
God is love: let earth rejoice;
let creation sing before Him,
and exalt Him with one voice.
He who laid the earth's foundation,
He who spread the heavens above,
He who breathes through all creation,
He is love, eternal love.

2 God is love: and He enfoldeth
all the world in one embrace;
with unfailing grasp He holdeth
every child of every race.
And when human hearts are breaking
under sorrow's iron rod,
all the sorrow, all the aching,
wrings with pain the heart of God.

3 God is love: and though with blindness
sin afflicts the souls of men,
God's eternal loving-kindness
holds and guides them even then.
Sin and death and hell shall never
o'er us final triumph gain;
God is love, so love for ever
o'er the universe must reign.

188
From Psalm 46
© Richard Bewes/Jubilate Hymns

1 **God is our strength and refuge,**
our present help in trouble;
and we therefore will not fear,
though the earth should change!
Though mountains shake and tremble,
though swirling floods are raging,
God the Lord of hosts
is with us evermore!

2 There is a flowing river,
within God's holy city;
God is in the midst of her –
she shall not be moved!
God's help is swiftly given,
thrones vanish at His presence –
God the Lord of hosts
is with us evermore!

3 Come, see the works of our maker,
   learn of His deeds all-powerful;
   wars will cease across the world
   when He shatters the spear!
   Be still and know your Creator,
   uplift Him in the nations –
   God the Lord of hosts
      is with us evermore!

4 All we can do is nothing worth
   unless God blesses the deed;
   vainly we hope for the harvest-tide
   till God gives life to the seed:
   nearer and nearer draws the time,
   the time that shall surely be,
   when the earth shall be filled
   with the glory of God,
   as the waters cover the sea.

189 Arthur Campbell Ainger (1841–1919)
© in this version Jubilate Hymns

1 **God is working His purpose out,**
   as year succeeds to year:
   God is working His purpose out,
   and the time is drawing near:
   nearer and nearer draws the time,
   the time that shall surely be,
   when the earth shall be filled
   with the glory of God,
   as the waters cover the sea.

2 From utmost east to utmost west
   wherever man has trod,
   by the mouth of many messengers
   rings out the voice of God:
   listen to me, you continents,
   you islands, look to me,
   that the earth may be filled
   with the glory of God,
   as the waters cover the sea.

3 We shall march in the strength of God,
   with the banner of Christ unfurled,
   that the light of the glorious gospel
      of truth
   may shine throughout the world;
   we shall fight with sorrow and sin
   to set their captives free,
   that the earth may be filled
   with the glory of God,
   as the waters cover the sea.

190 Philip Coutts
© 1988 Oxford University Press

1 **God of all ages**
      and Lord for all time,
   Creator of all things in perfect design:
   for fields ripe for harvest,
      for rich golden grain,
   for beauty in nature,
      we thank You again.

2 God of all nations
      and Lord of all lands,
   who placed the world's wealth
      in the palm of our hands,
   we pray for Your guidance
      to guard against greed.
   though great the resources,
      still great is the need.

3 God of compassion and Lord of all life,
   we pray for Your people
      in conflict and strife.
   The earth You created
      a vast treasure store,
   yet hunger still thrives
      while men fight to gain more.

4 God of all wisdom, take us by the hand
   and insight bestow
      when we ruin Your land.
   For rivers polluted,
      for forests laid bare,
   we pray Your forgiveness
      for failing to care.

5 God of all greatness and giver of light,
with each sunlit morning
we worship Your might,
our half-hearted service
Your only reward:
for love beyond measure,
we thank You, O Lord.

191 David Fellingham
© 1982 Kingsway's Thankyou Music

God of glory, we exalt Your name,
You who reign in majesty;
we lift our hearts to You
and we will worship,
praise, and magnify
Your holy name.

In power resplendent
You reign in glory;
eternal King,
You reign for ever:
Your word is mighty,
releasing captives,
Your love is gracious –
You are my God.

192 Henry Emerson Fosdick (1878–1969)
© Elinor F Downs

1 **God of grace and God of glory,**
on Thy people pour Thy power;
crown Thine ancient Church's story;
bring her bud to glorious flower.
Grant us wisdom,
grant us courage,
for the facing of this hour.

2 Lo! the hosts of evil round us
scorn Thy Christ, assail His ways!
Fears and doubts
too long have bound us;
free our hearts to work and praise.
Grant us wisdom,
grant us courage,
for the living of these days.

3 Heal Thy children's warring madness;
bend our pride to Thy control;
shame our wanton, selfish gladness,
rich in things and poor in soul.
Grant us wisdom,
grant us courage,
lest we miss Thy kingdom's goal.

4 Set our feet on lofty places;
gird our lives that they may be
armoured with all Christ-like graces
in the fight to set men free.
Grant us wisdom,
grant us courage,
that we fail not man nor Thee.

5 Save us from weak resignation
to the evils we deplore;
let the search for Thy salvation
be our glory evermore.
Grant us wisdom,
grant us courage,
serving Thee whom we adore.

193 William Cowper (1731–1800)

1 **God moves in a mysterious way,**
His wonders to perform;
He plants His footsteps in the sea,
and rides upon the storm.

2 Deep in unfathomable mines
of never-failing skill,
He treasures up His bright designs,
and works His sovereign will.

3 Ye fearful saints, fresh courage take;
  the clouds ye so much dread
  are big with mercy, and shall break
  in blessings on your head.

4 Judge not the Lord by feeble sense,
  but trust Him for His grace;
  behind a frowning providence
  He hides a smiling face.

5 His purposes will ripen fast,
  unfolding every hour;
  the bud may have a bitter taste,
  but sweet will be the flower.

6 Blind unbelief is sure to err,
  and scan His work in vain;
  God is His own interpreter,
  and He will make it plain.

194 Anon

1 **God save our gracious Queen,**
  long live our noble Queen,
  God save the Queen!
  Send her victorious,
  happy and glorious,
  long to reign over us;
  God save the Queen!

2 Thy choicest gifts in store
  on her be pleased to pour,
  long may she reign!
  May she defend our laws,
  and ever give us cause
  to sing with heart and voice
  God save the Queen!

195 © 1986 Peter Horrobin

1 **God whose Son**
  was once a man on earth
  gave His life that men may live.
  Risen, our ascended Lord
  fulfilled His promised word.

When the Spirit came,
  the Church was born,
God's people shared
  in a bright new dawn.
They healed the sick,
they taught God's word,
they sought the lost,
they obeyed the Lord.
And it's all because the Spirit came
that the world will never be the same,
because the Spirit came.

2 God whose power
  fell on the early Church,
  sent to earth from heaven above;
  Spirit-led, by Him ordained,
  they showed the world God's love.
  When the Spirit came . . .

3 Pour Your Spirit on the Church today,
  that Your life through me may flow;
  Spirit-filled, I'll serve Your name
  and live the truth I know.
  When the Spirit comes, new life is born,
  God's people share
    in a bright new dawn.
  We'll heal the sick,
  we'll teach God's word,
  we'll seek the lost,
  we'll obey the Lord.
  And it's all because the Spirit came
  that the world will never be the same,
  because the Spirit came.

196 John Mason Neale (1818–66)

1 **Good Christian men, rejoice**
  with heart and soul and voice!
  Give ye heed to what we say:
  News! News!
    Jesus Christ is born today.
  Ox and ass before Him bow,
  and He is in the manger now:
  Christ is born today,
  Christ is born today.

2 Good Christian men, rejoice
with heart and soul and voice!
Now ye hear of endless bliss:
Joy! Joy! Jesus Christ was born for this.
He hath ope'd the heavenly door,
and man is blest for evermore:
Christ was born for this,
Christ was born for this.

3 Good Christian men, rejoice
with heart and soul and voice!
Now ye need not fear the grave:
Peace! Peace!
    Jesus Christ was born to save;
calls you one, and calls you all,
to gain His everlasting hall:
Christ was born to save,
Christ was born to save.

197 Samuel Davies (1723–61) altd.

1 **Great God of wonders, all Thy ways**
are matchless, god-like and divine;
but the fair glories of Thy grace
more god-like and unrivalled shine:
    Who is a pardoning God like Thee?
    Or who has grace so rich and free?

2 Such dire offences to forgive,
such guilty daring souls to spare;
this is Thy grand prerogative,
and none shall in the honour share:
    Who is a pardoning God ...

3 In wonder lost, with trembling joy,
we take the pardon of our God,
pardon for sins of deepest dye,
a pardon sealed with Jesus' blood:
    Who is a pardoning God ...

4 O may this glorious matchless love,
this god-like miracle of grace,
teach mortal tongues, like those above,
to raise this song of lofty praise:
    Who is a pardoning God ...

198 Christopher Wordsworth (1807–85)

1 **Gracious Spirit, Holy Ghost,**
taught by You, we covet most,
of Your gifts at Pentecost,
holy, heavenly love.

2 Faith that mountains could remove,
tongues of earth or heaven above,
knowledge, all things, empty prove
without heavenly love.

3 Though I as a martyr bleed,
give my goods the poor to feed,
all is vain if love I need;
therefore give me love.

4 Love is kind, and suffers long;
love is meek, and thinks no wrong;
love, than death itself more strong:
therefore give us love.

5 Prophecy will fade away,
melting in the light of day;
love will ever with us stay:
therefore give us love.

6 Faith, and hope, and love we see
joining hand in hand, agree;
but the greatest of the three,
and the best, is love.

199 Steve McEwan
© 1985 Body Songs/CopyCare

Great is the Lord
        and most worthy of praise,
the city of our God, the holy place,
the joy of the whole earth.
Great is the Lord
        in whom we have the victory,
He aids us against the enemy,
we bow down on our knees.

And Lord, we want to lift Your name
    on high,
and Lord, we want to thank You,
for the works You've done in our lives;
and Lord, we trust in Your unfailing love,
for You alone are God eternal,
throughout earth and heaven above.

200 Thomas O Chisholm (1866–1960)
© 1951 Hope Publishing/CopyCare

1 **Great is Thy faithfulness,**
   O God my Father,
   there is no shadow of turning
       with Thee;
   Thou changest not,
       Thy compassions they fail not,
   as Thou hast been
       Thou for ever wilt be.
   Great is Thy faithfulness,
   great is Thy faithfulness;
   morning by morning
   new mercies I see;
   all I have needed
   Thy hand hath provided –
   great is Thy faithfulness, Lord, unto me!

2 Summer and winter,
       and spring-time and harvest,
   sun, moon and stars
       in their courses above,
   join with all nature in manifold witness
   to Thy great faithfulness,
       mercy and love.
   Great is Thy faithfulness . . .

3 Pardon for sin,
       and a peace that endureth,
   Thine own dear presence
       to cheer and to guide;
   strength for today
       and bright hope for tomorrow,
   blessings all mine,
       with ten thousand beside!
   Great is Thy faithfulness . . .

201 William Williams (1717–91) altd.

1 **Guide me, O Thou great Jehovah,**
   pilgrim through this barren land;
   I am weak, but Thou art mighty;
   hold me with Thy powerful hand:
       Bread of heaven,
   feed me now and evermore.

2 Open now the crystal fountain,
   whence the healing stream doth flow;
   let the fiery, cloudy pillar
   lead me all my journey through:
       strong deliverer,
   be Thou still my strength and shield.

3 When I tread the verge of Jordan,
   bid my anxious fears subside:
   death of death, and hell's destruction,
   land me safe on Canaan's side:
       songs of praises
   I will ever give to Thee.

202 Charles Wesley (1707–88)
and Thomas Cotterill (1779–1823)

1 **Hail the day that sees Him rise,**
   Alleluia,
   to His throne beyond the skies;
   Christ, the Lamb for sinners given,
   enters now the highest heaven.

2 There for Him high triumph waits:
   lift your heads, eternal gates,
   He has conquered death and sin,
   take the King of glory in.

3 See! the heaven its Lord receives,
   yet He loves the earth He leaves;
   though returning to His throne,
   still He calls mankind His own.

4 Still for us He intercedes,
   His prevailing death He pleads,
   near Himself prepares our place,
   He the first-fruits of our race.

5 Lord, though parted from our sight,
far beyond the starry height,
lift our hearts that we may rise
one with You beyond the skies.

6 There with You we shall remain,
share the glory of Your reign,
there Your face unclouded view,
find our heaven of heavens in You.

4 Worship, honour, power, and blessing,
Thou art worthy to receive;
loudest praises, without ceasing,
meet it is for us to give:
Help, ye bright angelic spirits!
bring your sweetest, noblest lays;
help to sing our Saviour's merits,
help to chant Immanuel's praise.

203 John Bakewell (1721–1819)

1 **Hail, Thou once despisèd Jesus,**
hail, Thou Galilean King!
Thou didst suffer to release us,
Thou didst free salvation bring.
Hail, Thou agonizing Saviour,
bearer of our sin and shame;
by Thy merits we find favour;
life is given through Thy name.

2 Paschal Lamb, by God appointed,
all our sins on Thee were laid;
by almighty love anointed,
Thou hast full atonement made.
All Thy people are forgiven
through the virtue of Thy blood;
opened is the gate of heaven,
peace is made 'twixt man and God.

3 Jesus, hail! enthroned in glory,
there for ever to abide;
all the heavenly hosts adore Thee,
seated at Thy Father's side:
there for sinners Thou art pleading,
there Thou dost our place prepare;
ever for us interceding,
till in glory we appear.

204 James Montgomery (1771–1854)

1 **Hail to the Lord's anointed,**
great David's greater Son!
Hail, in the time appointed,
His reign on earth begun!
He comes to break oppression,
to set the captive free,
to take away transgression,
and rule in equity.

2 He comes with succour speedy
to those who suffer wrong;
to help the poor and needy,
and bid the weak be strong;
to give them songs for sighing,
their darkness turn to light,
whose souls, condemned and dying,
were precious in His sight.

3 He shall come down like showers
upon the fruitful earth;
Love, joy, and hope, like flowers,
spring in His path to birth:
before Him, on the mountains,
shall peace the herald go,
and righteousness in fountains
from hill to valley flow.

4 Kings shall fall down before Him,
and gold and incense bring;
all nations shall adore Him,
His praise all people sing;
to Him shall prayer unceasing
and daily vows ascend;
His kingdom still increasing,
a kingdom without end.

5 O'er every foe victorious,
He on His throne shall rest;
from age to age more glorious,
all-blessing and all-blest.
The tide of time shall never
His covenant remove;
His name shall stand for ever,
His changeless name of Love.

205
Dale Garratt
© 1972 Scripture in Song/
Integrity Music/Kingsway's Thankyou Music

**Hallelujah! for the Lord our God
the almighty reigns.**
Hallelujah! for the Lord our God
the almighty reigns.
Let us rejoice and be glad and give
the glory unto Him.
Hallelujah! for the Lord our God
the almighty reigns.

206
Tim Cullen
© 1975 Celebration/Kingsway's Thankyou Music

Hallelujah, my Father,
for giving us Your Son;
sending Him into the world
to be given up for men,
knowing we would bruise Him
and smite Him from the earth.
Hallelujah, my Father,
in His death is my birth;
Hallelujah, my Father,
in His life is my life.

207
William Chatterton Dix (1837–98) altd.

1 **Hallelujah! sing to Jesus,**
His the sceptre, His the throne;
hallelujah! His the triumph,
His the victory alone.
Hark! the songs of peaceful Zion
thunder like a mighty flood;
Jesus out of every nation
hath redeemed us by His blood.

2 Hallelujah! not as orphans
are we left in sorrow now;
hallelujah! He is near us,
faith believes, nor questions how.
Though the cloud from sight
      received Him
when the forty days were o'er,
shall our hearts forget His promise,
'I am with you evermore'?

3 Hallelujah! bread of heaven!
Thou on earth our food, our stay;
Hallelujah! here the sinful
flee to Thee from day to day.
Intercessor, friend of sinners,
earth's Redeemer, plead for me,
where the songs of all the sinless
sweep across the crystal sea.

4 Hallelujah! Hallelujah!
Glory be to God on high;
to the Father, and the Saviour,
who has gained the victory;
glory to the Holy Spirit,
fount of love and sanctity.
Hallelujah! Hallelujah!
to the triune Majesty.

208
Steve and Gina Southworth
© 1985 Mercy/Vineyard Publishing/
CopyCare

**Hallelujah! sing to the Lord
songs of praise;**
we bless You, Lord,
we give to You glory due Your holy name.
We stretch out our hands,
we stretch out our hands unto You, Lord.

We lift up our voice,
we lift up our voice
    inviting You into this place.
Hear us, O God,
as one, we bring our praise,
a pleasing sacrifice to You,
O Ancient of Days,
Ancient of Days.

209 William Cowper (1731–1800)

1 **Hark, my soul! it is the Lord;**
'Tis thy Saviour, hear His word;
Jesus speaks, and speaks to thee,
'Say, poor sinner, lov'st thou Me?'

2 'I delivered thee when bound,
and, when bleeding, healed thy wound;
sought thee wandering, set thee right,
turned thy darkness into light.'

3 'Can a woman's tender care
cease towards the child she bare?
Yes, she may forgetful be,
yet will I remember Thee.'

4 'Mine is an unchanging love,
higher than the heights above,
deeper than the depths beneath,
free and faithful, strong as death.'

5 'Thou shalt see My glory soon,
when the work of grace is done;
partner of My throne shalt be;
say, poor sinner, lov'st thou Me?'

6 Lord! it is my chief complaint
that my love is weak and faint;
yet I love Thee, and adore:
O for grace to love Thee more!

210 Philip Dodderidge (1702–51)
altered © 1986 Horrobin/Leavers

1 **Hark, the glad sound!**
   the Saviour comes,
the Saviour promised long;
let every heart prepare a throne,
and every voice a song.

2 He comes, the prisoners to release
in Satan's bondage held;
the chains of sin before Him break,
the iron fetters yield.

3 He comes to free the captive mind
where evil thoughts control;
and for the darkness of the blind,
gives light that makes them whole.

4 He comes the broken heart to bind,
the wounded soul to cure;
and with the treasures of His grace
to enrich the humble poor.

5 Our glad hosannas, Prince of peace,
Your welcome shall proclaim;
and heaven's eternal arches ring
with Your belovèd name.

211 Charles Wesley (1707–88) and others

1 **Hark! the herald-angels sing,**
'Glory to the new-born King!
Peace on earth, and mercy mild,
God and sinners reconciled.'
Joyful, all you nations rise,
join the triumph of the skies;
with the angelic host proclaim,
'Christ is born in Bethlehem!'
   Hark! the herald-angels sing,
   'Glory to the new-born King!'

2 Christ by highest heaven adored,
Christ, the everlasting Lord,
late in time behold Him come,
offspring of a virgin's womb!
Veiled in flesh the Godhead see!
Hail, the incarnate Deity!
Pleased as man with man to dwell,
Jesus, our Immanuel.
Hark! the herald-angels sing,
'Glory to the new-born King!'

3 Hail, the heaven-born Prince of peace!
Hail, the Sun of righteousness!
Light and life to all He brings,
risen with healing in His wings.
Mild He lays His glory by,
born that man no more may die;
born to raise the sons of earth,
born to give them second birth.
Hark! the herald-angels sing,
'Glory to the new-born King!'

4 Have Thine own way, Lord,
  have Thine own way;
hold o'er my being absolute sway;
fill with Thy Spirit till all shall see
Christ only, always, living in me.

213
Robert Manzano
© 1984 Kingsway's Thankyou Music

He gave me beauty for ashes,
the oil of joy for mourning,
the garment of praise
for the spirit of heaviness;
that we might be trees of righteousness,
the planting of the Lord,
that He might be glorified.

212
Adelaide Addison Pollard (1862–1934)
© Alexander Copyright Trust

1 **Have Thine own way, Lord,**
  have Thine own way;
Thou art the potter, I am the clay;
mould me and make me after Thy will,
while I am waiting, yielded and still.

2 Have Thine own way, Lord,
  have Thine own way;
search me and try me, Master, today.
Whiter than snow, Lord,
  wash me just now,
as in Thy presence humbly I bow.

3 Have Thine own way, Lord,
  have Thine own way;
wounded and weary, help me, I pray.
Power, all power, surely is Thine;
touch me and heal me, Saviour divine.

214
© Christopher Porteous/Jubilate Hymns

1 **He gave His life in selfless love,**
for sinful man He came;
He had no stain of sin Himself
but bore our guilt and shame:
He took the cup of pain and death,
His blood was freely shed;
we see His body on the cross,
we share the living bread.

2 He did not come to call the good
but sinners to repent;
it was the lame, the deaf, the blind
for whom His life was spent:
to heal the sick, to find the lost –
it was for such He came,
and round His table all may come
to praise His holy name.

3 They heard Him call
    His Father's name –
then, 'Finished!' was His cry;
like them we have forsaken Him
and left Him there to die:
the sins that crucified Him then
are sins His blood has cured;
the love that bound Him to a cross
our freedom has ensured.

4 His body broken once for us
is glorious now above;
the cup of blessing we receive,
a sharing of His love:
as in His presence we partake,
His dying we proclaim
until the hour of majesty
when Jesus comes again.

215 Graham Kendrick
© 1987 Make Way Music

He has showed you, O man,
    what is good –
and what does the Lord require of you?
He has showed you, O man, what is good –
and what does the Lord require of you,
but to act justly, and to love mercy,
and to walk humbly with your God;
but to act justly, and to love mercy,
and to walk humbly with your God.
He has showed . . .

216 Jimmy Owens
© Bud John Songs/EMI Christian Music Publishing/
CopyCare

1 **He is born, our Lord and Saviour:**
    He is born, our heavenly King:
give Him honour, give Him glory,
earth rejoice and heaven sing!
Born to be our sanctuary,
born to bring us light and peace;
for our sins to bring forgiveness,
from our guilt to bring release.

2 He who is from everlasting
now becomes the incarnate Word;
He whose name endures for ever
now is born the Son of God:
born to bear our griefs and sorrows,
born to banish hate and strife;
born to bear the sin of many,
born to give eternal life!

3 Hail, the Holy One of Israel,
chosen heir to David's throne;
hail the brightness of His rising –
to His light the Gentiles come:
plunderer of Satan's kingdom,
downfall of his evil power;
rescuer of all His people,
Conqueror in death's dark hour!

4 He shall rule with righteous judgement,
and His godly rule extend;
governor among the nations,
His great kingdom has no end:
He shall reign, the King of glory,
higher than the kings of earth –
alleluia, alleluia!
Praise we now His holy birth!

217 Twila Paris
© 1985 Straightway/Mountain Spring/
EMI Christian Music Publishing/CopyCare

He is exalted,
the King is exalted on high;
I will praise Him.
He is exalted,
for ever exalted
and I will praise His name!

He is the Lord;
for ever His truth shall reign.
Heaven and earth
rejoice in His holy name.
He is exalted,
the King is exalted on high.

218
Jimmy Owens
© 1972 Bud John Songs/EMI Christian
Music Publishing/CopyCare

1 **He is here, He is here,**
He is moving among us;
He is here, He is here,
as we gather in His name!
He is here, He is here,
and He wants to work a wonder;
He is here as we gather in His name.

2 He is Lord, He is Lord,
let us worship before Him;
He is Lord, He is Lord,
as we gather in His name!
He is Lord, He is Lord,
let us praise and adore Him
yesterday and today
and for evermore the same.

219
Graham Kendrick
© 1986 Kingsway's Thankyou Music

He that is in us is greater
than he that is in the world;
He that is in us is greater
than he that is in the world.

1 Therefore I will sing and I will rejoice,
for His Spirit lives in me.
Christ the living One has overcome,
and we share in His victory.
He that is in us . . .

2 All the powers of death and hell and
sin
lie crushed beneath His feet.
Jesus owns the name above all names,
crowned with honour and majesty.
He that is in us . . .

(*Repeat verse 2, slowly and majestically*)

220
Marvin Frey
Copyright control

He is Lord, He is Lord,
He is risen from the dead
and He is Lord!
Every knee shall bow,
every tongue confess
that Jesus Christ is Lord.

221
Graham Kendrick
© 1988 Make Way Music

EACH LINE OF VERSE SUNG FIRST
BY LEADER, THEN BY ALL
1 **He walked where I walk,**
He stood where I stand,
He felt what I feel,
He understands.
He knows my frailty,
shared my humanity,
tempted in every way,
yet without sin.
God with us, so close to us,
God with us, Immanuel!

2 One of a hated race,
stung by the prejudice,
suffering injustice,
yet He forgives.
Wept for my wasted years,
paid for my wickedness,
He died in my place,
that I might live.
God with us . . .

222
Maggi Dawn
© 1987 Kingsway's Thankyou Music

1 **He was pierced for our**
transgressions,
and bruised for our iniquities;
and to bring us peace He was
punished,
and by His stripes we are healed.

2   He was led like a lamb to the slaughter,
    although He was innocent of crime;
    and cut off from the land of the living,
    He paid for the guilt that was mine.

    We like sheep have gone astray,
    turned each one to his own way,
    and the Lord has laid on Him
    the iniquity of us all.
    We like sheep . . .

223

Chris Bowater
© 1988 Sovereign Lifestyle Music

WOMEN
He who dwells, he who dwells
in the shelter of the Most High,
MEN
he who dwells, he who dwells
in the shelter of the Most High
WOMEN
will rest in the shadow,
the shadow of the Almighty,
MEN
will rest in the shadow,
the shadow of the Almighty.
ALL
And I'll say of the Lord, 'He is my refuge';
and I'll say of the Lord,
    'He is my strength'.
And I'll make of the Most High One
    my dwelling-place,
and I'll say, 'He is my God',
I'll say, 'He is my God',
I will say, 'He is my God in whom I trust'.

224

after John Bunyan (1628–88)
Percy Dearmer (1867–1936)
by permission of Oxford University Press

1   **He who would valiant be**
    'gainst all disaster,
    let him in constancy
    follow the Master.
    There's no discouragement
    shall make him once relent,
    his first avowed intent
    to be a pilgrim.

2   Who so beset him round
    with dismal stories,
    do but themselves confound –
    his strength the more is.
    No foes shall stay his might,
    though he with giants fight:
    he will make good his right
    to be a pilgrim.

3   Since, Lord, Thou dost defend
    us with Thy Spirit,
    we know we at the end
    shall life inherit.
    Then fancies flee away!
    I'll fear not what men say,
    I'll labour night and day
    to be a pilgrim.

225

Anon
© Copyright control

1   **He's got the whole wide world
    in His hands,**
    He's got the whole wide world
    in His hands,
    He's got the whole wide world
    in His hands,
    He's got the whole world in His hands.

2   He's got everybody here,
    in His hands . . .

3   He's got the tiny little baby,
    in His hands . . .

4   He's got you and me, brother,
    in His hands . . .

226

© 1981 John Richards/
Renewal Servicing

1   **Healing God, almighty Father,**
    active throughout history;
    ever saving, guiding, working
    for Your children to be free.
    Shepherd, King, inspiring prophets
    to foresee Your suffering role –
    Lord, we raise our prayers and voices;
    make us one and make us whole.

2 Healing Christ, God's Word incarnate,
reconciling man to man;
God's atonement, dying for us
in His great redemptive plan.
Jesus, Saviour, healer, victor,
drawing out for us death's sting;
Lord, we bow our hearts in worship,
and united praises bring.

3 Healing Spirit, Christ-anointing,
raising to new life in Him;
help the poor; release to captives;
cure of body; health within.
Life-renewing and empowering
Christ-like service to the lost;
Lord, we pray, 'Renew Your wonders
as of a new Pentecost!'

4 Healing Church, called-out and chosen
to enlarge God's kingdom here;
Lord-obeying; Spirit-strengthened
to bring God's salvation near:
for creation's reconciling
gifts of love in us release;
Father, Son and Holy Spirit,
make us instruments of peace.

227 © 1986 Andy Silver

Hear my cry, O God,
listen to my prayer;
from the ends of the earth
will I call to You.
Hear my cry, O God,
when my heart is overwhelmed;
lead me to the rock
that is higher than I.

Teach me to trust in You,
to pour out my heart to You;
You're my help,
my refuge and my strength.
Hear my cry, O God,
listen to my prayer;
from the ends of the earth
will I call to You;
hear my cry, O God.

228 Frances van Alstyne (1820 –1915)
(Fanny J Crosby)

1 **Here from the world we turn,**
   Jesus to seek;
   here may His loving voice
      graciously speak!
   Jesus, our dearest friend,
      while at Thy feet we bend,
      oh, let Thy smile descend!
      'tis Thee we seek.

2 Come, Holy Comforter,
      Presence divine,
   now in our longing hearts
      graciously shine!
   O for Thy mighty power!
      O for a blessèd shower,
      filling this hallowed hour
      with joy divine.

3 Saviour, Thy work revive!
      Here may we see
   those who are dead in sin
      quickened by Thee!
   Come to our hearts' delight,
      make every burden light,
   cheer Thou our waiting sight;
      we long for Thee.

229 Chris Bowater
© 1981 Sovereign Lifestyle Music

Here I am, wholly available –
as for me, I will serve the Lord.

1 The fields are white unto harvest
but oh, the labourers are so few;
so, Lord, I give myself
    to help the reaping,
to gather precious souls unto You.
    Here I am, wholly available –
    as for me, I will serve the Lord.

2 The time is right in the nation
for works of power and authority;
God's looking for a people
    who are willing
to be counted in His glorious victory.
    Here I am . . .

3 As salt are we ready to savour,
in darkness are we ready to be light?
God's seeking out a very special people
to manifest His truth and His might.
    Here I am . . .

3 Too soon we rise,
    the symbols disappear;
the feast, though not the love,
    is past and gone;
the bread and wine remove,
    but Thou art here,
nearer than ever,
    still my shield and sun.

4 I have no help but Thine; nor do I need
another arm save Thine to lean upon;
it is enough, my Lord, enough indeed;
my strength is in Thy might,
    Thy might alone.

5 Mine is the sin,
    but Thine the righteousness;
mine is the guilt,
    but Thine the cleansing blood;
here is my robe, my refuge,
    and my peace –
Thy blood, Thy righteousness,
    O Lord my God.

6 Feast after feast thus comes
    and passes by,
yet passing,
    points to the glad feast above,
giving sweet foretaste of the festal joy,
the Lamb's great bridal feast
    of bliss and love.

230

Horatius Bonar (1808–89)

1 **Here, O my Lord,**
    I see Thee face to face;
here would I touch
    and handle things unseen,
here grasp with firmer hand
    th'eternal grace,
and all my weariness upon Thee lean.

2 Here would I feed
    upon the bread of God,
here drink with Thee
    the royal wine of heaven;
here would I lay aside
    each earthly load,
here taste afresh
    the calms of sin forgiven.

231

Chorus: Israeli traditional song
Verses: © Michael Baughen/Jubilate Hymns

Hévénu shalom aléchem,
Hévénu shalom aléchem,
Hévénu shalom aléchem,
Hévénu shalom,
shalom, shalom aléchem.

1 Because He died and is risen,
because He died and is risen,
because He died and is risen,
we now have peace with God
    through Jesus Christ our Lord.
    Hévénu shalom . . .

2 His peace destroys walls between us,
His peace destroys walls between us,
His peace destroys walls between us,
for only He can reconcile
us both to God.
Hévénu shalom ...

3 'My peace I give you,' said Jesus,
'My peace I give you,' said Jesus,
'My peace I give you,' said Jesus,
'don't let your heart be troubled,
do not be afraid.'
Hévénu shalom ...

4 The peace beyond understanding,
the peace beyond understanding,
the peace beyond understanding,
will guard the hearts and minds
of those who pray to Him.
Hévénu shalom ...

232 Douglas Woods
Copyright control

1 **His hands were pierced,
the hands that made**
the mountain range and everglade;
that washed the stains of sin away
and changed earth's darkness into day.

2 His feet were pierced, the feet that trod
the furthest shining star of God;
and left their imprint deep and clear
on every winding pathway here.

3 His heart was pierced,
the heart that burned
to comfort every heart that yearned;
and from it came a cleansing flood,
the river of redeeming blood.

4 His hands and feet and heart, all three
were pierced for me on Calvary;
and here and now, to Him I bring
my hands, feet, heart, an offering.

233 Anon
Copyright control

His name is higher than any other,
His name is Jesus, His name is Lord.
His name is wonderful,
His name is Counsellor,
His name is Prince of peace,
the mighty God.
His name is higher than any other,
His name is Jesus, His name is Lord.

234 Audrey Mieir
© 1959 Manna Music Inc/
Kingsway's Thankyou Music

His name is wonderful,
His name is wonderful,
His name is wonderful,
Jesus my Lord.

He is the mighty King,
Master of everything,
His name is wonderful,
Jesus my Lord.

He's the great shepherd,
the rock of all ages,
almighty God is He;
bow down before Him,
love and adore Him,
His name is wonderful,
Jesus my Lord!

235 Danny Daniels
© 1982 Mercy/Vineyard Publishing/
CopyCare

MEN AND WOMEN IN CANON
Hold me, Lord, in Your arms,
fill me, Lord, with Your Spirit;
touch my heart with Your love,
let my life glorify Your name.

Singing alleluia, singing alleluia,
singing alleluia, singing alleluia,
alleluia, (alleluia), allelu, (allelu),
alleluia, (alleluia), allelu, (allelu).

236 © Timothy Dudley-Smith

1 **Holy child, how still You lie!**
safe the manger, soft the hay;
faint upon the eastern sky
breaks the dawn of Christmas Day.

2 Holy child, whose birthday brings
shepherds from their field and fold,
angel-choirs and eastern kings,
myrrh and frankincense and gold:

3 Holy child, what gift of grace
from the Father freely willed!
In Your infant form we trace
all God's promises fulfilled.

4 Holy child, whose human years
span like ours delight and pain;
one in human joys and tears,
one in all but sin and stain:

5 Holy child, so far from home,
all the lost to seek and save,
to what dreadful death You come,
to what dark and silent grave!

6 Holy child, before whose name
powers of darkness faint and fall;
conquered death and sin and shame –
Jesus Christ is Lord of all!

7 Holy child, how still You lie!
safe the manger, soft the hay;
clear upon the eastern sky
breaks the dawn of Christmas Day.

237 Reginald Heber (1783–1826)

1 **Holy, holy, holy,**
     Lord God almighty!
early in the morning
     our song shall rise to Thee;
Holy, holy, holy! – merciful and mighty
God in three Persons, blessèd Trinity!

2 Holy, holy, holy!
     All the saints adore Thee,
casting down their golden crowns
     around the glassy sea;
cherubim and seraphim
     falling down before Thee,
which wert, and art,
     and evermore shall be.

3 Holy, holy, holy! –
     though the darkness hide Thee,
though the eye of sinful man
     Thy glory may not see;
only Thou art holy,
     there is none beside Thee,
perfect in power, in love, and purity.

4 Holy, holy, holy, Lord God almighty!
all Thy works shall praise Thy name,
     in earth, and sky, and sea:
Holy, holy, holy! – merciful and mighty
God in three Persons, blessèd Trinity!

238 Jimmy Owens
© 1972 Bud John Songs/EMI Christian
Music Publishing/CopyCare

1 **Holy, holy, holy, holy,**
holy, holy, Lord God almighty!
And we lift our hearts before You
as a token of our love:
holy, holy, holy, holy.

2 Gracious Father, gracious Father,
   we're so glad to be Your children,
      gracious Father;
   and we lift our heads before You
   as a token of our love,
   gracious Father, gracious Father.

3 Precious Jesus, precious Jesus,
   we're so glad that You've redeemed us,
      precious Jesus;
   and we lift our hands before You
   as a token of our love,
   precious Jesus, precious Jesus.

4 Holy Spirit, Holy Spirit,
   come and fill our hearts anew,
      Holy Spirit! –
   and we lift our voice before You
   as a token of our love,
   Holy Spirit, Holy Spirit.

5 Hallelujah, hallelujah,
   hallelujah, hallelujah –
   and we lift our hearts before You
   as a token of our love,
   hallelujah, hallelujah.

239 Anon
Copyright control

1 **Holy, holy, holy is the Lord;**
   holy is the Lord God almighty!
   Holy, holy, holy is the Lord;
   holy is the Lord God almighty,
   who was, and is, and is to come!
   Holy, holy, holy is the Lord!

2 Jesus, Jesus, Jesus is the Lord;
   Jesus is the Lord God almighty!
   Jesus, Jesus, Jesus is the Lord;
   Jesus is the Lord God almighty,
   who was, and is, and is to come!
   Jesus, Jesus, Jesus is the Lord!

3 Worthy, worthy, worthy is the Lord;
   worthy is the Lord God almighty!
   Worthy, worthy, worthy is the Lord;
   worthy is the Lord God almighty,
   who was, and is, and is to come!
   Worthy, worthy, worthy is the Lord!

4 Glory, glory, glory to the Lord;
   glory to the Lord God almighty!
   Glory, glory, glory to the Lord;
   glory to the Lord God almighty,
   who was, and is, and is to come!
   Glory, glory, glory to the Lord!

240 Kelly Green
© 1982 Mercy/Vineyard Publishing/
CopyCare

MEN AND WOMEN IN CANON
Holy is the Lord.
Holy is the Lord.
Holy is the Lord.
Holy is the Lord.
Righteousness and mercy,
judgement and grace.
Faithfulness and sovereignty;
Holy is the Lord,
Holy is the Lord.

241 Chris Bowater
© 1987 Sovereign Lifestyle Music

1 **Holy Spirit, we welcome You,**
   Holy Spirit, we welcome You!
   Move among us with holy fire
   as we lay aside all earthly desire,
   hands reach out and our hearts aspire.
   Holy Spirit, Holy Spirit,
   Holy Spirit, we welcome You!

2 Holy Spirit, we welcome You,
  Holy Spirit, we welcome You!
  Let the breeze of Your presence blow
  that Your children here
      might truly know
  how to move in the Spirit's flow.
  Holy Spirit, Holy Spirit,
  Holy Spirit, we welcome You!

3 Holy Spirit, we welcome You,
  Holy Spirit, we welcome You!
  Please accomplish in us today
  some new work of loving grace,
      we pray –
  unreservedly – have Your way.
  Holy Spirit, Holy Spirit,
  Holy Spirit, we welcome You!

242 Carl Tuttle
© 1985 Mercy/Vineyard Publishing/
CopyCare

1 **Hosanna, hosanna,
      hosanna in the highest;**
  hosanna, hosanna,
      hosanna in the highest:
  Lord, we lift up Your name,
  with hearts full of praise.
  Be exalted, O Lord my God –
  hosanna in the highest.

2 Glory, glory, glory to the King of kings;
  glory, glory, glory to the King of kings:
  Lord, we lift up Your name
  with hearts full of praise.
  Be exalted, O Lord my God –
  glory to the King of kings.

243 'K' in Rippon's *Selection* 1787 altd.

1 **How firm a foundation,
      ye saints of the Lord,**
  is laid for your faith
      in His excellent word;
  what more can He say
      than to you He hath said,
  you who unto Jesus
      for refuge have fled?

2 Fear not, He is with thee,
      O be not dismayed;
  for He is thy God,
      and will still give thee aid:
  He'll strengthen thee, help thee,
      and cause thee to stand,
  upheld by His righteous,
      omnipotent hand.

3 In every condition,
      in sickness, in health,
  in poverty's vale,
      or abounding in wealth;
  at home and abroad,
      on the land, on the sea,
  as thy days may demand
      shall thy strength ever be.

4 When through the deep waters
      He calls thee to go,
  the rivers of grief
      shall not thee overflow;
  for He will be with thee
      in trouble to bless,
  and sanctify to thee
      thy deepest distress.

5 When through fiery trials
      thy pathway shall lie,
  His grace all-sufficient
      shall be thy supply;
  the flame shall not hurt thee,
      His only design
  thy dross to consume
      and thy gold to refine.

6   The soul that on Jesus
        has leaned for repose
    He will not, He will not,
        desert to its foes;
    that soul, though all hell
        should endeavour to shake,
    He'll never, no never, no never forsake.

244   Joseph Hart (1712–68)

1   **How good is the God we adore!**
    Our faithful, unchangeable friend:
    His love is as great as His power
    and knows neither measure nor end.

2   For Christ is the First and the Last;
    His Spirit will guide us safe home:
    we'll praise Him for all that is past
    and trust Him for all that's to come.

245   Anon
          Copyright control

How great is our God,
how great is His name,
how great is His love
forever the same.

He rolled back the waters
of the mighty Red Sea,
and He said, 'I'll never leave you,
put your trust in Me.'

246   Keith and Melody Green
          © 1982 BMG Songs Inc/Ears to Hear Music/
          EMI Christian Music Publishing/CopyCare

How I love You:
You are the One,
You are the One;
how I love You:
You are the One for me!

1   I was so lost,
    but You showed the way –
    'cause You are the way;
    I was so lost,
    but You showed the way to me.
        How I love You . . .

2   I was lied to,
    but You told the truth –
    'cause You are the truth;
    I was lied to,
    but You showed the truth to me.
        How I love You . . .

3   I was dying,
    but You gave me life –
    'cause You are the life;
    I was dying,
    and You gave Your life for me.
        How I love You:
        You are the One,
        You are the One;
        how I love You:
        You are the One –
        God's risen Son,
        You are the One for me!

4   Hallelujah!
    You are the One,
    You are the One;
    hallelujah!
    You are the One for me!
        How I love You . . .

247   From Psalm 84
          Copyright control

1   **How lovely is Thy dwelling-place,**
    O Lord of hosts, to me;
    my soul is longing and fainting
    the courts of the Lord to see.
    My heart and flesh, they are singing
    for joy to the living God;
    how lovely is Thy dwelling-place,
    O Lord of hosts, to me.

2 Even the sparrow finds a home
   where he can settle down;
   and the swallow, she can build a nest
   where she may lay her young,
   within the courts of the Lord of hosts,
   my King, my Lord, and my God;
   and happy are those
       who are dwelling where
   the song of praise is sung.

3 And I'd rather be a door-keeper
   and only stay a day,
   than live the life of a sinner
   and have to stay away.
   For the Lord is shining as the sun,
   and the Lord, He's like a shield;
   and no good thing does He withhold
   from those who walk His way.

4 How lovely is Thy dwelling-place,
   O Lord of hosts, to me;
   my soul is longing and fainting
   the courts of the Lord to see.
   My heart and flesh, they are singing
   for joy to the living God;
   how lovely is Thy dwelling-place,
   O Lord of hosts, to me.

248 From Psalm 84
Copyright control

**How lovely is Thy dwelling-place,
O Lord of hosts,**
my soul longs and yearns for Your courts,
and my heart and flesh
    sing for joy to the living God.

One day in Thy presence
    is far better to me than gold,
or to live my whole life somewhere else,
and I would rather be a door-keeper
    in Your house
than to take my fate upon myself.

You are my sun and my shield,
You are my lover from the start,
and the highway to Your city
    runs through my heart.

249 Leonard E Smith Jr
© 1974 Kingsway's Thankyou Music

1 **How lovely on the mountains
   are the feet of him**
   who brings good news, good news,
   proclaiming peace,
       announcing news of happiness,
   our God reigns, our God reigns!
       Our God reigns, our God reigns,
       our God reigns, our God reigns!

POPULAR VERSION

2 You watchmen,
       lift your voices joyfully as one,
   shout for your King, your King.
   See eye to eye the Lord restoring Zion:
   your God reigns, your God reigns!
       Your God reigns, your God reigns,
       your God reigns, your God reigns!

3 Waste places of Jerusalem
       break forth with joy,
   we are redeemed, redeemed.
   The Lord has saved
       and comforted His people:
   your God reigns, your God reigns!
       Your God reigns, your God reigns,
       your God reigns, your God reigns!

4 Ends of the earth,
       see the salvation of your God,
   Jesus is Lord, is Lord.
   Before the nations
       He has bared His holy arm:
   your God reigns, your God reigns!
       Your God reigns, your God reigns,
       your God reigns, your God reigns!

2 He had no stately form,
    He had no majesty,
that we should be drawn to Him.
He was despised and we took no
    account of Him,
yet now He reigns with the Most High.
    Now He reigns, now He reigns,
    now He reigns with the Most High!

3 It was our sin and guilt that bruised
    and wounded Him,
it was our sin that brought Him down.
When we like sheep had gone astray,
    our shepherd came
and on His shoulders bore our shame.
    On His shoulders, on His shoulders,
    on His shoulders
    He bore our shame.

4 Meek as a lamb that's led out
    to the slaughterhouse,
dumb as a sheep before its shearer,
His life ran down upon the ground
    like pouring rain,
that we might be born again.
    That we might be, that we might be,
    that we might be born again.

5 Out from the tomb He came
    with grace and majesty,
He is alive, He is alive.
God loves us so – see here His hands,
    His feet, His side,
yes, we know He is alive.
    He is alive, He is alive,
    He is alive, He is alive!

6 How lovely on the mountains
    are the feet of him
who brings good news, good news,
announcing peace, proclaiming news of
    happiness:
our God reigns, our God reigns.
    Our God reigns, our God reigns,
    our God reigns, our God reigns!

250

From Romans 10; Matthew 28; Isaiah 6
© Timothy Dudley-Smith

1 **How shall they hear,**
    who have not heard
news of a Lord who loved and came?
nor known His reconciling word,
nor learned to trust
    the Saviour's name?

2 To all the world, to every place,
neighbours and friends
    and far-off lands,
preach the good news of saving grace;
go while the great commission stands.

3 'Whom shall I send?'
    Who hears the call,
constant in prayer,
    through toil and pain,
telling of One who died for all,
to bring a lost world home again?

4 'Lord, here am I,' Your fire impart
to this poor cold self-centred soul;
touch but my lips, my hands, my heart,
and make a world for Christ my goal.

5 Spirit of love, within us move:
Spirit of truth, in power come down!
So shall they hear and find and prove
Christ is their life, their joy,
    their crown.

251

John Newton (1725–1807) altd.

1 **How sweet the name**
    of Jesus sounds
in a believer's ear!
It soothes his sorrows,
    heals his wounds,
and drives away his fear.

2 It makes the wounded spirit whole,
and calms the troubled breast;
'tis manna to the hungry soul,
and to the weary rest.

3 Dear name! the rock on which I build,
my shield and hiding-place,
my never-failing treasury, filled
with boundless stores of grace.

4 Jesus! my shepherd, brother, friend,
my Prophet, Priest and King;
my Lord, my life, my way, my end,
accept the praise I bring.

5 Weak is the effort of my heart,
and cold my warmest thought;
but when I see Thee as Thou art,
I'll praise Thee as I ought.

6 Till then I would Thy love proclaim
with every fleeting breath;
and may the music of Thy name
refresh my soul in death!

252 Phil Rogers
© 1982 Kingsway's Thankyou Music

How precious, O Lord,
is Your unfailing love;
we find refuge
in the shadow of Your wings.
We feast, Lord Jesus,
on the abundance of Your house
and drink from Your river of delights.

With You is the fountain of life,
in Your light we see light,
with You is the fountain of life,
in Your light we see light.

253 James Drummond Burns (1823–64)
altered © 1986 Horrobin/Leavers

1 **Hushed was the evening hymn,**
the temple courts were dark;
the lamp was burning dim
before the sacred ark,
when suddenly a voice divine
rang through the silence of the shrine.

2 The old man, meek and mild,
the priest of Israel, slept;
his watch the temple child,
the little Samuel, kept:
and what from Eli's sense was sealed
the Lord to Hannah's son revealed.

3 O give me Samuel's ear,
the open ear, O Lord,
alive and quick to hear
each whisper of Your word –
like him to answer at Your call,
and to obey You first of all.

4 O give me Samuel's heart,
a lowly heart, that waits
to serve and play the part
You show us at Your gates,
by day and night, a heart that still
moves at the breathing of Your will.

5 O give me Samuel's mind,
a sweet, unmurmuring faith,
obedient and resigned
to You in life and death,
that I may read with childlike eyes
truths that are hidden from the wise.

254 Dave Bilbrough
© 1983 Kingsway's Thankyou Music

I am a new creation,
no more in condemnation,
here in the grace of God I stand.

My heart is over-flowing,
my love just keeps on growing,
here in the grace of God I stand.

And I will praise You, Lord,
yes I will praise You, Lord,
and I will sing of all that You have done.

A joy that knows no limit,
a lightness in my spirit –
here in the grace of God I stand.

255
Danny Daniels
© 1982 Mercy/Vineyard Publishing/
CopyCare

I am a wounded soldier
but I will not leave the fight,
because the Great Physician is healing me.

So I'm standing in the battle,
in the armour of His light,
because His mighty power is real in me.

I am loved, I am accepted
by the Saviour of my soul;
I am loved, I am accepted,
and my wounds will be made whole.

256
Chris Bowater
© 1985 Sovereign Lifestyle Music

1 **I am not mine own,**
   I've been bought with a price.
   Precious blood of Christ,
   I am not mine own.

2 I belong to You,
   I've been bought with a price.
   Precious blood of Christ,
   I belong to You.

3 How could I ever say,
   'I will choose another way',
   knowing the price that's paid;
   precious blood of Christ.

257
Dora Greenwell (1821–82) altd.
altered © 1987 Horrobin/Leavers

1 **I am not skilled to understand**
   what God has willed,
       what God has planned;
   I only know at His right hand
   stands one who is my Saviour.

2 I take Him at His word indeed:
   'Christ died for sinners,' this I read;
   and in my heart I find a need
   of Him to be my Saviour.

3 That He should leave His place on high
   and come for sinful man to die,
   you count it strange? so once did I,
   before I knew my Saviour.

4 And O that He fulfilled may see
   the glory of His life in me,
   and with His work contented be,
   as I with my dear Saviour.

5 Yea, living, dying, let me bring
   my life, to Him an offering,
   that He who lives to be my King
   once died to be my Saviour.

258
Frances Ridley Havergal (1836–79)

1 **I am trusting Thee, Lord Jesus,**
   trusting only Thee;
   trusting Thee for full salvation,
   great and free.

2 I am trusting Thee for pardon,
   at Thy feet I bow;
   for Thy grace and tender mercy,
   trusting now.

3 I am trusting Thee for cleansing
   in the crimson flood;
   trusting Thee to make me holy
   by Thy blood.

4 I am trusting Thee to guide me;
   Thou alone shalt lead,
   every day and hour supplying
   all my need.

5 I am trusting Thee for power,
   Thine can never fail;
   words which Thou Thyself
       shalt give me
   must prevail.

6 I am trusting Thee, Lord Jesus;
   never let me fall;
   I am trusting Thee for ever,
   and for all.

259 Andy and Becky Silver
© 1987 Andy Silver

I am trusting in You, O God,
in the power of Your name;
and I know that as long as I wait for You
my hope will not be in vain.
There may be problems,
there may be pain,
but my hope will not be in vain.

260 © Brian Hoare / Jubilate Hymns

1 **I am the bread,**
   the bread of life;
   who comes to Me will never hunger.
   I am the bread,
   the bread of heaven;
   who feeds on Me will never die.
   And as you eat, remember Me –
   My body broken on the tree:
   My life was given to set you free,
   and I'm alive for evermore.

2 I am the vine,
   the living vine;
   apart from Me you can do nothing.
   I am the vine,
   the real vine:
   abide in Me and I in you.
   And as you drink, remember Me –
   My blood was shed upon the tree:
   My life was given to set you free,
   and I'm alive for evermore.

3 So eat this bread,
   and drink this wine,
   and as you do, receive this life of Mine.
   All that I am I give to you,
   that you may live for evermore.

261 S Suzanne Toolan
© 1971 GIA Publications Inc

1 **I am the bread of life;**
   he who comes to Me shall not hunger;
   he who believes in Me shall not thirst.
   No-one can come to Me
       unless the Father draw him.
   And I will raise him up,
   and I will raise him up,
   and I will raise him up
   on the last day.

2 The bread that I will give
   is My flesh for the life of the world;
   and he who eats of this bread,
   he shall live for ever,
       he shall live for ever.
   And I will raise . . .

3 Unless you eat
   of the flesh of the Son of Man
   and drink of His blood,
   and drink of His blood,
       you shall not have life within you.
   And I will raise . . .

4 I am the Resurrection,
   I am the Life;
   he who believes in Me,
   even if he die, he shall live for ever.
   And I will raise . . .

5 Yes, Lord, we believe
   that You are the Christ,
   the Son of God,
   who has come into the world.
   And I will raise . . .

262
Samuel Trevor Francis (1834–1925)

1 **I am waiting for the dawning**
of the bright and blessèd day,
when the darksome night of sorrow
shall have vanished far away:
when for ever with the Saviour
far beyond this vale of tears,
I shall swell the song of worship
through the everlasting years.

2 I am looking at the brightness –
see, it shineth from afar –
of the clear and joyous beaming
of the bright and morning Star.
Through the dark grey mist of morning
do I see its glorious light;
then away with every shadow
of this sad and weary night.

3 I am waiting for the coming
of the Lord who died for me;
O His words have thrilled my spirit,
'I will come again for Thee.'
I can almost hear His footfall,
on the threshold of the door,
and my heart, my heart is longing
to be with Him evermore.

263
Anon
Copyright control

1 **I am weak but Thou art strong,**
Jesus, keep me from all wrong;
I'll be satisfied as long
as I walk, let me walk, close with Thee.
Just a closer walk with Thee,
grant it Jesus, this my plea;
daily walking close with Thee,
let it be, dear Lord, let it be.

2 Through this world of toils and snares,
if I falter, Lord, who cares?
Who with me my burden shares?
None but Thee, dear Lord,
none but Thee.
Just a closer walk . . .

3 When my feeble life is o'er,
time for me will be no more,
guide me gently, safely home,
to Thy kingdom's shore, to Thy shore.
Just a closer walk . . .

264
Marc Nelson
© 1987 Mercy/Vineyard Publishing/
CopyCare

1 **I believe in Jesus,**
I believe He is the Son of God.
I believe He died and rose again,
I believe He paid for us all.
And I believe He's here now,
standing in our midst,
here with the power to heal now,
and the grace to forgive.

2 I believe in You, Lord,
I believe You are the Son of God.
I believe You died and rose again,
I believe You paid for us all.
MEN   And I believe You're here now,
WOMEN I believe that You're here,
ALL   standing in our midst,
MEN   here with the power
              to heal now,
WOMEN with the power to heal,
ALL   and the grace to forgive.

3 I believe in You, Lord . . .
     (repeat verse 2)

And I believe He's here now,
standing in our midst,
here with the power to heal now,
and the grace to forgive.

265
Phil Rogers
© 1989 Kingsway's Thankyou Music

1 **I cannot count Your blessings, Lord,
     they're wonderful;**
   I can't begin to measure
       Your great love;
   I cannot count the times
       You have forgiven me
   and changed me by Your Spirit
       from above.
       How I worship You, my Father,
       You are wonderful;
       how I glorify You, Jesus,
       You're my Lord.
       How I praise You, Holy Spirit,
       You have changed my life,
       and You're now at work in me
       to change the world.

2 When I was blind
       You opened up my eyes to see;
   when I was dead
       You gave me life anew;
   when I was lost You found me
       and You rescued me,
   and carried me, rejoicing,
       home with You.
       How I worship You . . .

3 I cannot count Your mercies, Lord,
       they're marvellous;
   I can't begin to measure
       Your great grace;
   I cannot count the times
       that You have answered me,
   whenever I have prayed
       and sought Your face.
       How I worship You . . .

4 Whenever I consider what I am to You,
   my heart is filled with wonder,
       love and awe.
   I want to share with others
       that You love them too,
   and tell the world of Jesus,
       more and more.
       How I worship You . . .

266
William Young Fullerton (1857–1932)
© The Baptist Union of Great Britain

1 **I cannot tell why He,
     whom angels worship,**
   should set His love
       upon the sons of men,
   or why, as Shepherd,
       He should seek the wanderers,
   to bring them back,
       they know not how or when.
   But this I know,
       that He was born of Mary,
   when Bethlehem's manger
       was His only home,
   and that He lived
       at Nazareth and laboured,
   and so the Saviour,
       Saviour of the world, is come.

2 I cannot tell how silently He suffered,
   as with His peace
       He graced this place of tears,
   or how His heart
       upon the cross was broken,
   the crown of pain
       to three and thirty years.
   But this I know,
       He heals the broken-hearted,
   and stays our sin,
       and calms our lurking fear,
   and lifts the burden
       from the heavy-laden,
   for yet the Saviour,
       Saviour of the world, is here.

3 I cannot tell
       how He will win the nations,
   how He will claim His earthly heritage,
   how satisfy the needs and aspirations
   of east and west, of sinner and of sage.
   But this I know,
       all flesh shall see His glory,
   and He shall reap the harvest
       He has sown,

and some glad day
His sun shall shine in splendour
when He the Saviour,
Saviour of the world, is known.

4   I cannot tell
how all the lands shall worship,
when, at His bidding,
every storm is stilled,
or who can say how great the jubilation
when all the hearts of men
with love are filled.
But this I know,
the skies will thrill with rapture,
and myriad, myriad human voices sing,
and earth to heaven,
and heaven to earth, will answer:
At last the Saviour,
Saviour of the world, is King!

267   Chris Bowater
© 1981 Sovereign Lifestyle Music

I confess that Jesus Christ is Lord,
I confess that Jesus Christ is Lord.
He's omnipotent, magnificent,
all-glorious, victorious;
I confess that Jesus Christ is Lord.

268   Chris Bowater
© 1981 Sovereign Lifestyle Music

I delight greatly in the Lord,
my soul rejoices in my God.
I delight greatly in the Lord,
my soul rejoices in my God.

For He has clothed me
with garments of salvation,
and arrayed me in a robe of righteousness;
He has clothed me
with garments of salvation,
and arrayed me in a robe of righteousness.

269   Alfred B Smith and Eugene Clarke
© 1947, 1958 Singspiration Music/Brentwood Benson
Music Publishing/CopyCare

1   **I do not know what lies ahead,**
the way I cannot see;
yet one stands near to be my guide,
He'll show the way to me:
I know who holds the future,
and He'll guide me with His hand;
with God things don't just happen,
everything by Him is planned.
So as I face tomorrow,
with its problems large and small,
I'll trust the God of miracles,
give to Him my all.

2   I do not know how many days
of life are mine to spend;
but one who knows and cares for me
will keep me to the end:
I know who holds . . .

3   I do not know the course ahead,
what joys and griefs are there;
but one is near who fully knows,
I'll trust His loving care:
I know who holds . . .

270   Mick Ray
© 1978 Kingsway's Thankyou Music

1   **I get so excited, Lord,**
every time I realize
I'm forgiven, I'm forgiven.
Jesus, Lord, You've done it all,
You've paid the price:
I'm forgiven, I'm forgiven.
Hallelujah, Lord,
my heart just fills with praise,
my feet start dancing, my hands rise up,
and my lips they bless Your name.
I'm forgiven, I'm forgiven, I'm forgiven.
I'm forgiven, I'm forgiven, I'm forgiven.

2 Living in Your presence, Lord,
   is life itself;
   I'm forgiven, I'm forgiven.
   with the past behind, grace for today,
   and a hope to come;
   I'm forgiven, I'm forgiven.
      Hallelujah, Lord,
      my heart just fills with praise,
      my feet start dancing, my hands rise up,
      and my lips they bless Your name.
      I'm forgiven, I'm forgiven, I'm forgiven.
      I'm forgiven, I'm forgiven, I'm forgiven.

271 Carl Tuttle
© 1982 Mercy/Vineyard Publishing/
CopyCare

1 **I give You all the honour**
   and praise that's due Your name,
   for You are the King of glory,
   the Creator of all things.
      And I worship You,
      I give my life to You,
      I fall down on my knees.
      Yes, I worship You,
      I give my life to You,
      I fall down on my knees.

2 As Your Spirit moves upon me now,
   You meet my deepest need,
   and I lift my hands up to Your throne,
   Your mercy I've received.
      And I worship . . .

3 You have broken chains that bound me,
   You've set this captive free,
   I will lift my voice to praise Your name
   for all eternity.
      And I worship . . .

272 Anon
Copyright control

1 **I have decided to follow Jesus,**
      (*3 times*)
   no turning back, no turning back.

2 The world behind me, the cross before
      me, (*3 times*)
   no turning back, no turning back.

3 Though none go with me, I still will
      follow, (*3 times*)
   no turning back, no turning back.

4 Will you decide now to follow Jesus?
      (*3 times*)
   no turning back, no turning back.

273 Dave Moody
© 1984 C A Music/Music Services/
CopyCare

I hear the sound
      of the army of the Lord;
I hear the sound of the army of the Lord;
it's the sound of praise,
it's the sound of war;
the army of the Lord,
the army of the Lord,
the army of the Lord is marching on.

274 Ronnie Wilson
© 1979 Kingsway's Thankyou Music

1 **I hear the sound of rustling**
      in the leaves of the trees,
   the Spirit of the Lord
      has come down on the earth.
   The Church that seemed in slumber
      has now risen from its knees
   and dry bones are responding
      with the fruits of new birth.
   O this is now a time for declaration,
   the Word will go to all men
      everywhere,
   the Church is here
      for healing of the nations,
   behold the day of Jesus drawing near.

My tongue will be the pen
of a ready writer,
and what the Father gives to me
I'll sing,
I only want to be His breath,
I only want to glorify the King.

2 And all around the world
          the body waits expectantly,
    the promise of the Father
          is now ready to fall.
    The watchmen on the tower
          all exhort us to prepare,
    and the Church responds –
          a people who will answer the call.
    And this is not a phase
          which is passing,
    it's the start of an age that is to come;
    and where is the wise man
          and the scoffer?
    Before the face of Jesus they are dumb.
    My tongue will be . . .

3 A body now prepared by God
          and ready for war,
    the prompting of the Spirit
          is our word of command.
    We rise, a mighty army,
          at the bidding of the Lord,
    the devils see and fear,
          for their time is at hand.
    And children of the Lord
          hear our commission,
    that we should love and serve our God
          as one.
    The Spirit won't be hindered
          by division,
    in the perfect work
          that Jesus has begun.
    My tongue will be . . .

275   Horatius Bonar (1808–89)

1 **I heard the voice of Jesus say,**
    'Come unto Me and rest;
    lay down, thou weary one, lay down
    thy head upon My breast':
    I came to Jesus as I was,
    weary, and worn, and sad;
    I found in Him a resting-place,
    and He has made me glad.

2 I heard the voice of Jesus say,
    'Behold, I freely give
    the living water; thirsty one,
    stoop down and drink, and live':
    I came to Jesus, and I drank
    of that life-giving stream;
    my thirst was quenched,
          my soul revived,
    and now I live in Him.

3 I heard the voice of Jesus say,
    'I am this dark world's light;
    look unto Me, thy morn shall rise,
    and all thy day be bright':
    I looked to Jesus and I found
    in Him my star, my sun;
    and in that light of life I'll walk
    till travelling days are done.

276   Arthur Tannous
          © 1984 Kingsway's Thankyou Music

I just want to praise You;
lift my hands and say: 'I love You.'
You are everything to me,
and I exalt Your holy name on high.

I just want to praise You;
lift my hands and say: 'I love You.'
You are everything to me,
and I exalt Your holy name;
I exalt Your holy name,
I exalt Your holy name on high.

277
Avis M Christiansen
© 1993 Singspiration Music/Brentwood Benson
Music Publishing/CopyCare

1 **Sweet is the hope**
    that is thrilling my soul:
  I know I'll see Jesus some day!
  Then what if the dark clouds of sin
        o'er me roll,
  I know I'll see Jesus some day!
    I know I'll see Jesus some day!
    I know I'll see Jesus some day!
    What a joy it will be
    when His face I shall see,
    I know I'll see Jesus some day!

2 Though I must travel by faith
        not by sight,
  I know I'll see Jesus some day!
  No evil can harm me,
        no foe can affright,
  I know I'll see Jesus some day!
    I know I'll see Jesus . . .

3 Darkness is gathering,
        but hope shines within,
  I know I'll see Jesus some day!
  What joy when He comes
        to wipe out every sin;
  I know I'll see Jesus some day!
    I know I'll see Jesus . . .

278 Samuel Medley (1738–99)

1 **I know that my Redeemer lives!**
  What joy the blest assurance gives!
  He lives, He lives, who once was dead;
  He lives, my everlasting Head!

2 He lives, to bless me with His love;
  He lives, to plead for me above;
  He lives, my hungry soul to feed;
  He lives, to help in time of need.

3 He lives, and grants me daily breath;
  He lives, and I shall conquer death;
  He lives, my mansion to prepare;
  He lives, to lead me safely there.

4 He lives, all glory to His name;
  He lives, my Saviour, still the same;
  What joy the blest assurance gives!
  I know that my Redeemer lives!

279 Daniel Webster Whittle (1840–1901)

1 **I know not why God's wondrous**
    grace
  to me has been made known;
  nor why – unworthy as I am –
  He claimed me for His own.
    But, 'I know whom I have believed;
    and am persuaded that He is able
    to keep that which I've committed
    unto Him against that day.'

2 I know not how this saving faith
  to me He did impart;
  or how believing in His word
  wrought peace upon my heart.
    But 'I know . . .

3 I know not how the Spirit moves,
  convincing men of sin;
  revealing Jesus through the word,
  creating faith in Him.
    But 'I know . . .

4 I know not what of good or ill
  may be reserved for me –
  of weary ways or golden days
  before His face I see.
    But 'I know . . .

280
Eddie Espinosa
© 1982 Mercy/Vineyard Publishing/
CopyCare

1 **I lift my hands,**
I raise my voice,
I give my heart to You, my Lord,
and I rejoice.
There are many, many reasons
why I do the things I do,
O but most of all I praise You,
most of all I praise You,
Jesus, most of all I praise You
because You're You.

2 I lift my hands,
I raise my voice,
I give my life to You my Lord,
and I rejoice.
There are many, many reasons
why I do the things I do,
O but most of all I love You,
most of all I love You,
Jesus, most of all I love You
because You're You.

3 I lift my hands,
I raise my voice,
I give my love to You my Lord,
and I rejoice.
There are many, many reasons
why I love You like I do,
O but most of all I love You,
most of all I love You,
Jesus, most of all I love You
because You're You.

281
From Psalm 121
© Timothy Dudley-Smith

1 **I lift my eyes**
to the quiet hills,
in the press of a busy day;
as green hills stand
in a dusty land,
so God is my strength and stay.

2 I lift my eyes
to the quiet hills,
to a calm that is mine to share;
secure and still
in the Father's will
and kept by the Father's care.

3 I lift my eyes
to the quiet hills,
with a prayer as I turn to sleep;
by day, by night,
through the dark and light
my Shepherd will guard His sheep.

4 I lift my eyes
to the quiet hills,
and my heart to the Father's throne;
in all my ways,
to the end of days
the Lord will preserve His own.

282
Rich Cook
© 1976 John T Benson Publishing Co/Brentwood
Benson Music Publishing/CopyCare

I live, I live because He is risen,
I live, I live with power over sin;
I live, I live because He is risen,
I live, I live to worship Him.

Thank You Jesus, thank You Jesus,
because You're alive,
because You're alive,
because You're alive I live.

283
From Psalm 121
© 1989 Greg Leavers

I look to the hills
from where shall my help come;
my help comes from the Lord,
maker of heaven and earth.

1 He will not allow
your foot to ever slip;
He who keeps you will not sleep.
I look to the hills
from where shall my help come;
my help comes from the Lord,
maker of heaven and earth.

2 He watches over you
as your shade from moon and sun;
He will keep you from all harm.
I look to the hills . . .

3 He will guard your ways
as you come and as you go;
from this time and for evermore.
I look to the hills . . .

284 © J M Barnes

1 **I love my Lord**
because He heard my voice.
My God, He listens to my prayer.
Because He hears me
when I call on Him,
through all my days I shall pray.

2 My soul was saved from death;
my eyes from tears;
my feet now walk before the Lord;
yet in despair
I thought my end was near,
my faith in life disappeared.

3 What can I do
to thank God for His love –
for all His benefits to me?
I will lift up salvation's cup on high
and call on Him by His name.

4 My vows to Him I promise to fulfil,
to Him I sacrifice my life.
He freed me from the servitude of sin
and now I serve as His slave.

5 Unite in praise, great family of God,
His children,
bring to Him your thanks.
City of peace,
where God has made His home
with one accord, praise His name!

285 Kathleen Thomerson
© 1970 Celebration/Kingsway's Thankyou Music

1 **I love the name of Jesus,**
King of my heart,
He is everything to me.
I bless the name of Jesus,
reign in my life,
show the Father's love so free.
Spirit of love,
Spirit of power,
shine through eternity.
I love the name of Jesus,
Light of the world,
let me walk each day with Thee.

2 I love the name of Jesus,
risen above,
and He loves and prays for me.
I bless the name of Jesus,
ruling on high
with a glorious majesty.
Spirit of love,
Spirit of power,
shine through eternity.
I praise the name of Jesus,
Lord of my life,
for He died to set me free.

3 I love the name of Jesus,
splendour of God,
and His face I long to see.
I bless the name of Jesus,
Shepherd of men;
by His side I now can be.

Spirit of love,
Spirit of power,
shine through eternity.
I praise the name of Jesus,
for He is love,
and that love He gives to me.

287
Laurie Klein
© 1978, 1980 Maranatha! Music/
CopyCare

I love You, Lord,
and I lift my voice
to worship You,
O my soul rejoice!
Take joy, my King,
in what You hear,
may it be a sweet,
sweet sound in Your ear.

286
From Psalm 18
© Christopher Idle/Jubilate Hymns

1 **I love You, O Lord, You alone,**
my refuge on whom I depend;
my maker, my Saviour, my own,
my hope and my trust without end.
The Lord is my strength and my song,
defender and guide of my ways;
my Master to whom I belong,
my God who shall have all my praise.

2 The dangers of death gathered round,
the waves of destruction came near;
but in my despairing I found
the Lord who released me from fear.
I called for His help in my pain,
to God my salvation I cried;
He brought me His comfort again,
I live by the strength He supplied.

3 The earth and the elements shake
with thunder and lightning and hail;
the cliffs and the mountaintops break
and mortals are feeble and pale.
His justice is full and complete,
His mercy to us has no end;
the clouds are a path for His feet,
He comes on the wings of the wind.

4 My hope is the promise He gives,
my life is secure in His hand;
I shall not be lost, for He lives!
He comes to my side – I shall stand!
Lord God, You are powerful to save,
Your Spirit will spur me to pray;
Your Son has defeated the grave:
I trust and I praise You today!

288
Annie Sherwood Hawks (1835–1918)

1 **I need Thee every hour,**
most gracious Lord:
no tender voice like Thine
can peace afford.
    I need Thee, O I need Thee!
    every hour I need Thee;
    O bless me now, my Saviour!
    I come to Thee.

2 I need Thee every hour,
stay Thou near by;
temptations lose their power
when Thou art nigh.
    I need Thee . . .

3 I need Thee every hour,
in joy or pain;
come quickly and abide,
or life is vain.
    I need Thee . . .

4 I need Thee every hour,
teach me Thy will;
and Thy rich promises
in me fulfil.
    I need Thee . . .

5 I need Thee every hour,
most Holy One;
O make me Thine indeed,
Thou blessèd Son!
I need Thee, O I need Thee!
every hour I need Thee;
O bless me now, my Saviour!
I come to Thee.

289 John Lai
© 1982 Mercy/Vineyard Publishing/
CopyCare

1 **I receive You, O Spirit of love;**
how I need Your healing from above.
I receive You, I receive You,
I receive Your healing from above.

2 I can feel You, touching me right now;
come reveal Your power on me now.
I can feel You, I can feel You,
I can feel Your power on me now,
I can feel Your power on me now.

290 Paul Armstrong
© 1980 Word's Spirit of Praise Music/
CopyCare

1 **I receive Your love,**
I receive Your love,
in my heart I receive Your love,
O Lord,
I receive Your love;
by Your Spirit within me
I receive, I receive Your love.

2 I confess Your love,
I confess Your love,
in my heart I confess Your love,
O Lord,
I confess Your love;
by Your Spirit within me
I confess, I confess Your love.

291 John Daniels
© 1985 Sovereign Music UK

I rest in God alone,
from Him comes my salvation;
my soul finds rest in Him,
my fortress – I'll not be shaken.

1 My hope is in the Lord,
my honour and strength;
my refuge is in Him for ever,
my trust and all of my heart –
in Him alone my soul finds rest.
I rest in God alone . . .

2 O trust in Him, you people,
pour out your hearts,
for God is our refuge for ever,
my trust and all of my heart –
in Him alone my soul finds rest.
O trust in Him, you people . . .

292 Chris Eaton
© 1983 Patch Music

1 **I see perfection**
as I look in Your eyes, Lord;
there's no rejection
as I look in Your eyes, Lord.
You are a river that is never dry,
You are the star
that lights the evening sky,
You are my God
and I will follow You,
and now I know
just where I'm going to.
We are children,
children of the King;
we will praise Your name,
glorify You, magnify You.
Jesus, we can never deny
Your love for us on the cross
now You've made us
children of the King.

2 Your Holy Spirit
       will for ever control me!
   I give my present, future, past,
       to You completely.
   You are a river . . .
       now You've made us
       children of the King!

293 Isaac Watts (1674–1748)

1 **I sing the almighty power of God,**
   that made the mountains rise,
   that spread the flowing seas abroad,
   and built the lofty skies.

2 I sing the wisdom that ordained
   the sun to rule the day;
   the moon shines full at His command,
   and all the stars obey.

3 I sing the goodness of the Lord,
   that filled the earth with food;
   He formed the creatures
       with His word,
   and then pronounced them good.

4 Creatures, as numerous as they be,
   are subject to His care;
   there's not a place where we can flee
   but God is present there.

5 Lord, how Thy wonders are displayed
   where'er I turn mine eye,
   if I survey the ground I tread,
   or gaze upon the sky.

6 God's hand is my perpetual guard,
   He guides me with His eye;
   why should I then forget the Lord,
   whose love is ever nigh?

294 Carl Tuttle and John Wimber
© 1982 Mercy/Vineyard Publishing/
CopyCare

1 **I sing a new song
       to the Lord, my God,**
   I lift my voice to Jesus, the King;
   and I worship You, I worship You,
   I worship You, I worship You.

2 I bow down my face
       at the footstool of the Lamb,
   I lay down my life at the altar of God;
   and I worship You, I worship You,
   I worship You, I worship You.

295 Alfred Henry Ackley (1872–1958)
© 1933, 1961 The Rodeheaver Co/
Word Music/CopyCare

1 **I serve a risen Saviour,**
   He's in the world today;
   I know that He is living,
   whatever men may say.
   I see His hand of mercy,
   I hear His voice of cheer;
   and just the time I need Him,
   He's always near.
       He lives, He lives,
       Christ Jesus lives today!
       He walks with me and talks with me
       along life's narrow way.
       He lives, He lives,
       salvation to impart!
       You ask me how I know He lives?
       He lives within my heart.

2 In all the world around me
   I see His loving care,
   and though my heart grows weary
   I never will despair;
   I know that He is leading,
   through all the stormy blast,
   the day of His appearing
   will come at last.
       He lives . . .

3   Rejoice, rejoice, O Christian,
    lift up your voice and sing
    eternal hallelujahs
    to Jesus Christ the King!
    The hope of all who seek Him,
    The help of all who find,
    none other is so loving,
    so good and kind.

    He lives, He lives,
    Christ Jesus lives today!
    He walks with me and talks with me
    along life's narrow way.
    He lives, He lives,
    salvation to impart!
    You ask me how I know He lives?
    He lives within my heart.

296   Charles Hutchinson Gabriel (1858–1932)

1   **I stand amazed in the presence**
    of Jesus the Nazarene,
    and wonder how He could love me,
    a sinner, condemned, unclean.

    How marvellous! how wonderful!
    and my song shall ever be:
    How marvellous! how wonderful!
    is my Saviour's love for me!

2   For me it was in the garden
    He prayed – 'Not My will, but Thine';
    He had no tears for His own griefs,
    but sweat drops of blood for mine.
    How marvellous . . .

3   In pity angels beheld Him,
    and came from the world of light,
    to comfort Him in the sorrows
    He bore for my soul that night.
    How marvellous . . .

4   He took my sins and my sorrows,
    He made them His very own;
    He bore the burden to Calvary,
    and suffered, and died alone.
    How marvellous . . .

5   When with the ransomed in glory
    His face I at last shall see,
    'twill be my joy through the ages
    to sing of His love for me.
    How marvellous . . .

297   Mavis Ford
© 1980 Word's Spirit of Praise Music/ CopyCare

I stand before the presence
of the Lord God of hosts,
a child of my Father
and an heir of His grace.
For Jesus paid the debt for me,
the veil was torn in two,
and the Holy of Holies
has become my dwelling-place.

298   John Kennett
© 1980 Kingsway's Thankyou Music

I want to learn to appreciate You,
Lord, in every way,
I want to learn to walk with You,
Lord, day by day;
with You always there to guide me,
hand in hand,
there beside me,
walking in the Spirit day by day.

299   M Warrington
© 1972 Aquila Publishing/Copyright control

1   **I trust in Thee, O Lord;**
    I say, 'Thou art my God.'
    My times are in Thy hand,
    my times are in Thy hand.

2   Blessèd be the Lord,
    for He has wondrously shown
    His steadfast love to me,
    His steadfast love to me.

300

I want to see Your face,
I want to see Your face,
give You the worship of my heart,
of my heart,
giving up my life to You.
Knowing You (knowing You),
loving You (loving You), Lord.

301

Colin Waller

I want to thank You,
I want to praise You,
I want to love You more each day.
I want to thank You,
I want to praise You,
Yours is the power, the truth, the way.

1 Father, Your love I feel;
   help me to show it to be real.
   Then I can openly say,
   'Yours is the power, the truth, the way.'
   I want to thank You . . .

2 Jesus, Your word I hear;
   help me to see its truth so clear.
   So I can openly say,
   'Yours is the power, the truth, the way.'
   I want to thank You . . .

3 Spirit, Your power I know;
   help me to feel it, and to grow
   stronger in every way, – 'cause
   Yours is the power, the truth, the way.
   I want to thank You . . . (twice)

302

1 **I want to walk with Jesus Christ,**
   all the days I live of this life on earth;
   to give to Him complete control
   of body and of soul.

Follow Him, follow Him,
yield your life to Him –
He has conquered death,
He is King of kings;
accept the joy which He gives to those
who yield their lives to Him.

2 I want to learn to speak to Him,
   to pray to Him, confess my sin,
   to open my life and let Him in,
   for joy will then be mine.
   Follow Him, follow Him . . .

3 I want to learn to speak of Him –
   my life must show that He lives in me;
   my deeds, my thoughts, my words
       must speak
   all of His love for me.
   Follow Him, follow Him . . .

4 I want to learn to read His word,
   for this is how I know the way
   to live my life as pleases Him,
   in holiness and joy.
   Follow Him, follow Him . . .

5 O Holy Spirit of the Lord,
   enter now into this heart of mine;
   take full control of my selfish will
   and make me wholly Thine!
   Follow Him, follow Him . . .

303

Chris Rolinson

1 **I want to serve You, Lord,**
   in total abandonment,
   I want to yield my heart to You;
   I want to give my life in all surrender,
   I want to live for You alone.

2 I want to give my all
   in total abandonment,
   releasing all within my grasp;
   I want to live my life in all its fulness,
   I want to worship Christ alone.

3 I want to come to You
   in total abandonment –
   Lord, will You set my heart ablaze?
   I want to love You with all my soul
      and strength,
   I want to give You all my days.

304

Robert Cameron
© 1986 Word's Spirit of Praise Music/
CopyCare

I want to worship the Lord
   with all of my heart,
give Him my all
   and not just a part,
lift up my hands
   to the King of kings,
praise Him in everything.

305

Graham Kendrick
© 1988 Make Way Music

MEN   **'I will build my Church,**
WOMEN   I will build my Church,
MEN   and the gates of hell,
WOMEN   and the gates of hell,
MEN   shall not prevail,
WOMEN   shall not prevail,
ALL   against it.'
MEN   I will build . . .

ALL
So you powers in the heavens above,
bow down!
And you powers on the earth below,
bow down!
And acknowledge that Jesus,
Jesus, Jesus is Lord,
is Lord!

306

Michael O'Shields
© 1981 Lorenz Publishing Co/
MCA Music Publishing/CopyCare

MEN AND WOMEN IN CANON
I will call upon the Lord,
who is worthy to be praised.
So shall I be saved from my enemies.
ALL
The Lord liveth and blessèd be my rock,
and may the God of my salvation
      be exalted.
The Lord liveth and blessèd be my rock,
and may the God of my salvation
      be exalted.

307

Leona van Brethorst
© 1976 Maranatha! Music/CopyCare

I will enter His gates
with thanksgiving in my heart,
I will enter His courts with praise;
I will say, 'This is the day
that the Lord has made,
I will rejoice for He has made me glad.'
He has made me glad,
      He has made me glad;
I will rejoice for He has made me glad.
He has made me glad,
      He has made me glad;
I will rejoice for He has made me glad.

308

Brent Chambers
© 1977 Scripture in Song/Integrity Music/
Kingsway's Thankyou Music

I will give thanks to Thee,
   O Lord, among the peoples,
I will sing praises to Thee
   among the nations.
For Thy steadfast love is great,
   is great to the heavens,
and Thy faithfulness, Thy faithfulness,
   to the clouds.

Be exalted, O God, above the heavens,
let Thy glory be over all the earth!
Be exalted, O God, above the heavens,
let Thy glory, let Thy glory,
let Thy glory be over all the earth!

You anoint my head with oil,
and my cup surely overflows;
goodness and love shall follow me
all the days that I dwell in Your house.

309 Tommy Walker
© 1985 Kingsway's Thankyou Music

I will give You praise,
I will sing Your song,
I will bless Your holy name;
For there is no other God
who is like unto You,
You're the only way.
Only You are the author of life,
only You can bring the blind their sight,
only You are called Prince of peace,
only You promised You'd never leave,
only You are God.

310 Scott Palazzo
© 1985 Mercy/Vineyard Publishing/
CopyCare

I will magnify Thy name
above all the earth;
I will magnify Thy name
above all the earth.
I will sing unto Thee
the praises in my heart;
I will sing unto Thee
the praises in my heart.

311 David Fellingham
© 1982 Kingsway's Thankyou Music

I will rejoice, I will rejoice,
I will rejoice in the Lord
with my whole heart;
I will rejoice, I will rejoice,
I will rejoice in the Lord.

312 Anon
Copyright control

I will rejoice in You and be glad,
I will extol Your love more than wine;
draw me after You and let us run together,
I will rejoice in You and be glad.

313 Max Dyer
© 1974 Celebration/Kingsway's Thankyou Music

1 **I will sing, I will sing a song**
   unto the Lord, (*3 times*)
   alleluia, glory to the Lord.
   Allelu, alleluia, glory to the Lord,
   allelu, alleluia, glory to the Lord,
   allelu, alleluia, glory to the Lord,
   alleluia, glory to the Lord.

2 We will come, we will come as one
   before the Lord, (*3 times*)
   alleluia, glory to the Lord.
   Allelu, alleluia . . .

3 If the Son, if the Son shall make you
   free, (*3 times*)
   you shall be free indeed.
   Allelu, alleluia . . .

4 They that sow in tears shall reap in joy,
   (*3 times*)
   alleluia, glory to the Lord!
   Allelu, alleluia . . .

5 Every knee shall bow and every tongue
   confess, (*3 times*)
   that Jesus Christ is Lord.
   Allelu, alleluia . . .

6 In His name, in His name we have the
    victory. (*3 times*)
  Alleluia, glory to the Lord.
  Allelu, alleluia, glory to the Lord,
  allelu, alleluia, glory to the Lord,
  allelu, alleluia, glory to the Lord,
  alleluia, glory to the Lord.

3 He will keep me till the river
    rolls its waters at my feet:
    then He'll bear me safely over,
    made by grace for glory meet.
    Yes, I'll sing the wondrous story
    of the Christ who died for me –
    sing it with His saints in glory,
    gathered by the crystal sea.

314

Phil Potter
© 1981 Kingsway's Thankyou Music

I will sing about Your love,
I will magnify Your name,
I will be glad and rejoice in You,
I will praise You again.
Praise the Lord, lift your voices high,
praise the Lord, tell them He's alive,
praise the Lord, praise the Lord.

315

Francis Harold Rawley (1854–1952)
© HarperCollins*Religious*/CopyCare

1 **I will sing the wondrous story**
  of the Christ who died for me –
  how He left the realms of glory
  for the cross on Calvary.
  Yes, I'll sing the wondrous story
  of the Christ who died for me –
  sing it with His saints in glory,
  gathered by the crystal sea.

2 I was lost: but Jesus found me,
  found the sheep that went astray,
  raised me up and gently led me
  back into the narrow way.
  Days of darkness still may meet me,
  sorrow's path I oft may tread;
  but His presence still is with me,
  by His guiding hand I'm led.

316

Donya Brockway
© 1972 His Eye Music/Multisongs/
EMI Christian Music Publishing/CopyCare

I will sing unto the Lord
  as long as I live,
I will sing praise to my God
  while I have my being,
my meditation of Him shall be sweet,
I will be glad, I will be glad in the Lord.
Bless thou the Lord, O my soul,
praise ye the Lord;
bless thou the Lord, O my soul,
praise ye the Lord;
bless thou the Lord, O my soul,
praise ye the Lord;
bless thou the Lord, O my soul,
praise ye the Lord.

317

© 1985 Andy Silver

I will wait upon the Lord,
my hope is all in Him;
He only is my rock and strength,
my refuge is in God;
I will trust Him at all times,
pour out my heart to Him.

He only is my rock and strength,
my refuge is in God;
I will wait upon the Lord,
my hope is all in Him;
He only is my rock and strength,
my refuge is in God.

318
Graham Kendrick
© 1987 Make Way Music

If My people who bear My name
will humble themselves and pray;
if they seek My presence
and turn their backs on their wicked ways;
then I will hear from heaven,
I'll hear from heaven and will forgive.
I will forgive their sins
and will heal their land –
yes, I will heal their land.

319
Rhea F Miller (1894–1966)
© The Rodeheaver Co/Word Music/
CopyCare

1   **I'd rather have Jesus
       than silver or gold,**
    I'd rather be His
       than have riches untold;
    I'd rather have Jesus
       than houses or lands,
    I'd rather be led by
       His nail-pierced hand.
    Than to be the king of a vast domain
    and be held in sin's dread sway;
    I'd rather have Jesus than anything
    this world affords today.

2   I'd rather have Jesus
       than men's applause,
    I'd rather be faithful to His dear cause;
    I'd rather have Jesus
       than world-wide fame,
    I'd rather be true to His holy name.
    Than to be the king . . .

3   He's fairer than lilies of rarest bloom,
    He's sweeter than honey
       from out the comb;
    He's all that my hungering spirit needs,
    I'd rather have Jesus and let Him lead.
    Than to be the king . . .

320
Isaac Watts (1674–1748)

1   **I'll praise my maker
       while I've breath,**
    and when my voice is lost in death,
    praise shall employ my nobler powers:
    my days of praise shall ne'er be past,
    while life and thought and being last,
    or immortality endures.

2   Happy the man whose hopes rely
    on Israel's God! He made the sky
    and earth and sea, with all their train:
    His truth for ever stands secure;
    He saves the oppressed,
       He feeds the poor,
    and none shall find His promise vain.

3   The Lord gives eyesight to the blind;
    the Lord supports the fainting mind;
    He sends the labouring conscience
       peace:
    He helps the stranger in distress,
    the widow and the fatherless,
    and grants the prisoner sweet release.

4   I'll praise Him
       while He lends me breath;
    and when my voice is lost in death,
    praise shall employ my nobler powers.
    My days of praise shall ne'er be past,
    while life and thought and being last,
    or immortality endures.

321
Rob Hayward
© 1985 Kingsway's Thankyou Music

I'm accepted, I'm forgiven,
I am fathered by the true and living God.
I'm accepted, no condemnation,
I am loved by the true and living God.
There's no guilt or fear as I draw near
to the Saviour and Creator of the world.
There is joy and peace as I release
my worship to You, O Lord.

322 From Philippians 1
Copyright control

MEN AND WOMEN IN CANON
I'm confident of this very thing:
that He who has begun
    a good work in you,
ALL
He will perform it
    until the day of Jesus Christ,
He will perform it
    until the day of Jesus Christ,
He will perform it
    until the day of Jesus Christ.

323 Isaac Watts (1674–1748)

1 **I'm not ashamed to own my Lord,**
  or to defend His cause;
  maintain the honour of His word,
  the glory of His cross.

2 Jesus, my God, I know His name;
  His name is all my trust;
  nor will He put my soul to shame,
  nor let my hope be lost.

3 Firm as His throne His promise stands;
  and He can well secure
  what I've committed to His hands,
  till the decisive hour.

4 Then will He own my worthless name
  before His Father's face;
  and in the new Jerusalem
  appoint my soul a place.

324 Tony Humphries
© 1980 Kingsway's Thankyou Music

I'm redeemed, yes I am,
by the blood of the Lamb,
Jesus Christ has done it all for me.
I am His, He is mine,
I'm part of the royal vine,
all my sins were washed away at Calvary.

Once I was lost, I had nowhere to go,
my life was just a lonely round of sin;
till Jesus said to me,
'By My blood shed on the tree,
I've paid the price,
brought you back,
you're mine.'
O what a friend!

I'm redeemed, yes I am,
by the blood of the Lamb,
Jesus Christ has done it all for me.
I am His, He is mine,
I'm part of the royal vine,
all my sins were washed away at Calvary.

325 Graham Kendrick
© 1986 Kingsway's Thankyou Music

I'm special because God has loved me,
for He gave the best thing that He had
    to save me:
His own Son Jesus,
    crucified to take the blame,
for all the bad things I have done.

Thank You Jesus, thank You Lord,
for loving me so much;
I know I don't deserve anything,
help me feel Your love right now,
to know deep in my heart
    that I'm Your special friend.

326 Graham Kendrick
© 1988 Make Way Music

Immanuel, O Immanuel,
bowed in awe I worship at Your feet,
and sing, 'Immanuel, God is with us!'
Sharing my humanness, my shame,
feeling my weaknesses, my pain,
taking the punishment, the blame,
Immanuel.

And now my words cannot explain
all that my heart cannot contain,
how great are the glories of Your name,
Immanuel.

327
Walter Chalmers Smith (1824–1908)

1 **Immortal, invisible, God only wise,**
in light inaccessible hid from our eyes,
most blessèd, most glorious,
    the Ancient of Days,
almighty, victorious,
    Thy great name we praise.

2 Unresting, unhasting,
    and silent as light,
nor wanting, nor wasting,
    Thou rulest in might;
Thy justice like mountains
    high soaring above
Thy clouds, which are fountains
    of goodness and love.

3 To all, life Thou givest,
    to both great and small;
in all life Thou livest, the true life of all;
we blossom and flourish
    as leaves on the tree,
and wither and perish,
    but nought changeth Thee.

4 Great Father of glory,
    pure Father of light,
Thine angels adore Thee,
    all veiling their sight;
All laud we would render;
    O help us to see
'tis only the splendour
    of light hideth Thee.

5 Immortal, invisible, God only wise,
in light inaccessible hid from our eyes,
most blessed, most glorious,
    the Ancient of Days,
almighty, victorious,
    Thy great name we praise.

328
John Greenleaf Whittier (1807–92)

1 **Immortal Love, for ever full,**
    for ever flowing free,
for ever shared, for ever whole,
    a never-ebbing sea:

2 Our outward lips confess the name
    all other names above;
love only knoweth whence it came
    and comprehendeth love.

3 We may not climb the heavenly steeps
    to bring the Lord Christ down:
in vain we search the lowest deeps,
    for Him no depths can drown.

4 In joy of inward peace, or sense
    of sorrow over sin,
He is His own best evidence,
    His witness is within.

5 For warm, sweet, tender, even yet
    a present help is He;
and faith still has its Olivet,
    and love its Galilee.

6 The healing of His seamless dress
    is by our beds of pain;
we touch Him
    in life's throng and press,
and we are whole again.

7 Through Him the first fond prayers
    are said
our lips of childhood frame,
the last low whispers of our dead
    are burdened with His name.

8 O Lord and Master of us all,
    whate'er our name or sign,
we own Thy sway, we hear Thy call,
    we test our lives by Thine.

329
John Oxenham (1852–1941)
By permission of Desmond Dunkerley

1 **In Christ there is no east or west,**
in Him no south or north,
but one great fellowship of love
throughout the whole wide earth.

2 In Him shall true hearts everywhere
their high communion find:
His service is the golden cord
close-binding all mankind.

3 Join hands then, brothers of the faith,
whate'er your race may be!
Who serves my Father as a son
is surely kin to me.

4 In Christ now meet both east and west,
in Him meet south and north,
all Christly souls are one in Him,
throughout the whole wide earth.

330 Frances Ridley Havergal (1836–79)

1 **In full and glad surrender,**
I give myself to Thee,
Thine utterly and only
and evermore to be.

2 O Son of God, who lov'st me,
I will be Thine alone;
and all I have and am, Lord,
shall henceforth be Thine own!

3 Reign over me, Lord Jesus,
O make my heart Thy throne;
it shall be Thine, dear Saviour,
it shall be Thine alone.

4 O come and reign, Lord Jesus,
rule over everything!
and keep me always loyal
and true to Thee, my King.

331 Anna Laetitia Waring (1823–1910)

1 **In heavenly love abiding,**
no change my heart shall fear;
and safe is such confiding,
for nothing changes here.
The storm may roar without me,
my heart may low be laid,
but God is round about me,
and can I be dismayed?

2 Wherever He may guide me,
no want shall turn me back;
my shepherd is beside me,
and nothing can I lack.
His wisdom ever waketh,
His sight is never dim,
He knows the way He taketh,
and I will walk with Him.

3 Green pastures are before me,
which yet I have not seen;
bright skies will soon be o'er me,
where the dark clouds have been.
My hope I cannot measure,
my path to life is free,
my Saviour has my treasure,
and He will walk with me.

332 Randy Speir
© 1981 Integrity's Hosanna! Music
Kingsway's Thankyou Music

**In Him we live and move
and have our being;**
in Him we live and move
and have our being.
Make a joyful noise, sing unto the Lord,
tell Him of your love, dance before Him;
make a joyful noise, sing unto the Lord,
tell Him of your love, hallelujah!

333 Charles Hutchinson Gabriel (1856–1932)

1 **In loving-kindness Jesus came,**
my soul in mercy to reclaim,
and from the depths of sin and shame
through grace He lifted me.
From sinking sand He lifted me;
with tender hand He lifted me;
from shades of night to plains of light,
O praise His name, He lifted me!

2 He called me long before I heard,
   before my sinful heart was stirred;
   but when I took Him at His word,
   forgiven He lifted me.
       From sinking sand . . .

3 His brow was pierced
          with many a thorn,
   His hands by cruel nails were torn,
   when from my guilt and grief, forlorn,
   in love He lifted me.
       From sinking sand . . .

4 Now on a higher plane I dwell,
   and with my soul I know 'tis well;
   yet how or why, I cannot tell,
   He should have lifted me.
       From sinking sand . . .

334 David Graham
          © 1980 C A Music/Music Services/
          CopyCare

**In moments like these
          I sing out a song,**
I sing out a love-song to Jesus;
in moments like these I lift up my hands,
I lift up my hands to the Lord:
singing, 'I love You, Lord',
singing, 'I love You, Lord',
singing, 'I love You, Lord,
I love You.'

335 Bob Kilpatrick
          © 1978 Bob Kilpatrick Music/
          Lorenz Publishing Co/CopyCare

1 **In my life, Lord, be glorified,
          be glorified;**
   in my life, Lord, be glorified today.

2 In your Church, Lord, be glorified,
          be glorified;
   in your Church, Lord,
          be glorified today.

336 Gordon Brattle (1917–91)
          © David Brattle

In my need Jesus found me,
put His strong arm around me,
brought me safe home,
into the shelter of the fold.

Gracious shepherd that sought me,
precious life-blood that bought me;
out of the night,
into the light and near to God.

337 Christina Georgina Rossetti (1830–94)

1 **In the bleak mid-winter,**
   frosty wind made moan,
   earth stood hard as iron,
   water like a stone;
   snow had fallen, snow on snow,
   snow on snow,
   in the bleak mid-winter,
   long ago.

2 Our God, heaven cannot hold Him,
   nor earth sustain,
   heaven and earth shall flee away
   when He comes to reign;
   in the bleak mid-winter
   a stable-place sufficed
   the Lord God almighty,
   Jesus Christ.

3 Angels and archangels
   may have gathered there,
   cherubim and seraphim
   thronged the air;
   but His mother only,
   in her maiden bliss,
   worshipped the Belovèd
   with a kiss.

4   What can I give Him,
    poor as I am?
    If I were a shepherd,
    I would bring a lamb;
    if I were a wise man,
    I would do my part;
    yet what I can I give Him –
    give my heart.

338   John Bowring (1792–1872)

1   **In the cross of Christ I glory,**
    towering o'er the wrecks of time:
    all the light of sacred story
    gathers round its head sublime.

2   When the woes of life o'ertake me,
    hopes deceive, and fears annoy,
    never shall the cross forsake me;
    Lo! it glows with peace and joy.

3   When the sun of bliss is beaming
    light and love upon my way,
    from the cross the radiance streaming
    adds more lustre to the day.

4   Bane and blessing, pain and pleasure,
    by the cross are sanctified;
    peace is there that knows no measure,
    joys that through all time abide.

5   In the cross of Christ I glory,
    towering o'er the wrecks of time:
    all the light of sacred story
    gathers round its head sublime.

339   Anon
    Copyright control

In the name of Jesus,
in the name of Jesus,
we have the victory.
In the name of Jesus,
in the name of Jesus,
demons will have to flee.

Who can tell what God can do?
Who can tell of His love for you?
In the name of Jesus, Jesus,
we have the victory.

340   Graham Kendrick
    © 1986 Kingsway's Thankyou Music

1   **In the tomb so cold they laid Him,**
    death its victim claimed;
    powers of hell,
        they could not hold Him –
    back to life He came!
    Christ is risen,
    (Christ is risen),
    death has been conquered,
    (death has been conquered),
    Christ is risen,
    (Christ is risen):
    He shall reign for ever!

2   Hell had spent its fury on Him,
    left Him crucified;
    yet by blood He boldly conquered,
    sin and death defied.
    Christ is risen . . .

3   Now the fear of death is broken,
    Love has won the crown.
    Prisoners of the darkness – listen,
    walls are tumbling down!
    Christ is risen . . .

4   Raised from death,
        to heaven ascending,
    Love's exalted King:
    let His song of joy unending
    through the nations ring!
    Christ is risen . . .

341

Brent Chambers
© 1977 Scripture in Song/
Integrity Music/Kingsway's Thankyou Music

In the presence of Your people
I will praise Your name,
for alone You are holy,
    enthroned on the praises of Israel.
Let us celebrate Your goodness
    and Your steadfast love;
may Your name be exalted
    here on earth and in heaven above!

342

From a Polish carol
tr. E M G Reed (1885–1933)
Copyright control

1 **Infant holy, infant lowly,**
for His bed a cattle stall;
oxen lowing, little knowing
Christ the babe is Lord of all.
Swift are winging angels singing,
nowells ringing, tidings bringing:
Christ the babe is Lord of all;
Christ the babe is Lord of all!

2 Flocks were sleeping,
    shepherds keeping
vigil till the morning new,
saw the glory, heard the story –
tidings of a gospel true.
Thus rejoicing, free from sorrow,
praises voicing, greet the morrow:
Christ the babe was born for you;
Christ the babe was born for you!

343

© 1987 Anne Horrobin and Stephen Poxon/
Copyright control

1 **Is this the Church of our God?**
Is this the Church of the word?
Is this the Church of His Son
    Jesus Christ?
Is this the Church of His Spirit?

2 If we're dependent on Him,
if we believe God's own word,
if we're redeemed
    by the blood of His Son,
if we are filled with His Spirit:

3 Then this is the Church of our God,
then this is the Church of His word,
then this is the Church of His Son
    Jesus Christ,
then this is the Church of our Lord.

4 Yes, this is the Church of our God,
yes, this is the Church of His word,
yes, this is the Church of His Son
    Jesus Christ,
yes, this is the Church of our Lord!

344

John Wimber
© 1980 Mercy/Vineyard Publishing/
CopyCare

1 **Isn't He beautiful;**
beautiful, isn't He?
Prince of peace,
Son of God,
isn't He?
Isn't He wonderful,
wonderful, isn't He?
Counsellor,
Almighty God,
isn't He, isn't He,
isn't He, isn't He?

2 Yes, You are beautiful,
beautiful, yes, You are!
Prince of peace,
Son of God,
yes, You are!
Yes, You are wonderful,
wonderful, yes, You are!
Counsellor,
Almighty God,
yes, You are, yes, You are,
yes, You are, yes, You are,
yes, You are!

345 Edward Hamilton Sears (1810–76)
© in this version Jubilate Hymns

1 **It came upon the midnight clear,**
that glorious song of old,
from angels bending near the earth
to touch their harps of gold:
'Peace on the earth, goodwill to men
from heaven's all-gracious king!'
The world in solemn stillness lay
to hear the angels sing.

2 With sorrow brought by sin and strife
the world has suffered long,
and, since the angels sang, have passed
two thousand years of wrong;
for man at war with man hears not
the love-song which they bring:
O hush the noise, you men of strife,
and hear the angels sing!

3 And those whose journey now is hard,
whose hope is burning low,
who tread the rocky path of life
with painful steps and slow:
O listen to the news of love
which makes the heavens ring!
O rest beside the weary road
and hear the angels sing!

4 And still the days are hastening on –
by prophets seen of old –
towards the fulness of the time
when comes the age foretold:
then earth and heaven renewed
shall see
the Prince of peace, their king;
and all the world repeat the song
which now the angels sing.

346 William Walsham How (1823–97)

1 **It is a thing most wonderful,**
almost too wonderful to be,
that God's own Son
should come from heaven
and die to save a child like me.

2 And yet I know that it is true;
He chose a poor and humble lot,
and wept, and toiled,
and mourned, and died,
for love of those who loved Him not.

3 I sometimes think about the cross,
and shut my eyes and try to see
the cruel nails and crown of thorns,
and Jesus crucified for me.

4 But even could I see Him die,
I could but see a little part
of that great love, which, like a fire,
is always burning in His heart.

5 I cannot tell how He could love
a child so weak and full of sin;
His love must be most wonderful,
if He could die my love to win.

6 It is most wonderful to know
His love for me so free and sure;
but 'tis more wonderful to see
my love for Him so faint and poor.

7 And yet I want to love Thee, Lord;
O light the flame within my heart,
and I will love Thee more and more,
until I see Thee as Thou art.

347 H L Turner (19th century)

1 **It may be at morn,**
when the day is awaking,
when sunlight through darkness
and shadow is breaking,
that Jesus will come
in the fulness of glory,
to receive from the world His own.
O Lord Jesus, how long?
How long ere we shout the glad song?
Christ returneth,
hallelujah, hallelujah, amen,
hallelujah, amen!

2 It may be at mid-day,
  it may be at twilight,
it may be, perchance,
    that the blackness of midnight
will burst into light
    in the blaze of His glory,
when Jesus receives His own.
  O Lord Jesus . . .

3 While hosts cry, 'Hosanna',
    from heaven descending,
with glorified saints
      and the angels attending,
with grace on His brow,
    like a halo of glory,
will Jesus receive His own.
  O Lord Jesus . . .

4 O joy! O delight!
    should we go without dying;
no sickness, no sadness,
    no dread and no crying;
caught up through the clouds
    with our Lord into glory,
when Jesus receives His own.
  O Lord Jesus . . .

348 Kurt Kaiser
© 1969 Bud John Songs/EMI Christian
Music Publishing/CopyCare

1 **It only takes a spark
  to get a fire going,**
and soon all those around
    can warm up in its glowing;
that's how it is with God's love,
    once you've experienced it:
you spread His love to everyone;
you want to pass it on.

2 What a wondrous time is spring
      when all the trees are budding,
the birds begin to sing;
      the flowers start their blooming;

that's how it is with God's love,
once you've experienced it
    you want to sing,
it's fresh like spring;
    you want to pass it on.

3 I wish for you, my friend,
    this happiness that I've found;
you can depend on Him, it matters not
    where you're bound;
I'll shout it from the mountaintop,
I want my world to know;
The Lord of love has come to me,
    I want to pass it on.

349 Mary Shekleton (1827–83)

1 **It passeth knowledge,
    that dear love of Thine,**
my Saviour, Jesus! yet this soul of mine
would of Thy love,
    in all its breadth and length,
its height and depth,
    and everlasting strength,
    know more and more.

2 It passeth telling,
    that dear love of Thine,
my Saviour, Jesus!
    yet these lips of mine
would fain proclaim,
    to sinners, far and near,
a love which can remove all guilty fear,
    and love beget.

3 It passeth praises,
    that dear love of Thine,
my Saviour, Jesus!
    yet this heart of mine
would sing that love,
    so full, so rich, so free,
which brings a rebel sinner,
    such as me,
    nigh unto God.

4 O fill me, Saviour, Jesus, with Thy love;
lead, lead me to the living fount above;
thither may I, in simple faith,
draw nigh,
and never to another fountain fly,
but unto Thee.

5 And then, when Jesus face to face I see,
when at His lofty throne
I bow the knee,
then of His love,
in all its breadth and length,
its height and depth,
its everlasting strength,
my soul shall sing.

350 Sally Ellis
© 1980 Kingsway's Thankyou Music

It is no longer I that liveth
but Christ that liveth in me;
it is no longer I that liveth
but Christ that liveth in me.
He lives, He lives,
Jesus is alive in me;
it is no longer I that liveth
but Christ that liveth in me.

351 Michael Christ
© 1985 Mercy/Vineyard Publishing/
CopyCare

It's Your blood that cleanses me,
it's Your blood that gives me life,
it's Your blood that took my place
in redeeming sacrifice,
and washes me whiter than the snow,
than the snow.
My Jesus, God's precious sacrifice.

352 James Grindlay Small (1817–88)

1 **I've found a friend;**
   O such a friend!
He loved me ere I knew Him;
He drew me with the cords of love,
and thus He bound me to Him:
and round my heart still closely twine
those ties which nought can sever,
for I am His, and He is mine,
for ever and for ever.

2 I've found a friend; O such a friend!
He bled, He died to save me;
and not alone the gift of life,
but His own self He gave me:
nought that I have mine own I call,
I hold it for the giver;
my heart, my strength, my life, my all,
are His, and His for ever.

3 I've found a friend; O such a friend!
all power to Him is given;
to guard me on my onward course,
and bring me safe to heaven.
Eternal glories gleam afar,
to nerve my faint endeavour;
so now to watch, to work, to war,
and then to rest for ever.

4 I've found a friend; O such a friend!
so kind, and true, and tender!
So wise a counsellor and guide,
so mighty a defender!
From Him who loves me now so well
what power my soul shall sever?
Shall life or death? Shall earth or hell?
No! I am His for ever.

353 Traditional

I've got peace like a river,
   peace like a river,
I've got peace like a river in my soul;
I've got peace like a river,
   peace like a river,
I've got peace like a river in my soul.

354
Merla Watson
© 1974 Lorenz Publishing Co/
MCA Publishing Co/CopyCare

Jehovah Jireh, my provider,
His grace is sufficient for me,
for me, for me.
Jehovah Jireh, my provider,
His grace is sufficient for me.
My God shall supply all my need
according to His riches in glory;
He gives His angels charge over me.
Jehovah Jireh cares for me, for me, for me.
Jehovah Jireh cares for me.

355
Chris Bowater
© 1982 Sovereign Lifestyle Music

Jesus, at Your name we bow the knee,
Jesus, at Your name we bow the knee,
Jesus, at Your name we bow the knee,
and acknowledge You as Lord.
Jesus, at Your name . . .

You are the Christ, You are the Lord,
through Your Spirit in our lives
we know who You are.
You are the Christ . . .

356
Peter and Diane Fung
© 1983 Kingsway's Thankyou Music

Jesus Christ, our great Redeemer,
mighty victor and strong deliverer,
King of kings and Lord of lords,
We praise You, praise Your name –
   Alleluia, alleluia;
King of kings and Lord of lords –
   Alleluia, alleluia!
Your victory is assured.

357
From *Lyra Davidica*, 1708

1 **Jesus Christ is risen today,**
   hallelujah!
   our triumphant holy day,
   who did once, upon the cross,
   suffer to redeem our loss.

2 Hymns of praise then let us sing,
   unto Christ, our heavenly King,
   who endured the cross and grave,
   sinners to redeem and save.

3 But the pains which He endured,
   our salvation have procured,
   now in heaven above He's King,
   where the angels ever sing:

358
Anon
Copyright control

Jesus Christ is alive today,
I know, I know it's true.
Sovereign of the universe,
I give Him homage due.
Seated there at God's right hand,
I am with Him in the promised land.
Jesus lives and reigns in me,
that's how I know it's true.

359
Cecil Frances Alexander (1818–95)

1 **Jesus calls us; o'er the tumult**
   of our life's wild restless sea,
   day by day His voice is sounding,
   saying, 'Christian, follow me.'

2 As of old, apostles heard it
   by the Galilean lake,
   turned from home, and toil,
      and kindred,
   leaving all for His dear sake.

3 Jesus calls us from the worship
of the vain world's golden store,
from each idol that would keep us,
saying, 'Christian, love Me more.'

4 In our joys and in our sorrows,
days of toil and hours of ease,
still He calls, in cares and pleasures,
'Christian, love Me more than these.'

5 Jesus calls us! By Thy mercies,
Saviour, may we hear Thy call,
give our hearts to Thine obedience,
serve and love Thee best of all.

3 Jesus is now living in His Church:
men who have been purchased
  by His blood –
they will serve their God,
a royal priesthood,
and they will reign on earth.
  For the government . . .

4 Sound the trumpet –
  good news to the poor!
Captives will go free, the blind will see,
the kingdom of this world
  will soon become
the kingdom of our God.
  For the government . . .

360 Jonathan Wallis
© 1983 Kingsway's Thankyou Music

1 **Jesus has sat down
  at God's right hand,**
He is reigning now on David's throne;
God has placed all things
  beneath His feet,
His enemies will be His footstool.
  *For the government
  is now upon His shoulder,
  for the government
  is now upon His shoulder;
  and of the increase
  of His government and peace
  there will be no end,
  there will be no end,
  there will be no end.*

2 God has now exalted Him on high,
given Him a name above all names;
every knee will bow,
  and tongue confess
that Jesus Christ is Lord.
  For the government . . .

361 David Bolton
© 1975 Kingsway's Thankyou Music

Jesus, how lovely You are!
You are so gentle, so pure and kind,
You shine like the morning star:
Jesus, how lovely You are.

1 Alleluia, Jesus is my Lord and King;
Alleluia, Jesus is my everything.
  Jesus, how lovely . . .

2 Alleluia, Jesus died and rose again;
Alleluia, Jesus forgave all my sin.
  Jesus, how lovely . . .

3 Alleluia, Jesus is meek and lowly;
Alleluia, Jesus is pure and holy.
  Jesus, how lovely . . .

4 Alleluia, Jesus is the bridegroom;
Alleluia, Jesus will take His bride soon.
  Jesus, how lovely . . .

362 Jean Sophia Pigott (1845–82)

1 **Jesus, I am resting, resting,**
in the joy of what Thou art;
I am finding out the greatness
of Thy loving heart.
Thou hast bid me gaze upon Thee,
and Thy beauty fills my soul,
for, by Thy transforming power,
Thou hast made me whole.

Jesus, I am resting, resting,
in the joy of what Thou art;
I am finding out the greatness
of Thy loving heart.

2 O how great Thy loving-kindness,
vaster, broader than the sea!
O how marvellous Thy goodness,
lavished all on me!
Yes, I rest in Thee, Belovèd,
know what wealth of grace is Thine,
know Thy certainty of promise,
and have made it mine.

Jesus, I am resting . . .

3 Simply trusting Thee, Lord Jesus,
I behold Thee as Thou art;
and Thy love so pure, so changeless,
satisfies my heart.
Satisfies its deepest longings,
meets, supplies its every need,
compasseth me round with blessings;
Thine is love indeed.

Jesus, I am resting . . .

4 Ever lift Thy face upon me,
as I work and wait for Thee;
resting 'neath Thy smile, Lord Jesus,
earth's dark shadows flee.
Brightness of my Father's glory,
sunshine of my Father's face,
keep me ever trusting, resting,
fill me with Thy grace.

Jesus, I am resting . . .

363 Trish Morgan
© 1986 Kingsway's Thankyou Music

Jesus, I love You,
love You more and more each day;
Jesus, I love You,
Your gentle touch renews my heart.
It's really no wonder why
no other love can satisfy;
Jesus, I love You,
You've won this heart of mine!

364 Chris Bowater
© 1982 Sovereign Lifestyle Music

Jesus, I worship You,
worship, honour and adore
Your lovely name;
Jesus, I worship You,
Lord of lords and King of kings,
I worship You;
from a thankful heart I sing,
I worship You.

365 Marilyn Baker
© 1983 Word Music/CopyCare

1 **Jesus is Lord of all,**
Satan is under His feet,
Jesus is reigning on high,
and all power is given to Him
in heaven and earth.

2 We are joined to Him,
Satan is under our feet,
we are seated on high,
and all authority is given
to us through Him.

3 One day we'll be like Him,
perfect in every way,
chosen to be His bride,
ruling and reigning with Him
for evermore.

366
Wendy Churchill
© 1981 Springtide/Word Music/
CopyCare

1 **Jesus is King**
  and I will extol Him,
  give Him the glory,
    and honour His name;
  He reigns on high,
    enthroned in the heavens –
  Word of the Father,
    exalted for us.

2 We have a hope
    that is steadfast and certain,
  gone through the curtain
    and touching the throne;
  we have a priest
    who is there interceding,
  pouring His grace
    on our lives day by day.

3 We come to Him,
    our Priest and Apostle,
  clothed in His glory
    and bearing His name,
  laying our lives
    with gladness before Him –
  filled with His Spirit
    we worship the King:

4 'O Holy One,
    our hearts do adore You;
  thrilled with Your goodness
    we give You our praise!'
  Angels in light
    with worship surround Him,
  Jesus, our Saviour,
    for ever the same.

367
David Mansell
© 1982 Word's Spirit of Praise Music/
CopyCare

1 **Jesus is Lord!**
    Creation's voice proclaims it,
  for by His power each tree and flower
    was planned and made.
  Jesus is Lord! The universe declares it;
  sun, moon and stars in heaven cry:
    'Jesus is Lord!'

Jesus is Lord! Jesus is Lord!
Praise Him with hallelujahs,
  for Jesus is Lord!

2 Jesus is Lord!
    Yet from His throne eternal
  in flesh He came to die in pain
    on Calvary's tree.
  Jesus is Lord!
    From Him all life proceeding,
  yet gave His life a ransom
    thus setting us free.
  Jesus is Lord . . .

3 Jesus is Lord!
    O'er sin the mighty conqueror,
  from death He rose and all His foes
    shall own His name.
  Jesus is Lord!
    God sends His Holy Spirit
  to show by works of power
    that Jesus is Lord.
  Jesus is Lord . . .

368
Dennis Merry
© 1981 Word's Spirit of Praise Music/
CopyCare

Jesus is the Lord,
  Jesus the Lord reigns,
we will take the kingdoms of this world
  in His name.
Every tribe and nation, every situation,
must declare that Jesus is the Lord.

For the Lord our God
    has delivered Him from death
and established Jesus as Lord;
He has given Him the power
    over all that He has made,
for our God has made Him
    Christ the Lord.

369
© 1987 Ruth Hooke

1 **Jesus, Jesus,**
You are my Lord and my heart's desire;
Jesus, Jesus,
keep us in Your love.

2 Jesus, Jesus,
You are my King
    and my Sovereign Master;
Jesus, Jesus,
I will serve You, Lord.

370
Chris Bowater
© 1979 Sovereign Lifestyle Music

Jesus, Jesus, Jesus,
Your love has melted my heart;
Jesus, Jesus, Jesus,
Your love has melted my heart.

371
Betty Pulkingham
© 1974, 1975 Celebration/
Kingsway's Thankyou Music

Jesus, Lamb of God,
have mercy on us.
Jesus, bearer of our sins,
have mercy on us.
Jesus, Redeemer of the world,
give us your peace,
give us your peace.

Jesus, Lamb of God,
have mercy on us.
Jesus, bearer of our sins,
have mercy on us.
Jesus, Redeemer of the world,
give us your peace.

372
Charles Wesley (1707–88) altd.

1 **Jesus, lover of my soul,**
let me to Thy bosom fly,
while the nearer waters roll,
while the tempest still is high:
hide me, O my Saviour, hide,
till the storm of life is past;
safe into the haven guide;
O receive my soul at last!

2 Other refuge have I none,
hangs my helpless soul on Thee;
leave, ah! leave me not alone,
still support and comfort me:
all my trust on Thee is stayed;
all my help from Thee I bring;
cover my defenceless head
with the shadow of Thy wing.

3 Thou, O Christ, art all I want;
more than all in Thee I find;
raise the fallen, cheer the faint,
heal the sick, and lead the blind.
Just and holy is Thy name,
I am all unrighteousness;
false, and full of sin I am,
Thou art full of truth and grace.

4 Plenteous grace with Thee is found,
grace to cover all my sin;
let the healing streams abound,
make and keep me pure within.
Thou of life the fountain art,
freely let me take of Thee;
spring Thou up within my heart,
rise to all eternity.

373
Christian Furchtegott Gellert (1715–69)
tr. Frances Elizabeth Cox (1812–97)

1 **Jesus lives! thy terrors now**
can, O death, no more appal us;
Jesus lives! by this we know,
thou, O grave, canst not enthral us.
    Hallelujah!

2 Jesus lives! henceforth is death
but the gate of life immortal;
this shall calm our trembling breath,
when we pass its gloomy portal.
Hallelujah!

3 Jesus lives! for us He died;
then, alone to Jesus living,
pure in heart may we abide,
glory to our Saviour giving.
Hallelujah!

4 Jesus lives! our hearts know well,
naught from us His love shall sever;
life, nor death, nor powers of hell,
tear us from His keeping ever.
Hallelujah!

5 Jesus lives! to Him the throne
over all the world is given:
may we go where He is gone,
rest and reign with Him in heaven.
Hallelujah!

374 Norman J Clayton
© 1938, 1943 Wordspring/CopyCare

1 **Jesus my Lord will love me for ever,**
from Him no power of evil can sever,
He gave His life to ransom my soul,
now I belong to Him:
Now I belong to Jesus,
Jesus belongs to me,
not for the years of time alone,
but for eternity.

2 Once I was lost in sin's degradation,
Jesus came down to bring me salvation,
lifted me up from sorrow and shame,
now I belong to Him:
Now I belong . . .

3 Joy floods my soul,
for Jesus has saved me,
freed me from sin
that long had enslaved me,
His precious blood He gave to redeem,
now I belong to Him:
Now I belong . . .

375 Naida Hearn
© 1974, 1979 Scripture in Song/
Integrity Music/Kingsway's Thankyou Music

Jesus, name above all names,
beautiful Saviour, glorious Lord;
Emmanuel, God is with us,
blessèd Redeemer, living Word.

376 Graham Kendrick
© 1986 Kingsway's Thankyou Music

1 **Jesus put this song into our hearts,**
Jesus put this song into our hearts;
it's a song of joy no-one can take away.
Jesus put this song into our hearts.

2 Jesus taught us how to live in harmony,
Jesus taught us how to live in harmony;
different faces, different races,
He made us one –
Jesus taught us how to live in harmony.

3 Jesus taught us how to be a family,
Jesus taught us how to be a family;
loving one another
with the love that He gives –
Jesus taught us how to be a family.

4 Jesus turned our sorrow into dancing,
Jesus turned our sorrow into dancing,
changed our tears of sadness
into rivers of joy –
Jesus turned our sorrow into a dance.

377 © Timothy Dudley-Smith

1 **Jesus, Prince and Saviour,**
Lord of life who died;
Christ, the friend of sinners,
mocked and crucified.
For a world's salvation,
He His body gave,
lay at last death's victim,
lifeless in the grave.
Lord of life triumphant,
risen now to reign!
King of endless ages,
Jesus lives again!

2 In His power and Godhead
every victory won;
pain and passion ended,
all His purpose done.
Christ the Lord is risen!
sighs and sorrows past,
death's dark night is over,
morning comes at last!
Lord of life . . .

3 Resurrection morning!
sinners' bondage freed;
Christ the Lord is risen –
He is risen indeed!
Jesus, Prince and Saviour,
Lord of life who died,
Christ the King of glory
now is glorified!
Lord of life . . .

378 Chris Bowater
© 1988 Sovereign Lifestyle Music

Jesus shall take the highest honour,
Jesus shall take the highest praise,
let all earth join heaven in exalting
the name which is above all other names.
Let's bow the knee in humble adoration,
for at His name every knee must bow;
let every tongue confess He is Christ,
    God's only Son.

Sovereign Lord, we give You glory now,
for all honour and blessing and power
belongs to You, belongs to You.
All honour and blessing and power
belongs to You, belongs to You,
Lord Jesus Christ, Son of the living God.

379 Isaac Watts (1674–1748)

1 **Jesus shall reign where'er the sun**
does His successive journeys run;
His kingdom stretch from shore
        to shore,
till moons shall rise and set no more.

2 To Him shall endless prayer be made,
and princes throng to crown His head;
His name, like sweet perfume, shall rise
with every morning sacrifice.

3 People and realms of every tongue
dwell on His love with sweetest song;
and infant voices shall proclaim
their early blessings on His name.

4 Blessings abound where'er He reigns;
the prisoner leaps to lose his chains,
the weary find eternal rest,
and all the sons of want are blest.

5 Let every creature rise and bring
the highest honours to our King;
angels descend with songs again,
and earth repeat the loud 'Amen'.

380 William Pennefather (1816–73)

1 **Jesus, stand among us**
in Thy risen power;
let this time of worship
be a hallowed hour.

2 Breathe the Holy Spirit
   into every heart;
   bid the fears and sorrows
   from each soul depart.

3 Thus with quickened footsteps
   we'll pursue our way,
   watching for the dawning
   of eternal day.

382 Dave Bryant
© 1978 Kingsway's Thankyou Music

Jesus, take me as I am,
I can come no other way.
Take me deeper into You,
make my flesh life melt away.
Make me like a precious stone,
crystal clear and finely honed,
life of Jesus shining through,
giving glory back to You.

381 Graham Kendrick
© 1977 Kingsway's Thankyou Music

1 **Jesus, stand among us**
   at the meeting of our lives,
   be our sweet agreement
      at the meeting of our eyes;
   O Jesus, we love You,
      so we gather here,
   join our hearts in unity
      and take away our fear.

2 So to You we're gathering
      out of each and every land,
   Christ the love between us
      at the joining of our hands;
   O Jesus, we love You,
      so we gather here,
   join our hearts in unity
      and take away our fear.

OPTIONAL VERSE FOR COMMUNION

3 Jesus stand among us
      at the breaking of the bread;
   join us as one body
      as we worship You, our Head.
   O Jesus, we love You,
      so we gather here;
   join our hearts in unity
      and take away our fear.

383 From the Latin (12th century)
Ray Palmer (1808–87)

1 **Jesus, the joy of loving hearts,**
   true source of life, and light of men:
   from the best bliss that earth imparts
   we turn unfilled to You again.

2 Your truth unchanged has ever stood,
   You rescue those who on You call:
   to those yet seeking, You are good –
   to those who find You, all-in-all.

3 We taste of You, the living bread,
   and long to feast upon You still;
   we drink from You, the fountain-head,
   our thirsty souls from You we fill.

4 Our restless spirits long for You,
   whichever way our lot is cast,
   glad when Your gracious smile we view,
   blest when our faith can hold You fast.

5 Jesus, for ever with us stay,
   make all our moments calm and bright;
   chase the dark night of sin away,
   spread through the world
         Your holy light.

384
Translated from Urdu
Dermott Monahan (1906–57)
© Trustees for Methodist Church Purposes

1 **Jesus the Lord said:**
   'I am the bread,
   the bread of life for mankind am I,
   the bread of life for mankind am I,
   the bread of life for mankind am I.'
   Jesus the Lord said: 'I am the bread,
   the bread of life for mankind am I.'

2 Jesus the Lord said: 'I am the way,
   the true and living way am I,
   the true and living way am I,
   the true and living way am I.'
   Jesus the Lord said: 'I am the way,
   the true and living way am I.'

3 Jesus the Lord said: 'I am the Light,
   the one true Light of the world am I,
   the one true Light of the world am I,
   the one true Light of the world am I.'
   Jesus the Lord said: 'I am the Light,
   the one true Light of the world am I.'

4 Jesus the Lord said: 'I am the shepherd,
   the one good shepherd
       of the sheep am I,
   the one good shepherd
       of the sheep am I,
   the one good shepherd
       of the sheep am I.'
   Jesus the Lord said: 'I am the shepherd,
   the one good shepherd
       of the sheep am I.'

5 Jesus the Lord said: 'I am the Life,
   the Resurrection and the Life am I,
   the Resurrection and the Life am I,
   the Resurrection and the Life am I.'
   Jesus the Lord said: 'I am the Life,
   the Resurrection and the Life am I.'

385
Charles Wesley (1707–88)

1 **Jesus, the name high over all,**
   in hell, or earth, or sky:
   angels and men before it fall,
   and devils fear and fly.

2 Jesus, the name to sinners dear,
   the name to sinners given;
   it scatters all their guilty fear,
   it turns their hell to heaven.

3 Jesus, the prisoner's fetters breaks,
   and bruises Satan's head;
   power into strengthless souls
       He speaks,
   and life into the dead.

4 O that the world might taste and see
   the riches of His grace!
   The arms of love that compass me,
   would all mankind embrace.

5 His only righteousness I show,
   His saving truth proclaim:
   'tis all my business here below
   to cry: 'Behold the Lamb!'

6 Happy, if with my latest breath
   I may but gasp His name:
   preach Him to all, and cry in death:
   'Behold, behold the Lamb!'

386
Bernard of Clairvaux (1091–1153)
tr. Edward Caswall (1814–78)

1 **Jesus, the very thought of Thee**
   with sweetness fills the breast;
   but sweeter far Thy face to see,
   and in Thy presence rest.

2 Nor voice can sing,
       nor heart can frame,
   nor can the memory find
   a sweeter sound than Thy blest name,
   O Saviour of mankind!

3 O hope of every contrite heart,
   O joy of all the meek,
   to those who ask, how kind Thou art!
   how good to those who seek!

4 But what to those who find? Ah, this
   nor tongue nor pen can show:
   the love of Jesus, what it is
   none but His loved ones know.

5 Jesus, our only joy be Thou,
   as Thou our prize wilt be;
   in Thee be all our glory now,
   and through eternity.

387
John Gibson
© 1987 Kingsway's Thankyou Music

Jesus, we celebrate Your victory,
Jesus, we revel in Your love,
Jesus, we rejoice You've set us free,
Jesus, Your death has brought us life.

1 It was for freedom
      that Christ has set us free,
   no longer to be subject
      to a yoke of slavery.
   So we're rejoicing in God's victory,
   our hearts responding to His love.
      Jesus, we celebrate ...

2 His Spirit in us releases us from fear,
   the way to Him is open,
      with boldness we draw near;
   and in His presence
      our problems disappear,
   our hearts responding to His love.
      Jesus, we celebrate ...

388
Paul Kyle
© 1980 Kingsway's Thankyou Music

Jesus, we enthrone You,
we proclaim You our King.
Standing here in the midst of us
we raise You up with our praise,
and as we worship build a throne,
and as we worship build a throne,
and as we worship build a throne,
come, Lord Jesus, and take Your place.

389
Marilyn Baker
© 1981 Word's Spirit of Praise Music/
CopyCare

Jesus, You are changing me,
by Your Spirit You're making me like You;
Jesus, You're transforming me,
that Your loveliness may be seen in all I do.

You are the potter and I am the clay;
help me to be willing
      to let You have Your way;
Jesus, You are changing me
as I let You reign supreme
      within my heart.

390
David Fellingham
© 1987 Kingsway's Thankyou Music

Jesus, You are the power,
You are the wisdom
that comes from the Lord God,
who has revealed His love.
Our faith now rests on Your power, Lord,
which Your Spirit has poured out on us.
We declare the mystery
      hid before the ages,
which God had planned for our glory.
For we have received
      a glorious inheritance,
pledged by the Spirit.
And our eyes have not seen,
and our ears have not heard,
what is in store for the hearts
of the ones who love the Lord.

391
David Fellingham
© 1985 Kingsway's Thankyou Music

Jesus, You are the radiance
of the Father's glory,
You are the Son,
the appointed heir,
through whom all things are made;

You are the one
who sustains all things
by Your powerful word,
You have purified us from sin,
You are exalted, O Lord,
exalted, O Lord,
to the right hand of God:

Jesus, You are . . .

Crowned with glory,
crowned with honour –
we worship You.

5   Now let my soul arise,
    and tread the tempter down:
    my captain leads me forth
    to conquest and a crown:
    march on, nor fear to win the day,
    though death and hell obstruct the way.

6   Should all the hosts of death,
    and powers of hell unknown,
    put their most dreadful forms
    of rage and malice on,
    I shall be safe; for Christ displays
    superior power and guardian grace.

392   Isaac Watts (1674–1748)

1 **Join all the glorious names**
  of wisdom, love, and power,
  that ever mortals knew,
  that angels ever bore:
  all are too mean to speak His worth,
  too mean to set my Saviour forth.

2 Great Prophet of my God,
  my tongue would bless Thy name:
  by Thee the joyful news
  of our salvation came:
  the joyful news of sins forgiven,
  of hell subdued and peace with heaven.

3 Jesus, my great High Priest,
  offered His blood, and died;
  my guilty conscience seeks
  no sacrifice beside:
  His powerful blood did once atone,
  and now it pleads before the throne.

4 My Saviour and my Lord,
  my Conqueror and my King,
  Thy sceptre and Thy sword,
  Thy reigning grace I sing:
  Thine is the power; behold, I sit
  in willing bonds beneath Thy feet.

393   Isaac Watts (1674–1748)

1 **Joy to the world,**
    the Lord has come!
  let earth receive her King;
  let every heart prepare Him room
    and heaven and nature sing,
    and heaven and nature sing,
    and heaven,
      and heaven and nature sing!

2 Joy to the earth, the Saviour reigns!
  your sweetest songs employ
  while fields and streams
    and hills and plains
  repeat the sounding joy,
  repeat the sounding joy,
  repeat, repeat the sounding joy.

3 He rules the world
    with truth and grace,
  and makes the nations prove
  the glories of His righteousness,
    the wonders of His love,
    the wonders of His love,
    the wonders, wonders of His love.

394
From Psalm 100, Fred Dunn
© 1977 Kingsway's Thankyou Music

Jubilate, everybody,
serve the Lord in all your ways, and
come before His presence singing:
enter now His courts with praise.
For the Lord our God is gracious,
and His mercy everlasting.
Jubilate, jubilate,
jubilate Deo!

395
Henry Scott Holland (1847–1918) altd.

1 **Judge eternal,**
   throned in splendour,
   Lord of lords and King of kings,
   with Your living fire of judgement
   purge this realm of bitter things;
   solace all its wide dominion
   with the healing of Your wings.

2 Still the weary folk are pining
   for the hour that brings release;
   and the city's crowded clangour
   cries aloud for sin to cease;
   and the homesteads and the woodlands
   plead in silence for their peace.

3 Crown, O God, Your own endeavour;
   cleave our darkness with Your sword;
   feed the faithless and the hungry
   with the richness of Your word;
   cleanse the body of this nation
   through the glory of the Lord.

396
Charlotte Elliott (1789–1871)

1 **Just as I am, without one plea,**
   but that Thy blood was shed for me,
   and that Thou bidd'st me
         come to Thee,
   O Lamb of God, I come! I come!

2 Just as I am, and waiting not
   to rid my soul of one dark blot,
   to Thee, whose blood can cleanse
         each spot
   O Lamb of God, I come! I come!

3 Just as I am, though tossed about
   with many a conflict, many a doubt,
   fightings within, and fears without,
   O Lamb of God, I come! I come!

4 Just as I am, poor, wretched, blind;
   sight, riches, healing of the mind,
   yea, all I need, in Thee to find,
   O Lamb of God, I come! I come!

5 Just as I am, Thou wilt receive,
   wilt welcome, pardon, cleanse, relieve:
   because Thy promise I believe,
   O Lamb of God, I come! I come!

6 Just as I am, Thy love unknown
   hath broken every barrier down;
   now, to be Thine, yea, Thine alone,
   O Lamb of God, I come! I come!

397
George Herbert (1593–1633)

1 **King of glory, King of peace,**
      I will love Thee;
   and, that love may never cease,
      I will move Thee.
   Thou hast granted my request,
      Thou hast heard me;
   Thou didst note my working breast,
      Thou hast spared me.

2 Wherefore with my utmost art
      I will sing Thee,
   and the cream of all my heart
      I will bring Thee.
   Though my sins against me cried,
      Thou didst clear me;
   and alone, when they replied,
      Thou didst hear me.

3　Seven whole days, not one in seven,
　　I will praise Thee;
　in my heart, though not in heaven,
　　I can raise Thee.
　Small it is, in this poor sort
　　to enrol Thee:
　e'en eternity's too short
　　to extol Thee.

398　Sophie Conty and Naomi Batya
　　　　© 1980 Maranatha! Music/CopyCare

King of kings and Lord of lords,
　glory, hallelujah!
King of kings and Lord of lords,
　glory, hallelujah!
Jesus, Prince of peace,
　glory, hallelujah!
Jesus, Prince of peace,
　glory, hallelujah!

(*may be sung as a round*)

399　John Henry Newman (1801–90)

1　**Lead, kindly Light,**
　　amid the encircling gloom,
　lead Thou me on;
　the night is dark,
　　and I am far from home;
　lead Thou me on.
　Keep Thou my feet; I do not ask to see
　the distant scene;
　　one step enough for me.

2　I was not ever thus,
　　nor prayed that Thou
　shouldst lead me on;
　I loved to choose
　　and see my path; but now
　lead Thou me on.
　I loved the garish day,
　　and, spite of fears,
　pride ruled my will:
　　remember not past years.

3　So long Thy power has blest me,
　　sure it still
　　will lead me on
　o'er moor and fen,
　　o'er crag and torrent, till
　　the night is gone;
　and with the morn
　　those angel faces smile
　which I have loved long since,
　　and lost awhile.

400　James Edmeston (1791–1867)

1　**Lead us, heavenly Father, lead us**
　o'er the world's tempestuous sea;
　guard us, guide us, keep us, feed us –
　for we have no help but Thee,
　yet possessing every blessing
　if our God our Father be.

2　Saviour, breathe forgiveness o'er us:
　all our weakness Thou dost know:
　Thou didst tread this earth before us,
　Thou didst feel its keenest woe;
　lone and dreary, faint and weary,
　through the desert Thou didst go.

3　Spirit of our God, descending,
　fill our hearts with heavenly joy,
　love with every passion blending,
　pleasure that can never cloy:
　thus provided, pardoned, guided,
　nothing can our peace destroy.

401

Melvin Harrell
© 1963 Gospel Publishing House/
Lorenz Publishing Co/CopyCare

1 **Let all that is within me cry, 'holy';**
let all that is within me cry, 'holy';
holy, holy, holy
is the Lamb that was slain.

2 Let all that is within me cry, 'worthy';
let all that is within me cry, 'worthy';
worthy, worthy, worthy
is the Lamb that was slain.

3 Let all that is within me cry, 'Jesus';
let all that is within me cry, 'Jesus';
Jesus, Jesus, Jesus
is the Lamb that was slain.

4 Let all that is within me cry, 'glory';
let all that is within me cry, 'glory';
glory, glory, glory
to the Lamb that was slain.

402

Graham Kendrick
© 1983 Kingsway's Thankyou Music

1 **Led like a lamb to the slaughter,**
in silence and shame,
there on Your back You carried a world
of violence and pain;
Bleeding, dying, bleeding, dying.
You're alive,
You're alive,
You have risen!
Alleluia!
And the power
and the glory
is given,
Alleluia!
Jesus, to You.

2 At break of dawn, poor Mary,
still weeping she came,
when through her grief
she heard Your voice,
now speaking her name.
Mary! Master! Mary! Master!
You're alive . . .

3 At the right hand of the Father,
now seated on high,
You have begun Your eternal reign
of justice and joy.
Glory, glory, glory, glory.
You're alive . . .

403

Graham Kendrick
© 1985 Kingsway's Thankyou Music

1 **Let all the earth hear His voice,**
let the people rejoice
at the sound of His name;
let all the valleys and hills
burst with joy,
and the trees of the field
clap their hands.
Justice and love
He will bring to the world,
His kingdom will never fail;
held like a two-edgèd sword
in our hand,
His word and truth shall prevail,
shall prevail!

2 Let all the earth hear His voice,
let the prisoners rejoice –
He is coming to save.
Satan's dark strongholds crash down
as with prayer we surround,
as the cross we proclaim.
Justice and love . . .

3 Let all the earth hear His song;
sing it loud, sing it strong –
it's the song of His praise.
Silent no more, we cry out –
let the world hear the shout:
in the earth the Lord reigns.
  Justice and love . . .

404 George Herbert (1593–1632)

1 **Let all the world**
   in every corner sing,
   'My God and King!'
   The heavens are not too high;
   His praise may thither fly:
   the earth is not too low;
   His praises there may grow.
   Let all the world in every corner sing,
   'My God and King!'

2 Let all the world in every corner sing,
   'My God and King!'
   The Church with psalms must shout,
   no door can keep them out:
   but, above all, the heart
   must bear the longest part.
   Let all the world in every corner sing,
   'My God and King!'

405 Graham Kendrick
© 1984 Kingsway's Thankyou Music

Let God arise,
and let His enemies be scattered,
and let those who hate Him
flee before Him;
let God arise,
and let His enemies be scattered,
and let those who hate Him
flee away.

MEN	But let the righteous be glad,
WOMEN	the righteous be glad,
MEN	let them exult before God,
WOMEN	let them exult before God,
MEN	let them rejoice with gladness,
WOMEN	O let them rejoice,
MEN	building up a highway
ALL	for the King.
MEN	We go in the name of the Lord,
	let the shout go up
ALL	in the name of the Lord!

Let God arise . . .

406 Graham Kendrick
© 1988 Make Way Music

Let it be to me according to Your word;
let it be to me according to Your word.
I am Your servant,
      no rights shall I demand.
Let it be to me, let it be to me,
let it be to me according to Your word.

407 Graham Kendrick
© 1977 Kingsway's Thankyou Music

1 **Let Me have My way among you,**
   do not strive, do not strive;
   let Me have My way among you,
   do not strive, do not strive;
   for Mine is the power and the glory
   for ever and ever the same.
   Let Me have My way among you,
   do not strive, do not strive.

2 We'll let You have Your way among us,
   we'll not strive, we'll not strive;
   we'll let You have Your way among us,
   we'll not strive, we'll not strive;
   for Yours is the power and the glory
   for ever and ever the same.
   We'll let You have Your way among us,
   we'll not strive, we'll not strive.

3 Let My peace rule within your hearts,
do not strive, do not strive;
let My peace rule within your hearts,
do not strive, do not strive;
for Mine is the power and the glory
for ever and ever the same.
Let My peace rule within your hearts,
do not strive, do not strive.

4 We'll let Your peace
rule within our hearts,
we'll not strive, we'll not strive;
we'll let Your peace
rule within our hearts,
we'll not strive, we'll not strive;
for Yours is the power and the glory
for ever and ever the same.
We'll let You have Your way among us,
we'll not strive, we'll not strive.

408 Brent Chambers
© 1979 Scripture in Song/Integrity Music/
Kingsway's Thankyou Music

Let our praise to You be as incense,
let our praise to You
be as pillars of Your throne;
let our praise to You be as incense,
as we come before You
and worship You alone.

As we see You in Your splendour,
as we gaze upon Your majesty,
as we join the hosts of angels,
and proclaim together Your holiness.

Let our praise to You . . .

Holy, holy, holy;
holy is the Lord!
Holy, holy, holy;
holy is the Lord!

409 Charles Wesley (1707–88)
© in this version Jubilate Hymns

1 **Let saints on earth together sing**
with those whose work is done;
for all the servants of our King
in earth and heaven, are one.

2 One family, we live in Him,
one Church above, beneath,
though now divided by the stream,
the narrow stream of death.

3 One army of the living God,
to His command we bow;
part of His host have crossed the flood
and part are crossing now.

4 But all unite in Christ their head,
and love to sing His praise:
Lord of the living and the dead,
direct our earthly ways!

5 So shall we join our friends above
who have obtained the prize;
and on the eagle wings of love
to joys celestial rise.

410 Albert Orsborn
© R McCurdy Jones

Let the beauty of Jesus be seen in me,
all His wondrous compassion and purity:
O Thou Spirit divine,
all my nature refine,
till the beauty of Jesus be seen in me.

411 Dave Bilbrough
© 1979 Kingsway's Thankyou Music

Let there be love shared among us,
let there be love in our eyes;
may now Your love sweep this nation,
cause us, O Lord, to arise:
give us a fresh understanding
of brotherly love that is real;
let there be love shared among us,
let there be love.

412
Gloria and William J Gaither
© Gaither Music Company/
WJG Inc/Kingsway's Thankyou Music

Let's just praise the Lord!
Praise the Lord!
Let's just lift our hearts* to heaven
and praise the Lord;
Let's just praise the Lord!
Praise the Lord!
Let's just lift our hearts* to heaven
and praise the Lord!

* Alternative lyrics, 'voices', 'hands'.

413
© 1986 Andy Silver

Let us acknowledge the Lord,
let us press on to acknowledge Him,
let us acknowledge the Lord.
Let us acknowledge Him
as surely as the sun rises;
He will appear, He will come to us
like the winter rains,
like the spring rains
that water the earth.

414
James E Seddon (1915–83)
© Mavis Seddon/Jubilate Hymns

TRADITIONAL VERSION

1   **Let us break bread together
      on our knees,**
    let us break bread together
        on our knees:
    *When I fall on my knees,
    with my face to the rising sun,
    O Lord, have mercy on me!*

2   Let us drink wine together
        on our knees,
    let us drink wine together
        on our knees:
    When I fall . . .

3   Let us praise God together
        on our knees,
    let us praise God together
        on our knees:
    When I fall . . .

ALTERNATIVE VERSION

1   Let us praise God together,
        let us praise;
    let us praise God together all our days:
    He is faithful in all His ways,
    He is worthy of all our praise,
    His name be exalted on high!

2   Let us seek God together, let us pray;
    let us seek His forgiveness as we pray:
    He will cleanse us from all sin,
    He will help us the fight to win,
    His name be exalted on high!

3   Let us serve God together, Him obey;
    let our lives show His goodness
            through each day:
    Christ the Lord
        is the world's true light –
    let us serve Him with all our might,
    His name be exalted on high!

415
John Milton (1608–74)

1   **Let us with a gladsome mind**
    praise the Lord for He is kind;
    *For His mercies shall endure,
    ever faithful, ever sure.*

2   He, with all-commanding might,
    filled the new-made world with light:
    For His mercies . . .

3   All things living He doth feed,
    His full hand supplies their need:
    For His mercies . . .

4 He His chosen race did bless
in the wasteland wilderness:
For His mercies shall endure,
ever faithful, ever sure.

5 He hath, with a piteous eye,
looked upon our misery:
For His mercies ...

6 Let us then with gladsome mind,
praise the Lord for He is kind!
For His mercies ...

416 Anon
Copyright control

Lift Jesus higher, lift Jesus higher,
lift Him up for the world to see.
He said, 'If I be lifted up from the earth
I will draw all men unto me.'

417 George William Kitchen (1827–1912)
and Michael Robert Newbolt (1874–1956)
and in this version Jubilee Hymns
© Hymns Ancient & Modern Ltd

Lift high the cross,
the love of Christ proclaim
till all the world
adores His sacred name!

1 Come, Christians,
follow where the captain trod,
the King victorious,
Christ, the Son of God:
Lift high the cross ...

2 Each new-born soldier of the crucified
bears on his brow
the seal of Him who died:
Lift high the cross ...

3 This is the sign that Satan's armies fear
and angels veil their faces to revere:
Lift high the cross ...

4 Saved by the cross
on which their Lord was slain,
see Adam's children
their lost home regain:
Lift high the cross ...

5 From north and south,
from east and west they raise
in growing unison their songs of praise:
Lift high the cross ...

6 Let every race and every language tell
of Him who saves our souls
from death and hell!
Lift high the cross ...

7 O Lord, once lifted on the tree of pain,
draw all the world
to seek You once again:
Lift high the cross ...

8 Set up Your throne,
that earth's despair may cease
beneath the shadow
of its healing peace:
Lift high the cross ...

418 Steven L Fry © 1974 BMG Songs/Birdwing
Music/EMI Christian Music Publishing
CopyCare

Lift up your heads to the coming King;
bow before Him and adore Him, sing
to His majesty: let your praises be
pure and holy, giving glory
to the King of kings.

419 Michael Perry (1942–96)
© Mrs B Perry/Jubilee Hymns

1 **Like a mighty river flowing,**
like a flower in beauty growing,
far beyond all human knowing
is the perfect peace of God.

2 Like the hills serene and even,
like the coursing clouds of heaven,
like the heart that's been forgiven,
is the perfect peace of God.

3 Like the summer breezes playing,
like the tall trees softly swaying,
like the lips of silent praying
is the perfect peace of God.

4 Like the morning sun ascended,
like the scents of evening blended,
like a friendship never ended
is the perfect peace of God.

5 Like the azure ocean swelling,
like the jewel all-excelling,
far beyond our human telling
is the perfect peace of God.

420 Graham Kendrick
© 1988 Make Way Music

1 **Like a candle flame,**
flick'ring small in our darkness,
uncreated light
shines through infant eyes.
MEN *God is with us, alleluia,*
WOMEN *God is with us, alleluia,*
MEN *come to save us, alleluia,*
WOMEN *come to save us,*
ALL *alleluia!*

2 Stars and angels sing,
yet the earth sleeps in the shadows;
can this tiny spark
set a world on fire?
God is with us . . .

3 Yet His light shall shine
from our lives, Spirit blazing,
as we touch the flame
of His holy fire.
God is with us . . .

421 Frances Ridley Havergal (1836–79)

1 **Like a river glorious**
is God's perfect peace,
over all victorious,
in its bright increase:
perfect, yet it floweth
fuller every day;
perfect, yet it groweth
deeper all the way.
Stayed upon Jehovah,
hearts are fully blest;
finding, as He promised,
perfect peace and rest.

2 Hidden in the hollow
of His blessèd hand,
never foe can follow
never traitor stand;
not a surge of worry,
not a shade of care,
not a blast of hurry
touch the spirit there.
Stayed upon Jehovah . . .

3 Every joy or trial
falleth from above,
traced upon our dial
by the sun of love.
We may trust Him fully
all for us to do;
they who trust Him wholly
find Him wholly true.
Stayed upon Jehovah . . .

422 Graham Kendrick
© 1988 Make Way Music

1 **Light has dawned**
   that ever shall blaze,
darkness flees away;
Christ the light has shone in our hearts,
turning night to day.

We proclaim Him King of kings,
we lift high His name;
heaven and earth shall bow at His feet,
when He comes to reign.

WOMEN
2 Saviour of the world is He,
heaven's King come down;
judgement, love and mercy meet
at His thorny crown.
ALL *We proclaim ...*

MEN
3 Life has sprung from hearts of stone,
by the Spirit's breath;
hell shall let her captives go,
life has conquered death.
ALL *We proclaim ...*

4 Blood has flowed
that cleanses from sin,
God His love has proved;
man may mock
and demons may rage –
we shall not be moved!
We proclaim ...

We proclaim ...

423 David Hadden and Bob Silvester
© 1983 Restoration Music Ltd/
Sovereign Music UK

1 **Living under the shadow**
of His wing
we find security.
Standing in His presence we will bring
our worship, worship, worship
to the King.

2 Bowed in adoration at His feet
we dwell in harmony,
voices joined together that repeat,
'Worthy, worthy, worthy is the Lamb.'

3 Heart to heart embracing in His love
reveals His purity,
soaring in my spirit like a dove;
holy, holy, holy is the Lord.

424 Charles Wesley (1707–88)

1 **Lo! He comes,**
with clouds descending,
once for favoured sinners slain:
thousand thousand saints attending
swell the triumph of His train;
hallelujah, hallelujah, hallelujah!
God appears on earth to reign.

2 Every eye shall now behold Him
robed in dreadful majesty;
those who set at nought and sold Him,
pierced, and nailed Him to the tree,
deeply wailing ...
shall the true Messiah see.

3 Now redemption, long expected,
see in solemn pomp appear!
All His saints, by man rejected,
now shall meet Him in the air.
Hallelujah ...
see the day of God appear.

4 Yea, amen! let all adore Thee
high on Thy eternal throne;
Saviour, take the power and glory,
claim the kingdom of Thine own;
hallelujah ...
everlasting God, come down!

425
Graham Kendrick
© 1984 Kingsway's Thankyou Music

1 **Look to the skies,**
   there's a celebration;
   lift up your heads, join the angel-song,
   for our Creator becomes our Saviour,
   as a baby born!
   Angels amazed bow in adoration:
   'Glory to God in the highest heaven!' –
   Send the good news
       out to every nation,
   for our hope has come.
   Worship the King –
       come, see His brightness;
   worship the King, His wonders tell:
   Jesus our King is born today –
   we welcome You, Emmanuel!

2 Wonderful counsellor, Mighty God,
   Father for ever, the Prince of peace:
   there'll be no end
       to Your rule of justice,
   for it shall increase.
   Light of Your face,
       come to pierce our darkness;
   joy of Your heart
       come to chase our gloom;
   Star of the morning,
       a new day dawning,
   make our hearts Your home.
   Worship the King . . .

3 Quietly He came as a helpless baby –
   one day in power He will come again;
   swift through the skies
       He will burst with splendour
   on the earth to reign.
   Jesus, I bow at Your manger lowly:
   now in my life let Your will be done;
   live in my flesh by Your Spirit holy
   till Your kingdom comes.
   Worship the King . . .

426
Thomas Kelly (1769–1854)

1 **Look, ye saints,**
   the sight is glorious,
   see the Man of sorrows now
   from the fight returned victorious!
   Every knee to Him shall bow:
       Crown Him! Crown Him!
       Crown Him! Crown Him!
   Crowns become the victor's brow.

2 Crown the Saviour, angels, crown Him!
   Rich the trophies Jesus brings;
   in the seat of power enthrone Him,
   while the vault of heaven rings:
       Crown Him! Crown Him!
       Crown Him! Crown Him!
   Crown the Saviour King of kings!

3 Sinners in derision crowned Him,
   mocking thus the Saviour's claim;
   saints and angels crowd around Him,
   own His title, praise His name:
       Crown Him! Crown Him!
       Crown Him! Crown Him!
   Spread abroad the victor's fame.

4 Hark, those bursts of acclamation!
   Hark, those loud triumphant chords!
   Jesus takes the highest station:
   O what joy the sight affords!
       Crown Him! Crown Him!
       Crown Him! Crown Him!
   King of kings, and Lord of lords!

427
Chris Rolinson
© 1988 Kingsway's Thankyou Music

1 **Lord, come and heal Your Church,**
   take our lives
       and cleanse with Your fire;
   let Your deliverance flow
   as we lift Your name up higher.

We will draw near
and surrender our fear:
lift our hands to proclaim,
'Holy Father, You are here!'

2 Spirit of God, come in
and release our hearts to praise You;
make us whole, for
holy we'll become and serve You.
We will draw near . . .

3 Show us Your power, we pray,
that we may share in Your glory:
we shall arise, and go
to proclaim Your works most holy.
We will draw near . . .

4 Lord, for our world where men
disown and doubt You,
loveless in strength,
and comfortless in pain,
hungry and helpless,
lost indeed without You:
Lord of the world,
we pray that Christ may reign.

5 Lord, for ourselves;
in living power remake us –
self on the cross
and Christ upon the throne,
past put behind us,
for the future take us:
Lord of our lives,
to live for Christ alone.

428 © Timothy Dudley-Smith

1 **Lord, for the years Your love
has kept and guided,**
urged and inspired us,
cheered us on our way,
sought us and saved us,
pardoned and provided:
Lord of the years,
we bring our thanks today.

2 Lord, for that word,
the word of life which fires us,
speaks to our hearts
and sets our souls ablaze,
teaches and trains,
rebukes us and inspires us:
Lord of the word,
receive Your people's praise.

3 Lord, for our land
in this our generation,
spirits oppressed by pleasure,
wealth and care:
for young and old,
for commonwealth and nation,
Lord of our land,
be pleased to hear our prayer.

429 Gerald Markland
© 1978 Kevin Mayhew Ltd

Lord, have mercy,
Lord, have mercy,
Lord, have mercy on Your people.
Lord, have mercy, Lord, have mercy,
Lord, have mercy on Your people.

1 Give me the heart of stone within you,
and I'll give you a heart of flesh.
Clean water I will use
to cleanse all your wounds,
My Spirit I give to you.
Lord, have mercy . . .

2 You'll find Me near the
broken-hearted,
those crushed in spirit I will save.
So turn to Me for My pardon is great,
My word will heal all your wounds.
Lord, have mercy . . .

430 Graham Kendrick

Lord, have mercy on us,
come and heal our land;
cleanse with Your fire,
heal with Your touch:
    humbly we bow
    and call upon You now,
O Lord, have mercy on us,
O Lord, have mercy on us.

Lord, have mercy on us . . .
O Lord, have mercy on us.

431 George Hugh Bourne (1840–1925)

1 **Lord, enthroned in heavenly
    splendour,**
    glorious first-born from the dead,
    You alone our strong defender,
    lifting up Your people's head.
        Alleluia, alleluia,
        Jesus, true and living bread!

2 Prince of life, for us now living,
    by Your body souls are healed;
    Prince of peace, Your pardon giving,
    by Your blood our peace is sealed.
        Alleluia, alleluia,
        Word of God in flesh revealed.

3 Paschal Lamb! Your offering, finished
    once for all when You were slain,
    in its fulness undiminished
    shall for evermore remain,
        Alleluia, alleluia,
        cleansing souls from every stain.

4 Great High Priest of our profession,
    through the veil You entered in,
    by Your mighty intercession
    grace and mercy there to win,
        Alleluia, alleluia,
        only sacrifice for sin.

5 Life-imparting heavenly manna,
    stricken rock with streaming side,
    heaven and earth with loud hosanna
    worship You, the Lamb who died,
        Alleluia, alleluia,
        risen, ascended, glorified!

432 Eddie Espinosa

Lord, I love You,
You alone did hear my cry;
only You can mend
this broken heart of mine.
Yes, I love You,
and there is no doubt,
Lord, You've touched me
from the inside out.

433 William Tidd Matson (1833–99)

1 **Lord, I was blind; I could not see**
    in Your marred visage any grace:
    but now the beauty of Your face
    in radiant vision dawns on me.

2 Lord, I was deaf; I could not hear
    the thrilling music of Your voice:
    but now I hear You and rejoice,
    and all Your spoken words are dear.

3 Lord, I was dumb; I could not speak
    the grace and glory of Your name:
    but now as touched with living flame
    my lips will speak for Jesus' sake.

4 Lord, I was dead; I could not move
    my lifeless soul from sin's dark grave:
    but now the power of life You gave
    has raised me up to know Your love.

5   Lord, You have made the blind to see,
the deaf to hear, the dumb to speak,
the dead to live – and now I break
the chains of my captivity!

434   Colin Sterne (1862–1926)

1   **Lord, it is eventide:**
the light of day is waning;
far o'er the golden land
earth's voices faint and fall;
lowly we pray to You
for strength and love sustaining,
lowly we ask of You
Your peace upon us all.
O grant unto our souls
light that grows not pale
with day's decrease,
love that never can fail
till life shall cease;
joy no trial can mar,
hope that shines afar,
faith serene as a star,
and Christ's own peace.

2   Lord, it is eventide:
we turn to You for healing,
like those of Galilee
who came at close of day;
speak to our waiting souls,
their hidden needs revealing;
touch us with hands divine
that take our sin away.
O grant unto our souls
light that grows . . .

3   Saviour, You know of every trial
and temptation,
know of the wilfulness
and waywardness of youth,
help us to hold to You,
our strength and our salvation,
help us to find in You
the one eternal truth.
O grant unto our souls
light that grows . . .

4   Lord, it is eventide:
our hearts await Your giving,
wait for that peace divine
that none can take away,
peace that shall lift our souls
to loftier heights of living,
till we abide with You
in everlasting day.
O grant unto our souls
light that grows . . .

435   Patrick Appleford
© 1960 Josef Weinberger Ltd

1   **Lord Jesus Christ,**
You have come to us,
You are one with us, Mary's son;
cleansing our souls from all their sin,
pouring Your love and goodness in:
Jesus, our love for You we sing –
living Lord!

2   Lord Jesus Christ, now and every day
teach us how to pray, Son of God;
You have commanded us to do
this in remembrance, Lord, of You:
into our lives
Your power breaks through –
living Lord!

3 Lord Jesus Christ,
    You have come to us,
born as one of us, Mary's son;
led out to die on Calvary,
risen from death to set us free:
living Lord Jesus, help us see
    You are Lord!

4 Lord Jesus Christ,
    I would come to You,
live my life for You, Son of God;
all Your commands I know are true,
Your many gifts will make me new:
into my life
    Your power breaks through –
    living Lord!

436
Paul Field
© 1983 Waif Productions Ltd

1 **Lord, make me a mountain
    standing tall for You,**
strong and free and holy
    in everything I do.
Lord, make me a river of water
    pure and sweet,
Lord, make me the servant
    of everyone I meet.

2 Lord, make me a candle
    shining with Your light,
steadfastly unflickering,
    standing for the right.
Lord, make me a fire
    burning strong for You,
Lord, make me be humble
    in everything I do.

3 Lord, make me a mountain,
    strong and tall for You,
Lord, make me a fountain of water
    clear and new,
Lord, make me a shepherd
    that I may feed Your sheep,
Lord, make me the servant
    of everyone I meet.

437
Robert Bicknell
© 1977 Zion Song/CopyCare

1 **Lord, make me an instrument,**
an instrument of worship;
I lift up my hands in Your name.
Lord, make me an instrument,
an instrument of worship;
I lift up my hands in Your name.

2 I'll sing You a love-song,
a love-song of worship;
I lift up my hands in Your name.
I'll sing You a love-song,
a love-song to Jesus;
I lift up my hands in Your name.

3 Lord, make us a symphony,
a symphony of worship;
we lift up our hands in Your name.
Lord, make us a symphony,
a symphony of worship;
we lift up our hands in Your name.

438
© Christopher Porteous/Jubilate Hymns

1 **Lord, may we see Your hands
    and side,**
touch You and feel Your presence near;
Lord, could our eyes
    behold those clouds
and watch You rising disappear.
Help us to pray for Your return,
to watch until You come to reign;
and be Your witnesses
    through the world,
to speak and glorify Your name.

2 Lord, unto You we lift our eyes,
help us to live as You desire.
Bring down upon us power to win
through tongues of Holy Spirit, fire.
Lord, breathe upon us to receive
the grace and love Your Spirit gives;
and may we know You with us now
because in us Your Spirit lives.

439

Oliver Wendell Holmes (1809–94)

1 **Lord of all being, throned afar,**
Thy glory flames from sun and star;
centre and soul of every sphere,
yet to each loving heart how near.

2 Sun of our life, Thy quickening ray
sheds on our path the glow of day;
Star of our hope, Thy softened light
cheers the long watches of the night.

3 Our midnight is Thy smile withdrawn,
our noontide is Thy gracious dawn,
our rainbow arch Thy mercy's sign;
all, save the clouds of sin, are Thine.

4 Lord of all life, below, above,
whose light is truth,
whose warmth is love,
before Thy ever-blazing throne
we ask no lustre of our own.

5 Grant us Thy truth to make us free,
and kindling hearts that burn for Thee,
till all Thy living altars claim
one holy light, one heavenly flame.

3 Lord of all wisdom,
I give You my mind,
rich truth that surpasses
man's knowledge to find;
what eye has not seen
and what ear has not heard
is taught by Your Spirit
and shines from Your word.

4 Lord of all bounty, I give You my heart;
I praise and adore You
for all You impart,
Your love to inspire me,
Your counsel to guide,
Your presence to cheer me,
whatever betide.

5 Lord of all being, I give You my all;
for if I disown You I stumble and fall;
but, sworn in glad service
Your word to obey,
I walk in Your freedom
to the end of the way.

440

Jack C Winslow (1882–1974)
© Mrs J Tyrrell

1 **Lord of creation,**
to You be all praise!
Most mighty Your working,
most wondrous Your ways!
Your glory and might
are beyond us to tell,
and yet in the heart of the humble
You dwell.

2 Lord of all power, I give You my will,
in joyful obedience Your tasks to fulfil;
Your bondage is freedom,
Your service is song,
and, held in Your keeping,
my weakness is strong.

441

Philip Pusey (1799–1855)
based on the German of
M A von Löwenstern (1594–1648)

1 **Lord of our life,**
and God of our salvation,
Star of our night,
and hope of every nation,
hear and receive
Thy Church's supplication,
Lord God almighty.

2 Lord, Thou canst help
when earthly armour faileth,
Lord, Thou canst save
when sin itself assaileth;
Lord, o'er Thy Church
nor death nor hell prevaileth;
grant us Thy peace, Lord.

3 Peace in our hearts,
   our evil thoughts assuaging;
peace in Thy Church
   when disputes are engaging;
peace, when the world
   its busy war is waging:
calm Thy foes' raging.

4 Grant us Thy help
   till backward they are driven,
grant them Thy truth,
   that they may be forgiven;
grant peace on earth,
   and after we have striven,
peace in Thy heaven.

3 Lord of the Church,
   we long for our uniting,
true to one calling,
   by one vision stirred;
one cross proclaiming
   and one creed reciting,
one in the truth of Jesus and His word!
So lead us on;
   till toil and trouble ended,
one Church triumphant
   one new song shall sing,
to praise His glory, risen and ascended,
Christ over all, the everlasting King!

442 © Timothy Dudley-Smith

1 **Lord of the Church,**
   we pray for our renewing:
Christ over all, our undivided aim;
fire of the Spirit, burn for our enduing,
wind of the Spirit, fan the living flame!
We turn to Christ
   amid our fear and failing,
the will
   that lacks the courage to be free,
the weary labours, all but unavailing,
to bring us nearer
   what a church should be.

2 Lord of the Church,
   we seek a Father's blessing,
a true repentance and a faith restored,
a swift obedience
   and a new possessing,
filled with the Holy Spirit of the Lord!
We turn to Christ
   from all our restless striving,
unnumbered voices
   with a single prayer –
the living water for our souls' reviving,
in Christ to live,
   and love and serve and care.

443 © Michael Saward/Jubilate Hymns

1 **Lord of the cross of shame,**
set my cold heart aflame
with love for You,
   my Saviour and my Master;
   who on that lonely day
   bore all my sins away,
and saved me from the judgement
   and disaster.

2 Lord of the empty tomb,
born of a virgin's womb,
triumphant over death,
   its power defeated;
   how gladly now I sing
   Your praise, my risen King,
and worship You,
   in heaven's splendour seated.

3 Lord of my life today,
teach me to live and pray
as one who knows the joy
   of sins forgiven;
   so may I ever be,
   now and eternally,
one with my fellow-citizens in heaven.

444 Frances Ridley Havergal (1836–79)

1 **Lord, speak to me, that I may speak**
in living echoes of Thy tone;
as Thou hast sought, so let me seek
Thy erring children, lost and lone.

2 O lead me, Lord, that I may lead
the wandering and the wavering feet;
O feed me, Lord, that I may feed
Thy hungering ones with manna sweet.

3 O strengthen me, that, while I stand
firm on the rock, and strong in Thee,
I may stretch out a loving hand
to wrestlers with the troubled sea.

4 O teach me, Lord, that I may teach
the precious things Thou dost impart;
and wing my words,
that they may reach
the hidden depths of many a heart.

5 O give Thine own sweet rest to me,
that I may speak with soothing power
a word in season, as from Thee,
to weary ones in needful hour.

6 O fill me with Thy fulness, Lord,
until my very heart o'erflow
in kindling thought and glowing word,
Thy love to tell, Thy praise to show.

7 O use me, Lord, use even me,
just as Thou wilt,
and when, and where,
until Thy blessèd face I see,
Thy rest, Thy joy, Thy glory share.

445 Graham Kendrick
© 1987 Make Way Music

1 **Lord, the light of Your love**
is shining,
in the midst of the darkness, shining:
Jesus, Light of the world,
shine upon us;
set us free
by the truth You now bring us –
shine on me, shine on me.

Shine, Jesus, shine,
fill this land with the Father's glory;
blaze, Spirit, blaze,
set our hearts on fire.
Flow, river, flow,
flood the nations with grace and mercy;
send forth Your word, Lord,
and let there be light!

2 Lord, I come to Your awesome
presence,
from the shadows into Your radiance;
by Your blood
I may enter Your brightness:
search me, try me,
consume all my darkness –
shine on me, shine on me.
Shine, Jesus, shine . . .

3 As we gaze on Your kingly brightness
so our faces display Your likeness,
ever changing from glory to glory:
mirrored here,
may our lives tell Your story –
shine on me, shine on me.
Shine, Jesus, shine . . .

446 Henry Williams Baker (1821–77)

1 **Lord, Thy word abideth,**
and our footsteps guideth;
who its truth believeth
light and joy receiveth.

2 Who can tell the pleasure,
who recount the treasure,
by Thy word imparted
to the simple-hearted?

3 When the storms are o'er us,
and dark clouds before us,
then its light directeth,
and our way protecteth.

4 When our foes are near us,
   then Thy word doth cheer us,
   word of consolation,
   message of salvation.

5 Word of mercy, giving
   succour to the living;
   word of life, supplying
   comfort to the dying.

6 O that we discerning
   its most holy learning,
   Lord, may love and fear Thee,
   evermore be near Thee!

447 © 1985 Lynn DeShazo/
Integrity's Hosanna! Music/
Kingsway's Thankyou Music

**Lord, You are more precious
than silver,**
Lord, You are more costly than gold;
Lord, You are more beautiful
   than diamonds,
and nothing I desire compares with You.

448 Trish Morgan, Ray Goudie,
Ian Townend and Dave Bankhead
© 1986 Kingsway's Thankyou Music

1 **Lord, we long for You
   to move in power.**
   There's a hunger
      deep within our hearts,
   to see healing in our nation.
   Send Your Spirit to revive us:
      Heal our nation!
      Heal our nation!
      Heal our nation!
      Pour out Your Spirit on this land!

2 Lord, we hear Your Spirit
      coming closer,
   a mighty wave to break upon our land,
   bringing justice, and forgiveness,
   God, we cry to You, 'Revive us':
      Heal our nation . . .

449 Charles Wesley (1707–88)

1 **Love divine, all loves excelling,**
   joy of heaven, to earth come down:
   fix in us Thy humble dwelling,
   all Thy faithful mercies crown.
   Jesus, Thou art all compassion,
   pure, unbounded love Thou art;
   visit us with Thy salvation,
   enter every trembling heart.

2 Breathe, O breathe Thy loving Spirit
   into every troubled breast;
   let us all in Thee inherit,
   let us find Thy promised rest.
   Take away the love of sinning,
   Alpha and Omega be;
   end of faith, as its beginning,
   set our hearts at liberty.

3 Come, almighty to deliver,
   let us all Thy grace receive;
   suddenly return, and never,
   never more Thy temples leave.
   Thee we would be always blessing,
   serve Thee as Thy hosts above,
   pray, and praise Thee without ceasing,
   glory in Thy perfect love.

4 Finish then Thy new creation:
   pure and spotless let us be;
   let us see Thy great salvation,
   perfectly restored in Thee:
   changed from glory into glory,
   till in heaven we take our place,
   till we cast our crowns before Thee,
   lost in wonder, love, and praise.

450 James Rowe (1865–1933)
© R H Coleman/Copyright control

1 **I was sinking deep in sin,**
sinking to rise no more,
overwhelmed by guilt within,
mercy I did implore.
Then the Master of the sea
heard my despairing cry,
Christ my Saviour lifted me,
now safe am I.
Love lifted me!
Love lifted me!
When no-one but Christ could help,
love lifted me!
Love lifted me!
Love lifted me!
When no-one but Christ could help,
love lifted me!

2 Souls in danger, look above,
Jesus completely saves;
He will lift you by His love
out of the angry waves.
He's the Master of the sea,
billows His will obey;
He your Saviour wants to be,
be saved today!
Love lifted me ...

3 When the waves of sorrow roll,
when I am in distress,
Jesus takes my hand in His,
ever He loves to bless.
He will every fear dispel,
satisfy every need;
all who heed His loving call,
find rest indeed.
Love lifted me ...

451 Christina Georgina Rossetti (1830–94)

1 **Love came down at Christmas,**
Love all lovely, Love divine;
Love was born at Christmas,
star and angels gave the sign.

2 Worship we the Godhead,
Love incarnate, Love divine;
worship we our Jesus:
but wherewith for sacred sign?

3 Love shall be our token,
love be yours and love be mine,
love to God and all men,
love for plea and gift and sign.

452 George Wade Robinson (1838–77)

1 **Loved with everlasting love,**
led by grace that love to know;
Spirit, breathing from above,
You have taught me it is so.
O this full and perfect peace!
O this presence so divine!
In a love which cannot cease
I am His, and He is mine.
(repeat last two lines)

2 Heaven above is softer blue,
earth around is sweeter green;
something lives in every hue,
Christless eyes have never seen:
birds with gladder songs o'erflow,
flowers with deeper beauties shine,
since I know, as now I know,
I am His, and He is mine.
(repeat last two lines)

3 His for ever, only His:
who the Lord and me shall part?
Ah, with what a rest of bliss
Christ can fill the loving heart!
Heaven and earth may fade and flee,
first-born light in gloom decline;
but while God and I shall be,
I am His, and He is mine.
(repeat last two lines)

453
Robert Lowry (1826–99)

1 **Low in the grave He lay,**
  Jesus, my Saviour;
  waiting the coming day,
  Jesus, my Lord.

  Up from the grave He arose,
  with a mighty triumph o'er His foes;
  He arose a victor from the dark domain,
  and He lives for ever
    with His saints to reign:
  He arose! He arose! Hallelujah! Christ
  arose!

2 Vainly they watch His bed,
  Jesus, my Saviour;
  vainly they seal the dead,
  Jesus, my Lord.
  Up from the grave . . .

3 Death cannot keep his prey,
  Jesus, my Saviour,
  He tore the bars away,
  Jesus, my Lord.
  Up from the grave . . .

454
Jack Hayford
© 1981 Rocksmith Music/
Leosong Copyright Services Ltd

Majesty, worship His majesty;
unto Jesus be glory, honour and praise.
Majesty, kingdom, authority,
  flows from His throne
unto His own, His anthem raise.
So exalt, lift up on high the name of Jesus,
magnify, come glorify,
  Christ Jesus the King.
Majesty, worship His majesty,
Jesus who died, now glorified,
  King of all kings.

455
George Matheson (1842–1906)

1 **Make me a captive, Lord,**
  and then I shall be free;
  force me to render up my sword,
  and I shall conqueror be.
  I sink in life's alarms
  when by myself I stand;
  imprison me within Thine arms,
  and strong shall be my hand.

2 My heart is weak and poor
  until its master find;
  it has no spring of action sure –
  it varies with the wind.
  It cannot freely move,
  till Thou hast wrought its chain;
  enslave it with Thy matchless love,
  and deathless it shall reign.

3 My power is faint and low
  till I have learned to serve;
  it wants the needed fire to glow,
  it wants the breeze to nerve;
  it cannot drive the world,
  until itself be driven;
  its flag can only be unfurled
  when Thou shalt breathe from heaven.

4 My will is not my own
  till Thou hast made it Thine;
  if it would reach a monarch's throne
  it must its crown resign;
  it only stands unbent,
  amid the clashing strife,
  when on Thy bosom it has leant
  and found in Thee its life.

456
Sebastian Temple
© 1967 OCP Publications

1 **Make me a channel of Your peace.**
  Where there is hatred
    let me bring Your love;
  where there is injury,
    Your pardon, Lord;
  and where there's doubt,
    true faith in You.

O Master, grant that I may never seek
so much to be consoled as to console;
to be understood as to understand;
to be loved, as to love with all my soul.

2 Make me a channel of Your peace.
Where there's despair in life
    let me bring hope;
where there is darkness, only light;
and where there's sadness, ever joy.
    O Master ...

3 Make me a channel of Your peace.
It is in pardoning
    that we are pardoned,
in giving to all men that we receive;
and in dying
    that we're born to eternal life.

457 Graham Kendrick
© 1986 Kingsway's Thankyou Music

1 **Make way, make way,**
for Christ the King
    in splendour arrives;
fling wide the gates
and welcome Him into your lives.
    Make way, make way,
    for the King of kings;
    make way, make way,
    and let His kingdom in!

2 He comes the broken hearts to heal,
the prisoners to free;
    the deaf shall hear,
        the lame shall dance,
the blind shall see.
    Make way ...

3 And those who mourn
    with heavy hearts,
who weep and sigh,
with laughter, joy and royal crown
He'll beautify.
    Make way ...

4 We call you now to worship Him
as Lord of all,
to have no gods before Him,
their thrones must fall!
    Make way ...

458 Philipp Paul Bliss (1838–76)

1 **Man of Sorrows! what a name**
for the Son of God, who came
ruined sinners to reclaim!
Hallelujah! what a Saviour!

2 Bearing shame and scoffing rude,
in my place condemned He stood;
sealed my pardon with His blood;
hallelujah! what a Saviour!

3 Guilty, vile and helpless we;
spotless Lamb of God was He:
full atonement – can it be?
hallelujah! what a Saviour!

4 Lifted up was He to die,
'It is finished!' was His cry;
now in heaven exalted high;
hallelujah! what a Saviour!

5 When He comes, our glorious King,
all His ransomed home to bring,
then anew this song we'll sing:
'Hallelujah! what a Saviour!'

459 Frances Ridley Havergal (1836–79)

1 **Master, speak! Thy servant heareth,**
waiting for Thy gracious word,
longing for Thy voice that cheereth;
Master, let it now be heard.
I am listening, Lord, for Thee;
what hast Thou to say to me?

2 Speak to me by name, O Master!
let me know it is to me;
speak, that I may follow faster,
with a step more firm and free,
where the shepherd leads the flock
in the shadow of the rock.

3 Master, speak! though least and lowest,
let me not unheard depart;
Master, speak! for O Thou knowest
all the yearning of my heart;
knowest all its truest need;
speak, and make me blest indeed.

4 Master, speak! and make me ready,
when Thy voice is truly heard,
with obedience glad and steady
still to follow every word.
I am listening, Lord, for Thee;
Master, speak, O speak to me!

460 © 1982 Cliff Barrows

**May God's blessing
surround you each day,**
as you trust Him and walk in His way.
May His presence within
guard and keep you from sin,
go in peace, go in joy, go in love.

461 Graham Kendrick
© 1988 Make Way Music

May our worship be acceptable
in Your sight, O Lord;
may our worship be acceptable
in Your sight, O Lord;
may the words of my mouth be pure,
and the meditation of my heart;
may our worship be acceptable
in Your sight, O Lord.

462 Graham Kendrick
© 1986 Kingsway's Thankyou Music

1 MEN   **May the fragrance of Jesus
fill this place,**
 WOMEN may the fragrance of Jesus
fill this place,
 MEN   may the fragrance of Jesus
fill this place,
 WOMEN lovely fragrance of Jesus,
 ALL   rising from the sacrifice
of lives laid down in adoration.

2 MEN   May the glory of Jesus
fill His Church,
 WOMEN may the glory of Jesus
fill His Church,
 MEN   may the glory of Jesus
fill His Church;
 WOMEN radiant glory of Jesus,
 ALL   shining from our faces
as we gaze in adoration.

3 MEN   May the beauty of Jesus
fill my life,
 WOMEN may the beauty of Jesus
fill my life,
 MEN   may the beauty of Jesus
fill my life:
 WOMEN perfect beauty of Jesus,
 ALL   fill my thoughts, my words,
my deeds,
my all I give in adoration;
fill my thoughts, my words,
my deeds,
my all I give in adoration.

463 Kate B Wilkinson (1859–1928)
Copyright control

1 **May the mind of Christ my Saviour**
live in me from day to day,
by His love and power controlling
all I do and say.

2   May the word of God dwell richly
    in my heart from hour to hour,
    so that all may see I triumph
    only through His power.

3   May the peace of God my Father
    rule my life in everything,
    that I may be calm to comfort
    sick and sorrowing.

4   May the love of Jesus fill me,
    as the waters fill the sea;
    Him exalting, self abasing,
    this is victory.

5   May I run the race before me,
    strong and brave to face the foe,
    looking only unto Jesus,
    as I onward go.

464 Susie Hare
© 1983 Kingsway's Thankyou Music

May the Lord bless you and keep you,
make His face to shine upon you
and be gracious unto you.
May the Lord lift up the light
of His countenance upon you
and give you peace.

465 Graham Kendrick
© 1986 Kingsway's Thankyou Music

1   **Meekness and majesty,**
    manhood and deity,
    in perfect harmony,
    the man who is God:
    Lord of eternity
    dwells in humanity,
    kneels in humility
    and washes our feet.

O what a mystery,
meekness and majesty:
bow down and worship,
for this is your God,
this is your God!

2   Father's pure radiance,
    perfect in innocence,
    yet learns obedience
    to death on a cross:
    suffering to give us life,
    conquering through sacrifice;
    and, as they crucify,
    prays, 'Father, forgive.'
    O what a mystery . . .

3   Wisdom unsearchable,
    God the invisible,
    Love indestructible
    in frailty appears.
    Lord of infinity,
    stooping so tenderly,
    lifts our humanity
    to the heights of His throne.
    O what a mystery . . .
    this is your God!

466 Mavis Ford
© 1984 Word's Spirit of Praise Music/
CopyCare

Mighty in victory, glorious in majesty:
every eye shall see Him when He appears,
coming in the clouds
    with power and glory.
    Hail to the King!
We must be ready, watching and praying,
serving each other, building His kingdom;
then every knee shall bow,
    then every tongue confess,
    Jesus is Lord!

467
Eleanor Farjeon (1881–1965)
© David Higham Associates Ltd
from *The Children's Bells*
published by Oxford University Press

1 **Morning has broken**
   like the first morning;
   blackbird has spoken
   like the first bird.
   Praise for the singing!
   Praise for the morning!
   Praise for them, springing
   fresh from the Word!

2 Sweet the rain's new fall
   sunlit from heaven,
   like the first dewfall
   on the first grass.
   Praise for the sweetness
   of the wet garden,
   sprung in completeness
   where His feet pass.

3 Mine is the sunlight!
   Mine is the morning
   born of the one light
   Eden saw play!
   Praise with elation,
   praise every morning,
   God's re-creation
   of the new day!

468
Frederick William Faber (1814–63)
altered © 1987 Horrobin/Leavers

1 **My God, how wonderful You are,**
   Your majesty how bright!
   How beautiful Your mercy-seat,
   in depths of burning light!

2 In awe I glimpse eternity,
   O everlasting Lord;
   by angels worshipped day and night,
   incessantly adored!

3 O how I love You, living God,
   who my heart's longing hears,
   and worship You with certain hope
   and penitential tears!

4 Yes, I may love You, O my Lord,
   almighty King of kings,
   for You have stooped to live in me,
   with joy my heart now sings:

5 How wonderful, how beautiful,
   Your loving face must be,
   Your endless wisdom,
       boundless power,
   and awesome purity!

469
Ray Palmer (1808–87)

1 **My faith looks up to Thee,**
   Thou Lamb of Calvary,
   Saviour divine:
   now hear me while I pray;
   take all my guilt away;
   O let me from this day
   be wholly Thine.

2 May Thy rich grace impart
   strength to my fainting heart,
   my zeal inspire.
   As Thou hast died for me,
   O may my love to Thee
   pure, warm, and changeless be,
   a living fire.

3 While life's dark maze I tread,
   and griefs around me spread,
   be Thou my guide;
   bid darkness turn to day,
   wipe sorrow's tears away,
   nor let me ever stray
   from Thee aside.

4 When ends life's transient dream,
   when death's cold sullen stream
   shall o'er me roll,
   blest Saviour, then in love,
   fear and distrust remove;
   O bear me safe above,
   a ransomed soul.

470
F Brook
Copyright control

1 **My goal is God Himself,**
   not joy nor peace,
   nor even blessing,
      but Himself, my God:
   'tis His to lead me there,
      not mine, but His,
   'At any cost, dear Lord, by any road!'

2 So faith bounds forward
      to its goal in God,
   and love can trust her Lord
      to lead her there;
   upheld by Him
      my soul is following hard,
   till God hath full fulfilled
      my deepest prayer.

3 No matter if the way
      be sometimes dark,
   no matter though the cost
      be oft-times great,
   He knoweth how
      I best shall reach the mark,
   the way that leads to Him
      must needs be strait.

4 One thing I know,
      I cannot say Him nay;
   one thing I do, I press toward my Lord:
   My God, my glory here,
      from day to day,
   and in the glory there my great reward.

2 I thank You, Lord, that You have made
      joy to abound;
   so many gentle thoughts and deeds
      circling us round,
   that in the darkest spot of earth
      some love is found.

3 I thank You too that all our joy
      is touched with pain;
   that shadows fall on brightest hours,
      that thorns remain:
   so that earth's bliss may be our guide,
      and not our chain.

4 For You, O Lord, know well how soon
      our weak heart clings,
   has given us joys, tender and true,
      yet all with wings;
   so that we see, gleaming on high,
      diviner things.

5 I thank You, Lord, that You have kept
      the best in store;
   we have enough, yet not too much
      to long for more;
   a yearning for a deeper peace
      not known before.

6 I thank You, Lord, that here our souls,
      though amply blest,
   can never find, although they seek,
      a perfect rest,
   nor ever shall, until they lean
      on Jesus' breast.

471 Adelaide Anne Procter (1825–64)

1 **My God, I thank You, who has made**
      the earth so bright,
   so full of splendour and of joy,
      beauty and light;
   so many glorious things are here,
      noble and right.

472
Carolyn Govier
© 1979 Word's Spirit of Praise Music/
CopyCare

My heart overflows
   with a goodly theme,
I will address my verses to the King;
my heart overflows
   with praise to my God,
I'll give Him the love of my heart.

1 For He is Lord of all the earth,
    He's risen above,
    He's seated at God's right hand;
    and from Him and through Him
        and to Him are all things,
    that His glory might fill the land.
    My heart overflows . . .

2 For He has chosen Mount Zion
        as His resting-place,
    He says, 'Here will I dwell,
    I will abundantly bless and satisfy,
    and her saints will shout for joy.'
    My heart overflows . . .

3 'Lift up your eyes round about and see,
    your heart shall thrill and rejoice,
    for the abundance of the nations
        is coming to you,
    I am glorifying My house.'
    My heart overflows . . .

4 When the last trumpet's voice shall
        sound,
    O may I then in Him be found!
    clothed in His righteousness alone,
    faultless to stand before His throne.
    On Christ, the solid rock . . .

474   © 1987 Ruth Hooke

My life is Yours, O Lord,
my life is Yours, O Lord;
so do as You will,
do what is pleasing to You,
for my life belongs to You.

Teach me the fear of the Lord,
let me see Your righteousness;
I will kneel before You
and worship Christ my King.

473   Edward Mote (1797–1874)
    © in this version Jubilate Hymns

1 **My hope is built on nothing less**
    than Jesus' blood and righteousness;
    no merit of my own I claim,
    but wholly trust in Jesus' name.
    On Christ, the solid rock, I stand –
    all other ground is sinking sand,
    all other ground is sinking sand.

2 When weary in this earthly race,
    I rest on His unchanging grace;
    in every wild and stormy gale
    my anchor holds and will not fail.
    On Christ, the solid rock . . .

3 His vow, His covenant and blood
    are my defence against the flood;
    when earthly hopes are swept away
    He will uphold me on that day.
    On Christ, the solid rock . . .

475   Joan Parsons
    © 1978 Kingsway's Thankyou Music

My Lord, He is the fairest of the fair,
He is the lily of the valley,
the bright and morning star;
His love is written deep within my heart,
He is the never-ending fountain
of everlasting life:
and He lives, He lives,
He lives, He lives in me.

476   Graham Kendrick
    © 1989 Make Way Music

1 **My Lord, what love is this**
    that pays so dearly,
    that I, the guilty one,
    may go free!

Amazing love, O what sacrifice,
the Son of God given for me.
My debt He pays,
   and my death He dies,
that I might live, that I might live.

2 And so, they watched Him die
   despised, rejected:
   but O the blood He shed
   flowed for me!
   Amazing love ...

3 And now this love of Christ
   shall flow like rivers;
   come wash your guilt away,
   live again!
   Amazing love ...

477 Keith Routledge
© 1975 Sovereign Music UK

1 **My peace I give unto you,**
   it's a peace that the world cannot give,
   it's a peace
      that the world cannot understand:
   peace to know, peace to live,
   My peace I give unto you.

2 My joy I give unto you,
   it's a joy that the world cannot give,
   it's a joy
      that the world cannot understand:
   joy to know, joy to live,
   My joy I give unto you.

3 My love I give unto you,
   it's a love that the world cannot give,
   it's a love
      that the world cannot understand:
   love to know, love to live,
   My love I give unto you.

478 Samuel Crossman (1624–83)

1 **My song is love unknown;**
   my Saviour's love to me;
   love to the loveless shown,
   that they might lovely be.
   O who am I,
   that for my sake,
   my Lord should take
   frail flesh, and die?

2 He came from His blest throne,
   salvation to bestow;
   but men made strange, and none
   the longed-for Christ would know.
   But O my friend,
   my friend indeed,
   who at my need
   His life did spend.

3 Sometimes they strew His way,
   and His sweet praises sing;
   resounding all the day,
   hosannas to their King.
   Then: 'Crucify!'
   is all their breath,
   and for His death
   they thirst and cry.

4 Why, what hath my Lord done?
   What makes this rage and spite?
   He made the lame to run,
   He gave the blind their sight.
   Sweet injuries!
   yet they at these
   themselves displease,
   and 'gainst Him rise.

5 They rise and needs will have
   my dear Lord made away:
   a murderer they save,
   the Prince of life they slay.
   Yet cheerful He
   to suffering goes,
   that He His foes
   from thence might free.

6   In life, no house, no home
    my Lord on earth might have;
    in death, no friendly tomb,
    but what a stranger gave.
    What may I say?
    Heaven was His home;
    but mine the tomb
    wherein He lay.

7   Here might I stay and sing,
    no story so divine;
    never was love, dear King,
    never was grief like Thine.
    This is my friend,
    in whose sweet praise
    I all my days
    could gladly spend.

479   From Luke 1
          Copyright control

My soul doth magnify the Lord,
and my spirit hath rejoiced
        in God my Saviour.
For He that is mighty
        hath done great things,
and holy is His name.

My soul doth magnify the Lord,
my soul doth magnify the Lord,
and my spirit hath rejoiced
        in God my Saviour.
For He that is mighty
        hath done great things,
and holy is His name.

My soul doth magnify the Lord,
my soul doth magnify the Lord,
and my spirit hath rejoiced
        in God my Saviour.
For He that is mighty
        hath done great things,
and holy is His name.

480   John Keble (1792–1866)

1   **New every morning is the love**
    our waking and uprising prove:
    through sleep and darkness
            safely brought,
    restored to life and power and thought.

2   New mercies, each returning day,
    surround Your people as they pray:
    new dangers past, new sins forgiven,
    new thoughts of God,
            new hopes of heaven.

3   If in our daily life our mind
    be set to honour all we find,
    new treasures still, of countless price,
    God will provide for sacrifice.

4   The trivial round, the common task,
    will give us all we ought to ask:
    room to deny ourselves, a road
    to bring us daily nearer God.

5   Prepare us, Lord, in Your dear love
    for perfect rest with You above,
    and help us, this and every day,
    to grow more like You as we pray.

481   © Timothy Dudley-Smith

1   **Name of all majesty,**
    fathomless mystery,
    King of the ages
    by angels adored;
        power and authority,
        splendour and dignity,
        bow to His mastery,
    Jesus is Lord!

2 Child of our destiny,
God from eternity,
love of the Father
on sinners outpoured;
see now what God has done
sending His only Son,
Christ the belovèd One,
Jesus is Lord!

3 Saviour of Calvary,
costliest victory,
darkness defeated
and Eden restored;
born as a man to die,
nailed to a cross on high,
cold in the grave to lie,
Jesus is Lord!

4 Source of all sovereignty,
light, immortality,
life everlasting
and heaven assured;
so with the ransomed, we
praise Him eternally,
Christ in His majesty –
Jesus is Lord!

482 Sarah Flower Adams (1805–48)

1 **Nearer, my God, to Thee,**
nearer to Thee:
e'en though it be a cross
that raiseth me,
still all my song would be
nearer, my God, to Thee,
nearer to Thee, nearer to Thee.

2 Though, like the wanderer,
the sun gone down,
darkness be over me,
my rest a stone,
yet in my dreams I'd be
nearer, my God, to Thee,
nearer to Thee, nearer to Thee.

3 There let the way appear,
steps up to heaven;
all that Thou sendest me,
in mercy given;
angels to beckon me
nearer, my God, to Thee,
nearer to Thee, nearer to Thee.

4 Then, with my waking thoughts
bright with Thy praise,
out of my stony griefs
Bethel I'll raise;
so by my woes to be
nearer, my God, to Thee,
nearer to Thee, nearer to Thee.

5 Or, if on joyful wing
cleaving the sky,
sun, moon, and stars forgot,
upwards I fly,
still all my song shall be,
nearer, my God, to Thee,
nearer to Thee, nearer to Thee.

483 Tom Dowell

No weapon formed, or army or king,
shall be able to stand
against the Lord and His anointed.

All principalities and powers
shall crumble before the Lord;
and men's hearts shall be released,
and they shall come unto the Lord.

No weapon formed, or army or king,
shall be able to stand
against the Lord and His anointed.

484

Graham Kendrick
© 1988 Make Way Music

1 **Now dawns the Sun of
   righteousness,**
   and the darkness will never
   His brightness dim;
   true light that lights the hearts of men,
   only Son of the Father,
   Jesus Christ.
   *Tell out, tell out the news,
   on every street proclaim,
   a child is born, a Son is given
   and Jesus is His name!
   Tell out, tell out the news,
   our Saviour Christ has come,
   in every tribe and nation,
   let songs of praise be sung,
   let songs of praise be sung!*

2 Laughter and joy He will increase,
   all our burdens be lifted,
   oppression cease;
   the blood-stained battle-dress
   be burned,
   and the art of our warfare
   never more be learned.
   Tell out . . .

3 So let us go, His witnesses,
   spreading news of His kingdom
   of righteousness,
   till the whole world has heard the song,
   till the harvest is gathered,
   then the end shall come.
   Tell out . . .

2 Father, Your everlasting grace
   our human thought surpassing far,
   Your heart still melts with tenderness,
   Your arms of love still open are:
   returning sinners will receive
   eternal life as they believe.

3 Your love, eternal hope, no less,
   my sins consumed at Calvary!
   Covered is my unrighteousness,
   no spot of guilt remains on me,
   while Jesu's blood
        through earth and skies
   mercy, free, boundless mercy! cries.

4 Though waves and storms
        go o'er my head,
   though strength, and health,
        and friends be gone,
   though joys be withered all and dead,
   though every comfort be withdrawn,
   on this my steadfast soul relies –
   Father, Your mercy never dies!

5 Fixed on this ground will I remain,
   though my heart fail and flesh decay;
   this anchor shall my soul sustain,
   when earth's foundations melt away:
   mercy's full power I then shall prove,
   loved with an everlasting love.

485

Johann Andreas Rothe (1688–1758)
tr. John Wesley (1703–91)
altered © 1987 Horrobin/Leavers

1 **Now I have found the ground
   wherein**
   sure my soul's anchor may remain –
   the wounds of Jesus, for my sin
   before the world's foundation slain;
   whose mercy shall unshaken stay,
   when heaven and earth are fled away.

486

Martin Rinkart (1586–1649)
tr. Catherine Winkworth (1829–78)

1 **Now thank we all our God,**
   with hearts, and hands, and voices;
   who wondrous things hath done,
   in whom His world rejoices;
   Who, from our mothers' arms,
   hath blest us on our way
   with countless gifts of love,
   and still is ours today.

2 O may this bounteous God
   through all our life be near us,
   with ever-joyful hearts
   and blessèd peace to cheer us;
   and keep us in His grace,
   and guide us when perplexed,
   and free us from all ills
   in this world and the next.

3 All praise and thanks to God
   the Father now be given,
   the Son, and Him who reigns
   with Them in highest heaven;
   the one eternal God,
   whom heaven and earth adore;
   for thus it was, is now,
   and shall be evermore.

487 Horatius Bonar (1808–89)

1 **Not what these hands have done**
   can save this guilty soul,
   not what this toiling flesh has borne
   can make my spirit whole.

2 Not what I feel or do
   can give me peace with God;
   not all my prayers, and sighs, and tears
   can bear my awful load.

3 Thy work alone, O Christ,
   can ease this weight of sin;
   Thy blood alone, O Lamb of God,
   can give me peace within.

4 Thy love to me, O God,
   not mine, O Lord, to Thee,
   can rid me of this dark unrest,
   and set my spirit free.

5 Thy grace alone, O God,
   to me can pardon speak;
   Thy power alone, O Son of God,
   can this sore bondage break.

6 I bless the Christ of God,
   I rest on love divine,
   and with unfaltering lip and heart,
   I call this Saviour mine.

488 Elizabeth Ann Porter Head (1850–1936)
Copyright control

1 **O Breath of Life,**
   come sweeping through us,
   revive Your Church
      with life and power;
   O Breath of Life,
      come, cleanse, renew us
   and fit Your Church to meet this hour.

2 O Breath of Love,
      come breathe within us,
   renewing thought and will and heart;
   come, Love of Christ, afresh to win us,
   revive Your Church in every part!

3 O Wind of God, come bend us,
      break us
   till humbly we confess our need;
   then, in Your tenderness remake us,
   revive, restore – for this we plead.

4 Revive us, Lord; is zeal abating
   while harvest fields are vast and white?
   Revive us, Lord, the world is waiting –
   equip Thy Church to spread the light.

489 Graham Kendrick
© 1988 Make Way Music

1 LEADER **O come and join the dance**
      that all began so long ago,
   ALL   when Christ the Lord was
      born in Bethlehem.
   LEADER Through all the years
      of darkness
      still the dance goes on and on,
   ALL   O take my hand and come
      and join the song.

MEN	*Rejoice!*
WOMEN	*Rejoice!*
MEN	*Rejoice!*
WOMEN	*Rejoice!*
ALL	*O lift your voice and sing,*
	and open up your heart
	to welcome Him.
MEN	*Rejoice!*
WOMEN	*Rejoice!*
MEN	*Rejoice!*
WOMEN	*Rejoice!*
ALL	*and welcome now your King,*
	for Christ the Lord was born
	in Bethlehem.

2 LEADER Come shed your heavy load
    and dance your worries
    all away,
ALL for Christ the Lord was born
    in Bethlehem.
LEADER He came to break the power
    of sin
    and turn your night to day,
ALL O take my hand and come
    and join the song.
    Rejoice . . .

3 (*Instrumental verse and chorus*)

4 LEADER Let laughter ring
    and angels sing
    and joy be all around,
ALL for Christ the Lord was born
    in Bethlehem.
LEADER And if you seek
    with all your heart
    He surely can be found,
ALL O take my hand and come
    and join the song.
    Rejoice . . .
    Rejoice . . .
    for Christ the Lord was born
    in Bethlehem,
    for Christ the Lord was born
    in Bethlehem.

490 Anon
Copyright control

1 **O come, let us adore Him,**
O come, let us adore Him,
O come, let us adore Him,
Christ the Lord.

2 We'll give Him all the glory . . .

3 For He alone is worthy . . .

491 From the Latin (18th century)
tr. Frederick Oakley (1802–80)
altered © 1986 Horrobin/Leavers

1 **O come, all you faithful,**
joyful and triumphant,
O come now, O come now
    to Bethlehem;
come and behold Him,
born the King of angels:
    O come, let us adore Him,
    O come, let us adore Him,
    O come, let us adore Him,
    Christ the Lord!

2 True God of true God,
light of light eternal,
He, who abhors not the virgin's womb;
Son of the Father,
begotten not created:
    O come, let us adore Him . . .

3 Sing like the angels,
sing in exultation,
sing with the citizens of heaven above,
'Glory to God,
glory in the highest':
    O come, let us adore Him . . .

4 Yes, Lord, we greet You,
born that/*this* happy morning,
Jesus, to You be glory given!
Word of the Father,
then/*now* in flesh appearing:
    O come, let us adore Him . . .

492
Iain Anderson
© 1981 Word's Spirit of Praise Music/
CopyCare

O come, let us worship and bow down,
let us kneel before the Lord our King;
let us whisper His name, wonderful name,
Jesus our Lord and King.

For He is Lord of all the earth,
His glory outshines the sun;
see Him clothed in His robes
        of righteousness,
God's belovèd Son.

O come, let us worship and bow down,
let us kneel before the Lord our King;
let us whisper His name, wonderful name,
Jesus our Lord and King.

493
From the Latin (12th century)
tr. John Mason Neale (1818–66)

1   **O come, O come, Emmanuel,**
    and ransom captive Israel,
    that mourns in lonely exile here
    until the Son of God appear.
    Rejoice, rejoice! Emmanuel
    shall come to thee, O Israel.

2   O come, O come, Thou Lord of might,
    who to Thy tribes, on Sinai's height
    in ancient times didst give the law
    in cloud and majesty and awe.
    Rejoice, rejoice . . .

3   O come, Thou rod of Jesse, free
    Thine own from Satan's tyranny;
    from depths of hell Thy people save,
    and give them victory o'er the grave.
    Rejoice, rejoice . . .

4   O come, Thou dayspring,
        come and cheer
    our spirits by Thine advent here;
    disperse the gloomy clouds of night,
    and death's dark shadows put to flight.
    Rejoice, rejoice . . .

5   O come, Thou key of David, come
    and open wide our heavenly home;
    make safe the way that leads on high,
    and close the path to misery.
    Rejoice, rejoice . . .

494
William Cowper (1731–1800)

1   **O for a closer walk with God,**
    a calm and heavenly frame,
    a light to shine upon the road
    that leads me to the Lamb.

2   Where is the blessèdness I knew
    when I first saw the Lord?
    Where is that soul-refreshing view
    of Jesus and His word?

3   What peaceful hours I once enjoyed!
    how sweet their memory still!
    But they have left an aching void
    the world can never fill.

4   Return, O holy Dove! return,
    sweet messenger of rest!
    I hate the sins that made Thee mourn,
    and drove Thee from my breast.

5   The dearest idol I have known,
    whate'er that idol be,
    help me to tear it from Thy throne,
    and worship only Thee.

6   So shall my walk be close with God,
    calm and serene my frame;
    so purer light shall mark the road
    that leads me to the Lamb.

495
Charles Wesley (1707–88)

1   **O for a heart to praise my God,**
    a heart from sin set free,
    a heart that always feels Thy blood
    so freely shed for me.

2 A heart resigned, submissive, meek,
my great Redeemer's throne;
where only Christ is heard to speak,
where Jesus reigns alone:

3 A humble, lowly, contrite heart,
believing, true, and clean;
which neither life nor death can part
from Him that dwells within:

4 A heart in every thought renewed,
and full of love divine;
perfect, and right, and pure, and good,
a copy, Lord, of Thine.

5 Thy nature, gracious Lord, impart;
come quickly from above,
write Thy new name upon my heart,
Thy new, best name of love.

6 My gracious Master, and my God,
assist me to proclaim,
to spread through all the earth abroad,
the honours of Thy name.

497
Joanne Pond
© 1980 Kingsway's Thankyou Music

O give thanks to the Lord,
all you His people,
O give thanks to the Lord,
    for He is good.
Let us praise, let us thank,
let us celebrate and dance;
O give thanks to the Lord,
    for He is good.

496
Charles Wesley (1707–88) altd.

1 **O for a thousand tongues to sing**
my great Redeemer's praise,
the glories of my God and King,
the triumphs of His grace!

2 Jesus! the name that charms our fears,
that bids our sorrows cease;
'tis music in the sinner's ears,
'tis life, and health, and peace.

3 He breaks the power of cancelled sin,
He sets the prisoner free;
His blood can make the foulest clean;
His blood availed for me.

4 He speaks, and, listening to His voice,
new life the dead receive,
the mournful, broken hearts rejoice,
the humble poor believe.

5 Hear Him, ye deaf;
    His praise, ye dumb,
your loosened tongues employ:
ye blind, behold your Saviour come;
and leap, ye lame, for joy.

498
Isaac Watts (1674–1748) altd.

1 **O God, our help in ages past,**
our hope for years to come,
our shelter from the stormy blast,
and our eternal home.

2 Under the shadow of Your throne
Your saints have dwelt secure;
sufficient is Your arm alone,
and our defence is sure.

3 Before the hills in order stood,
or earth received her frame,
from everlasting You are God,
to endless years the same.

4 A thousand ages in Your sight
are like an evening gone,
short as the watch that ends the night
before the rising sun.

5 Time, like an ever-rolling stream,
bears all its sons away;
they fly forgotten, as a dream
dies with the dawning day.

6   O God, our help in ages past,
    our hope for years to come,
    be our defence while life shall last,
    and our eternal home.

499   Philip Doddridge (1702–51)

1   **O happy day! that fixed my choice**
    on Thee, my Saviour and my God!
    Well may this glowing heart rejoice,
    and tell its raptures all abroad.
      O happy day! O happy day!
      when Jesus washed my sins away;
      He taught me how to watch and pray,
      and live rejoicing every day;
      (hallelujah!)
      O happy day! O happy day!
      when Jesus washed my sins away.

2   'Tis done, the great transaction's done!
    I am my Lord's and He is mine!
    He drew me, and I followed on,
    charmed to confess the voice divine.
      O happy day . . .

3   Now rest, my long-divided heart,
    fixed on this blissful centre, rest;
    nor ever from the Lord depart,
    with Him of every good possessed.
      O happy day . . .

4   High heaven,
      that heard the solemn vow,
    that vow renewed shall daily hear;
    till in life's latest hour I bow,
    and bless in death a bond so dear.
      O happy day . . .

500   © 1980 Norman Warren/Jubilate Hymns

1   **O Holy Spirit, breathe on me,**
    O Holy Spirit, breathe on me,
    and cleanse away my sin,
    fill me with love within:
    O Holy Spirit, breathe on me!

2   O Holy Spirit, fill my life,
    O Holy Spirit, fill my life,
    take all my pride from me,
    give me humility:
    O Holy Spirit, breathe on me!

3   O Holy Spirit, make me new,
    O Holy Spirit, make me new,
    make Jesus real to me,
    give me His purity:
    O Holy Spirit, breathe on me!

4   O Holy Spirit, wind of God,
    O Holy Spirit, wind of God,
    give me Your power today,
    to live for You always:
    O Holy Spirit, breathe on me!

501   John Ernest Bode (1816–74)

1   **O Jesus, I have promised**
    to serve Thee to the end;
    be Thou for ever near me,
    my Master and my friend.
    I shall not fear the battle
    if Thou art by my side,
    nor wander from the pathway
    if Thou wilt be my guide.

2   O let me feel Thee near me;
    the world is ever near;
    I see the sights that dazzle,
    the tempting sounds I hear;
    my foes are ever near me,
    around me and within;
    but, Jesus, draw Thou nearer,
    and shield my soul from sin.

3   O let me hear Thee speaking
    in accents clear and still,
    above the storms of passion,
    the murmurs of self-will;
    O speak to reassure me,
    to hasten or control;
    O speak, and make me listen,
    Thou guardian of my soul.

4 O Jesus, Thou hast promised,
   to all who follow Thee,
   that where Thou art in glory
   there shall Thy servant be;
   and, Jesus, I have promised
   to serve Thee to the end;
   O give me grace to follow
   my Master and my friend.

5 O let me see Thy footmarks,
   and in them plant mine own;
   my hope to follow duly
   is in Thy strength alone;
   O guide me, call me, draw me,
   uphold me to the end;
   and then in heaven receive me,
   my Saviour and my friend!

502

John Wimber
© 1979 Mercy/Vineyard Publishing/
CopyCare

1 **O let the Son of God enfold you**
   with His Spirit and His love;
   let Him fill your heart
         and satisfy your soul.
   O let Him have the things
         that hold you,
   and His Spirit, like a dove,
   will descend upon your life
         and make you whole.
      Jesus, O Jesus,
      come and fill Your lambs;
      Jesus, O Jesus,
      come and fill Your lambs.

2 O come and sing this song
         with gladness,
   as your hearts are filled with joy;
   lift your hands in sweet surrender
         to His name.
   O give Him all your tears and sadness,
   give Him all your years of pain,
   and you'll enter into life in Jesus' name.
      Jesus, O Jesus . . .

503

Phillips Brooks (1835–93)

1 **O little town of Bethlehem,**
   how still we see you lie!
   Above your deep and dreamless sleep
   the silent stars go by:
   yet in your dark streets shining
   is everlasting light;
   the hopes and fears of all the years
   are met in you tonight.

2 For Christ is born of Mary;
   and, gathered all above,
   while mortals sleep, the angels keep
   their watch of wondering love.
   O morning stars, together
   proclaim the holy birth,
   and praises sing to God the King,
   and peace to men on earth.

3 How silently, how silently,
   the wondrous gift is given!
   So God imparts to human hearts
   the blessings of His heaven.
   No ear may hear His coming;
   but in this world of sin,
   where meek souls will receive Him, still
   the dear Christ enters in.

4 O holy Child of Bethlehem,
   descend to us, we pray;
   cast out our sin, and enter in;
   be born in us today.
   We hear the Christmas angels
   the great glad tidings tell;
   O come to us, abide with us,
   our Lord Immanuel.

504

Carl Tuttle
© 1982 Mercy/Vineyard Publishing/
CopyCare

1 **O Lord, have mercy on me,**
      and heal me;
   O Lord, have mercy on me,
      and free me.

Place my feet upon a rock,
put a new song in my heart,
in my heart,
O Lord, have mercy on me.

2   O Lord, may Your love
        and Your grace protect me;
    O Lord, may Your ways
        and Your truth direct me.
    Place my feet upon a rock,
    put a new song in my heart,
    in my heart,
    O Lord, have mercy on me.

    Place my feet upon a rock,
    put a new song in my heart,
    in my heart,
    O Lord, have mercy on me,
    O Lord, have mercy on me, on me.

505   Wendy Churchill
          © 1980 Word's Spirit of Praise Music/
          CopyCare

1   **O Lord, most Holy God,**
    great are Your purposes,
    great is Your will for us,
    great is Your love.
    And we rejoice in You,
    and we will sing to You,
    O Father, have Your way,
    Your will be done.

2   For You are building
    a temple without hands,
    a city without walls,
    enclosed by fire.
    A place for You to dwell,
    built out of living stones,
    shaped by a Father's hand
    and joined in love.

506   Russian hymn
          tr. Stuart Wesley Keene Hine (1899–1989)
          © 1953 Stuart Wesley Keene Hine/
          Kingsway's Thankyou Music

1   **O Lord my God!**
    when I in awesome wonder
    consider all the works
        Thy hand hath made,
    I see the stars,
        I hear the mighty thunder,
    the power throughout the universe
        displayed;
        Then sings my soul,
        my Saviour God, to Thee,
        how great Thou art,
            how great Thou art!
        Then sings my soul,
        my Saviour God, to Thee,
        how great Thou art,
            how great Thou art!

2   When through the woods
        and forest glades I wander
    and hear the birds sing sweetly
        in the trees;
    when I look down
        from lofty mountain grandeur,
    and hear the brook,
        and feel the gentle breeze;
        Then sings my soul . . .

3   And when I think
        that God His Son not sparing,
    sent Him to die –
        I scarce can take it in,
    that on the cross
        my burden gladly bearing,
    He bled and died to take away my sin:
        Then sings my soul . . .

4   When Christ shall come
        with shout of acclamation
    and take me home –
        what joy shall fill my heart!
    Then shall I bow in humble adoration
    and there proclaim,
        my God, how great Thou art!
        Then sings my soul . . .

507
Phil Lawson Johnston
© 1982 Kingsway's Thankyou Music

1   **O Lord our God,
       how majestic is Your name,**
   the earth is filled with Your glory.
   O Lord our God,
       You are robed in majesty,
   You've set Your glory
       above the heavens.
       We will magnify, we will magnify
       the Lord enthroned in Zion;
       We will magnify, we will magnify
       the Lord enthroned in Zion.

2   O Lord our God,
       You have established a throne,
   You reign in righteousness
       and splendour.
   O Lord our God, the skies are ringing
       with Your praise,
   soon those on earth
       will come to worship.
       We will magnify . . .

3   O Lord our God, the world was made
       at Your command,
   in You all things now hold together.
   Now to Him who sits on the throne
       and to the Lamb,
   be praise and glory and power for ever.
       We will magnify . . .

508
Michael W Smith
© 1981 Meadowgreen Music/
EMI Christian Music Publishing/CopyCare

O Lord, our Lord,
how majestic is Your name in all the earth;
O Lord, our Lord,
how majestic is Your name in all the earth;
O Lord, we praise Your name;
O Lord, we magnify Your name.
Prince of peace, mighty God,
O Lord God almighty!

509
Graham Kendrick
© 1987 Make Way Music

1   **O Lord, the clouds are gathering,**
   the fire of judgement burns.
   How we have fallen!
   O Lord, You stand appalled to see
   Your laws of love so scorned
   and lives so broken.
   MEN   *Have mercy, Lord,*
   WOMEN   *have mercy, Lord.*
   MEN   *Forgive us, Lord,*
   WOMEN   *forgive us, Lord.*
   ALL   *Restore us, Lord;*
                 revive Your Church again.
   MEN   *Let justice flow,*
   WOMEN   *let justice flow,*
   MEN   *like rivers,*
   WOMEN   *like rivers;*
   ALL   *and righteousness*
                 like a never-failing stream.

2   O Lord, over the nations now,
   where is the dove of peace?
   Her wings are broken,
   O Lord, while precious children starve,
   the tools of war increase,
   their bread is stolen.
   MEN *Have mercy, Lord . . .*

3   O Lord, dark powers are poised
   to flood our streets with hate and fear.
   We must awaken!
   O Lord, let love reclaim the lives
   that sin would sweep away,
   and let Your kingdom come!
   MEN *Have mercy, Lord . . .*

4   Yet, O Lord, Your glorious cross
   shall tower triumphant in this land,
   evil confounding;
   through the fire, Your suffering Church
   display the glories of her Christ,
   praises resounding.
   MEN *Have mercy, Lord . . .*

       A never-failing stream.

510 David Fellingham
© 1983 Kingsway's Thankyou Music

O Lord, You are my light,
O Lord, You are my salvation;
You have delivered me from all my fear,
for You are the defence of my life.

For my life is hidden with Christ in God,
You have concealed me in Your love;
You've lifted me up,
        placed my feet on a rock;
I will shout for joy in the house of God.

O Lord, You are my light . . .

511 Graham Kendrick
© 1986 Kingsway's Thankyou Music

O Lord, Your tenderness –
melting all my bitterness!
    O Lord, I receive Your love.
O Lord, Your loveliness,
changing all my ugliness,
    O Lord, I receive Your love,
    O Lord, I receive Your love,
    O Lord, I receive Your love.

512 Carolyn Govier
© 1979 Word's Spirit of Praise Music/
CopyCare

**O Lord, You've done great things,
    and I will praise You,**
I will extol You and magnify Your name.
O Lord, You've done great things,
    and I will praise You,
I will extol You and magnify Your name.

I will sing praises unto You
    and remember Your goodness,
my past is forgiven and now I have life;
You crown me with steadfast love
    and tender mercy,
I'll do Your will and bless You, O Lord.

513 Keith Green
© 1980 BMG Songs/Birdwing Music/
EMI Christian Music Publishing/CopyCare

1 **O Lord, You're beautiful,**
    Your face is all I seek;
    for when Your eyes are on this child,
    Your grace abounds to me.

2 O Lord, please light the fire
    that once burned bright and clear;
    replace the lamp of my first love
    that burns with holy fear!

        I want to take Your word
            and shine it all around,
        but first help me just to live it, Lord!
        And when I'm doing well,
        help me to never seek a crown,
        for my reward is giving glory to You.

3 O Lord, You're beautiful,
    Your face is all I seek;
    for when Your eyes are on this child,
    Your grace abounds to me.

514 Horatius Bonar (1808–89)

1 **O love of God, how strong and true!**
    eternal and yet ever new;
    uncomprehended and unbought,
    beyond all knowledge and all thought.

2 O heavenly love, how precious still,
    in days of weariness and ill,
    in nights of pain and helplessness,
    to heal, to comfort, and to bless!

3 O wide-embracing, wondrous love,
    we see You in the sky above;
    we see You in the earth below,
    in seas that swell and streams that flow.

4 We see You best in Him who came
    to bear for us the cross of shame,
    sent by the Father from on high,
    our life to live, our death to die.

5 We see Your power to bless and save
e'en in the darkness of the grave;
still more in resurrection-light,
we see the fulness of Your might.

6 O love of God, our shield and stay
through all the perils of our way;
eternal Love, in You we rest,
for ever safe, for ever blest!

515 George Matheson (1842–1906)

1 **O Love that wilt not let me go,**
I rest my weary soul in Thee;
I give Thee back the life I owe,
that in Thine ocean depths its flow
may richer, fuller be.

2 O Light that followest all my way,
I yield my flickering torch to Thee;
my heart restores its borrowed ray,
that in Thy sunshine's blaze its day
may brighter, fairer be.

3 O Joy that seekest me through pain,
I cannot close my heart to Thee;
I trace the rainbow through the rain,
and feel the promise is not vain
that morn shall tearless be.

4 O cross that liftest up my head,
I dare not ask to fly from thee;
I lay in dust life's glory dead,
and from the ground
there blossoms red
life that shall endless be.

516 William Walsham How (1823–97)

1 **O my Saviour, lifted**
from the earth for me,
draw me, in Thy mercy,
nearer unto Thee.

2 Lift my earth-bound longings,
fix them, Lord, above;
draw me with the magnet
of Thy mighty love.

3 And I come, Lord Jesus;
dare I turn away?
No! Thy love hath conquered,
and I come today.

4 Bringing all my burdens,
sorrow, sin, and care;
at Thy feet I lay them,
and I leave them there.

517 Dorothy Gurney (1858–1932)
By permission of Oxford University Press

1 **O perfect Love, all human thought
transcending,**
lowly we kneel in prayer
before Your throne,
that theirs may be the love
which knows no ending,
whom You for evermore
now join as one.

2 O perfect Life,
be now their full assurance
of tender charity, and steadfast faith,
of patient hope,
and quiet brave endurance,
with childlike trust that fears
nor pain nor death.

3 Grant them the joy
which brightens earthly sorrow;
grant them the peace
which calms all earthly strife;
and to life's day
the glorious unknown morrow
that dawns upon eternal love and life.

518

Henry Williams Baker (1821–77)

1 **O praise ye the Lord!**
praise Him in the height;
rejoice in His word,
ye angels of light;
ye heavens adore Him
by whom ye were made,
and worship before Him,
in brightness arrayed.

2 O praise ye the Lord!
praise Him upon earth,
in tuneful accord,
ye sons of new birth;
praise Him who has brought you
His grace from above,
praise Him who has taught you
to sing of His love.

3 O praise ye the Lord!
all things that give sound;
each jubilant chord,
re-echo around;
loud organs, His glory
forth tell in deep tone,
and sweet harp, the story
of what He has done.

4 O praise ye the Lord!
thanksgiving and song
to Him be outpoured
all ages along:
for love in creation,
for heaven restored,
for grace of salvation,
O praise ye the Lord!

519

1 **O Saviour Christ, I now confess**
You are my Lord, my righteousness,
I follow Your example true,
and daily seek to be like You.

2 These waters have no power, I know,
to cleanse from sin or grace bestow.
'Tis in obedience to my Lord
that I am blest and He's adored.

3 Buried with Christ, I die to sin,
His risen life and power within.
And victory is to me assured
as I surrender to the Lord.

4 'Tis one more step along the road
that leads me onward with my Lord.
Now fill me with the Spirit's power,
make this a pentecostal hour.

5 Baptizing nations in Your name,
Father, Son, Spirit – still the same.
In full alignment to the Lord,
their guide, their strength –
the Living Word.

6 Then, only then, shall all men hear
the news, that Christ's return is near.
And men shall greet their coming Lord
by heaven and earth, for e'er adored.

520

attrib. Bernard of Clairvaux (1091–1153)
Paul Gerhardt (1607–76)
tr. James Waddell Alexander (1804–59)

1 **O sacred head, once wounded,**
with grief and pain weighed down,
how scornfully surrounded
with thorns, Thine only crown!
How pale art Thou with anguish,
with sore abuse and scorn!
How does that visage languish,
which once was bright as morn!

2 O Lord of life and glory,
what bliss till now was Thine!
I read the wondrous story,
I joy to call Thee mine.
Thy grief and Thy compassion
were all for sinners' gain;
mine, mine was the transgression,
but Thine the deadly pain.

3 What language shall I borrow
to praise Thee, heavenly friend,
for this, Thy dying sorrow,
Thy pity without end?
Lord, make me Thine for ever,
nor let me faithless prove;
O let me never, never
abuse such dying love!

4 Be near me, Lord, when dying;
O show Thyself to me;
and, for my succour flying,
come, Lord, to set me free:
these eyes, new faith receiving,
from Jesus shall not move;
for he who dies believing,
dies safely through Thy love.

521
Lucy Ann Bennett (1850–1927)

1 **O teach me what it meaneth,**
that cross uplifted high,
with One, the Man of Sorrows,
condemned to bleed and die!
O teach me what it cost Thee
to make a sinner whole;
and teach me, Saviour, teach me
the value of a soul!

2 O teach me what it meaneth,
that sacred crimson tide,
the blood and water flowing
from Thine own wounded side.
Teach me that if none other
had sinned, but I alone,
yet still Thy blood, Lord Jesus,
Thine only, must atone.

3 O teach me what it meaneth,
Thy love beyond compare,
the love that reacheth deeper
than depths of self-despair!
Yes, teach me, till there gloweth
in this cold heart of mine,
some feeble, pale reflection
of that pure love of Thine.

4 O teach me what it meaneth,
for I am full of sin;
and grace alone can reach me,
and love alone can win.
O teach me, for I need Thee,
I have no hope beside,
the chief of all the sinners
for whom the Saviour died!

5 O infinite Redeemer!
I bring no other plea,
because Thou dost invite me
I cast myself on Thee.
Because Thou dost accept me
I love and I adore;
because Thy love constraineth,
I'll praise Thee evermore!

522
Samuel Trevor Francis (1834–1925)

1 **O the deep, deep love of Jesus!**
Vast, unmeasured, boundless, free;
rolling as a mighty ocean
in its fulness over me.
Underneath me, all around me,
is the current of Thy love;
leading onward, leading homeward,
to my glorious rest above.

2 O the deep, deep love of Jesus!
   Spread His praise from shore to shore,
   how He loveth, ever loveth,
   changeth never, nevermore;
   how He watches o'er His loved ones,
   died to call them all His own;
   how for them He intercedeth,
   watches over them from the throne.

3 O the deep, deep love of Jesus!
   Love of every love the best:
   'tis an ocean vast of blessing,
   'tis a haven sweet of rest.
   O the deep, deep love of Jesus!
   'tis a heaven of heavens to me;
   and it lifts me up to glory,
   for it lifts me up to Thee.

523

Dave Bilbrough
© 1980 Kingsway's Thankyou Music

**O the valleys shall ring
  with the sound of praise,**
and the lion shall lie with the lamb.
Of His government there shall be no end,
and His glory shall fill the earth.

May Your will be done,
    may Your kingdom come!
let it rule, let it reign in our lives.
There's a shout in the camp
    as we answer the call,
Hail the King! Hail the Lord of lords!

524

Theodore Monod (1836–1921)
© in this version Jubilate Hymns

1 **O the bitter shame and sorrow**
   that a time could ever be
   when I let the Saviour's pity
   plead in vain, and proudly answered,
   'None of You and all of me!'

2 Yet You found me; there I saw You
   dying and in agony,
   heard You pray, 'Forgive them, Father',
   and my wistful heart said faintly,
   'Some of You and some of me.'

3 Day by day Your tender mercy,
   healing, helping, full and free,
   firm and strong, with endless patience
   brought me lower, while I whispered,
   'More of You and less of me.'

4 Higher than the highest heaven,
   deeper than the deepest sea,
   Lord, Your love at last has conquered:
   grant me now my spirit's longing,
   'All of You and none of me!'

525

Charles Wesley (1707–88)

1 **O Thou who camest from above**
   the pure, celestial fire to impart,
   kindle a flame of sacred love
   on the mean altar of my heart.

2 There let it for Thy glory burn,
   with inextinguishable blaze;
   and, trembling, to its source return
   in humble love and fervent praise.

3 Jesus, confirm my heart's desire
   to work and speak and think for Thee;
   still let me guard the holy fire,
   and still stir up Thy gift in me;

4 Ready for all Thy perfect will,
   my acts of faith and love repeat,
   till death Thine endless mercies seal,
   and make the sacrifice complete.

526
Pat Uhl Howard © 1967, 1970, 1978, 1979
American Catholic Press

O what a gift!
what a wonderful gift!
Who can tell the wonders of the Lord?
Let us open our eyes,
  our ears, and our hearts;
it is Christ the Lord, it is He!

1   In the stillness of the night
    when the world was asleep,
    the almighty Word leapt out.
    He came to Mary, He came to us;
    Christ came to the land of Galilee;
    Christ our Lord and our King!
      O what a gift . . .

2   On the night before He died
    it was Passover night,
    and He gathered His friends together;
    He broke the bread,
      He blessed the wine;
    it was the gift of His love and His life;
    Christ our Lord and our King!
      O what a gift . . .

3   On the hill of Calvary
    the world held its breath;
    for there, for the world to see,
    God gave His Son, His very own Son
    for the love of you and me;
    Christ our Lord and our King!
      O what a gift . . .

4   Early on that morning
    when the world was sleeping,
    back to life came He!
    He conquered death,
      He conquered sin,
    but the victory He gave to you and me!
    Christ our Lord and our King!
      O what a gift . . .

5   Some day with the saints
    we will come before our Father,
    and then we will shout and dance
      and sing.
    For in our midst for our eyes to see
    will be Christ our Lord and our King;
    Christ our Lord and our King!
      O what a gift . . .

527
William Walsham How (1823–97)

1   **O Word of God incarnate,**
    O wisdom from on high,
    O truth unchanged, unchanging,
    O light of our dark sky,
    we praise Thee for the radiance,
    that from the hallowed page,
    a lantern to our footsteps,
    shines on from age to age.

2   The Church from her dear Master
    received the gift divine,
    and still that light she lifteth
    o'er all the earth to shine:
    it is the golden casket
    where gems of truth are stored;
    it is the heaven-drawn picture
    of Christ, the living Word.

3   It floateth like a banner
    before God's host unfurled;
    it shineth like a beacon
    above the darkling world:
    it is the chart and compass
    that o'er life's surging sea,
    mid mists and rocks and quicksands
    still guide, O Christ, to Thee.

4 O make Thy Church, dear Saviour,
  a lamp of burnished gold,
  to bear before the nations
  Thy true light as of old;
  O teach Thy wandering pilgrims
  by this their path to trace,
  till, clouds and darkness ended,
  they see Thee face to face!

528
Robert Grant (1779–1838)

1 **O worship the King,**
  all-glorious above;
  O gratefully sing
  His power and His love;
  our shield and defender,
  the Ancient of Days,
  pavilioned in splendour,
  and girded with praise.

2 O tell of His might,
  O sing of His grace,
  whose robe is the light,
  whose canopy, space;
  His chariots of wrath
  the deep thunder-clouds form,
  and dark is His path
  on the wings of the storm.

3 The earth, with its store
  of wonders untold,
  Almighty, Thy power
  hath founded of old:
  hath stablished it fast
  by a changeless decree,
  and round it hath cast,
  like a mantle, the sea.

4 Thy bountiful care
  what tongue can recite?
  It breathes in the air,
  it shines in the light,
  it streams from the hills,
  it descends to the plain,
  and sweetly distils
  in the dew and the rain.

5 Frail children of dust,
  and feeble as frail,
  in Thee do we trust,
  nor find Thee to fail:
  Thy mercies, how tender,
  how firm to the end,
  our maker, defender,
  Redeemer, and friend!

6 O Lord of all might,
  how boundless Thy love!
  while angels delight
  to hymn Thee above,
  the humbler creation,
  though feeble their lays,
  with true adoration
  shall sing to Thy praise.

529
John Samuel Bewley Monsell (1811–75)

1 **O worship the Lord**
    in the beauty of holiness,
  bow down before Him,
    His glory proclaim;
  with gold of obedience
    and incense of lowliness,
  kneel and adore Him,
    the Lord is His name.

2 Low at His feet
    lay thy burden of carefulness,
high on His heart
    He will bear it for thee,
comfort thy sorrows,
    and answer thy prayerfulness,
guiding thy steps
    as may best for thee be.

3 Fear not to enter His courts
    in the slenderness
of the poor wealth
    thou wouldst reckon as thine:
truth in its beauty
    and love in its tenderness:
these are the offerings
    to lay on His shrine.

4 These, though we bring them
    in trembling and fearfulness,
He will accept
    for the name that is dear;
mornings of joy
    give for evenings of tearfulness,
trust for our trembling,
    and hope for our fear.

5 O worship the Lord
    in the beauty of holiness
bow down before Him,
    His glory proclaim;
with gold of obedience
    and incense of lowliness,
kneel and adore Him,
    the Lord is His name.

530 Shona Sauni
© 1982 Scripture in Song/Integrity Music/
Kingsway's Thankyou Music

O I will sing unto You with joy, O Lord,
for You're the rock of my salvation;
come before You with thanksgiving,
and extol You with a song.

For You're the greatest King above all else,
You hold the depths of the earth
    in Your hand.
O I will sing unto You with joy, O Lord,
for You're the rock of my salvation.

O I will sing unto You . . .

O I will sing unto You with joy, O Lord,
for You're the rock of my salvation.

531 © 1989 Greg Leavers

1 **O Lord, I turn my mind to You**
right away from the things
    that today I've been through.
I'm so sorry, Lord,
    when they've clouded the way
and then have stopped me
    trusting You.

2 O Lord, I turn my eyes to You
and see love in Your eyes
    as You look towards me.
I'm so unworthy, Lord,
    yet You died for me;
all I can say is, 'I love You.'

3 O Lord, please speak Your word to me,
just the message I need,
    out of Your loving heart.
May I grasp Your truth
    that will set my heart free
from the things that hold me back.

4 O Lord, please fill my heart anew;
I surrender my pride
    which stops me trusting You.
For I long that my life may glorify You;
I open up my life to You.

532 Anon
Copyright control

O! O! O! how good is the Lord,
O! O! O! how good is the Lord,
O! O! O! how good is the Lord,
I never will forget
what He has done for me.

1 He gives me salvation,
   how good is the Lord,
He gives me salvation,
   how good is the Lord,
He gives me salvation,
   how good is the Lord,
I never will forget
   what He has done for me.
   O! O! O! . . .

2 He gives me His blessings . . .
   O! O! O! . . .

3 He gives me His Spirit . . .
   O! O! O! . . .

4 He gives me His healing . . .
   O! O! O! . . .

5 He gives me His glory . . .
   O! O! O! . . .

OTHER SUITABLE VERSES MAY BE ADDED
He gives us each other . . .
He gives us His body . . .
He gives us His freedom . . . *etc.*

533 Henry Kirke White (1785–1806) and others

1 **Oft in danger, oft in woe,**
   onward, Christians, onward go;
   bear the toil, maintain the strife,
   strengthened with the bread of life.

2 Onward, Christians, onward go!
   join the war, and face the foe;
   will ye flee in danger's hour?
   know ye not your captain's power?

3 Let your drooping hearts be glad;
   march in heavenly armour clad;
   fight, nor think the battle long,
   victory soon shall tune your song.

4 Let not sorrow dim your eye,
   soon shall every tear be dry;
   let not fears your course impede,
   great your strength, if great your need.

5 Onward then in battle move;
   more than conquerors ye shall prove;
   though opposed by many a foe,
   Christian soldiers, onward go.

534 Dave Bilbrough
© 1988 Kingsway's Thankyou Music

O the joy of Your forgiveness,
slowly sweeping over me;
now in heartfelt adoration,
this praise I'll bring to You, my King;
I'll worship You, my Lord.

535 Graham Kendrick
© 1988 Make Way Music

1 **O what a mystery I see,**
   what marvellous design,
   that God should come as one of us,
   a Son in David's line.
   Flesh of our flesh, of woman born,
   our humanness He owns;
   and for a world of wickedness
   His guiltless blood atones.

2 This perfect Man, incarnate God,
   by selfless sacrifice
   destroyed our sinful history,
   all fallen Adam's curse.
   In Him the curse to blessing turns,
   my barren spirit flowers,
   as over the shattered power of sin
   the cross of Jesus towers.

WOMEN

3 By faith a child of His I stand,
an heir in David's line,
royal descendant by His blood
destined by love's design.

MEN

Fathers of faith, my fathers now!
because in Christ I am,

ALL

and all God's promises in Him
to me are, 'Yes, amen'!

4 No more then as a child of earth
must I my lifetime spend –
His history, His destiny
are mine to apprehend.
O what a Saviour, what a Lord,
O Master, brother, friend!
What miracle has joined me to
this life that never ends!

536

George Bennard (1873–1958)
© 1941 The Rodeheaver Co/
Word Music/CopyCare

1 **On a hill far away**
stood an old rugged cross,
the emblem of suffering and shame;
and I love that old cross
where the dearest and best
for a world of lost sinners was slain.
So I'll cherish the old rugged cross
till my trophies at last I lay down;
I will cling to the old rugged cross
and exchange it some day for a crown.

2 O, the old rugged cross,
so despised by the world,
has a wondrous attraction for me;
for the dear Lamb of God
left His glory above
to bear it to dark Calvary.
So I'll cherish . . .

3 In the old rugged cross,
stained with blood so divine,
a wondrous beauty I see;
for 'twas on that old cross
Jesus suffered and died
to pardon and sanctify me.
So I'll cherish . . .

4 To the old rugged cross
I will ever be true,
its shame and reproach gladly bear;
then He'll call me some day
to my home far away,
when His glory for ever I'll share.
So I'll cherish . . .

537

collected by Ralph Vaughan Williams
(1872–1958)

1 **On Christmas night**
all Christians sing
to hear the news the angels bring:
on Christmas night all Christians sing
to hear the news the angels bring:
news of great joy, news of great mirth,
news of our merciful King's birth.

2 Then why should we on earth
be so sad,
since our Redeemer made us glad,
then why should we on earth be so sad,
since our Redeemer made us glad,
when from our sin He set us free,
all for to gain our liberty?

3 When sin departs before His grace,
then life and health come in its place;
when sin departs before His grace,
then life and health come in its place;
angels and men with joy may sing,
all for to see the new-born King.

4 All out of darkness we have light,
which made the angels sing this night:
all out of darkness we have light,
which made the angels sing this night:
'Glory to God and peace to men,
now and for evermore. Amen.'

538   Charles Coffin (1676–1749)
tr. John Chandler (1806–76)
altered © 1986 Horrobin/Leavers

1 **On Jordan's bank the Baptist's cry**
announces that the Lord is nigh;
come then and listen for he brings
glad tidings from the King of kings.

2 Then cleansed be every heart from sin;
make straight the way for God within;
prepare we in our hearts a home,
where such a mighty guest may come.

3 For You are our salvation, Lord,
our refuge and our great reward;
without Your grace we waste away,
like flowers that wither and decay.

4 To heal the sick stretch out Your hand,
make wholeness flow
    at Your command;
sin's devastation now restore
earth's own true loveliness once more.

5 To Him who left the throne of heaven
to save mankind, all praise be given;
to God the Father, voices raise,
and Holy Spirit, let us praise.

539   Cecil Frances Alexander (1818–95)

1 **Once in royal David's city,**
stood a lowly cattle shed,
where a mother laid her baby,
in a manger for His bed.
Mary was that mother mild,
Jesus Christ her little child.

2 He came down to earth from heaven,
who is God and Lord of all;
and His shelter was a stable,
and His cradle was a stall:
with the poor and mean and lowly
lived on earth our Saviour holy.

3 And through all His wondrous
    childhood
He would honour and obey,
love, and watch the lowly mother,
in whose gentle arms He lay:
Christian children all should be,
kind, obedient, good as He.

4 For He is our childhood's pattern:
day by day like us He grew;
He was little, weak, and helpless,
tears and smiles like us He knew;
and He feels for all our sadness,
and He shares in all our gladness.

5 And our eyes at last shall see Him,
through His own redeeming love;
for that child, so dear and gentle,
is our Lord in heaven above;
and He leads His children on
to the place where He is gone.

6 Not in that poor lowly stable,
with the oxen standing by,
we shall see Him, but in heaven,
set at God's right hand on high;
there His children gather round,
bright like stars, with glory crowned.

540   J Wilbur Chapman (1859–1918)

1 **One day when heaven was filled**
    with His praises,
one day when sin
    was as black as could be,
Jesus came forth to be born of a virgin,
dwelt amongst men, my example is He!

Living, He loved me;
dying, He saved me;
buried, He carried my sins far away,
rising, He justified freely for ever:
one day He's coming: O glorious day.

2 One day they led Him
    up Calvary's mountain,
one day they nailed Him
    to die on the tree;
suffering anguish,
    despised and rejected;
bearing our sins, my Redeemer is He!
    Living, He loved me . . .

3 One day they left Him alone
    in the garden,
one day He rested, from suffering free;
angels came down o'er His tomb
    to keep vigil;
hope of the hopeless, my Saviour is He!
    Living, He loved me . . .

4 One day the grave could conceal Him
    no longer,
one day the stone rolled away
    from the door;
Then He arose,
    over death He had conquered;
now is ascended, my Lord evermore!
    Living, He loved me . . .

5 One day the trumpet will sound
    for His coming,
one day the skies with His glory
    will shine;
wonderful day,
    my beloved ones bringing;
glorious Saviour, this Jesus is mine!
    Living, He loved me . . .

541 Graham Kendrick
© 1981 Kingsway's Thankyou Music

1 **One shall tell another,**
and he shall tell his friends,
husbands, wives and children
shall come following on.
From house to house in families
shall more be gathered in;
and lights will shine in every street,
so warm and welcoming.
    Come on in
    and taste the new wine,
    the wine of the kingdom,
    the wine of the kingdom of God:
    here is healing and forgiveness,
    the wine of the kingdom,
    the wine of the kingdom of God.

2 Compassion of the Father
is ready now to flow;
through acts of love and mercy
we must let it show.
He turns now from His anger
to show a smiling face,
and longs
    that men should stand beneath
the fountain of His grace.
    Come on in . . .

3 He longs to do much more than
our faith has yet allowed,
to thrill us and surprise us
with His sovereign power.
Where darkness has been darkest,
the brightest light will shine;
His invitation comes to us –
it's yours and it is mine.
    Come on in . . .

542 John Newton (1725–1807)

1 **One there is, above all others,**
well deserves the name of friend;
His is love beyond a brother's,
costly, free, and knows no end:
they who once His kindness prove,
find it everlasting love.

2 Which of all our friends, to save us,
could, or would, have shed His blood?
Christ, the Saviour, died to have us
reconciled in Him to God:
this was boundless love indeed!
Jesus is a friend in need.

3 When He lived on earth abasèd,
'Friend of sinners' was His name;
now, above all glory raisèd,
He rejoices in the same:
still He calls them brethren, friends,
and to all their wants attends.

4 O for grace our hearts to soften!
teach us, Lord, at length to love.
We, alas! forget too often
what a friend we have above:
but when home our souls are brought,
we will love Thee as we ought.

543 Sabine Baring-Gould (1834–1924)

1 **Onward Christian soldiers,
marching as to war,**
with the cross of Jesus going on before.
Christ the royal Master
leads against the foe;
forward into battle,
see, His banners go!
*Onward, Christian soldiers,
marching as to war,
with the cross of Jesus going on before.*

2 At the name of Jesus
Satan's legions flee;
on then, Christian soldiers,
on to victory.
Hell's foundations quiver
at the shout of praise;
brothers, lift your voices,
loud your anthems raise.
Onward, Christian soldiers . . .

3 Like a mighty army
moves the Church of God;
brothers, we are treading
where the saints have trod;
we are not divided, all one body we,
one in hope and calling, one in charity.
Onward, Christian soldiers . . .

4 Crowns and thrones may perish,
kingdoms rise and wane,
but the Church of Jesus
constant will remain;
gates of hell can never
'gainst that Church prevail;
We have Christ's own promise,
and that cannot fail.
Onward, Christian soldiers . . .

5 Onward, then, ye people,
join our happy throng,
blend with ours your voices
in the triumph-song;
glory, praise and honour
unto Christ the King;
This through countless ages
men and angels sing.
Onward, Christian soldiers . . .

544 Clara Scott (1841–97)

1 **Open my eyes that I may see**
glimpses of truth Thou hast for me;
place in my hands the wonderful key
that shall unclasp and set me free.
*Silently now I wait for Thee,
ready, my God, Thy will to see;
open my eyes, illumine me,
Spirit divine!*

2 Open my ears that I may hear
voices of truth Thou sendest clear;
and while the wave-notes
fall on my ear,
everything false will disappear.
Silently now I wait . . .

3 Open my mouth and let me bear
tidings of mercy everywhere;
open my heart and let me prepare
love with Thy children thus to share.
Silently now I wait . . .

4 Open my mind, that I may read
more of Thy love in word and deed:
what shall I fear
while yet Thou dost lead?
Only for light from Thee I plead.
Silently now I wait . . .

545 Robert Cull
© 1976 Maranatha! Music/CopyCare

Open our eyes, Lord,
we want to see Jesus –
to reach out and touch Him
and say that we love Him.
Open our ears, Lord,
and help us to listen:
O open our eyes, Lord,
we want to see Jesus!

546 From Psalm 119
C C Kerr
© B M Kerr

Open Thou mine eyes,
that I may behold
wondrous, wondrous things
out of Thy law.

547 Carl Tuttle
© 1985 Mercy/Vineyard Publishing/
CopyCare

Open your eyes,
see the glory of the King;
lift up your voice,
and His praises sing!
I love You, Lord,
I will proclaim:
alleluia!
I bless Your name.

548 Henriette Auber (1773–1862)

1 **Our blest Redeemer,
ere He breathed**
His tender last farewell,
a guide, a Comforter bequeathed,
with us to dwell.

2 He came in semblance of a dove,
with sheltering wings outspread,
the holy balm of peace and love
on earth to shed.

3 He came in tongues of living flame,
to teach, convince, subdue;
all-powerful as the wind He came,
as viewless too.

4 He comes sweet influence to impart,
a gracious, willing guest,
where He can find one humble heart
wherein to rest.

5 And His that gentle voice we hear,
soft as the breath of even,
that checks each fault,
that calms each fear,
and speaks of heaven.

6 And every virtue we possess,
and every victory won,
and every thought of holiness,
are His alone.

7 Spirit of purity and grace,
our weakness, pitying, see;
O make our hearts Thy dwelling-place,
and worthier Thee.

549 © Roland Meredith

1 **Our eyes have seen the glory**
of our Saviour, Christ the Lord;
He is seated at His Father's side
in love and full accord;
from there upon the sons of men
His Spirit is out-poured,
all hail, ascended King!

Glory, glory, hallelujah,
glory, glory, hallelujah,
glory, glory, hallelujah,
all hail, ascended King!

2 He came to earth at Christmas
and was made a man like us;
He taught, He healed, He suffered –
and they nailed Him to the cross;
He rose again on Easter Day –
our Lord victorious,
all hail, ascended King!
    Glory, glory . . .

3 The good news of His kingdom
must be preached to every shore,
the news of peace and pardon,
and the end of strife and war;
the secret of His kingdom
is to serve Him evermore,
all hail, ascended King!
    Glory, glory . . .

4 His kingdom is a family
of men of every race,
they live their lives in harmony,
enabled by His grace;
they follow His example
till they see Him face to face,
all hail, ascended King!
    Glory, glory . . .

550 From *The Alternative Service Book 1980*
© 1980 The Archbishops' Council

Our Father in heaven,
hallowed be Your name,
Your kingdom come,
Your will be done,
on earth as in heaven.
Give us today our daily bread,
forgive us our sins,
as we forgive those who sin against us.
Lead us not into temptation,
but deliver us from evil.

For the kingdom, the power,
and the glory are Yours,
now and for ever, amen.
For the kingdom, the power,
and the glory are Yours,
now and for ever, amen.

551 William True Sleeper (1840–1920)

1 **Out of my bondage, sorrow,**
   and night,
   Jesus, I come: Jesus, I come;
   into Your freedom, gladness, and light,
   Jesus, I come to You.
   Out of my sickness into Your health,
   out of my want and into Your wealth,
   out of my sin and into Yourself,
   Jesus, I come to You.

2 Out of my shameful failure and loss,
   Jesus, I come: Jesus, I come;
   into the glorious gain of Your cross,
   Jesus, I come to You.
   Out of earth's sorrows into Your balm,
   out of life's storm and into Your calm,
   out of distress to jubilant psalm,
   Jesus, I come to You.

3 Out of unrest and arrogant pride,
   Jesus, I come: Jesus, I come;
   into Your blessèd will to abide,
   Jesus, I come to You.
   Out of myself to dwell in Your love,
   out of despair into joy from above,
   upward for ever on wings like a dove,
   Jesus, I come to You.

4 Out of the fear and dread of the tomb,
   Jesus, I come: Jesus, I come;
   into the joy and light of Your home,
   Jesus, I come to You.
   Out of the depths of ruin untold,
   into the peace of Your sheltering fold,
   ever Your glorious face to behold,
   Jesus, I come to You.

552

1 **Our Father who is in heaven,**
hallowed be Your name,
Your Kingdom come,
Your will be done,
hallowed be Your name.

2 On earth as it is in heaven,
hallowed be Your name,
give us this day our daily bread,
hallowed be Your name.

3 Forgive us all our trespasses,
hallowed be Your name,
as we forgive those
who trespass against us,
hallowed be Your name.

4 And lead us not into temptation,
hallowed be Your name,
but deliver us from all that is evil,
hallowed be Your name.

5 For Yours is the kingdom,
the power and the glory,
hallowed be Your name,
for ever and for ever,
hallowed be Your name.

6 Amen, amen, it shall be so,
hallowed be Your name,
amen, amen, it shall be so,
hallowed be Your name.

553
Graham Kendrick

1 **Peace I give to you,**
I give to you My peace;
peace I give to you,
I give to you My peace.
Let it flow to one another,
let it flow, let it flow;
let it flow to one another,
let it flow, let it flow.

2 Love I give to you,
I give to you My love;
love I give to you,
I give to you My love.
Let it flow . . .

3 Hope I give to you,
I give to you My hope;
hope I give to you,
I give to you My hope.
Let it flow . . .

4 Joy I give to you, I give to you My joy;
joy I give to you, I give to you My joy.
Let it flow . . .

554
Anon

Peace is flowing like a river,
flowing out through you and me,
spreading out into the desert,
setting all the captives free,
setting all the captives free.

Love is flowing . . .
Joy is flowing . . .
Faith is flowing . . .
Hope is flowing . . . *etc.*

555
Edward Henry Bickersteth (1825–1906)

1 **Peace, perfect peace,**
in this dark world of sin?
The blood of Jesus
whispers peace within.

2 Peace, perfect peace,
by thronging duties pressed?
To do the will of Jesus, this is rest.

3 Peace, perfect peace,
with sorrows surging round?
In Jesus' presence
nought but calm is found.

4 Peace, perfect peace,
   with loved ones far away?
   In Jesus' keeping we are safe, and they.

5 Peace, perfect peace,
   our future all unknown?
   Jesus we know,
   and He is on the throne.

6 Peace, perfect peace,
   death shadowing us and ours?
   Jesus has vanquished death
   and all its powers.

7 It is enough: earth's struggles
   soon shall cease,
   and Jesus call us
   to heaven's perfect peace.

praise Him on the loud cymbals,
praise Him on the loud cymbals;
let everything that has breath
   praise the Lord!

Hallelujah, praise the Lord;
hallelujah, praise the Lord:
let everything that has breath
   praise the Lord!

Hallelujah, praise the Lord;
hallelujah, praise the Lord:
let everything that has breath
   praise the Lord!

556 Graham Kendrick
© 1988 Make Way Music

Peace to you,
we bless you now
in the name of the Lord,
Peace to you.
We bless you now
in the name of the Prince of peace.
Peace to you, peace to you,
peace to you, peace to you.

557 Thomas Ken (1637–1710)

**Praise God from whom
all blessings flow;**
praise Him all creatures here below,
praise Him above, ye heavenly host;
praise Father, Son, and Holy Ghost.

558 John Kennett
© 1981 Kingsway's Thankyou Music

**Praise Him on the trumpet,
the psaltery and harp;**
praise Him on the timbrel and the dance;
praise Him with stringed instruments too;

559 Frances van Alstyne (1820–1915)
(Fanny J Crosby)

1 **Praise Him, praise Him!
   Jesus, our blessèd Redeemer!**
   Sing, O earth –
      His wonderful love proclaim!
   Hail Him! hail Him!
      highest archangels in glory;
   strength and honour
      give to his holy name!
   Like a shepherd,
      Jesus will guard His children,
   in His arms He carries them
      all day long.
   *Praise Him, praise Him!
   tell of His excellent greatness;
   Praise Him, praise Him
   ever in joyful song!*

2 Praise Him, praise Him!
   Jesus, our blessèd Redeemer!
   for our sins He suffered,
      and bled, and died;
   He – our rock,
      our hope of eternal salvation,

hail Him, hail Him! Jesus the crucified!
Sound His praises –
     Jesus who bore our sorrows,
love unbounded, wonderful,
     deep and strong.
     Praise Him . . .

3   Praise Him, praise Him!
       Jesus, our blessèd Redeemer!
    heavenly portals,
       loud with hosannas ring!
    Jesus, Saviour,
       reigneth for ever and ever:
    crown Him, crown Him!
       Prophet, and Priest, and King!
    Christ is coming,
       over the world victorious,
    power and glory unto the Lord belong.
       Praise Him . . .

3   Father-like He tends and spares us;
    well our feeble frame He knows;
    in His hands He gently bears us,
    rescues us from all our foes.
       Praise Him! Praise Him!
       Praise Him! Praise Him!
    Widely as His mercy flows.

4   Angels, help us to adore Him;
    ye behold Him face to face;
    sun and moon, bow down before Him;
    dwellers all in time and space.
       Praise Him! Praise Him!
       Praise Him! Praise Him!
    Praise with us the God of grace.

561 From Psalm 150
© 1980 Bible Society

Praise the Lord!
Praise Him in His temple!
Praise Him for the mighty things
     He has done!
Praise the Lord!
Praise Him for His greatness!
Praise Him with trumpets, harps and lyres.
All living creatures, praise! O praise,
O praise, praise the Lord!

560 Henry Francis Lyte (1793–1847)

1   **Praise, my soul,
       the King of heaven;**
    to His feet thy tribute bring;
    ransomed, healed, restored, forgiven,
    who like thee His praise should sing?
       Praise Him! Praise Him!
       Praise Him! Praise Him!
    Praise the everlasting King.

2   Praise Him for His grace and favour
    to our fathers, in distress;
    praise Him still the same for ever,
    slow to chide, and swift to bless.
       Praise Him! Praise Him!
       Praise Him! Praise Him!
    Glorious in His faithfulness.

562 David Hadden
© 1983 Restoration Music Ltd/
Sovereign Music UK

Praise the Lord,
praise God in His sanctuary,
praise Him in His mighty heavens;
praise Him for His greatness,
and praise Him for His power.
Praise the Lord . . .

1 Praise Him
    with the sound of trumpets,
 praise Him with the harp and lyre,
 praise Him with the tambourine
    and with dancing;
 let everything that has breath
    praise the Lord.
 Praise the Lord,
 praise God in His sanctuary,
 praise Him in His mighty heavens;
 praise Him for His greatness,
 and praise Him for His power.
 Praise the Lord . . .

2 Praise Him with the clash of cymbals,
 praise Him with the strings and flute,
 praise Him with the tambourine
    and with dancing;
 let everything that has breath
    praise the Lord.
 Praise the Lord . . .

5 O generous love! that He, who smote
 in man for man the foe,
 the double agony in man
 for man should undergo.

6 And in the garden secretly,
 and on the cross on high,
 should teach His brethren, and inspire
 to suffer and to die.

7 Praise to the Holiest in the height
 and in the depth be praise:
 in all His words most wonderful;
 most sure in all His ways.

563 John Henry Newman (1801–90)

1 **Praise to the Holiest in the height,**
 and in the depth be praise;
 in all His words most wonderful;
 most sure in all His ways.

2 O loving wisdom of our God!
 when all was sin and shame,
 a second Adam to the fight,
 and to the rescue came.

3 O wisest love! that flesh and blood
 which did in Adam fail,
 should strive afresh against the foe,
 should strive and should prevail.

4 And that a higher gift than grace
 should flesh and blood refine,
 God's presence, and His very self
 and essence all-divine.

564 Joachim Neander (1650–80)
tr. Catherine Winkworth (1829–78)

1 **Praise to the Lord, the Almighty,**
    the King of creation;
 O my soul, praise Him,
    for He is thy health and salvation;
 all ye who hear,
 brothers and sisters, draw near,
 praise Him in glad adoration.

2 Praise to the Lord, who o'er all things
    so wondrously reigneth,
 shelters thee under His wings,
    yea, so gently sustaineth:
 hast thou not seen?
 all that is needful hath been
 granted in what He ordaineth.

3 Praise to the Lord, who doth prosper
    thy work, and defend thee!
 surely His goodness and mercy
    here daily attend thee.
 Ponder anew
 what the Almighty can do,
 who with His love doth befriend thee.

4 Praise to the Lord!
O let all that is in me adore Him!
All that hath life and breath come now
with praises before Him!
Let the amen
sound from His people again:
gladly for aye we adore Him.

566 Roy Hicks
© 1979 Latter Rain Music/
EMI Christian Music Publishing/CopyCare

Praise the name of Jesus,
praise the name of Jesus,
He's my rock, He's my fortress,
He's my deliverer,
in Him will I trust;
praise the name of Jesus.

565 Nettie Rose
© 1977 Kingsway's Thankyou Music

1 **Praise You, Lord,**
for the wonder of Your healing;
praise You, Lord,
for Your love so freely given;
out-pouring, anointing,
flowing in to heal our wounds –
praise You, Lord,
for Your love for me.

2 Praise You, Lord,
for Your gift of liberation;
praise You, Lord,
You have set the captives free;
the chains that bind are broken
by the sharpness of Your sword –
praise You, Lord,
You gave Your life for me.

3 Praise You, Lord,
You have borne the depths of sorrow;
praise You, Lord,
for Your anguish on the tree;
the nails that tore Your body
and the pain that tore Your soul –
praise You, Lord,
Your tears, they fell for me.

4 Praise You, Lord,
You have turned our thorns to roses;
glory, Lord, as they bloom
upon Your brow;
the path of pain is hallowed,
for Your love has made it sweet –
praise You, Lord,
and may I love You now.

567 James Montgomery (1771–1854)

1 **Prayer is the soul's sincere desire,**
uttered or unexpressed,
the motion of a hidden fire
that trembles in the breast.

2 Prayer is the burden of a sigh,
the falling of a tear,
the upward glancing of an eye,
when none but God is near.

3 Prayer is the simplest form of speech
that infant lips can try;
prayer the sublimest strains that reach
the majesty on high.

4 Prayer is the contrite sinner's voice,
returning from his ways;
while angels in their songs rejoice,
and cry, 'Behold, he prays!'

5 Prayer is the Christian's vital breath,
the Christian's native air,
his watchword at the gates of death;
he enters heaven with prayer.

6 No prayer is made on earth alone;
the Holy Spirit pleads;
and Jesus on the eternal throne,
for sinners intercedes.

7 O Thou by whom we come to God,
the life, the truth, the way,
the path of prayer Thyself hast trod;
Lord, teach us how to pray!

568
Mike Kerry
© 1984 Kingsway's Thankyou Music

1 **Reconciled, I'm reconciled,**
I'm reconciled to God for ever;
know He took away my sin,
I know His love will leave me never.
Reconciled, I am His child,
I know it was on me He smiled;
I'm reconciled, I'm reconciled to God,
hallelujah!

2 I'm justified, I'm justified,
it's just as if I'd never sinned;
and once I knew such guilty fear,
but now I know His peace within.
Justified, I'm justified,
it's all because my Jesus died;
I'm justified, I'm justified by God,
hallelujah!

3 I'll magnify, I'll magnify,
I'll magnify His name for ever;
wear the robe of righteousness
and bless the name of Jesus, Saviour;
magnify the One who died,
the One who reigns for me on high;
I'll magnify, I'll magnify my God.

569
Bill Harmon
© 1958, 1986, Gospel Publishing House/
Lorenz Publishing Co/CopyCare

**Reach out and touch the Lord
as He goes by;**
you'll find He's not too busy
to hear your heart's cry.
He's passing by this moment,
your needs to supply;
reach out and touch the Lord
as He goes by.

570
Chris Bowater
© 1985 Sovereign Lifestyle Music

**Reign in me, sovereign Lord,
reign in me,**
reign in me, sovereign Lord, reign in me.
Captivate my heart,
let Your kingdom come,
establish there Your throne,
let Your will be done!

Reign in me, sovereign Lord, reign in me.
Reign in me, sovereign Lord, reign in me.

571
Dave Bilbrough
© 1984 Kingsway's Thankyou Music

Reigning in all splendour –
victorious love;
Christ Jesus the Saviour,
transcendent above.
All earthly dominions
and kingdoms shall fall,
for His name is Jesus
and He is the Lord.
He is Lord, He is Lord,
He is Lord, He is Lord.

572
Graham Kendrick
© 1983 Kingsway's Thankyou Music

*Rejoice, rejoice! Christ is in you –
the hope of glory in our hearts.
He lives, He lives!
His breath is in you.
Arise! A mighty army we arise!*

1 Now is the time for us
to march upon the land –
into our hands
He will give the ground we claim;
He rides in majesty
to lead us into victory,
the world shall see that Christ is Lord.
Rejoice, rejoice . . .

2 God is at work in us,
    His purpose to perform –
building a kingdom
    of power not of words;
where things impossible
    by faith shall be made possible:
let's give the glory to Him now.
    Rejoice, rejoice . . .

3 Though we are weak,
    His grace is everything we need –
we're made of clay,
    but this treasure is within;
He turns our weaknesses
    into His opportunities,
so that the glory goes to Him.
    Rejoice, rejoice . . .
    We arise! We arise! We arise!

4 Rejoice and be glad!
    now the pardon is free;
the just for the unjust
    has died on the tree.
    Sound His praises . . .

5 Rejoice and be glad!
    for the Lamb that was slain
o'er death is triumphant,
    and now lives again.
    Sound His praises . . .

6 Rejoice and be glad!
    for our King is on high;
He pleads now for us
    on His throne in the sky.
    Sound His praises . . .

7 Rejoice and be glad!
    for He's coming again;
He'll come in great glory,
    the Lamb that was slain.
    Sound His praises . . .

573
Horatius Bonar (1808–89)

1 **Rejoice and be glad!**
    the Redeemer has come:
go, look on His cradle,
    His cross, and His tomb.
    Sound His praises, tell the story
    of Him who was slain;
    sound His praises, tell with gladness
    He now lives again.

2 Rejoice and be glad!
    it is sunshine at last;
the clouds have departed,
    the shadows are past.
    Sound His praises . . .

3 Rejoice and be glad!
    for the blood has been shed;
redemption is finished,
    the price has been paid.
    Sound His praises . . .

574
Chris Bowater
© 1986 Sovereign Lifestyle Music

Rejoice, rejoice, rejoice,
rejoice, rejoice, rejoice;
my soul rejoices in the Lord.
Rejoice . . .

My soul magnifies the Lord,
and my spirit rejoices in God my Saviour;
my soul magnifies the Lord,
and my spirit rejoices in my God.
Rejoice . . .

575
Charles Wesley (1707–88)

1 **Rejoice, the Lord is King!**
    your Lord and King adore;
mortals, give thanks and sing,
    and triumph evermore:

Lift up your heart, lift up your voice;
rejoice, again I say, rejoice.

2 Jesus the Saviour reigns,
the God of truth and love;
when He had purged our stains,
He took His seat above:
Lift up your heart ...

3 His kingdom cannot fail,
He rules o'er earth and heaven;
the keys of death and hell
are to our Jesus given:
Lift up your heart ...

4 He sits at God's right hand,
till all His foes submit,
and bow to His command,
and fall beneath His feet:
Lift up your heart ...

5 Rejoice in glorious hope;
Jesus the Judge shall come,
and take His servants up
to their eternal home:
We soon shall hear the archangel's voice;
the trump of God shall sound, rejoice!

576 Moira Austin
© 1986 M C and M M Austin

1 **Rejoice, the Lord is risen!**
He is the King of glory;
mighty Redeemer,
He has made us His own:
rejoice, the Lord is risen!
opened, the gate of heaven:
bow down before Him
for He comes to claim His own!
Glory to the King of kings!
Glory to the Lord of lords!
Jesus, we proclaim
that You are Lord enthroned in majesty!
Glory to the King of kings!
Glory to the Lord of lords!
Jesus, You are reigning
now on high for evermore!

2 Rejoice, the Lord is risen!
We are His holy nation,
ransomed, forgiven,
washed in His precious blood:
rejoice, the Lord is risen!
Worthy His new creation,
perfect and spotless,
as the Lamb upon the throne.
Glory to the King ...

3 Rejoice, the Lord is risen!
Blessing and honour give Him;
wisdom, authority,
belong to His name:
rejoice, the Lord is risen!
Angels and saints adore Him,
worship and praise Him,
singing, 'Jesus Christ is Lord!'
Glory to the King ...

577 From Philippians 4
Copyright control

Rejoice in the Lord always,
and again I say rejoice!
Rejoice in the Lord always,
and again I say rejoice!
Rejoice, rejoice, and again I say rejoice!
Rejoice, rejoice, and again I say rejoice!

578 Albert Midlane (1825–1909)

1 **Revive Thy work, O Lord,**
Thy mighty arm make bare;
speak with the voice
that wakes the dead
and make Thy people hear.

2 Revive Thy work, O Lord,
disturb this sleep of death;
quicken the smouldering embers now
by Thine almighty breath.

3 Revive Thy work, O Lord,
create soul-thirst for Thee;
and hungering for the bread of life
O may our spirits be!

4 Revive Thy work, O Lord,
exalt Thy precious name;
and, by the Holy Ghost, our love
for Thee and Thine inflame.

5 Revive Thy work, O Lord,
give pentecostal showers;
the glory shall be all Thine own,
the blessing, Lord, be ours.

579
Graham Kendrick and Chris Rolinson
© 1981 Kingsway's Thankyou Music

1 **Restore, O Lord,**
the honour of Your name!
In works of sovereign power
come shake the earth again,
that men may see,
and come with reverent fear
to the living God,
whose kingdom shall outlast the years.

2 Restore, O Lord,
in all the earth Your fame,
and in our time revive
the Church that bears Your name,
and in Your anger,
Lord, remember mercy,
O living God,
whose mercy shall outlast the years.

3 Bend us, O Lord,
where we are hard and cold,
in Your refiner's fire;
come purify the gold:
though suffering comes,
and evil crouches near,
still our living God
is reigning, He is reigning here.

580
Henry Hart Milman (1791–1868)

1 **Ride on, ride on in majesty!**
Hark, all the tribes, 'Hosanna!' cry,
O Saviour meek, pursue Your road
with palms and scattered garments
    strowed.

2 Ride on, ride on in majesty!
in lowly pomp ride on to die:
O Christ, Your triumphs now begin
o'er captive death and conquered sin.

3 Ride on, ride on in majesty!
The angel armies of the sky
look down with sad and wondering
    eyes
to see the approaching sacrifice.

4 Ride on, ride on in majesty!
Your last and fiercest strife is nigh;
the Father on His sapphire throne
awaits His own anointed Son.

5 Ride on, ride on in majesty!
in lowly pomp ride on to die;
bow Your meek head to mortal pain,
then take, O God, Your power,
    and reign.

581
Dougie Brown
© 1980 Kingsway's Thankyou Music

1 **River, wash over me,**
cleanse me and make me new;
bathe me, refresh me
    and fill me anew –
river, wash over me.

2 Spirit, watch over me,
lead me to Jesus' feet;
cause me to worship and fill me anew –
Spirit, watch over me.

3 Jesus, rule over me,
  reign over all my heart;
  teach me to praise You
   and fill me anew –
  Jesus, rule over me.

582 Augustus Montague Toplady (1740–78)

1 **Rock of ages, cleft for me,**
  let me hide myself in Thee;
  let the water and the blood,
  from Thy riven side which flowed,
  be of sin the double cure,
  cleanse me from its guilt and power.

2 Not the labour of my hands
  can fulfil Thy law's demands;
  could my zeal no respite know,
  could my tears for ever flow,
  all for sin could not atone;
  Thou must save, and Thou alone.

3 Nothing in my hand I bring,
  simply to Thy cross I cling;
  naked, come to Thee for dress,
  helpless, look to Thee for grace;
  foul, I to the fountain fly;
  wash me, Saviour, or I die.

4 While I draw this fleeting breath,
  when mine eyes shall close in death,
  when I soar through tracts unknown,
  see Thee on Thy judgement throne;
  Rock of ages, cleft for me,
  let me hide myself in Thee.

583 From Psalm 91
  © Timothy Dudley-Smith

1 **Safe in the shadow of the Lord**
  beneath His hand and power,
   I trust in Him,
   I trust in Him,
  my fortress and my tower.

2 My hope is set on God alone
  though Satan spreads his snare;
   I trust in Him,
   I trust in Him,
  to keep me in His care.

3 From fears and phantoms of the night,
  from foes about my way,
   I trust in Him,
   I trust in Him,
  by darkness as by day.

4 His holy angels keep my feet
  secure from every stone;
   I trust in Him,
   I trust in Him,
  and unafraid go on.

5 Strong in the everlasting name,
  and in my Father's care,
   I trust in Him,
   I trust in Him,
  who hears and answers prayer.

6 Safe in the shadow of the Lord,
  possessed by love divine,
   I trust in Him,
   I trust in Him,
  and meet His love with mine.

584 John Ellerton (1826–93)

1 **Saviour, again to Thy dear name**
   we raise
  with one accord
   our parting hymn of praise;
  we stand to bless Thee
   ere our worship cease,
  then, lowly kneeling,
   wait Thy word of peace.

2 Grant us Thy peace
  upon our homeward way;
with Thee began,
  with Thee shall end the day;
guard Thou the lips from sin,
  the hearts from shame,
that in this house
  have called upon Thy name.

3 Grant us Thy peace, Lord,
  through the coming night;
turn Thou for us its darkness into light;
from harm and danger
  keep Thy children free,
for dark and light
  are both alike to Thee.

4 Grant us Thy peace
  throughout our earthly life,
our balm in sorrow,
  and our stay in strife;
then, when Thy voice shall bid
  our conflict cease,
call us, O Lord, to Thine eternal peace.

585 © 1986 Greg Leavers

Saviour of the world,
thank You for dying on the cross.
All praise to You our risen Lord,
hallelujah! Jesus.

1 In the garden of Gethsemane
  Jesus knelt and prayed;
for He knew the time was near
  when He would be betrayed.
God gave Him the strength to cope
  with all that people did to hurt
  Him;
soldiers laughed and forced a crown of
  thorns upon His head.
Saviour of the world . . .

2 On a cross outside the city
  they nailed Jesus high;
innocent, but still He suffered
  as they watched Him die.
Nothing that the soldiers did could
  make Him lose control, for Jesus
knew the time to die, then,
  'It is finished!' was His cry.
Saviour of the world . . .

3 Three days later by God's power
  He rose up from the dead,
for the tomb could not hold Jesus:
  it was as He'd said;
victor over sin and death,
  He conquered Satan's power;
so let us
celebrate that Jesus
  is alive for evermore.
Saviour of the world . . .

586 Sylvanus Dryden Phelps (1816–95)

1 **Saviour, Thy dying love**
  Thou gavest me,
nor should I aught withhold,
  my Lord, from Thee;
in love my soul would bow,
my heart fulfil its vow,
some offering bring Thee now,
  something for Thee.

2 At the blest mercy-seat
  pleading for me,
my feeble faith looks up,
  Jesus, to Thee:
help me the cross to bear,
Thy wondrous love declare,
some song to raise, or prayer –
  something for Thee.

3 Give me a faithful heart,
      likeness to Thee,
   that each departing day
   henceforth may see
   some work of love begun,
   some deed of kindness done,
   some wanderer sought and won –
   something for Thee.

4 All that I am and have,
      Thy gifts so free,
   in joy, in grief, through life,
      O Lord, for Thee.
   And when Thy face I see,
   my ransomed soul shall be,
   through all eternity,
   something for Thee.

587 J Edwin Orr (1912–87)
© 1936 Maranatha! Music/CopyCare

1 **Search me, O God,**
      and know my heart today;
   try me, O Lord,
      and know my thoughts I pray:
   see if there be some wicked way in me,
   cleanse me from every sin
      and set me free.

2 I praise Thee, Lord,
      for cleansing me from sin;
   fulfil Thy word,
      and make me pure within;
   fill me with fire,
      where once I burned with shame,
   grant my desire to magnify Thy name.

3 Lord, take my life,
      and make it wholly Thine;
   fill my poor heart
      with Thy great love divine;
   take all my will, my passion,
      self and pride;
   I now surrender – Lord, in me abide.

4 O Holy Ghost,
      revival comes from Thee;
   send a revival – start the work in me:
   Thy word declares
      Thou wilt supply our need;
   for blessing now, O Lord,
      I humbly plead.

588 Edward Caswall (1814–78)

1 **See, amid the winter's snow,**
   born for us on earth below,
   see, the Lamb of God appears,
   promised from eternal years.
      Hail, thou ever-blessèd morn!
      Hail, redemption's happy dawn!
      Sing through all Jerusalem,
      Christ is born in Bethlehem!

2 Lo, within a manger lies
   He who built the starry skies,
   He who, throned in height sublime,
   sits amid the cherubim.
      Hail, thou ever-blessèd morn . . .

3 Say, ye holy shepherds, say,
   what your joyful news today;
   wherefore have ye left your sheep
   on the lonely mountain steep?
      Hail, thou ever-blessèd morn . . .

4 As we watched at dead of night,
   Lo, we saw a wondrous light:
   angels singing, 'Peace on earth!'
   told us of the Saviour's birth.
      Hail, thou ever-blessèd morn . . .

5 Sacred infant, all divine,
   what a tender love was Thine,
   thus to come from highest bliss
   down to such a world as this!
      Hail, thou ever-blessèd morn . . .

6 Teach, O teach us, holy child,
by Thy face so meek and mild,
teach us to resemble Thee
in Thy sweet humility.
Hail, thou ever-blessèd morn . . .

589 Michael Perry (1942–96)
© Mrs B Perry/Jubilate Hymns

1 **See Him lying on a bed of straw:**
a draughty stable with an open door;
Mary cradling the babe she bore –
the Prince of glory is His name.
O now carry me to Bethlehem
to see the Lord appear to men –
just as poor as was the stable then,
the Prince of glory when He came.

2 Star of silver, sweep across the skies,
show where Jesus in the manger lies;
shepherds, swiftly from your stupor rise
to see the Saviour of the world!
O now carry . . .

3 Angels, sing the song that you began,
bring God's glory to the heart of man;
sing that Bethl'em's little baby can
be salvation to the soul.
O now carry . . .

4 Mine are riches, from Your poverty,
from Your innocence, eternity;
mine forgiveness by Your death for me,
child of sorrow for my joy.
O now carry . . .

590 Karen Lafferty
© 1972 Maranatha! Music/CopyCare

1 **Seek ye first the kingdom of God,**
and His righteousness,
and all these things
shall be added unto you.
Allelu, alleluia.
Seek ye first . . .

2 Man shall not live by bread alone,
but by every word
that proceeds from the mouth of God.
Allelu, alleluia.
Man shall not . . .

3 Ask and it shall be given unto you,
seek and ye shall find;
knock and the door shall be opened
up to you.
Allelu, alleluia.
Ask and it shall . . .

591 Joan Parsons
© 1978 Kingsway's Thankyou Music

1 **Seek ye the Lord, all ye people,**
turn to Him while He is near;
let the wicked forsake his own way,
and call on Him while He may hear.

2 Ho, everyone who is thirsty,
come to the waters of life;
come and drink of the milk
and the wine,
come without money and price.

And there is peace like a river,
and glory divine,
if you'll come to the water,
if you'll taste of His wine.
There is love ever flowing,
and joy ever full;
and there's life everlasting
for us all.

592 © 1987 Ruth Hooke

1 **See Him on the cross of shame**
dying for me,
bearing all my guilt and pain,
dying for me.
And how I love You,
Jesus my Redeemer;
You gave Your life for me, O Lord,
now I give my life to You.

Jesus lives, Jesus lives,
Jesus lives in me:
I will praise Your name.

2 They laid Him in a garden tomb,
and sealed it with a stone.
Mary wept her tears of grief –
her precious Lord had gone:
'And how I love You,
Jesus my Redeemer';
then she looked –
    the stone was rolled away –
He had triumphed over death.
    Jesus lives . . .

593 Henry Elliott Fox (1841–1926)
Copyright control

1 **Send forth the gospel! Let it run**
southward and northward,
    east and west:
tell all the earth Christ died and lives,
He offers pardon, life, and rest.

2 Send forth Your gospel, mighty Lord!
Out of the chaos bring to birth
Your own creation's promised hope;
the better days of heaven on earth.

3 Send forth Your gospel, gracious Lord!
Yours was the blood for sinners shed;
Your voice still pleads in human hearts;
to You may all Your sheep be led.

4 Send forth Your gospel, holy Lord!
Kindle in us love's sacred flame;
love giving all and grudging naught
for Jesus' sake, in Jesus' name.

5 Send forth the gospel! Tell it out!
Go, brothers, at the Master's call;
prepare His way, who comes to reign
the King of kings and Lord of all.

594 John Pantry
© 1986 HarperCollins*Religious*/CopyCare

Send me out from here, Lord,
to serve a world in need;
may I know no man
    by the coat he wears,
but the heart that Jesus sees.
And may the light of Your face
shine upon me, Lord –
You have filled my heart
    with the greatest joy
and my cup is overflowing.

1 Go now and carry the news
    to all creation –
every race and every tongue;
take no purse with you,
    take nothing to eat
for He will supply your every need.
    Send me out . . .

2 Go now, bearing the light,
    living for others,
fearlessly walking into the night;
take no thought for your lives –
    like lambs among wolves –
full of the Spirit, ready to die.
    Send me out . . .
    . . . and my cup
    is overflowing with joy!

595 Anon
Copyright control

Set my spirit free
    that I might worship You;
set my spirit free
    that I might praise Your name.
Let all bondage go
    and let deliverance flow;
set my spirit free to worship You.

596 Graham Kendrick
© 1988 Make Way Music

1 **Show Your power, O Lord,**
demonstrate the justice
   of Your kingdom;
prove Your mighty word,
vindicate Your name
before a watching world.
Awesome are Your deeds, O Lord –
renew them for this hour.
   Show Your power, O Lord,
   among the people now.

2 Show Your power, O Lord,
cause Your Church
   to rise and take action;
let all fear be gone;
powers of the age to come
are breaking through.
We Your people are ready to serve,
to arise and to obey.
   Show Your power, O Lord,
   and set the people –
   show Your power, O Lord,
   and set the people –
   show Your power, O Lord,
   and set the people free!

597 Joseph Mohr (1792–1848)
tr. Stopford Augustus Brooke (1832–1916)

1 **Silent night, holy night!**
Sleeps the world; hid from sight,
Mary and Joseph in stable bare
watched o'er the child belovèd and fair
   sleeping in heavenly rest,
   sleeping in heavenly rest.

· 2 Silent night, holy night!
Shepherds first saw the light,
heard resounding clear and long,
far and near, the angel-song:
   'Christ the Redeemer is here,
   Christ the Redeemer is here.'

3 Silent night, holy night!
Son of God, O how bright
love is smiling from Your face!
Strikes for us now the hour of grace,
   Saviour, since You are born,
   Saviour, since You are born.

598 Anon
Copyright control

1 **Peter and John went to pray,**
they met a lame man on the way;
he asked for alms
   and held out his palms,
and this is what Peter did say:

2 'Silver and gold have I none,
but such as I have give I thee.
In the name of Jesus Christ
   of Nazareth,
   rise up and walk!'

3 He went walking and leaping
   and praising God,
walking and leaping and praising God.
'In the name of Jesus Christ
   of Nazareth,
   rise up and walk!'

599 From Psalm 98
© Timothy Dudley-Smith

1 **Sing a new song to the Lord,**
He to whom wonders belong;
rejoice in His triumph
   and tell of His power,
O sing to the Lord a new song!

2 Now to the ends of the earth,
see His salvation is shown;
and still He remembers
   His mercy and truth,
unchanging in love to His own.

3 Sing a new song and rejoice,
publish His praises abroad;
let voices in chorus,
    with trumpet and horn,
resound for the joy of the Lord!

4 Join with the hills and the sea,
thunders of praise to prolong;
in judgement and justice
    He comes to the earth,
O sing to the Lord a new song!

600 From Psalm 98
© Michael Baughen/Jubilate Hymns

1 **Sing to God new songs of worship –**
all His deeds are marvellous;
He has brought salvation to us
with His hand and holy arm:
He has shown to all the nations
righteousness and saving power;
He recalled His truth and mercy
to His people Israel.

2 Sing to God new songs of worship –
earth has seen His victory;
let the lands of earth be joyful
praising Him with thankfulness:
sound upon the harp His praises,
play to Him with melody;
let the trumpets sound His triumph,
show your joy to God the King!

3 Sing to God new songs of worship –
let the sea now make a noise;
all on earth and in the waters
sound your praises to the Lord:
let the hills be joyful together,
let the rivers clap their hands,
for with righteousness and justice
He will come to judge the earth.

601 © 1974 Linda Stassen/
New Song Ministries

1 **Sing alleluia to the Lord,**
sing alleluia to the Lord,
sing alleluia, sing alleluia,
sing alleluia to the Lord!

2 Jesus is risen from the dead,
Jesus is risen from the dead,
Jesus is risen, Jesus is risen,
Jesus is risen from the dead!

3 Jesus is Lord of heaven and earth,
Jesus is Lord of heaven and earth,
Jesus is Lord, Jesus is Lord,
Jesus is Lord of heaven and earth.

4 Jesus is coming for His own,
Jesus is coming for His own,
Jesus is coming, Jesus is coming,
Jesus is coming for His own.

602 Charles Silvester Horne (1865–1914)

1 **Sing we the King**
    who is coming to reign,
glory to Jesus, the Lamb that was slain;
life and salvation
    His empire shall bring,
joy to the nations when Jesus is King.
Come, let us sing: praise to our King.
Jesus our King, Jesus our King:
this is our song, who to Jesus belong:
glory to Jesus, to Jesus our King.

2 All men shall dwell
    in His marvellous light,
races long severed His love shall unite;
justice and truth
    from His sceptre shall spring,
wrong shall be ended
    when Jesus is King.
Come, let us sing . . .

3 All shall be well
    in His kingdom of peace,
freedom shall flourish
    and wisdom increase;
foe shall be friend
    when His triumph we sing,
sword shall be sickle
    when Jesus is King.
    Come, let us sing . . .

4 Souls shall be saved
    from the burden of sin;
doubt shall not darken
    His witness within;
hell hath no terrors,
    and death hath no sting;
love is victorious, when Jesus is King.
    Come, let us sing . . .

5 Kingdom of Christ,
    for thy coming we pray,
hasten, O Father, the dawn of the day;
when this new song
    Thy creation shall sing,
Satan is vanquished and Jesus is King.
    Come, let us sing . . .

603
Dave Bilbrough
© 1983 Kingsway's Thankyou Music

1 **So freely**
flows the endless love You give to me;
so freely,
not dependent on my part.
As I am reaching out,
reveal the love within Your heart;
as I am reaching out,
reveal the love within Your heart.

2 Completely –
that's the way You give Your love to me,
completely,
not dependent on my part.

As I am reaching out,
reveal the love within Your heart,
as I am reaching out,
reveal the love within Your heart.

3 So easy,
I receive the love You give to me;
so easy,
not dependent on my part.
Flowing out to me –
the love within Your heart;
flowing out to me –
the love within Your heart.

604
Charles Wesley (1707–88)

1 **Soldiers of Christ, arise,**
and put your armour on,
strong in the strength
    which God supplies
through His eternal Son.
Strong in the Lord of hosts,
and in His mighty power;
who in the strength of Jesus trusts
is more than conqueror.

2 Stand then in His great might,
with all His strength endued;
and take, to arm you for the fight,
the panoply of God:
to keep your armour bright,
attend with constant care,
still walking in your Captain's sight
and watching unto prayer.

3 From strength to strength go on,
wrestle and fight and pray;
tread all the powers of darkness down
and win the well-fought day.
That, having all things done,
and all your conflicts past,
ye may o'ercome through Christ alone,
and stand entire at last.

605 Andrae Crouch

1 **Soon, and very soon,**
we are going to see the King;
soon, and very soon,
we are going to see the King;
soon, and very soon,
we are going to see the King;
alleluia, alleluia,
we're going to see the King!

2 No more crying there . . .
alleluia . . .

3 No more dying there . . .
alleluia . . .
Alleluia, alleluia, alleluia, alleluia.

4 Soon and very soon . . .
alleluia . . .
Alleluia, alleluia, alleluia, alleluia.

606 Graham Kendrick

Soften my heart, Lord,
soften my heart;
from all indifference set me apart;
to feel Your compassion,
to weep with Your tears –
come soften my heart, O Lord,
soften my heart.

607 Frederick William Faber (1814–63)

1 **Souls of men, why will ye scatter**
like a crowd of frightened sheep?
Foolish hearts, why will ye wander
from a love so true and deep?

2 Was there ever kindest shepherd
half so gentle, half so sweet,
as the Saviour who would have us
come and gather round His feet?

3 There's a wideness in God's mercy,
like the wideness of the sea;
there's a kindness in His justice,
which is more than liberty.

4 There is plentiful redemption
in the blood that has been shed;
there is joy for all the members
in the sorrows of the Head.

5 For the love of God is broader
than the measures of man's mind;
and the heart of the Eternal
is most wonderfully kind.

6 If our love were but more simple,
we should take Him at His word,
and our lives would be all sunshine
in the sweetness of our Lord.

608 Emily Mary Crawford (1864–1927)

1 **Speak, Lord, in the stillness,**
while I wait on Thee;
hushed my heart to listen
in expectancy.

2 Speak, O blessèd Master,
in this quiet hour;
let me see Thy face, Lord,
feel Thy touch of power.

3 For the words Thou speakest,
they are life indeed;
living bread from heaven,
now my spirit feed!

4 All to Thee is yielded,
I am not my own;
blissful, glad surrender –
I am Thine alone.

5 Speak, Thy servant heareth!
be not silent, Lord;
waits my soul upon Thee
for the quickening word!

6   Fill me with the knowledge
    of Thy glorious will;
    all Thine own good pleasure
    in Thy child fulfil.

609 Chris Bowater
         © 1978 Sovereign Lifestyle Music

Spirit of God, show me Jesus;
remove the darkness,
        let truth shine through.
Spirit of God, show me Jesus;
reveal the fulness of His love to me!

610 © 1984 Colin Preston

1   **Spirit of God divine,**
    fill this heart of mine
    with holy flame,
    to praise the name
    of Jesus my Lord.
        Fill me again,
        fill me again,
        fill me again,
        O Spirit of the Lord.

2   Spirit of God divine,
    fill this mouth of mine
    with holy praise,
    to set the earth ablaze
    and glorify Your name.
        Fill me again . . .

3   Spirit of God divine,
    take this heart of mine
    to Your throne this day;
    help me, I pray,
    my offering to give.
        Fill me again . . .

611 © Christopher Idle/Jubilate Hymns

Spirit of holiness,
wisdom and faithfulness,
Wind of the Lord,
blowing strongly and free;
strength of our serving
and joy of our worshipping,
Spirit of God,
bring Your fulness to me!

1   You came to interpret
        and teach us effectively
    all that the Saviour
        has spoken and done;
    to glorify Jesus is all Your activity,
    promise and gift of the Father and Son:
        Spirit of holiness . . .

2   You came with Your gifts
        to supply all our poverty,
    pouring Your love
        on the church in her need;
    You came with Your fruit
        for our growth to maturity,
    richly refreshing the souls
        that You feed:
        Spirit of holiness . . .

612 Paul Armstrong
         © 1984 Restoration Music Ltd/
         Sovereign Music UK

Spirit of the living God,
fall afresh on me;
Spirit of the living God,
fall afresh on me;
fill me anew, fill me anew;
Spirit of the Lord,
fall afresh on me.

613

Daniel Iverson
© 1935, 1963 Birdwing Music/
EMI Christian Music Publishing/CopyCare

Spirit of the living God,
  fall afresh on me;
Spirit of the living God,
  fall afresh on me;
break me, melt me,
  mould me, fill me;
Spirit of the living God,
  fall afresh on me.

614

Andrew Reed (1787–1862)

1 **Spirit divine, attend our prayers,**
  and make this house Thy home;
  descend with all Thy gracious powers,
  O come, great Spirit, come!

2 Come as the light; to us reveal
  our emptiness and woe;
  and lead us in those paths of life
  where all the righteous go.

3 Come as the fire; and purge our hearts
  like sacrificial flame;
  let our whole soul an offering be
  to our Redeemer's name.

4 Come as the dove;
      and spread Thy wings,
  the wings of perfect love;
  and let Thy Church on earth become
  blest as the Church above.

5 Spirit divine, attend our prayers,
  make a lost world Thy home;
  descend with all Thy gracious powers,
  O come, great Spirit, come!

615

James Montgomery (1771–1854)

1 **Stand up and bless the Lord,**
  ye people of His choice;
  stand up and bless the Lord your God,
  with heart and soul and voice.

2 Though high above all praise,
  above all blessing high;
  who would not fear His holy name?
  and laud and magnify?

3 O for the living flame
  from His own altar brought,
  O touch our lips, our minds inspire,
  and wing to heaven our thought!

4 There, with benign regard,
  our hymns He deigns to hear;
  though unrevealed to mortal sense,
  our spirits feel Him near.

5 God is our strength and song,
  and His salvation ours;
  then be His love in Christ proclaimed
  with all our ransomed powers.

6 Stand up and bless the Lord,
  the Lord your God adore;
  stand up and bless His glorious name
  henceforth for evermore.

616

© 1986 Andy Silver

Stand up and bless the Lord your God,
stand up and bless the Lord;
His name is exalted above all names;
stand up and bless the Lord.

For our God is good to us,
always ready to forgive;
He is gracious and merciful,
slow to anger and very kind.

So, stand up and bless the Lord your God,
stand up and bless the Lord;
stand up and bless the Lord your God,
stand up.

617 George Duffield (1818–88)

1 **Stand up! stand up for Jesus!**
ye soldiers of the cross,
lift high His royal banner;
it must not suffer loss.
From victory unto victory
His army shall He lead,
till every foe is vanquished
and Christ is Lord indeed.

2 Stand up! stand up for Jesus!
the trumpet-call obey;
forth to the mighty conflict
in this His glorious day.
Ye that are men, now serve Him
against unnumbered foes;
let courage rise with danger,
and strength to strength oppose.

3 Stand up! stand up for Jesus!
stand in His strength alone;
the arm of flesh will fail you,
ye dare not trust your own.
Put on the gospel armour,
each piece put on with prayer;
where duty calls, or danger,
be never wanting there.

4 Stand up! stand up for Jesus!
the strife will not be long;
this day the noise of battle,
the next the victor's song.
To him that overcometh
a crown of life shall be;
he with the King of glory
shall reign eternally.

618 John Keble (1792–1866)

1 **Sun of my soul, my Saviour dear,**
it is not night if You are near;
O may no earth-born cloud arise
to hide You from Your servant's eyes.

2 When the soft dews of kindly sleep
my wearied eyelids gently steep,
be my last thought, how sweet to rest
for ever on my Saviour's breast!

3 Abide with me from morn till eve,
for without You I cannot live;
abide with me when night is nigh,
for without You I dare not die.

4 If some poor wandering child of Yours
have spurned today Your holy voice,
now, Lord, the gracious work begin;
let them no more be ruled by sin.

5 Watch by the sick; enrich the poor
with blessings from Your boundless
       store;
be every mourner's sleep tonight,
like infant's slumbers, pure and light.

6 Come near and bless us when we wake,
ere through the world our way we take;
till in the ocean of Your love
we lose ourselves in heaven above.

619 Graham Kendrick
© 1988 Make Way Music

1 **Such love,**
   pure as the whitest snow;
such love weeps for the shame I know;
such love, paying the debt I owe;
O Jesus, such love.

2 Such love, stilling my restlessness;
such love, filling my emptiness;
such love, showing me holiness;
O Jesus, such love.

3 Such love springs from eternity;
such love, streaming through history;
such love, fountain of life to me;
O Jesus, such love.

620

Isaac Watts (1674–1748)

1 **Sweet is the work, my God,
my King,**
to praise Thy name,
give thanks and sing,
to show Thy love by morning light,
and talk of all Thy truth at night.

2 Sweet is the day of sacred rest,
no mortal cares disturb my breast;
O may my heart in tune be found,
like David's harp of solemn sound.

3 My heart shall triumph in the Lord,
and bless His works,
and bless His word;
Thy works of grace,
how bright they shine,
how deep Thy counsels, how divine!

4 And I shall share a glorious part,
when grace has well refined my heart,
and fresh supplies of joy are shed,
like holy oil, to cheer my head.

5 Then shall I see and hear and know
all I desired or wished below;
and every power find sweet employ
in that eternal world of joy.

621

Chris Bowater
© 1986 Sovereign Lifestyle Music

Swing wide the gates,
let the King come in.
Swing wide the gates,
make a way for Him.
Swing wide the gates,
let the King come in.
Swing wide the gates,
make a way for Him.

Here He comes,
the King of glory;
here He comes,
mighty in victory;
here He comes
in splendour and majesty.

Swing wide the gates,
swing wide the gates,
let the King come in.
Swing wide the gates,
swing wide the gates,
let the King come in.

622

Paul Simmons
© 1985 Kingsway's Thankyou Music

Take, eat, this is My body,
broken for you;
for I am come that you might have life;
eat of My flesh and live,
eat of My flesh and live.

1 My blood was shed for many,
taking away your sin,
and if I shall make you free then
you shall be free indeed,
you shall be free indeed.
Take, eat ...

2 Though your sins be as scarlet
they shall be white as snow,
though they be red like crimson
they shall be as wool,
they shall be as wool.
Take, eat ...

3 For God so loved the world
He gave His only Son,
that whosoever believeth on Him
might have everlasting life,
might have everlasting life.
Take, eat ...

623

© David Mowbray/Jubilate Hymns

1 **Take heart and praise our God;**
rejoice and clap your hands –
His power our foe subdued,
His mercy ever stands:
Let trumpets sound and people sing,
The Lord through all the earth is King!

2 Take heart, but sing with fear,
exalt His worthy name;
with mind alert and clear
now celebrate His fame:
Let trumpets sound . . .

3 Take heart for future days,
for tasks as yet unknown –
the God whose name we praise
is seated on the throne:
Let trumpets sound . . .

4 Take heart and trust in God
the Father and the Son –
God is our strength and shield,
His Spirit guides us on:
Let trumpets sound . . .

624

Frances Ridley Havergal (1836–79)

1 **Take my life, and let it be**
consecrated, Lord, to Thee;
take my moments and my days,
let them flow in ceaseless praise.

2 Take my hands, and let them move
at the impulse of Thy love;
take my feet, and let them be
swift and beautiful for Thee.

3 Take my voice, and let me sing
always, only, for my King;
take my lips, and let them be
filled with messages from Thee.

4 Take my silver and my gold,
not a mite would I withhold;
take my intellect, and use
every power as Thou shalt choose.

5 Take my will, and make it Thine;
it shall be no longer mine:
take my heart, it is Thine own;
it shall be Thy royal throne.

6 Take my love; my Lord, I pour
at Thy feet its treasure store:
take myself, and I will be
ever, only, all, for Thee.

625

William Dunn Longstaff (1822–94)
© 1967 Good News Broadcasting Association/
Carlin Music Corp/IMP Ltd

1 **Take time to be holy,**
speak oft with Thy Lord;
abide in Him always,
and feed on His word.
Make friends of God's children,
help those who are weak;
forgetting in nothing
His blessing to seek.

2 Take time to be holy,
the world rushes on;
spend much time in secret
with Jesus alone –
by looking to Jesus,
like Him thou shalt be!
Thy friends in thy conduct
His likeness shall see.

3 Take time to be holy,
let Him be thy guide;
and run not before Him,
whatever betide;
in joy or in sorrow still follow thy Lord,
and, looking to Jesus,
still trust in His word.

4 Take time to be holy,
  be calm in thy soul;
  each thought and each temper
    beneath His control;
  thus led by His Spirit
    to fountains of love,
  thou soon shalt be fitted
    for service above.

626
Benjamin Mansell Ramsey (1849–1923)

1 **Teach me Thy way, O Lord,**
  teach me Thy way!
  Thy gracious aid afford,
  teach me Thy way!
  Help me to walk aright,
  more by faith, less by sight;
  lead me with heavenly light:
  teach me Thy way!

2 When doubts and fears arise,
  teach me Thy way!
  When storms o'erspread the skies,
  teach me Thy way!
  Shine through the cloud and rain,
  through sorrow, toil, and pain;
  make Thou my pathway plain:
  teach me Thy way!

3 Long as my life shall last,
  teach me Thy way!
  Where'er my lot be cast,
  teach me Thy way!
  Until the race is run,
  until the journey's done,
  until the crown is won,
  teach me Thy way!

627
© 1982 Elizabeth M Dyke

1 **Teach me to live, day by day,**
  in Your presence, Lord;
  day by day, in Your presence, Lord,
  teach me to live.

2 Teach me to praise, day by day,
  in Your Spirit, Lord;
  day by day, in Your Spirit, Lord,
  teach me to praise.

3 Teach me to love, day by day,
  in Your power, Lord;
  day by day, in Your power, Lord,
  teach me to love.

4 Teach me to give, day by day,
  from my wealth, O Lord;
  day by day, from my wealth, O Lord,
  teach me to give.

628
Arabella Catherine Hankey (1834–1911) altd.

1 **Tell me the old, old story**
  of unseen things above,
  of Jesus and His glory,
  of Jesus and His love.
  Tell me the story simply,
  as to a little child,
  for I am weak and weary,
  and helpless and defiled.
    Tell me the old, old story,
    tell me the old, old story,
    tell me the old, old story
    of Jesus and His love.

2 Tell me the story slowly,
  that I may take it in –
  that wonderful redemption,
  God's remedy for sin.
  Tell me the story often,
  for I forget so soon:
  the early dew of morning
  has passed away at noon.
    Tell me the old . . .

3 Tell me the story softly,
with earnest tones and grave;
Remember! I'm the sinner
whom Jesus came to save.
Tell me the story always,
if you would really be,
in any time of trouble,
a comforter to me.
Tell me the old . . .

4 Tell me the same old story,
when you have cause to fear
that this world's empty glory
is costing me too dear.
Yes, and when that world's glory
is dawning on my soul,
tell me the old, old story;
'Christ Jesus makes you whole.'
Tell me the old . . .

629 William Henry Parker (1845–1929)
v.6 Hugh Martin (1890–1964)
adapted Horrobin/Leavers by permission of
the National Christian Education Council

1 **Tell me the stories of Jesus**
I love to hear;
things I would ask Him to tell me
if He were here;
scenes by the wayside,
tales of the sea,
stories of Jesus,
tell them to me.

2 First let me hear how the children
stood round His knee;
that I may know of His blessing
resting on me;
words full of kindness,
deeds full of grace,
signs of the love found
in Jesus' face.

3 Tell me, in words full of wonder,
how rolled the sea,
tossing the boat in a tempest
on Galilee.
Jesus then doing
His Father's will,
ended the storm saying,
'Peace, peace, be still.'

4 Into the city I'd follow
the children's band,
waving a branch of the palm-tree
high in my hand;
worshipping Jesus,
yes, I would sing
loudest hosannas,
for He is King!

5 Show me that scene in the garden,
of bitter pain;
and of the cross where my Saviour
for me was slain;
and, through the sadness,
help me to see
how Jesus suffered
for love of me.

6 Gladly I'd hear of His rising
out of the grave,
living and strong and triumphant,
mighty to save:
and how He sends us
all men to bring
stories of Jesus,
Jesus, their King.

630 Leonard Bartlotti and Jan Harrington
© 1975 Celebration/
Kingsway's Thankyou Music

Tell My people I love them,
tell My people I care;
when they feel far away from Me,
tell My people I am there.

1 Tell My people I came and died
   to give them liberty;
   and to abide in Me
   is to be really free.
    Tell My people I love them,
    tell My people I care;
    when they feel far away from Me,
    tell My people I am there.

2 Tell My people where'er they go
   My comfort they can know;
   My peace and joy and love
   I freely will bestow.
    Tell my people . . .

631
From Luke 1
© Timothy Dudley-Smith

1 **Tell out, my soul,**
    the greatness of the Lord!
   Unnumbered blessings
    give my spirit voice;
   tender to me the promise of His word;
   in God my Saviour
    shall my heart rejoice.

2 Tell out, my soul,
    the greatness of His name!
   Make known His might,
    the deeds His arm has done;
   His mercy sure,
    from age to age the same;
   His holy name, the Lord,
    the Mighty One.

3 Tell out, my soul,
    the greatness of His might!
   Powers and dominions
    lay their glory by.
   Proud hearts and stubborn wills
    are put to flight,
   the hungry fed, the humble lifted high.

4 Tell out, my soul,
    the glories of His word!
   Firm is His promise,
    and His mercy sure.

Tell out, my soul,
    the greatness of the Lord
   to children's children and for evermore!

632
Graham Kendrick
© 1985 Kingsway's Thankyou Music

1 **Thank You for the cross,**
   the price You paid for us,
   how You gave Yourself
   so completely,
   precious Lord, precious Lord.
   Now our sins are gone,
   all forgiven,
   covered by Your blood,
   all forgotten,
   thank You, Lord, thank You, Lord.
    O I love You, Lord,
    really love You, Lord.
    I will never understand
    why You love me.
    You're my deepest joy,
    You're my heart's delight,
    and the greatest thing of all,
    O Lord, I see:
    You delight in me!

2 For our healing there,
   Lord, You suffered,
   and to take our fear
   You poured out Your love,
   precious Lord, precious Lord.
   Calvary's work is done,
   You have conquered,
   able now to save
   so completely,
   thank You, Lord, thank You, Lord.
    O I love You . . .

633
Alison Revell
© 1978 Kingsway's Thankyou Music

1 **Thank You, Jesus, thank You, Jesus,**
   thank You, Lord, for loving me.
   Thank You, Jesus . . .

2 You went to Calvary,
       there You died for me,
   thank You, Lord, for loving me.
   You went to Calvary . . .

3 You rose up from the grave,
       to me new life You gave,
   thank You, Lord, for loving me.
   You rose up from the grave . . .

4 You're coming back again,
       and we with You shall reign,
   thank You, Lord, for loving me.
   You're coming back again . . .

634 Alison Revell
         © 1978 Kingsway's Thankyou Music

Thank You, Jesus, for Your love to me;
thank You, Jesus, for Your grace so free.
I'll lift my voice to praise Your name,
praise You again and again:
You are everything,
You are my Lord.

635 © 1987 Greg Leavers and Phil Burt

SELECT VERSES AS APPROPRIATE

1 **Thank You, Lord, thank You, Lord,**
   that nothing can separate us
       from Your love.

2 Thank You, Lord, thank You, Lord,
   that there is no condemnation
       when we're in You.

CONFESSION VERSES

3 Search my heart, search my heart,
   and show me the sin
       I need to confess to You.

4 Sorry, Lord, sorry, Lord,
   I humbly now ask forgiveness
       for my sin.

5 Cleanse me, Lord, cleanse me, Lord,
   through Your precious blood
       make my heart clean before You.

6 Thank You, Lord, thank You, Lord
   that You've now removed the guilt
       of all my sin.

COMMUNION

7 Take this bread, take this bread,
   for this is Christ's body
       which was broken for you.

8 Thank You, Lord, thank You, Lord
   for dying on Calvary
       so that I can know You.

9 Take this cup, take this cup
   and drink it remembering
       Jesus Christ died for you.

10 Thank You, Lord, thank You, Lord,
    that through Your shed blood
        we are made one with God.

PRAISE AND WORSHIP

11 Fill me, Lord, fill me, Lord,
    so that I might learn to live
        through Your power alone.

12 We love You, we love You,
    we open our hearts
        in adoration to You.

13 Holy Lord, holy Lord,
    Your name is far higher
        than any other name.

14 Worthy Lord, worthy Lord,
    we offer our sacrifice of worship
        to You.

15 Reigning King, reigning King,
    You're glorious in majesty,
        almighty in power.

636 © 1986 Roland Fudge

Thank You, Lord,
for Your presence here,
thank You, Lord, thank You, Lord.
Thank You, Lord, You remove all fear,
thank You, Lord, thank You, Lord.
For the love that You showed
as You poured out Your life,
we thank You, we bless You,
Christ Jesus our Lord,
we thank You, Lord, thank You, Lord.
Thank You, Lord . . .

637 Robert Stoodley
© 1978 Sovereign Music UK

Thanks be to God
who gives us the victory,
gives us the victory
through our Lord Jesus Christ;
thanks be to God
who gives us the victory,
gives us the victory
through our Lord Jesus Christ.

1 He is able to keep us from falling,
and to set us free from sin:
so let us each live up to our calling,
and commit our way to Him.
Thanks be to God . . .

2 Jesus knows all about our temptations –
He has had to bear them too;
He will show us how to escape them,
if we trust Him
He will lead us through.
Thanks be to God . . .

3 He has led us
from the power of darkness
to the kingdom of His blessèd Son:
so let us join in praise together,
and rejoice in what the Lord has done.
Thanks be to God . . .

4 Praise the Lord for sending Jesus
to the cross of Calvary:
now He's risen, reigns in power,
and death is swallowed up in victory.
Thanks be to God . . .

638 Anon
Copyright control

Thank You, God, for sending Jesus;
thank You, Jesus, that You came;
Holy Spirit, won't You teach us
more about His wondrous name?

639 Jamie Owens-Collins
© 1984 Fairhill Music/CopyCare

1 **In heavenly armour**
we'll enter the land –
the battle belongs to the Lord;
no weapon that's fashioned
against us will stand –
the battle belongs to the Lord.
We sing glory, honour,
power and strength to the Lord;
we sing glory, honour,
power and strength to the Lord!

2 When the power of darkness
comes in like a flood,
the battle belongs to the Lord;
He's raised up a standard,
the power of His blood –
the battle belongs to the Lord.
We sing glory . . .

3 When your enemy presses in hard,
do not fear –
the battle belongs to the Lord;
take courage, my friend,
your redemption is near –
the battle belongs to the Lord.

We sing glory, honour,
power and strength to the Lord;
we sing glory, honour,
power and strength to the Lord!
We sing glory, honour,
power and strength to the Lord;
we sing glory, honour,
power and strength to the Lord!
Power and strength to the Lord!

4　Mid toil and tribulation,
　　and tumult of her war,
　　she waits the consummation
　　of peace for evermore;
　　till with the vision glorious
　　her longing eyes are blest,
　　and the great Church victorious
　　shall be the Church at rest.

5　Yet she on earth hath union
　　with God the Three-in-One,
　　and mystic sweet communion
　　with those whose rest is won.
　　O happy ones and holy!
　　Lord, give us grace that we,
　　like them, the meek and lowly,
　　on high may dwell with Thee.

640　Samuel John Stone (1839–1900)

1　**The Church's one foundation**
　　is Jesus Christ our Lord:
　　she is His new creation
　　by water and the word;
　　from heaven He came and sought her
　　to be His holy bride;
　　with His own blood He bought her,
　　and for her life He died.

2　Elect from every nation,
　　yet one o'er all the earth,
　　her charter of salvation
　　one Lord, one faith, one birth;
　　one holy name she blesses,
　　partakes one holy food,
　　and to one hope she presses,
　　with every grace endued.

3　Though with a scornful wonder
　　men see her sore oppressed,
　　by schisms rent asunder
　　by heresies distressed;
　　yet saints their watch are keeping,
　　their cry goes up: 'How long?'
　　and soon the night of weeping
　　shall be the morn of song.

641　John Ellerton (1826–93)

1　**The day Thou gavest, Lord,**
　　is ended,
　　the darkness falls at Thy behest;
　　to Thee our morning hymns ascended,
　　Thy praise shall sanctify our rest.

2　We thank Thee
　　　　that Thy Church unsleeping,
　　while earth rolls onward into light,
　　through all the world
　　　　her watch is keeping,
　　and rests not now by day or night.

3　As o'er each continent and island
　　the dawn leads on another day,
　　the voice of prayer is never silent,
　　nor dies the strain of praise away.

4　The sun, that bids us rest, is waking
　　our brethren 'neath the western sky,
　　and hour by hour fresh lips are making
　　Thy wondrous doings heard on high.

5 So be it, Lord: Thy throne shall never,
like earth's proud empires, pass away;
Thy kingdom stands,
     and grows for ever,
till all Thy creatures own Thy sway.

642

Graham Kendrick
© 1986 Kingsway's Thankyou Music

MEN   **The earth is the Lord's**
WOMEN and everything in it.
MEN   The earth is the Lord's,
WOMEN the work of His hands.
MEN   The earth is the Lord's
WOMEN and everything in it,
ALL   and all things were made
           for His glory!

The mountains are His,
the seas and the islands,
the cities and towns,
the houses and streets:
let rebels bow down
and worship before Him,
for all things were made for His glory!
MEN   The earth is the Lord's . . .

The mountains are His . . .

MEN   The earth is the Lord's . . .

MEN   The earth is the Lord's
WOMEN and everything in it.
MEN   The earth is the Lord's,
WOMEN the work of His hands.
MEN   The earth is the Lord's
WOMEN and everything in it,
ALL   and all things were made,
           yes, all things were made,
           and all things were made
               for His glory!

643

John Daniels and Phil Thomson
© HarperCollins*Religious*/CopyCare

1 **The earth was dark
      until You spoke –**
then all was light and all was peace;
yet still, O God, so many wait
to see the flame of love released.
     Lights to the world! O Light divine,
     kindle in us a mighty flame,
     till every heart, consumed by love
     shall rise to praise Your holy name!

2 In Christ You gave Your gift of life
to save us from the depth of night:
O come and set our spirits free
and draw us to Your perfect light.
     Lights to the world . . .

3 Where there is fear may we bring joy
and healing to a world in pain:
Lord, build Your kingdom
           through our lives
till Jesus walks this earth again.
     Lights to the world . . .

4 O burn in us, that we may burn
with love that triumphs in despair;
and touch our lives with such a fire
that souls may search
           and find You there.
     Lights to the world . . .

644

Anon (17th century)
© in this version Jubilate Hymns

1 **The first nowell the angel did say,**
was to Bethlehem's shepherds
           in fields as they lay;
in fields where they
           lay keeping their sheep
on a cold winter's night
           that was so deep:
     Nowell, nowell, nowell, nowell,
     born is the King of Israel!

2 Then wise men from a country far
looked up and saw a guiding star;
they travelled on by night and day
to reach the place where Jesus lay:
Nowell, nowell . . .

3 At Bethlehem they entered in,
on bended knee they worshipped Him;
they offered there in His presence
their gold and myrrh and frankincense:
Nowell, nowell . . .

4 Then let us all with one accord
sing praises to our heavenly Lord;
for Christ has our salvation wrought
and with His blood
    mankind has bought:
Nowell, nowell . . .

3 The God of Abraham praise,
whose all-sufficient grace
shall guide us all our happy days,
in all our ways:
He is our faithful friend;
He is our gracious God;
and He will save us to the end,
through Jesus' blood.

4 He by Himself has sworn –
we on His oath depend –
we shall, on eagles' wings upborne,
to heaven ascend:
we shall behold His face,
we shall His power adore,
and sing the wonders of His grace
for evermore.

5 The whole triumphant host
give thanks to God on high:
'Hail, Father, Son, and Holy Ghost!'
they ever cry.
Hail, Abraham's God and ours!
We join the heavenly lays;
and celebrate with all our powers
His endless praise.

645 Thomas Olivers (1725–99) altd.

1 **The God of Abraham praise,**
who reigns enthroned above,
Ancient of everlasting days,
and God of love.
Jehovah, great I Am!
by earth and heaven confessed;
we bow and bless the sacred name,
for ever blest.

2 The God of Abraham praise,
at whose supreme command
from earth we rise, and seek the joys
at His right hand;
we all on earth forsake,
its wisdom, fame, and power;
and Him our only portion make,
our shield and tower.

646 Mark Prendergrass

1 **The greatest thing in all my life**
is knowing You;
the greatest thing in all my life
is knowing You;
I want to know You more;
I want to know You more.
The greatest thing in all my life
is knowing You.

2 The greatest thing in all my life
   is loving You;
the greatest thing in all my life
   is loving You;
I want to love You more;
   I want to love You more.
The greatest thing in all my life
   is loving You.

3 The greatest thing in all my life
   is serving You;
the greatest thing in all my life
   is serving You;
I want to serve You more;
   I want to serve You more.
The greatest thing in all my life
   is serving You.

648 © 1987 Andy Silver

The heavens declare the glory of God,
and the heavens proclaim
   the work of His hands;
and day after day they pour forth speech,
and night after night
   they display what He knows.

647 Thomas Kelly (1769–1855)

1 **The head that once was crowned
   with thorns**
is crowned with glory now;
a royal diadem adorns
the mighty victor's brow.

2 The highest place that heaven affords
is His by sovereign right;
the King of kings and Lord of lords,
He reigns in perfect light.

3 The joy of all who dwell above,
the joy of all below,
to whom He manifests His love,
and grants His name to know.

4 To them the cross, with all its shame,
with all its grace is given;
their name an everlasting name,
their joy the joy of heaven.

5 They suffer with their Lord below;
they reign with Him above;
their profit and their joy, to know
the mystery of His love.

649 Henry Williams Baker (1821–77)

1 **The King of love my shepherd is,**
whose goodness faileth never;
I nothing lack if I am His
and He is mine for ever.

2 Where streams of living water flow
my ransomed soul He leadeth,
and where the verdant pastures grow
with food celestial feedeth.

3 Perverse and foolish oft I strayed;
but yet in love He sought me,
and on His shoulder gently laid,
and home rejoicing brought me.

4 In death's dark vale I fear no ill
with Thee, dear Lord, beside me;
Thy rod and staff my comfort still,
Thy cross before to guide me.

5 Thou spread'st a table in my sight;
Thy unction grace bestoweth;
and O what transport of delight
from Thy pure chalice floweth!

6 And so through all the length of days
  Thy goodness faileth never;
  Good Shepherd, may I sing Thy praise
    within Thy house for ever!

650
Graham Kendrick
© 1981 Kingsway's Thankyou Music

1 **The King is among us,**
  His Spirit is here:
  let's draw near and worship,
  let songs fill the air!

2 He looks down upon us,
  delight in His face,
  enjoying His children's love,
  enthralled by our praise.

3 For each child is special,
  accepted and loved –
  a love gift from Jesus
  to His Father above.

4 And now He is giving
  His gifts to us all;
  for no-one is worthless
  and each one is called.

5 The Spirit's anointing
  on all flesh comes down,
  and we shall be channels
  for works like His own:

6 We come now believing
  Your promise of power,
  for we are Your people
  and this is Your hour.

651
Bryn Rees (1911–83)
© Alexander Scott

1 **The kingdom of God**
  is justice and joy,
  for Jesus restores
    what sin would destroy;
  God's power and glory
  in Jesus we know,
  and here and hereafter
    the kingdom shall grow.

2 The kingdom of God
  is mercy and grace,
  the captives are freed,
    the sinners find place,
  the outcast are welcomed
    God's banquet to share,
  and hope is awakened
    in place of despair.

3 The kingdom of God
  is challenge and choice,
  believe the good news,
    repent and rejoice!
  His love for us sinners
    brought Christ to His cross,
  our crisis of judgement
    for gain or for loss.

4 God's kingdom is come,
    the gift and the goal,
  in Jesus begun,
    in heaven made whole;
  the heirs of the kingdom
    shall answer His call,
  and all things cry, 'Glory!'
    to God all-in-all!

652
Donald Fishel
© 1974 Word of God/CopyCare

The light of Christ
  has come into the world;
the light of Christ
  has come into the world.

1 All men must be born again
    to see the kingdom of God;
  the water and the Spirit
    bring new life in God's love.
  The light of Christ . . .

2 God gave up His only Son
    out of love for the world,
  so that all men who believe in Him
    will live for ever.
  The light of Christ . . .

3 The light of God has come to us
   so that we might have salvation;
   from the darkness of our sins
   we walk into glory with Christ Jesus.
   The light of Christ
   has come into the world;
   the light of Christ
   has come into the world.

He has given to them
   the lands of the nations,
to possess the fruit and keep His laws,
and praise, praise His name.
The Lord has led forth His people
   with joy,
and His chosen ones with singing, singing;
the Lord has led forth His people with joy,
and His chosen ones with singing.

653
Anon
Copyright control

1 **The Lord has given**
   a land of good things,
   I will press on and make them mine;
   I'll know His power,
      I'll know His glory,
   and in His kingdom I will shine.
   With the high praises of God
      in our mouth,
   and a two-edged sword in our hand,
   we'll march right on to the victory side,
      right into Canaan's land.

2 Gird up your armour, ye sons of Zion,
   gird up your armour, let's go to war;
   we'll win the battle with great rejoicing
   and so we'll praise Him
      more and more.
   With the high praises ...

3 We'll bind their kings
      in chains and fetters,
   we'll bind their nobles tight in iron,
   to execute God's written judgement –
   march on to glory, sons of Zion!
   With the high praises ...

654
Chris Bowater
© 1982 Sovereign Lifestyle Music

The Lord has led forth His people
   with joy,
and His chosen ones with singing, singing;
the Lord has led forth His people with joy,
and His chosen ones with singing.

655
Diane Davis
© 1973 GIA Publications Inc

The Lord is a great and
   mighty King,
   just and gentle with everything;
   so with happiness we sing,
   and let His praises ring.

1 We are His voice, we His song;
   let us praise Him all day long. Alleluia.
   The Lord is a great ...

2 We are His body here on earth;
   from above He gave us birth. Alleluia.
   The Lord is a great ...

3 For our Lord we will stand,
   sent by Him to every land. Alleluia.
   The Lord is a great ...

4 The Lord our God is one,
   Father, Spirit, and the Son. Alleluia.
   The Lord is a great ...

656
Josiah Conder (1789–1855)

1 **The Lord is King! lift up thy voice,**
   O earth, and all ye heavens rejoice;
   from world to world the joy shall ring,
   'The Lord omnipotent is King!'

2 The Lord is King! who then shall dare
resist His will, distrust His care,
or murmur at His wise decrees,
or doubt His royal promises?

3 The Lord is King! Child of the dust,
the Judge of all the earth is just;
holy and true are all His ways:
let every creature speak His praise.

4 He reigns! ye saints, exalt your strains;
your God is King, your Father reigns;
and He is at the Father's side,
the man of love, the crucified.

5 One Lord, one empire, all secures;
He reigns, and life and death are yours,
through earth and heaven
    one song shall ring,
'The Lord omnipotent is King!'

657 Graham Kendrick
© 1983 Kingsway's Thankyou Music

1 **The Lord is King,**
    He is mighty in battle,
working wonders,
    glorious in majesty.

2 The Lord is King –
    so majestic in power!
His right hand
    has shattered the enemy.

3 A This is my God
    and I will praise Him;
  B this is my God
    and I will praise Him:

4 A My strength and song
    and my salvation,
  B my strength and song
    and my salvation.

(*The singers may divide at* A *and* B)

658 © 1982 Roland Fudge

The Lord is my strength and my song,
the Lord is my strength and my song,
and He has become my salvation.
Sing to the Lord, for He has done
    marvellous things;
sing to the Lord, for He has done
    marvellous things;
sing to the Lord, sing to the Lord,
sing to the Lord, for He has done
    marvellous things.
The Lord is my strength and my song,
the Lord is my strength and my song,
and He has become my salvation.

659 Angela Browning
© 1979 Word's Spirit of Praise Music/
CopyCare

The Lord reigns, the Lord reigns,
He is robed in majesty,
the Lord is robed in majesty,
and He is girded with strength.

1 The Lord has established the world,
it shall never be moved;
Thy throne is established of old,
Thou art from everlasting.
    The Lord reigns . . .

2 The floods have lifted up, O Lord,
lifted up their voice;
mightier than the thunder of the waves,
the Lord on high is mighty.
    The Lord reigns . . .

660 Francis Rous (1579–1659)
revised for *Scottish Psalter*, 1650

1 **The Lord's my shepherd,**
    I'll not want;
He makes me down to lie
in pastures green; He leadeth me
the quiet waters by.

2 My soul He doth restore again,
and me to walk doth make
within the paths of righteousness,
e'en for His own name's sake.

3 Yea, though I walk
through death's dark vale,
yet will I fear none ill;
for Thou art with me, and Thy rod
and staff me comfort still.

4 My table Thou hast furnishèd
in presence of my foes;
my head Thou dost with oil anoint,
and my cup overflows.

5 Goodness and mercy all my life
shall surely follow me;
and in God's house for evermore
my dwelling-place shall be.

661
The Lord's Prayer
Copyright control

Our Father which art in heaven,
hallowèd be Thy name,
Thy kingdom come,
Thy will be done,
in earth, as it is in heaven.
Give us this day our daily bread;
forgive us our trespasses
as we forgive them who trespass against us.
And lead us not into temptation,
but deliver us from evil.
For Thine is the kingdom,
the power and the glory
for ever and ever.
Amen, amen.

662
© Timothy Dudley-Smith

1 **The love of Christ who died for me**
is more than mind can know,
His mercy measureless and free
to meet the debt I owe.

2 He came my sinful cause to plead,
He laid His glories by,
for me a homeless life to lead,
a shameful death to die.

3 My sins I only see in part,
my self-regarding ways;
the secret places of my heart
lie bare before His gaze.

4 For me the price of sin He paid;
my sins beyond recall
are all alike on Jesus laid,
He died to bear them all.

5 O living Lord of life, for whom
the heavens held their breath,
to see, triumphant from the tomb,
a love that conquers death.

6 Possess my heart that it may be
Your kingdom without end,
O Christ who died for love of me
and lives to be my friend.

663
Graham Kendrick
© 1983 Kingsway's Thankyou Music

1 **The price is paid:**
come, let us enter in
to all that Jesus died
to make our own.
For every sin
more than enough He gave,
and bought our freedom
from each guilty stain.
The price is paid, alleluia –
amazing grace,
so strong and sure!
And so with all my heart,
my life in every part,
I live to thank You
for the price You paid.

2 The price is paid:
     see Satan flee away –
for Jesus, crucified,
     destroys his power.
No more to pay!
     Let accusation cease:
in Christ there is
     no condemnation now!
     The price is paid . . .

3 The price is paid:
     and by that scourging cruel,
He took our sicknesses
     as if His own.
And by His wounds,
     His body broken there,
His healing touch may now
     by faith be known.
     The price is paid . . .

4 The price is paid:
     'Worthy the Lamb!' we cry –
eternity shall never
     cease His praise.
The Church of Christ
     shall rule upon the earth:
in Jesus' name
     we have authority!
     The price is paid . . .

2 Jesus promised life to all,
walk, walk in the light;
the dead were wakened by His call,
walk, walk in the light.
     Walk in the light . . .

3 He died in pain on Calvary,
walk, walk in the light;
to save the lost like you and me,
walk, walk in the light.
     Walk in the light . . .

4 We know His death was not the end,
walk, walk in the light;
He gave His Spirit to be our friend,
walk, walk in the light.
     Walk in the light . . .

5 By Jesus' love our wounds are healed,
walk, walk in the light;
the Father's kindness is revealed,
walk, walk in the light.
     Walk in the light . . .

6 The Spirit lives in you and me,
walk, walk in the light;
His light will shine for all to see,
walk, walk in the light.
     Walk in the light . . .

664 Damien Lundy
© Kevin Mayhew Ltd

1 **The Spirit lives to set us free,**
walk, walk in the light;
He binds us all in unity,
walk, walk in the light.
     Walk in the light,
     walk in the light,
     walk in the light,
     walk in the light of the Lord.

665 Chris Bowater
© 1985 Sovereign Lifestyle Music

1 **The Spirit of the Lord,**
the sovereign Lord, is on me,
because He has anointed me
to preach good news to the poor:
     Proclaiming Jesus, only Jesus –
     it is Jesus, Saviour, healer and baptizer,
     and the mighty King,
     the victor and deliverer –
     He is Lord, He is Lord, He is Lord.

2 And He has called on me
to bind up all the broken hearts,
to minister release to every
captivated soul:
Proclaiming Jesus, only Jesus –
it is Jesus, Saviour, healer and baptizer,
and the mighty King,
the victor and deliverer –
He is Lord, He is Lord, He is Lord.

3 Let righteousness arise
and blossom as a garden;
let praise begin to spring in every
tongue and nation:
Proclaiming Jesus . . .

666 Edith McNeill
© 1974 Celebration/Kingsway's Thankyou Music

The steadfast love of the Lord
never ceases,
His mercies never come to an end;
they are new every morning,
new every morning:
great is Thy faithfulness, O Lord,
great is Thy faithfulness.

1 The Lord is my portion, says my soul,
therefore I will hope in Him.
The steadfast love . . .

2 The Lord is good to those
who wait for Him,
to the soul that seeks Him:
it is good that we should wait quietly
for the salvation of the Lord.
The steadfast love . . .

3 The Lord will not cast off for ever,
but will have compassion:
for He does not willingly afflict
or grieve the sons of men.
The steadfast love . . .

4 So let us examine all our ways,
and return to the Lord:
let us lift up our hearts and hands
to God in heaven.
The steadfast love . . .

667 Graham Kendrick
© 1989 Make Way Music

1 **The trumpets sound,**
   the angels sing,
the feast is ready to begin;
the gates of heaven are open wide,
and Jesus welcomes you inside.
The trumpets sound . . .
Sing with thankfulness
songs of pure delight,
come and revel
in heaven's love and light;
take your place at the table of the King,
the feast is ready to begin,
the feast is ready to begin.

2 Tables are laden with good things,
O taste the peace and joy He brings;
He'll fill you up with love divine,
He'll turn your water into wine.
Sing with thankfulness . . .

3 The hungry heart He satisfies,
offers the poor His paradise;
now hear all heaven and earth applaud
the amazing goodness of the Lord.
Sing with thankfulness . . .

668 vv.1–2 Seth Sykes, v.3 Glyn L Taylor
© Singspiration Music/Brentwood Benson
Music Publishing/CopyCare

1 **The world was in darkness,**
   in sin and shame;
mankind was lost, and then Jesus came.
He carried our sins to Calvary's tree,
He hung there, and bled there,
   for you and me.

Thank You, Lord, for saving my soul.
Thank You, Lord, for making me whole.
Thank You, Lord, for giving to me
Thy great salvation so rich and free.

2   Lord Jesus came down
  from His throne on high;
 ready to live and willing to die.
 For all of the pain and the suffering
  He bore,
 I'll love Him and thank Him
  for evermore.
 Thank You, Lord . . .

3   To You I surrender my all today,
 the debt I owe, I ne'er could repay,
 I'll serve You with joy
  wherever You lead,
 with this great assurance,
  You'll meet my need.
 Thank You, Lord . . .

669 © Christopher Idle / Jubilate Hymns

1   **Then I saw a new heaven and earth,**
 for the first had passed away;
 and the holy city,
  come down from God,
 like a bride on her wedding day:
 and I know how He loves His own,
 for I heard His great voice tell,
 they would be His people,
  and He their God,
 and among them He came to dwell.

2   He will wipe away every tear,
 even death shall die at last;
 there'll be no more sorrow,
  or grief, or pain,
 they belong to the world that's past:
 and the One on the throne said, 'Look!
 I am making all things new';
 He is A and Z, He is First and Last,
 and His words are exact and true.

3   So the thirsty can drink their fill
 at the fountain giving life;
 but the gates are shut on all evil things,
 on deceit and decay and strife:
 with foundations and walls and towers,
 like a jewel the city shines;
 with its streets of gold
  and its gates of pearl,
 in a glory where each combines.

4   As they measured its length
  and breadth
 I could see no temple there,
 for its only temple is God the Lord
 and the Lamb in that city fair:
 and it needs neither sun nor moon
 in a place which knows no night,
 for the city's lamp is the Lamb Himself
 and the glory of God its light.

5   And I saw by the sacred stream
 flowing water, crystal clear;
 and the tree of life
  with its healing leaves
 and its fruit growing all the year:
 so the worshippers of the Lamb
 bear His name, and see His face;
 and they reign and serve
  and for ever live
 to the praise of His glorious grace.

670 From the Latin
    tr. Francis Pott (1832–1909)

1   **The strife is o'er, the battle done;**
 the victory of life is won;
 the song of triumph has begun:
  hallelujah!

2   The powers of death
  have done their worst,
 but Christ their legions has dispersed;
 let shouts of holy joy outburst:
  hallelujah!

3 The three sad days have quickly sped:
He rises glorious from the dead;
all glory to our risen Head:
    hallelujah!

4 He broke the bonds of death and hell;
the bars from heaven's high portals fell;
let hymns of praise His triumph tell:
    hallelujah!

5 Lord, by the stripes
    which wounded Thee,
from death's dread sting
    Thy servants free,
that we may live, and sing to Thee;
    hallelujah!

671 William Cowper (1731–1800)

1 **There is a fountain filled with blood**
drawn from Emmanuel's veins;
and sinners,
    plunged beneath that flood,
lose all their guilty stains.

2 The dying thief rejoiced to see
that fountain in his day;
and there may I, as vile as he,
wash all my sins away.

3 Dear dying Lamb! Your precious blood
shall never lose its power,
till all the ransomed Church of God
be saved, to sin no more.

4 E'er since, by faith, I saw the stream
Your flowing wounds supply,
redeeming love has been my theme,
and shall be till I die.

5 Then in a nobler, sweeter song,
I'll sing Your power to save,
when this poor lisping,
    stammering tongue
lies silent in the grave.

672 Frederick Whitfield (1829–1904)

1 **There is a name I love to hear,**
I love to speak its worth;
it sounds like music in my ear,
the sweetest name on earth.
    O how I love the Saviour's name,
    O how I love the Saviour's name,
    O how I love the Saviour's name,
    the sweetest name on earth.

2 It tells me of a Saviour's love,
who died to set me free;
it tells me of His precious blood,
the sinner's perfect plea.
    O how I love . . .

3 It tells of One whose loving heart
can feel my deepest woe,
who in my sorrow bears a part
that none can bear below.
    O how I love . . .

4 It bids my trembling heart rejoice,
it dries each rising tear;
it tells me in a 'still, small voice'
to trust and never fear.
    O how I love . . .

5 Jesus, the name I love so well,
the name I love to hear!
No saints on earth its worth can tell,
no heart conceive how dear!
    O how I love . . .

673 Melody Green
© 1982 Birdwing Music/BMG Songs/
EMI Christian Music Publishing/CopyCare

1 **There is a Redeemer,**
Jesus, God's own Son,
precious Lamb of God, Messiah,
Holy One.
    Thank You, O my Father,
    for giving us Your Son,
    and leaving Your Spirit
    till the work on earth is done.

2 Jesus, my Redeemer,
  name above all names,
  precious Lamb of God, Messiah,
  O for sinners slain:
    Thank You . . .

3 When I stand in glory
  I will see His face,
  and there I'll serve my King for ever
  in that holy place.
    Thank You . . .

674 Cecil Frances Alexander (1818–95)

1 **There is a green hill far away**
  without a city wall,
  where the dear Lord was crucified,
  who died to save us all.

2 We may not know, we cannot tell
  what pains He had to bear;
  but we believe it was for us
  He hung and suffered there.

3 He died that we might be forgiven,
  He died to make us good,
  that we might go at last to heaven,
  saved by His precious blood.

4 There was no other good enough
  to pay the price of sin;
  He only could unlock the gate
  of heaven, and let us in.

5 O dearly, dearly has He loved,
  and we must love Him too,
  and trust in His redeeming blood,
  and try His works to do.

675 Joan Parsons
© 1978 Kingsway's Thankyou Music

1 **There is no condemnation**
      for those who are in Christ,
  for the Spirit of life in Christ
      has set me free.

O He's alive, He's alive, He's alive,
O He's alive, He's alive, He's alive,
praise the Lord.

2 If the Spirit of Him
      who raised Christ from the dead
  be born in you,
      then He will give you life.
    O He's alive . . .

3 If God be for us,
      who can be against us?
  For He who sent His Son
      will freely give us all things.
    O He's alive . . .

676 W E Littlewood (1831–86)

1 **There is no love**
      like the love of Jesus,
  never to fade or fall,
  till into the fold of the peace of God
  He has gathered us all.
    Jesus' love, precious love,
    boundless and pure and free!
    O turn to that love,
      weary wandering soul,
    Jesus pleadeth with thee.

2 There is no heart
      like the heart of Jesus,
  filled with a tender love,
  no throb nor throe
      that our hearts can know
  but He feels it above.
    Jesus' love . . .

3 O let us hark to the voice of Jesus!
  O may we never roam,
  till safe we rest on His loving breast
  in the dear heavenly home.
    Jesus' love . . .

677

Gary Garratt
© 1982 Scripture in Song/Integrity Music/
Kingsway's Thankyou Music

There is none holy as the Lord,
there is none beside Thee;
neither is there any rock like our God,
there is none holy as the Lord.

678

Tedd Smith
© 1973 Hope Publishing/CopyCare

1 **There's a quiet understanding**
when we're gathered in the Spirit,
it's a promise that He gives us,
when we gather in His name.
There's a love we feel in Jesus,
there's a manna that He feeds us,
it's a promise that He gives us
when we gather in His name.

2 And we know when we're together,
sharing love and understanding,
that our brothers and our sisters
feel the oneness that He brings.
Thank You, thank You,
thank You, Jesus,
for the way You love and feed us,
for the many ways You lead us;
thank You, thank You, Lord.

679

Henry Burton (1840–1930)
© Trustees for Methodist Church Purposes

1 **There's a light upon the mountains,
and the day is at the spring,**
when our eyes shall see the beauty
and the glory of the King;
weary was our heart with waiting,
and the night-watch seemed so
long;
but His triumph-day is breaking,
and we hail it with a song.

2 In the fading of the starlight
we can see the coming morn;
and the lights of men are paling
in the splendours of the dawn:
for the eastern skies are glowing
as with light of hidden fire,
and the hearts of men are stirring
with the throbs of deep desire.

3 There's a hush of expectation,
and a quiet in the air;
and the breath of God is moving
in the fervent breath of prayer:
for the suffering, dying Jesus
is the Christ upon the throne,
and the travail of our spirit
is the travail of His own.

4 He is breaking down the barriers,
He is casting up the way;
He is calling for His angels
to build up the gates of day:
but His angels here are human,
not the shining hosts above;
for the drum-beats of His army
are the heart-beats of our love.

5 Hark! we hear a distant music,
and it comes with fuller swell;
'tis the triumph-song of Jesus,
of our King, Immanuel:
Zion, go ye forth to meet Him;
and, my soul, be swift to bring
all thy sweetness and thy dearest
for the triumph of our King!

680

Albert Midlane (1825–1909)
© in this version Jubilate Hymns

1 **There's a song for all the children**
that makes the heavens ring,
a song that even angels
can never never sing;
they praise Him as their maker
and see Him glorified,
but we can call Him Saviour
because for us He died.

2 There's a place for all the children
where Jesus reigns in love,
a place of joy and freedom
that nothing can remove;
a home that is more friendly
than any home we know,
where Jesus makes us welcome
because He loves us so.

3 There's a friend for all the children
to guide us every day,
whose care is always faithful
and never fades away;
there's no-one else so loyal –
His friendship stays the same;
He knows us and He loves us,
and Jesus is His name.

4 Now the King of the ages
approaches the earth,
He will burst through
the gates of the sky;
and all men shall bow down
to His beautiful name;
we shall rise with a shout, we shall fly!
Come on . . .

(repeat verse 4)

682
E H Swinstead (d1976)
Copyright control

There's a way back to God
from the dark paths of sin;
there's a door that is open
and you may go in:
at Calvary's cross is where you begin,
when you come as a sinner to Jesus.

681
Graham Kendrick
© 1978 Kingsway's Thankyou Music

1 **There's a sound on the wind**
like a victory song;
listen now, let it rest on your soul.
It's a song that I learned
from a heavenly King,
it's a song of a battle royal.

2 There's a loud shout of victory
that leaps from our hearts,
as we wait for our conquering King.
There's a triumph resounding
from dark ages past,
to the victory song we now sing.
Come on, heaven's children,
the city is in sight.
There will be no sadness
on the other side.

3 There'll be crowns for the conquerors
and white robes to wear,
there will be no more sorrow or pain;
and the battles of earth
shall be lost in the sight,
of the glorious Lamb that was slain.

683
Frederick William Faber (1814–63) altd.

1 **There's a wideness in God's mercy**
like the wideness of the sea;
there's a kindness in His justice
which is more than liberty.

2 There is plentiful redemption
in the blood that has been shed;
there is joy for all the members
in the sorrows of the Head.

3 There is grace enough for thousands
of new worlds as great as this;
there is room for fresh creations
in that upper home of bliss.

4 For the love of God is broader
than the measures of man's mind;
and the heart of the Eternal
is most wonderfully kind.

5 But we make His love too narrow
by false limits of our own;
and we magnify His strictness
with a zeal He will not own.

6 If our love were but more simple
we should take Him at His word;
and our lives would be illumined
by the presence of our Lord.

They shall obtain gladness and joy,
and sorrow and mourning shall flee away.
Therefore the redeemed of the Lord
shall return,
and come with singing unto Zion,
and everlasting joy
shall be upon their head.

684 © Michael Baughen/Jubilate Hymns

1 **There's no greater name
than Jesus,**
name of Him who came to save us;
in that saving name so gracious
every knee shall bow.

2 Let everything
that's beneath the ground,
let everything in the world around,
let everything exalted on high
bow at Jesus' name.

3 In our minds, by faith professing,
in our hearts, by inward blessing,
on our tongues, by words confessing,
Jesus Christ is Lord.

685 Ruth Lake
© 1972 Scripture in Song/Integrity Music/
Kingsway's Thankyou Music

**Therefore the redeemed of the Lord
shall return,**
and come with singing unto Zion,
and everlasting joy
shall be upon their head.

Therefore the redeemed of the Lord
shall return,
and come with singing unto Zion,
and everlasting joy
shall be upon their head.

686 Colin Green
Copyright control

1 **Therefore we lift our hearts
in praise,**
sing to the living God who saves,
for grace poured out for you and me.

2 There for everyone to see,
there on the hill at Calvary,
Jesus died for you and me.

3 There for sad and broken men
He rose up from the grave again,
and reigns on high for you and me.

4 There for such great pain and cost
the Spirit came at Pentecost,
and comes in power for you and me.

5 Therefore we lift our hearts in praise,
sing to the living God who saves,
for grace poured out for you and me.

687 © Michael Saward/Jubilate Hymns

1 **These are the facts
as we have received them,**
these are the truths
that the Christian believes,
this is the basis of all of our preaching:
Christ died for sinners
and rose from the tomb.

2 These are the facts
    as we have received them:
Christ has fulfilled
    what the Scriptures foretold,
Adam's whole family
    in death had been sleeping,
Christ through His rising
    restores us to life.

3 These are the facts
    as we have received them:
we, with our Saviour,
    have died on the cross;
now, having risen, our Jesus lives in us,
gives us His Spirit
    and makes us His home.

4 These are the facts
    as we have received them:
we shall be changed
    in the blink of an eye,
trumpets shall sound
    as we face life immortal,
this is the victory
    through Jesus our Lord.

5 These are the facts
    as we have received them,
these are the truths
    that the Christian believes,
this is the basis of all of our preaching:
Christ died for sinners
    and rose from the tomb.

688 © 1987 Andy Silver

They that wait upon the Lord
shall renew their strength,
and mount on eagles' wings.
They that wait upon the Lord
shall renew their strength,
and mount on eagles' wings.

They will run and not grow weary,
they will walk and not be faint.
Those whose hope is in the Lord
shall renew their strength.

689 Edmond Budry (1854–1932)
tr. R Birch Hoyle (1875–1939)

1 **Thine be the glory,**
    risen, conquering Son,
endless is the victory
    Thou o'er death hast won;
angels in bright raiment
    rolled the stone away,
kept the folded grave-clothes
    where Thy body lay.
    Thine be the glory,
        risen, conquering Son,
    endless is the victory
        Thou o'er death hast won.

2 Lo! Jesus meets us,
    risen from the tomb;
lovingly He greets us,
    scatters fear and gloom;
let the Church with gladness
    hymns of triumph sing,
for her Lord now liveth;
    death hath lost its sting.
    Thine be the glory . . .

3 No more we doubt Thee,
    glorious Prince of life;
life is nought without Thee:
    aid us in our strife;
make us more than conquerors,
    through Thy deathless love:
bring us safe through Jordan
    to Thy home above.
    Thine be the glory . . .

690
Graham Kendrick
© 1988 Make Way Music

1 **This Child**
   secretly comes in the night,
   oh, this Child, hiding a heavenly light,
   oh, this Child,
     coming to us like a stranger,
   this heavenly Child.
     This Child, heaven come down
       now to be with us here,
     heavenly love and mercy appear,
     softly in awe and wonder come near
     to this heavenly Child.

2 This Child, rising on us like the sun,
   oh, this Child, given to light everyone,
   oh, this Child,
     guiding our feet on the pathway
   to peace on earth.
     This Child, heaven come down . . .

3 This Child,
     raising the humble and poor,
   oh, this Child,
     making the proud ones to fall;
   this Child, filling the hungry
     with good things,
   this heavenly Child.
     This Child, heaven come down . . .
     This Child, heaven come down . . .

691
Les Garrett
© 1967 Scripture in Song/Integrity Music/
Kingsway's Thankyou Music

1 **This is the day,**
   this is the day that the Lord has made,
   that the Lord has made.
   We will rejoice,
   we will rejoice and be glad in it,
   and be glad in it.
   This is the day that the Lord has made,
   we will rejoice and be glad in it.
   This is the day,
   this is the day that the Lord hath made.

2 This is the day,
   this is the day when He rose again,
   when He rose again.
   We will rejoice,
   we will rejoice and be glad in it,
   and be glad in it.
   This is the day when He rose again,
   we will rejoice and be glad in it.
   This is the day,
   this is the day when He rose again.

3 This is the day,
   this is the day when the Spirit came,
   when the Spirit came.
   We will rejoice,
   we will rejoice and be glad in it,
   and be glad in it.
   This is the day when the Spirit came,
   we will rejoice and be glad in it.
   This is the day,
   this is the day when the Spirit came.

692
© 1987 Greg Leavers and Phil Burt

1 **This is what our Saviour said,**
   He will return to the earth in power,
   coming on the clouds from heaven,
   all earth shall see Him
     and bow before Him.
   He is the Alpha and Omega,
   Who is, and who was,
     and who is to come;
   once He was dead
     and behold He now is
   living for evermore.

2 With a shout and trumpet sound
   He'll fetch His bride
     for the marriage feast,
   and then we'll see Him face to face,
   joining all heaven in praise
     and worship.

Blessing and glory and thanksgiving
be to the Lamb
    reigning now and forever;
honour and power belong to Jesus,
come quickly Lord, amen!

693 Josiah Conder (1789–1855)

1 **Thou art the everlasting Word,**
   the Father's only Son;
   God manifestly seen and heard,
   and Heaven's belovèd One:
      worthy, O Lamb of God, art Thou
      that every knee to Thee should bow.

2 In Thee most perfectly expressed
   the Father's glories shine;
   of the full Deity possessed,
   eternally divine:
      worthy, O Lamb of God . . .

3 True image of the infinite,
   whose essence is concealed;
   brightness of uncreated light;
   the heart of God revealed:
      worthy, O Lamb of God . . .

4 But the high mysteries of Thy name
   an angel's grasp transcend;
   the Father only – glorious claim!
   the Son can comprehend:
      worthy, O Lamb of God . . .

5 Throughout the universe of bliss,
   the centre Thou, and sun;
   the eternal theme of praise is this,
   to heaven's belovèd One:
      worthy, O Lamb of God . . .

694 Tony Hopkins
© 1972 Scripture in Song/Integrity Music/
Kingsway's Thankyou Music

Thou art my God
      and I will praise Thee;
Thou art my God, I will exalt Thee.
O give thanks unto the Lord,
      for He is good;
for His mercy endureth for ever.

695 George Washington Doane (1799–1859)

1 **Thou art the way: to Thee alone**
   from sin and death we flee:
   and he who would the Father seek,
   must seek Him, Lord, by Thee.

2 Thou art the truth: Thy word alone
   true wisdom can impart;
   Thou only canst inform the mind
   and purify the heart.

3 Thou art the life: the rending tomb
   proclaims Thy conquering arm;
   and those who put their trust in Thee
   nor death nor hell shall harm.

4 Thou art the way, the truth, the life;
   grant us that way to know,
   that truth to keep, that life to win,
   whose joys eternal flow.

696 Pauline Michael Mills
Verse 2: Tom Smail
© 1963 Fred Bock Music/
Kingsway's Thankyou Music

1 **Thou art worthy, Thou art worthy,**
   Thou art worthy, O Lord.
   Thou art worthy to receive glory,
   glory and honour and power.
   For Thou hast created,
      hast all things created,
   for Thou hast created all things;
   and for Thy pleasure they are created:
   Thou art worthy, O Lord.

2 Thou art worthy, Thou art worthy,
Thou art worthy, O Lamb.
Thou art worthy to receive glory
and power at the Father's right hand.
For Thou hast redeemed us;
hast ransomed and cleaned us,
by Thy blood setting us free.
In white robes arrayed us,
    kings and priests made us,
and we are reigning in Thee.

4 Thou camest, O Lord,
with the living word
that should set Thy people free;
but, with mocking scorn,
and with crown of thorn,
they bore Thee to Calvary:
O come to my heart, Lord Jesus,
Thy cross is my only plea.

5 When heaven's arches ring,
and her choirs shall sing,
at Thy coming to victory,
let Thy voice call me home,
saying, 'Yet there is room,
there is room at my side for thee!'
And my heart shall rejoice, Lord Jesus,
when Thou comest and callest for me.

697 Emily Elizabeth Steele Elliott (1836–97)

1 **Thou didst leave Thy throne**
and Thy kingly crown,
when Thou camest to earth for me;
but in Bethlehem's home
was there found no room
for Thy holy nativity:
O come to my heart, Lord Jesus,
there is room in my heart for Thee.

2 Heaven's arches rang
when the angels sang,
proclaiming Thy royal degree;
but of lowly birth
cam'st Thou, Lord, on earth,
and in great humility:
O come to my heart, Lord Jesus,
there is room in my heart for Thee.

3 The foxes found rest,
and the birds their nest,
in the shade of the cedar-tree;
but Thy couch was the sod,
O Thou Son of God,
in the deserts of Galilee;
O come to my heart, Lord Jesus,
there is room in my heart for Thee.

698 R D Browne
© C M Browne

1 **Thou, Lord, hast given Thyself
    for our healing;**
poured out Thy life
    that our souls might be freed;
love, from the heart of the Father,
    revealing
light for our darkness
    and grace for our need.

2 Saviour of men, our humanity sharing,
give us a passion for souls that are lost.
Help us to follow,
    Thy gospel declaring;
daily to serve Thee
    and count not the cost.

3 Pray we for men
    who today in their blindness
wander from Thee
    and Thy kingdom of truth:
grant them a sight
    of Thy great loving-kindness,
Lord of their manhood
    and guide of their youth.

4 Come, Holy Spirit,
       to cleanse and renew us:
   purge us from evil
       and fill us with power:
   thus shall the waters of healing
       flow through us;
   so shall revival be born in this hour.

5 Give to Thy Church,
       as she tells forth the story,
   strength for her weakness
       and trust for her fears;
   make her a channel of grace
       for Thy glory,
   answer her prayers
       in the midst of the years.

699 John Marriott (1780–1825)

1 **Thou, whose almighty word**
   chaos and darkness heard,
   and took their flight;
   hear us, we humbly pray,
   and where the gospel day
   sheds not its glorious ray,
   let there be light!

2 Thou, who didst come to bring,
   on Thy redeeming wing,
   healing and sight;
   health to the sick in mind,
   sight to the inly blind,
   O now to all mankind
   let there be light!

3 Spirit of truth and love,
   Life-giving, holy Dove,
   speed forth Thy flight;
   move on the water's face,
   bearing the lamp of grace,
   and in earth's darkest place
   let there be light!

4 Blessèd and holy Three,
   glorious Trinity,
   wisdom, love, might;
   boundless as ocean's tide,
   rolling in fullest pride,
   through the earth, far and wide
   let there be light!

700 Frank Houghton (1894–1972)
         © Mrs D Houghton

1 **Thou who wast rich**
       beyond all splendour,
   all for love's sake becamest poor,
   thrones for a manger didst surrender
   sapphire-paved courts for stable floor.
   Thou who wast rich
       beyond all splendour,
   all for love's sake becamest poor.

2 Thou who art God beyond all praising,
   all for love's sake becamest man;
   stooping so low, but sinners raising
   heavenwards by Thine eternal plan.
   Thou who art God beyond all praising,
   all for love's sake becamest man.

3 Thou who art love beyond all telling,
   Saviour and King, we worship Thee.
   Immanuel, within us dwelling,
   make us what Thou
       wouldst have us be.
   Thou who art love beyond all telling,
   Saviour and King, we worship Thee.

701 Anon
         Copyright control

1 **Thou wilt keep him in perfect**
       peace, (*3 times*)
   whose mind is stayed on Thee.

2 Marvel not that I say unto you,
       (*3 times*)
   ye must be born again.

3 Though your sins as scarlet be,
   (*3 times*)
   they shall be white as snow.

4 If the Son shall make you free, (*3 times*)
   ye shall be free indeed.

5 They that wait upon the Lord, (*3 times*)
   they shall renew their strength.

6 Whom shall I send and who will go?
   (*3 times*)
   Here I am Lord, send me.

702 Nahum Tate (1652–1715)
and Nicholas Brady (1639–1726)

1 **Through all the changing scenes of
   life,**
   in trouble and in joy,
   the praises of my God shall still
   my heart and tongue employ.

2 Of His deliverance I will boast,
   till all that are distressed
   from my example comfort take,
   and charm their griefs to rest.

3 O magnify the Lord with me,
   with me exalt His name;
   when in distress to Him I called,
   He to my rescue came.

4 The hosts of God encamp around
   the dwellings of the just;
   deliverance He affords to all
   who on His succour trust.

5 O make but trial of His love;
   experience will decide
   how blest they are, and only they,
   who in His truth confide.

6 Fear Him, ye saints, and you will then
   have nothing else to fear;
   make you His service your delight,
   He'll make your wants His care.

703 Dale Garratt
© 1979 Scripture in Song/Integrity Music/
Kingsway's Thankyou Music

**Through our God
  we shall do valiantly,**
it is He who will tread down our enemies;
we'll sing and shout His victory:
Christ is King!

For God has won the victory
and set His people free;
His word has slain the enemy,
the earth shall stand and see that –

Through our God we shall do valiantly,
it is He who will tread down our enemies;
we'll sing and shout His victory,
Christ is King,
Christ is King,
Christ is King!

704 Mary Peters (1813–56)

1 **Through the love of God
   our Saviour**
   all will be well;
   free and changeless is His favour,
   all, all is well.
   Precious is the blood that heals us,
   perfect is the grace that seals us,
   strong the hand stretched out
      to shield us;
   all must be well.

2 Though we pass through tribulation,
   all will be well;
   ours is such a full salvation,
   all, all is well.
   Happy, still in God confiding;
   fruitful, if in Christ abiding;
   holy, through the Spirit's guiding;
   all must be well.

3 We expect a bright tomorrow;
 all will be well;
 faith can sing, through days of sorrow,
  'All, all is well.'
 On our Father's love relying,
 Jesus every need supplying,
 or in living or in dying,
  all must be well.

4 Thy mercy will not fail us,
 nor leave Thy work undone;
 with Thy right hand to help us,
 the victory shall be won;
 and then, by men and angels,
 Thy name shall be adored,
 and this shall be their anthem:
 One Church, one faith, one Lord.

705
Edward Hayes Plumptre (1821–91)

1 **Thy hand, O God, has guided**
 Thy flock, from age to age;
 the wondrous tale is written,
 full clear on every page;
 our fathers owned Thy goodness,
 and we their deeds record;
 and both of this bear witness:
 One Church, one faith, one Lord.

2 Thy heralds brought glad tidings
 to greatest as to least;
 they bade men rise and hasten
 to share the great King's feast;
 and this was all their teaching
 in every deed and word;
 to all alike proclaiming:
 One Church, one faith, one Lord.

3 Through many a day of darkness,
 through many a scene of strife,
 the faithful few fought bravely
 to guard the nation's life.
 Their gospel of redemption,
 sin pardoned, man restored,
 was all in this enfolded:
 One Church, one faith, one Lord.

706
Hugh Mitchell
© 1956 Singspiration Music/Brentwood Benson
Music Publishing/CopyCare

1 **Thy loving-kindness
 is better than life,**
 Thy loving-kindness is better than life;
 my lips shall praise Thee,
  thus will I bless Thee;
 Thy loving-kindness is better than life.

2 I lift my hands up unto Thy name,
 I lift my hands up unto Thy name;
 my lips shall praise Thee,
  thus will I bless Thee;
 Thy loving-kindness is better than life.

707
From Psalm 89
© Timothy Dudley-Smith

1 **Timeless love! We sing the story,**
 praise His wonders, tell His worth;
 love more fair than heaven's glory,
 love more firm than ancient earth!
 Tell His faithfulness abroad:
 who is like Him? Praise the Lord!

2 By His faithfulness surrounded,
 north and south His hand proclaim;
 earth and heaven formed and founded,
 skies and seas declare His name!
 Wind and storm obey His word:
 who is like Him? Praise the Lord!

3 Truth and righteousness
    enthrone Him,
just and equal are His ways;
more than happy, those who own Him,
more than joy, their songs of praise!
Sun and shield and great reward,
who is like Him? Praise the Lord!

708 Frances van Alstyne (1820–1915)
(Fanny J Crosby)

1 **To God be the glory!**
    great things He hath done;
so loved He the world
    that He gave us His Son;
who yielded His life
    an atonement for sin,
and opened the life gate
    that all may go in.
    Praise the Lord, praise the Lord!
    let the earth hear His voice;
    praise the Lord, praise the Lord!
    let the people rejoice:
    O come to the Father,
    through Jesus the Son
    and give Him the glory;
    great things He hath done!

2 O perfect redemption,
    the purchase of blood!
to every believer the promise of God;
the vilest offender who truly believes,
that moment from Jesus
    a pardon receives.
    Praise the Lord . . .

3 Great things He hath taught us,
    great things He hath done,
and great our rejoicing
    through Jesus the Son;
but purer, and higher,
    and greater will be
our wonder, our rapture,
    when Jesus we see.
    Praise the Lord . . .

709 James E Seddon (1915–83)
© Mrs Mavis Seddon/Jubilate Hymns

1 **To Him we come –**
Jesus Christ our Lord,
God's own living Word,
His dear Son:
in Him there is no east and west,
in Him all nations shall be blest;
to all He offers peace and rest –
    loving Lord!

2 In Him we live –
Christ our strength and stay,
life and truth and way,
friend divine:
His power can break the chains of sin,
still all life's storms without, within,
help us the daily fight to win –
    living Lord!

3 For Him we go –
soldiers of the cross,
counting all things loss
Him to know;
going to every land and race,
preaching to all redeeming grace,
building His church in every place –
    conquering Lord!

4 With Him we serve –
His the work we share
with saints everywhere,
near and far;
one in the task which faith requires,
one in the zeal which never tires,
one in the hope His love inspires –
    coming Lord!

5 Onward we go –
faithful, bold, and true,
called His will to do
day by day
till, at the last, with joy we'll see
Jesus, in glorious majesty;
live with Him through eternity –
    reigning Lord!

710

To Him who is able to keep us,
to keep us from falling away,
who'll bring us, spotless and joyful,
into God's presence one day.
To the only God our Saviour,
through Jesus Christ our Lord
be glory, majesty, might and power,
now, always – amen.

3 True-hearted! Saviour,
        You know all our story,
    weak are the hearts
        that we lay at Your feet;
    sinful and treacherous,
        yet, for Your glory,
    heal them and cleanse them
        from sin and deceit.
        Peal out the watchword . . .

4 True-hearted, whole-hearted!
        Saviour, all-glorious,
    take Your great power
        and You reign alone,
    over our wills and affections
        victorious –
    freely surrendered
        and wholly Your own.
        Peal out the watchword . . .

711

1 **True-hearted, whole-hearted,**
        faithful and loyal,
    King of our lives,
        by Your grace we'll stay true!
    Under Your standard,
        exalted and royal,
    strong in Your strength,
        we will battle for You!
        Peal out the watchword,
        and silence it never,
        song of our spirits, rejoicing and free:
        'True-hearted, whole-hearted,
            now and for ever,
        King of our lives,
            by Your grace we will be!'

2 True-hearted, whole-hearted!
        fullest allegiance
    yielding each day to our glorious King!
    Valiant endeavour
        and loving obedience
    freely and joyously
        now would we bring.
        Peal out the watchword . . .

712

1 **O soul, are you weary**
        and troubled?
    No light in the darkness you see?
    There's light for a look at the Saviour,
    and life more abundant and free!
        Turn your eyes upon Jesus,
        look full in His wonderful face;
        and the things of earth
            will grow strangely dim
        in the light of His glory and grace.

2 Through death into life everlasting
    He passed and we follow Him there;
    over us sin no more hath dominion,
    for more than conquerors we are!
        Turn your eyes . . .

3 His word shall not fail you
    He promised;
  believe Him, and all will be well:
  then go to a world that is dying,
  His perfect salvation to tell.
  Turn your eyes upon Jesus,
  look full in His wonderful face;
  and the things of earth
    will grow strangely dim
  in the light of His glory and grace.

713 Graham Kendrick
© 1988 Make Way Music

1 **Tonight, while all the world was**
      sleeping,
  a light exploded in the skies.
  And then, as glory did surround us,
  a voice, an angel did appear!
  WOMEN *Glory to God in the highest,*
  MEN   *glory to God in the highest,*
        and on the earth,
  ALL   *be peace from heaven!*
  WOMEN *Glory to God in the highest,*
  MEN   *glory to God in the highest,*
        and on the earth,
  ALL   *be peace from heaven!*

2 Afraid, we covered up our faces,
  amazed at what our ears did hear.
  Good news of joy for all the people –
  today a Saviour has appeared!
      Glory to God . . .

  (*Bridge*)
  And so to Bethlehem
  to find it was all true;
  despised and worthless shepherds,
  we were the first to know!
      Glory to God . . .

714 German (15th century)
tr. Percy Dearmer (1867–1936)
© 1964 Oxford University Press

1 **Unto us a boy is born!**
  King of all creation,
  came He to a world forlorn,
    the Lord of every nation,
    the Lord of every nation.

2 Cradled in a stall was He
  with sleepy cows and asses;
  but the very beasts could see
    that He all men surpasses,
    that He all men surpasses.

3 Herod then with fear was filled:
  'A Prince,' he said, 'in Jewry!'
  All the little boys he killed
    at Bethlehem in his fury,
    at Bethlehem in his fury.

4 Now may Mary's Son, who came
  so long ago to love us,
  lead us all with hearts aflame
    unto the joys above us,
    unto the joys above us.

5 Alpha and Omega He!
  Let the organ thunder,
  while the choir with peals of glee
    doth rend the air asunder,
    doth rend the air asunder!

715 Diane Fung
© 1979 Word's Spirit of Praise Music/
CopyCare

Victory is on our lips and in our lives,
for Jesus has surely been raised
      from the dead;
and never shall the powers of darkness
      doubt that
Jesus is Lord over all.
Neither shall the powers of darkness
      triumph,
for Jesus is Lord! Jesus is Lord!
Jesus is Lord over all.

716

David Hadden
© 1981 Word's Spirit of Praise Music/
CopyCare

We are a chosen people,
a royal priesthood,
a holy nation belonging to God.

1 You have called us out of darkness
to declare Your praise;
we exalt You and enthrone You,
glorify Your name.
We are a chosen people . . .

2 You have placed us into Zion,
in the new Jerusalem;
thousand thousand are their voices,
singing to the Lamb.
We are a chosen people . . .

717

Graham Kendrick
© 1985 Kingsway's Thankyou Music

We are here to praise You,
lift our hearts and sing;
we are here to give You
the best that we can bring.
And it is our love
rising from our hearts –
everything within us cries:
'Abba Father!'
Help us now to give You
pleasure and delight –
heart and mind and will that say:
'I love You, Lord.'

O give thanks to the Lord,
for His love will never end.

2 It's a march of victory,
it's a march of triumph,
lifting Jesus higher
on a throne of praise,
with the banner of love
flying over us,
ever further and deeper
into the heart of God.
O give thanks . . .

3 We will go to the nations,
spreading wide the fragrance
of the knowledge of Jesus
into every place.
Hear the great cloud of witnesses
cheer us onward,
ever further and deeper
into the heart of God.
O give thanks . . .

4 And the whole creation
waits in expectation
of the full revelation
of the sons of God;
as we march through history
to our blood-bought destiny,
ever further and deeper
into the heart of God.

Ever further and deeper
into the heart of God.

718

Graham Kendrick
© 1985 Kingsway's Thankyou Music

1 **We are marching**
in the great procession,
singers and dancers,
and musicians;
with the great congregation
we are moving onward,
ever further and deeper
into the heart of God.

719

Ian Traynar
© 1977 Kingsway's Thankyou Music

1 **We are moving on into**
a deep appreciation
of the love which flows from Father out
to every child of God;
of the grace with which He handles
every minute situation,
how He wants the best for everyone
who gives to Him his all.

Grace, it seems, is all He has,
and one big open heart;
and it's so good
being loved by You, my Lord.

2 We will know and understand
His purposes more clearly,
O the mystery of the things He does
in making us more whole.
With His love He woos us,
by His grace He sets us free;
we can only trust Him
and just hold on to His hand.
Grace, it seems . . .

720 Graham Kendrick
© 1986 Kingsway's Thankyou Music

1 **We believe in God the Father,**
maker of the universe,
and in Christ His Son our Saviour,
come to us by virgin birth.
We believe He died to save us,
bore our sins, was crucified;
then from death He rose victorious,
ascended to the Father's side.
Jesus, Lord of all, Lord of all;
Jesus, Lord of all, Lord of all;
Jesus, Lord of all, Lord of all;
Jesus, Lord of all, Lord of all;
name above all names,
name above all names!

2 We believe He sends His Spirit
on His Church with gifts of power;
God, His word of truth affirming,
sends us to the nations now.
He will come again in glory,
judge the living and the dead:
every knee shall bow before Him,
then must every tongue confess.
Jesus, Lord of all . . .

Name above all names!

721 From *The Alternative Service Book 1980*
© 1980 The Archbishops' Council

1 MEN **We break this bread**
to share in the body of Christ:
WOMEN we break this bread
to share in the body of Christ:
ALL though we are many,
we are one body,
because we all share,
we all share in one bread.

2 MEN We drink this cup
to share in the body of Christ:
WOMEN we drink this cup
to share in the body of Christ:
ALL though we are many,
we are one body,
because we all share,
we all share in one cup.

722 Kirk Dearman
© 1984 Stamps Baxter Music/
Brentwood Benson Music Publishing/
CopyCare

We bring the sacrifice of praise
into the house of the Lord;
we bring the sacrifice of praise
into the house of the Lord;
we bring the sacrifice of praise
into the house of the Lord;
we bring the sacrifice of praise
into the house of the Lord;
and we offer up to You
the sacrifices of thanksgiving;
and we offer up to You
the sacrifices of joy.

723 © Timothy Dudley-Smith

1 **We come as guests invited**
when Jesus bids us dine,
His friends on earth united
to share the bread and wine;
the bread of life is broken,
the wine is freely poured
for us, in solemn token
of Christ our dying Lord.

2 We eat and drink, receiving
from Christ the grace we need,
and in our hearts believing
on Him by faith we feed;
with wonder and thanksgiving
for love that knows no end,
we find in Jesus living
our ever-present friend.

3 One bread is ours for sharing,
one single fruitful vine,
our fellowship declaring
renewed in bread and wine:
renewed, sustained and given
by token, sign and word,
the pledge and seal of heaven,
the love of Christ our Lord.

2 The fire divine, their steps that led,
still goeth bright before us;
the heavenly shield,
around them spread,
is still high holden o'er us;
the grace those sinners that subdued,
the strength those weaklings
that renewed,
doth vanquish, doth restore us.

3 The cleaving sins
that brought them low
are still our souls oppressing;
the tears that from their eyes did flow
fall fast, our shame confessing;
as with Thee, Lord, prevailed their cry,
so now our prayer ascends on high,
and bringeth down Thy blessing.

4 Their joy unto their Lord we bring;
their song to us descendeth:
the Spirit who in them did sing
to us His music lendeth.
His song in them, in us, is one;
we raise it high, we send it on –
the song that never endeth!

5 Ye saints to come, take up the strain,
the same sweet theme endeavour!
Unbroken be the golden chain,
keep on the song for ever!
Safe in the same dear dwelling-place,
rich with the same eternal grace,
bless the same boundless giver!

724 Thomas Hornblower Gill (1819–1906)

1 **We come unto our fathers' God:**
their rock is our salvation:
the eternal arms, their dear abode,
we make our habitation:
we bring Thee, Lord,
the praise they brought;
we seek Thee as Thy saints have sought
in every generation.

725 Mimi Farra
© 1975 Celebration/
Kingsway's Thankyou Music

We cry, 'Hosanna, Lord;
yes, hosanna, Lord;
yes, hosanna, Lord', to You:
we cry, 'Hosanna, Lord;
yes, hosanna, Lord;
yes, hosanna, Lord', to You!

1 Behold, our Saviour comes!
   behold the Son of our God!
   He offers Himself,
        and He comes among us,
   a lowly servant to all.
      We cry, 'Hosanna, Lord;
      yes, hosanna, Lord;
      yes, hosanna, Lord', to You:
      we cry, 'Hosanna, Lord;
      yes, hosanna, Lord;
      yes, hosanna, Lord', to You!

2 Children wave their palms
   as the King of all kings rides by;
   should we forget to praise our God,
   the very stones would sing.
      We cry, 'Hosanna . . .

3 He comes to set us free,
   He gives us liberty;
   His victory over death
        is the eternal sign
   of God's love for us.
      We cry, 'Hosanna . . .

726 Malcolm du Plessis
         © 1984 Kingsway's Thankyou Music

We declare Your majesty,
we proclaim that Your name is exalted;
for You reign magnificently,
        rule victoriously,
and Your power is shown
        throughout the earth.

And we exclaim, 'Our God is mighty!'
lift up Your name, for You are holy.
Sing it again, all honour and glory –
in adoration we bow before Your throne!

727 Anon
         Copyright control

1 **We are gathering together
   unto Him,**
   we are gathering together unto Him;
   unto Him shall the gathering
        of the people be;
   we are gathering together unto Him.

2 We are offering together unto Him,
   we are offering together unto Him;
   unto Him shall the offering
        of the people be;
   we are offering together unto Him.

3 We are singing together unto Him,
   we are singing together unto Him;
   unto Him shall the singing
        of the people be;
   we are singing together unto Him.

4 We are praying together unto Him,
   We are praying together unto Him;
   unto Him shall the praying
        of the people be;
   we are praying together unto Him.

728 © Edward Joseph Burns

1 **We have a gospel to proclaim,**
   good news for men in all the earth;
   the gospel of a saviour's name:
   we sing His glory, tell His worth.

2 Tell of His birth at Bethlehem,
   not in a royal house or hall
   but in a stable dark and dim:
   the Word made flesh, a light for all.

3 Tell of His death at Calvary,
   hated by those He came to save;
   in lonely suffering on the cross
   for all He loved, His life He gave.

4   Tell of that glorious Easter morn:
    empty the tomb, for He was free;
    He broke the power of death and hell
    that we might share His victory.

5   Tell of His reign at God's right hand,
    by all creation glorified;
    He sends His Spirit on His Church
    to live for Him, the Lamb who died.

6   Now we rejoice to name Him king:
    Jesus is Lord of all the earth;
    this gospel-message we proclaim:
    we sing His glory, tell His worth.

729   Bruce Ballinger
          © Lorenz Publishing Co/MCA Publishing Co/
          CopyCare

1   **We have come into His house,**
    and gathered in His name
        to worship Him.
    We have come into His house,
    and gathered in His name
        to worship Him.
    We have come into His house,
    and gathered in His name
        to worship Christ the Lord,
    worship Him, Christ the Lord.

2   So forget about yourself
    and concentrate on Him
        and worship Him.
    So forget about yourself
    and concentrate on Him
        and worship Him.
    So forget about yourself
    and concentrate on Him
        and worship Christ the Lord,
    worship Him, Christ the Lord.

3   Let us lift up holy hands
    and magnify His name
        and worship Him.
    Let us lift up holy hands
    and magnify His name
        and worship Him.

Let us lift up holy hands
and magnify His name
    and worship Christ the Lord,
worship Him, Christ the Lord.

730   Priscilla Owens (1829–1907)

1   **We have heard a joyful sound:**
    Jesus saves!
    Spread the gladness all around:
    Jesus saves!
    Bear the news to every land,
    climb the steeps and cross the waves;
    Onward! 'tis our Lord's command:
    Jesus saves!

2   Sing above the battle's strife:
    Jesus saves!
    By His death and endless life,
    Jesus saves!
    Sing it softly through the gloom,
    when the heart for mercy craves;
    sing in triumph o'er the tomb:
    Jesus saves!

3   Give the winds a mighty voice:
    Jesus saves!
    Let the nations now rejoice:
    Jesus saves!
    Shout salvation full and free
    to every strand that ocean laves –
    this our song of victory:
    Jesus saves!

731   William Bullock (1798–1874)
          and Henry Williams Baker (1821–77)

1   **We love the place, O God,**
    wherein Thine honour dwells;
    the joy of Thine abode
    all earthly joy excels.

2 It is the house of prayer,
wherein Thy servants meet;
and Thou, O Lord, art there,
Thy chosen flock to greet.

3 We love the word of life,
the word that tells of peace,
of comfort in the strife,
and joys that never cease.

4 We love to sing below
of mercies freely given;
but O we long to know
the triumph-song of heaven.

5 Lord Jesus, give us grace,
on earth to love Thee more,
in heaven to see Thy face,
and with Thy saints adore.

732 Matthias Claudius (1740–1815)
tr. Jane Montgomery Campbell (1817–78)
altered © 1986 Horrobin/Leavers

1 **We plough the fields and scatter**
the good seed on the land,
but it is fed and watered
by God's almighty hand;
He sends the snow in winter,
the warmth to swell the grain,
the breezes and the sunshine
and soft refreshing rain.
All good gifts around us
are sent from heaven above,
then thank the Lord, O thank the Lord,
for all His love.

2 He only is the maker
of all things near and far;
He paints the wayside flower,
He lights the evening star;
the wind and waves obey Him,
by Him the birds are fed;
much more to us, His children,
He gives our daily bread.
All good gifts . . .

3 We thank You then, O Father,
for all things bright and good,
the seed-time and the harvest,
our life, our health, our food.
Accept the gifts we offer
for all Your love imparts;
we come now, Lord, to give You
our humble, thankful hearts.
All good gifts . . .

733 Frances van Alstyne (1820 –1915)
(Fanny J Crosby)
altered © 1987 Horrobin/Leavers

1 **We praise You, we bless You,**
   our Saviour divine,
all power and dominion
   are Yours for all time!
We sing of Your mercy
   with joyful acclaim,
for You have redeemed us:
   all praise to Your name!

2 All honour and praise
   to Your excellent name,
Your love is unchanging –
   for ever the same!
We bless and adore You,
   O Saviour and King;
with joy and thanksgiving
   Your praises we sing!

3 The strength of the hills
   and the depths of the sea,
the earth and its fulness,
   Yours always shall be;
and yet to the lowly
   You listen with care,
so ready their humble petitions to hear.

4 Your infinite goodness
   our tongues shall employ;
You give to us richly all things to enjoy;
we'll follow Your footsteps,
   we'll rest in Your love,
and soon we shall praise You
   in mansions above!

734
Verses 1 and 2: Ed Baggett
© 1974, 1975 Celebration/
Kingsway's Thankyou Music
Verse 3 after Thomas Ken (1637–1710)

**We really want to thank You,
Lord,**
*we really want to bless Your name:
hallelujah! Jesus is our King!*

1 We thank You, Lord,
    for Your gift to us,
Your life so rich beyond compare,
the gift of Your body here on earth
of which we sing and share.
    We really want . . .

2 We thank You, Lord,
    for our life together,
to live and move in the love of Christ,
Your tenderness which sets us free
to serve You with our lives.
    We really want . . .

3 Praise God
    from whom all blessings flow,
praise Him all creatures here below,
praise Him above, you heavenly host,
praise Father, Son and Holy Ghost.
    We really want . . .

735
Edith Gilling Cherry (1872–97)

1 **We rest on Thee,**
    our shield and our defender!
we go not forth alone against the foe;
strong in Thy strength,
    safe in Thy keeping tender,
we rest on Thee,
    and in Thy name we go.
Strong in Thy strength,
    safe in Thy keeping tender,
we rest on Thee,
    and in Thy name we go.

2 Yes, in Thy name,
    O Captain of salvation!
in Thy dear name,
    all other names above;
Jesus our righteousness,
    our sure foundation,
our Prince of glory
    and our King of love.
Jesus our righteousness,
    our sure foundation,
our Prince of glory
    and our King of love.

3 We go in faith,
    our own great weakness feeling,
and needing more each day
    Thy grace to know:
yet from our hearts
    a song of triumph pealing,
'We rest on Thee,
    and in Thy name we go.'
Yet from our hearts
    a song of triumph pealing,
'We rest on Thee,
    and in Thy name we go.'

4 We rest on Thee,
    our shield and our defender!
Thine is the battle,
    Thine shall be the praise;
when passing through
    the gates of pearly splendour,
victors, we rest with Thee,
    through endless days.
When passing through
    the gates of pearly splendour,
victors, we rest with Thee,
    through endless days.

736 From Isaiah 6
Copyright control

We see the Lord,
we see the Lord,
and He is high and lifted up,
and His train fills the temple;
He is high and lifted up,
and His train fills the temple.
The angels cry, 'Holy',
the angels cry, 'Holy',
the angels cry, 'Holy is the Lord.'

DESCANT
We see Jesus,
we see Jesus.
High, He is high,
He is high.
Angels cry, 'Holy' . . .

737 Graham Kendrick
© 1988 Make Way Music

We shall stand,
with our feet on the rock;
whatever men may say,
we'll lift Your name up high –
and we shall walk
through the darkest night;
setting our faces like flint,
we'll walk into the light!

1 Lord, You have chosen me
        for fruitfulness
    to be transformed into Your likeness:
    I'm going to fight on through
        till I see You
    face to face.
    We shall stand . . .

2 Lord, as Your witnesses
        You've appointed us,
    and with Your Holy Spirit anointed us:
    and so I'll fight on through
        till I see You
    face to face.
    We shall stand . . .

738 Thomas Kelly (1769–1855)

1 **We sing the praise of Him**
        who died,
    of Him who died upon the cross;
    the sinner's hope let men deride,
    for this we count the world but lost.

2 Inscribed upon the cross we see,
    in shining letters, 'God is love';
    He bears our sins upon the tree,
    He brings us mercy from above.

3 The cross! it takes our guilt away,
    it holds the fainting spirit up;
    it cheers with hope the gloomy day
    and sweetens every bitter cup.

4 It makes the coward spirit brave,
    and nerves the feeble arm for fight;
    it takes the terror from the grave,
    and gilds the bed of death with light.

5 The balm of life, the cure of woe,
    the measure and the pledge of love;
    the sinners' refuge here below,
    the angels' theme in heaven above.

739 Gordon Brattle (1917–91)
© David Brattle

We will sing of our Redeemer,
    He's our King:
all His glory, all His praise
    to you we bring;
with our hearts and with our voices
    Him we sing,
we love the Lord, we love His word;
    He's our King.

740 John H Hopkins (1820–91)
altered © 1986 Horrobin/Leavers

1 **We three kings of Orient are,**
    bearing gifts we travel afar,
    field and fountain,
        moor and mountain,
    following yonder star:

O star of wonder, star of night,
star with royal beauty bright,
westward leading, still proceeding,
guide us to the perfect light.

2　Born a King on Bethlehem plain,
　gold I bring to crown Him again:
　King for ever, ceasing never,
　over us all to reign.
　　O star of wonder . . .

3　Frankincense for Jesus have I,
　God on earth yet Priest on high;
　prayer and praising all men raising:
　worship is earth's reply.
　　O star of wonder . . .

4　Myrrh is mine: its bitter perfume
　tells of His death and Calvary's gloom;
　sorrowing, sighing, bleeding, dying,
　sealed in a stone-cold tomb.
　　O star of wonder . . .

5　Glorious now, behold Him arise,
　King, and God, and sacrifice!
　Heaven sings out, 'Alleluia!',
　'Amen!' the earth replies.
　　O star of wonder . . .

741　Adrian Snell
　　　　© 1986 Serious Music UK

1　**We Your people bow before You**
　broken and ashamed;
　we have turned on Your creation,
　crushed the life You freely gave.

2　Lord, have mercy on Your children
　weeping and in fear:
　for You are our God and Saviour,
　Father, in Your love draw near.

3　Father, in this hour of danger
　we will turn to You:
　O forgive us, Lord, forgive us
　and our lives and faith renew.

4　Pour Your Holy Spirit on us,
　set our hearts aflame:
　all shall see Your power in the nations,
　may we bring glory to Your name.

742　Diane Fung
　　　　© 1978, 1979 Word's Spirit of Praise Music/
　　　　CopyCare

We'll sing a new song
　　of glorious triumph,
for we see the government of God
　　in our lives;
we'll sing a new song of glorious triumph,
for we see the government of God
　　in our lives.

He is crowned God of the whole world,
　　crowned,
King of creation, crowned,
　　ruling the nations now;
He is crowned God of the whole world,
　　crowned,
King of creation, crowned,
　　ruling the nations now.

743　Graham Kendrick
　　　　© 1989 Make Way Music

1　**We'll walk the land**
　　with hearts on fire;
　and every step will be a prayer.
　Hope is rising, new day dawning;
　sound of singing fills the air.

2　Two thousand years, and still the flame
　is burning bright across the land.
　Hearts are waiting, longing, aching,
　for awakening once again.
　　Let the flame burn brighter
　　in the heart of the darkness,
　　turning night to glorious day.
　　Let the song grow louder,
　　as our love grows stronger;
　　let it shine! let it shine!

3 We'll walk for truth, speak out for love;
in Jesus' name we shall be strong,
to lift the fallen, to save the children,
to fill the nation with Your song.
Let the flame burn brighter
in the heart of the darkness,
turning night to glorious day.
Let the song grow louder,
as our love grows stronger;
let it shine! let it shine!

744 Colin Sterne (1862–1926)

1 **We've a story to tell to the nations,**
that shall turn their hearts to the right;
a story of truth and sweetness,
a story of peace and light,
a story of peace and light:
For the darkness shall turn to dawning,
and the dawning to noon-day bright,
and Christ's great kingdom
shall come on earth,
the kingdom of love and light.

2 We've a song to be sung to the nations,
that shall lift their hearts to the Lord;
a song that shall conquer evil,
and shatter the spear and sword,
and shatter the spear and sword:
For the darkness . . .

3 We've a message to give to the nations,
that the Lord who reigneth above
hath sent us His Son to save us,
and show us that God is love,
and show us that God is love:
For the darkness . . .

4 We've a Saviour to show to the nations,
who the path of sorrow hath trod,
that all of the world's great peoples,
might come to the truth of God,
might come to the truth of God:
For the darkness . . .

745 American folk hymn
Copyright control

1 **Were you there**
when they crucified my Lord?
Were you there
when they crucified my Lord?
Oh! Sometimes it causes me to
tremble, tremble, tremble;
Were you there
when they crucified my Lord?

2 Were you there
when they nailed Him to the tree?
Were you there
when they nailed Him to the tree?
Oh! Sometimes it causes me to
tremble, tremble, tremble;
Were you there
when they nailed Him to the tree?

3 Were you there
when they laid Him in the tomb?
Were you there
when they laid Him in the tomb?
Oh! Sometimes it causes me to
tremble, tremble, tremble;
Were you there
when they laid Him in the tomb?

4 Were you there when God raised Him
from the dead?
Were you there when God raised Him
from the dead?
Oh! Sometimes it causes me to
tremble, tremble, tremble;
Were you there when God raised Him
from the dead?

746 Joseph Scriven (1819–86)

1 **What a friend we have in Jesus,**
all our sins and griefs to bear!
What a privilege to carry
everything to God in prayer!
O what peace we often forfeit,
O what needless pain we bear –
all because we do not carry
everything to God in prayer!

2 Have we trials and temptations?
Is there trouble anywhere?
We should never be discouraged:
take it to the Lord in prayer!
Can we find a friend so faithful,
who will all our sorrows share?
Jesus knows our every weakness –
take it to the Lord in prayer!

3 Are we weak and heavy-laden,
cumbered with a load of care?
Precious Saviour, still our refuge!
Take it to the Lord in prayer!
Do thy friends despise, forsake thee?
Take it to the Lord in prayer!
In His arms He'll take and shield thee,
thou wilt find a solace there.

747
Anon
Copyright control

1 **What a mighty God we serve . . .**
(4 times)

2 He created you and me . . .

3 He has all the power to save . . .

4 Let us praise the living God . . .

5 What a mighty God we serve . . .

748
Rufus Henry McDaniel (1850–1940)
© The Rodeheaver Co/Word Music/
CopyCare

1 **What a wonderful change
in my life has been wrought**
since Jesus came into my heart!
I have light in my soul
for which long I had sought,
since Jesus came into my heart!

*Since Jesus came into my heart,
since Jesus came into my heart,
floods of joy o'er my soul
like the sea billows roll,
since Jesus came into my heart!*

2 I have ceased from my wandering
and going astray
since Jesus came into my heart!
And my sins, which were many,
are all washed away
since Jesus came into my heart!
Since Jesus came . . .

3 I'm possessed of a hope
that is steadfast and sure,
since Jesus came into my heart!
And no dark clouds of doubt
now my pathway obscure,
since Jesus came into my heart!
Since Jesus came . . .

4 There's a light in the valley of death
now for me,
since Jesus came into my heart!
And the gates of the city beyond
I can see,
since Jesus came into my heart!
Since Jesus came . . .

5 I shall go there to dwell in that city,
I know,
since Jesus came into my heart!
and I'm happy, so happy,
as onward I go,
since Jesus came into my heart!
Since Jesus came . . .

749
William Chatterton Dix (1837–98)

1 **What child is this, who, laid to rest,**
on Mary's lap is sleeping?
Whom angels greet
with anthems sweet,
while shepherds watch are keeping?

This, this is Christ the King,
whom shepherds guard and angels sing:
haste, haste to bring Him praise,
the babe, the Son of Mary.

2 Why lies He in such mean estate,
   where ox and ass are feeding?
   Good Christian fear: for sinners here
   the silent Word is pleading.
   This, this is Christ . . .

3 So bring Him incense,
        gold, and myrrh,
   come, peasant, king, to own Him.
   The King of kings salvation brings,
   let loving hearts enthrone Him.
   This, this is Christ . . .

750 Bryn and Sally Haworth
© 1983 Signalgrade/
Kingsway's Thankyou Music

1 **What kind of love is this,**
   that gave itself for me?
   I am the guilty one,
   yet I go free.
   What kind of love is this?
   A love I've never known.
   I didn't even know His name,
   what kind of love is this?

2 What kind of man is this,
   that died in agony?
   He who had done no wrong
   was crucified for me.
   What kind of man is this,
   who laid aside His throne
   that I may know the love of God?
   What kind of man is this?

3 By grace I have been saved,
   it is the gift of God.
   He destined me to be His son,
   such is His love.
   No eye has ever seen,
   no ear has ever heard,
   nor has the heart of man conceived,
   what kind of love is this.

751 Joseph Addison (1672–1719)

1 **When all Your mercies, O my God,**
   my rising soul surveys,
   transported with the view, I'm lost
   in wonder, love, and praise.

2 Unnumbered comforts on my soul
   Your tender care bestowed,
   before my infant heart conceived
   from whom those comforts flowed.

3 Ten thousand thousand precious gifts
   my daily thanks employ,
   nor is the least a cheerful heart
   that tastes those gifts with joy.

4 Through every period of my life
   Your goodness I'll pursue,
   and after death, in distant worlds,
   the glorious theme renew.

5 Through all eternity to You
   a joyful song I'll raise;
   for O! eternity's too short
   to utter all Your praise!

752 Sue Read
© 1983 Kingsway's Thankyou Music

1 **When He comes**
        we'll see just a child;
   no warrior lord but a baby so mild.
   The Lord says: 'Bethlehem,
        though you are but small,
   in you shall be born the King.'
   When He comes, when He comes.

2 When He comes
  His reign shall bring peace;
when He comes all fighting shall cease.
Men shall hammer their spears
  into pruning hooks
and prepare for battle no more.
When He comes, when He comes.
And on that day there will be laughter;
on that day joy ever after, no more tears:
for the Lord will wipe them all away.
And on that day, men shall be brothers,
reconciled to God and each other;
the world shall see
  the King in His glory,
  when He comes.

3 When He comes
  He'll be of David's line,
the mighty God and ruler divine.
They'll call Him wonderful and
  counsellor,
and His kingdom shall never cease.
When He comes, when He comes.
And on that day . . .

753 Keri Jones and Dave Matthews
  © 1978 Word's Spirit of Praise Music/
  CopyCare

When I feel the touch
of Your hand upon my life,
it causes me to sing a song,
that I love You, Lord.
So from deep within
my spirit singeth unto Thee,
You are my King,
You are my God,
and I love You, Lord.

754 Wayne and Cathy Perrin
  © Integrity's Hosanna! Music/
  Kingsway's Thankyou Music

When I look into Your holiness,
when I gaze into Your loveliness,
when all things that surround
become shadows in the light of You.

When I've found the joy
  of reaching Your heart,
when my will becomes enthroned
  in Your love,
when all things that surround
become shadows in the light of You.

I worship You, I worship You;
the reason I live is to worship You.
I worship You, I worship You;
the reason I live is to worship You.

755 Isaac Watts (1674–1748)

1 **When I survey the wondrous cross**
on which the Prince of glory died,
my richest gain I count but loss,
and pour contempt on all my pride.

2 Forbid it, Lord, that I should boast,
save in the death of Christ my God:
all the vain things that charm me most,
I sacrifice them to His blood.

3 See from His head, His hands, His feet,
sorrow and love flow mingled down:
did e'er such love and sorrow meet,
or thorns compose so rich a crown?

4 Were the whole realm of nature mine,
that were an offering far too small,
love so amazing, so divine,
demands my soul, my life, my all.

756 tr. from the German by
  Edward Caswall (1814–78)

1 **When morning gilds the skies,**
my heart awaking cries:
  'May Jesus Christ be praised!'
Alike at work and prayer
to Jesus I repair;
  may Jesus Christ be praised!

2 Does sadness fill my mind?
a solace here I find –
   may Jesus Christ be praised!
When evil thoughts molest,
with this I shield my breast –
   may Jesus Christ be praised!

3 Be this, when day is past,
of all my thoughts the last:
   May Jesus Christ be praised!
The night becomes as day,
when from the heart we say:
   'May Jesus Christ be praised!'

4 To God, the Word, on high
the hosts of angels cry:
   'May Jesus Christ be praised!'
Let mortals, too, upraise
their voice in hymns of praise:
   May Jesus Christ be praised!

5 Let earth's wide circle round
in joyful notes resound:
   May Jesus Christ be praised!
Let air, and sea, and sky,
from depth to height, reply:
   May Jesus Christ be praised!

6 Be this while life is mine,
my canticle divine:
   May Jesus Christ be praised!
Be this the eternal song
through all the ages long:
   May Jesus Christ be praised!

757 Horatio Gates Spafford (1828–88)

1 **When peace like a river**
   attendeth my way,
when sorrows like sea-billows roll;
whatever my lot
   You have taught me to say,
'It is well, it is well with my soul.'
   It is well with my soul;
   it is well, it is well with my soul.

2 Though Satan should buffet,
   if trials should come,
let this blessèd assurance control,
that Christ has regarded
   my helpless estate,
and has shed His own blood
   for my soul.
   It is well . . .

3 My sin – O the bliss
   of this glorious thought –
my sin – not in part – but the whole
is nailed to His cross;
   and I bear it no more;
praise the Lord, praise the Lord,
   O my soul.
   It is well . . .

4 For me, be it Christ,
   be it Christ hence to live!
If Jordan above me shall roll,
no pang shall be mine,
   for in death as in life
You will whisper Your peace
   to my soul.
   It is well . . .

5 But Lord, it's for You –
   for Your coming we wait,
the sky, not the grave, is our goal:
O trump of the angel!
   O voice of the Lord!
Blessèd hope! blessèd rest of my soul.
   It is well . . .

758 © Timothy Dudley-Smith

1 **When the Lord in glory comes,**
not the trumpets, not the drums,
not the anthem, not the psalm,
not the thunder, not the calm,
not the shout the heavens raise,
not the chorus, not the praise,
not the silences sublime,
not the sounds of space and time,
but His voice when He appears
shall be music to my ears;
   but His voice when He appears
   shall be music to my ears.

2 When the Lord is seen again,
   not the glories of His reign,
   not the lightnings through the storm,
   not the radiance of His form,
   not His pomp and power alone,
   not the splendours of His throne,
   not His robe and diadems,
   not the gold and not the gems,
   but His face upon my sight
   shall be darkness into light;
       but His face upon my sight
       shall be darkness into light.

3 When the Lord to human eyes
   shall bestride our narrow skies,
   not the child of humble birth,
   not the carpenter of earth,
   not the man by all denied,
   not the victim crucified,
   but the God who died to save,
   but the victor of the grave,
   He it is to whom I fall,
   Jesus Christ, my all-in-all;
       He it is to whom I fall,
       Jesus Christ, my all-in-all.

759 James M Black (1856–1938)

1 **When the trumpet of the Lord
   shall sound, and time
   shall be no more,**
   and the morning breaks,
       eternal, bright, and fair;
   when the saved of earth shall gather
   over on the other shore,
   and the roll is called up yonder,
       I'll be there.
       When the roll is called up yonder,
       when the roll is called up yonder,
       when the roll is called up yonder,
       when the roll is called up yonder
       I'll be there.

2 On that bright and cloudless morning
       when the dead in Christ shall rise,
   and the glory of His resurrection share;
   when His chosen ones shall gather
       to their home beyond the skies,
   and the roll is called up yonder,
       I'll be there.
       When the roll is called . . .

3 Let us labour for the Master
       from the dawn till setting sun,
   let us talk
       of all His wondrous love and care;
   then when all of life is over,
       and our work on earth is done,
   and the roll is called up yonder,
       I'll be there.
       When the roll is called . . .

760 John Henry Sammis (1846–1919)

1 **When we walk with the Lord**
   in the light of His word,
   what a glory He sheds on our way!
   While we do His good will,
   He abides with us still,
   and with all who will trust and obey.
       Trust and obey,
       for there's no other way
       to be happy in Jesus,
       but to trust and obey.

2 Not a shadow can rise,
   not a cloud in the skies,
   but His smile quickly drives it away;
   not a doubt nor a fear,
   not a sigh nor a tear,
   can abide while we trust and obey.
       Trust and obey . . .

3   Not a burden we bear,
    not a sorrow we share,
    but our toil He doth richly repay;
    not a grief nor a loss,
    not a frown nor a cross,
    but is blest if we trust and obey.
    Trust and obey,
    for there's no other way
    to be happy in Jesus,
    but to trust and obey.

4   But we never can prove
    the delights of His love,
    until all on the altar we lay;
    for the favour He shows,
    and the joy He bestows
    are for them who will trust and obey.
    Trust and obey . . .

5   Then in fellowship sweet,
    we will sit at His feet,
    or we'll walk by His side in the way.
    What He says we will do,
    where He sends we will go,
    never fear, only trust and obey.
    Trust and obey . . .

761 © 1977 Timothy Dudley-Smith

1   **When to our world**
    the Saviour came,
    the sick and helpless heard His name;
    and in their weakness longed to see
    the healing Christ of Galilee.

2   That good physician! night and day
    the people thronged about His way;
    and wonder ran from soul to soul –
    'The touch of Christ
        has made us whole!'

3   His praises then were heard and sung
    by opened ears and loosened tongue,
    while lightened eyes
        could see and know
    the healing Christ of long ago.

4   Of long ago: yet living still,
    who died for us on Calvary's hill;
    who triumphed over cross and grave,
    His healing hands
        stretched forth to save.

5   Those wounded hands
        are still the same,
    and all who serve that saving name
    may share today in Jesus' plan –
    the healing Christ of every man.

6   Then grant us, Lord, in this our day,
    to hear the prayers the helpless pray;
    give to us hearts their pain to share,
    make of us hands to tend and care.

7   Make us Your hands! for Christ to live,
    in prayer and service, swift to give;
    till all the world rejoice to find
    the healing Christ of all mankind.

762 Anon
         Copyright control

Wherever I am, I'll praise Him,
whenever I can, I'll praise Him;
for His love surrounds me like a sea;
I'll praise the name of Jesus,
lift up the name of Jesus,
for the name of Jesus lifted me.

763 From the book of Nahum
         © 1987 Anne Horrobin and Sue Cartwright

Where the Lord walks,
    storms arise,
the clouds are the dust
    raised by His feet;
the earth shakes when the Lord appears,
the world and its people tremble.

1 You, Nineveh, are a wicked city,
your people plot against Me;
you've made My people Israel suffer,
but now I'm going to set them free.
Where the Lord walks . . .

2 The Lord will always protect
His people,
He'll care for those who trust Him;
but turn against Him, oppose the Lord,
and His judgement then is death.
Where the Lord walks . . .

3 I say to my people Israel,
a messenger is bringing good news;
stand in the victory I've given you,
for your enemy has been destroyed.
Where the Lord walks . . .

764 Nahum Tate (1652–1715)

1 **While shepherds watched their
flocks by night,**
all seated on the ground,
the angel of the Lord came down
and glory shone around.

2 'Fear not,' said he – for mighty dread
had seized their troubled mind –
'Glad tidings of great joy I bring
to you and all mankind:

3 'To you in David's town this day
is born of David's line,
a Saviour, who is Christ the Lord.
And this shall be the sign:

4 'The heavenly babe you there shall find
to human view displayed,
all meanly wrapped
in swaddling bands,
and in a manger laid.'

5 Thus spake the angel; and forthwith
appeared a shining throng
of angels praising God, who thus
addressed their joyful song:

6 'All glory be to God on high,
and to the earth be peace;
goodwill henceforth
from heaven to men
begin and never cease!'

765 Thoro Harris (1874–1955)
© 1931, 1959 Nazarene Publishing/
Lillenas Publishing Co/CopyCare

1 **Who can cheer the heart like Jesus,**
by His presence all-divine?
True and tender, pure and precious,
O how blest to call Him mine!
*All that thrills my soul is Jesus;
He is more than life to me;
and the fairest of ten thousand,
in my blessèd Lord I see.*

2 Love of Christ, so freely given,
grace of God beyond degree,
mercy higher than the heaven,
deeper than the deepest sea.
All that thrills . . .

3 What a wonderful redemption!
Never can a mortal know
how my sin, though red like crimson,
can be whiter than the snow.
All that thrills . . .

4 Every need His hand supplying,
every good in Him I see;
on His strength divine relying,
He is all-in-all to me.
All that thrills . . .

5 By the crystal flowing river,
with the ransomed I will sing,
and for ever and for ever,
praise and glorify the King.
All that thrills . . .

766

Graham Kendrick
© 1988 Make Way Music

1 **Who can sound the depths of
   sorrow**
   in the father heart of God,
   for the children we've rejected,
   for the lives so deeply scarred?
   And each light that we've extinguished
   has brought darkness to our land:
   upon the nation, upon the nation
   have mercy, Lord!

2 We have scorned the truth You gave us,
   we have bowed to other lords,
   we have sacrificed the children
   on the altars of our gods.
   O let truth again shine on us,
   let Your holy fear descend:
   upon the nation, upon the nation
   have mercy, Lord!

MEN

3 Who can stand before Your anger;
   who can face Your piercing eyes?
   For You love the weak and helpless,
   and You hear the victims' cries.

ALL

Yes, You are a God of justice,
and Your judgement surely comes:
upon the nation, upon the nation
have mercy, Lord!

WOMEN

4 Who will stand against the violence?
   Who will comfort those who mourn?
   In an age of cruel rejection,
   who will build for love a home?

ALL

Come and shake us into action,
come and melt our hearts of stone:
upon Your people, upon Your people,
have mercy, Lord!

5 Who can sound the depths of mercy
   in the father heart of God?
   For there is a Man of Sorrows
   who for sinners shed His blood.

He can heal the wounds of nations,
He can wash the guilty clean:
because of Jesus, because of Jesus,
have mercy, Lord!

767

Benjamin Russell Hanby (1833–67)

1 **Who is He, in yonder stall,**
   at whose feet the shepherds fall?
   'Tis the Lord! O wondrous story!
   'Tis the Lord! the King of glory!
   At His feet we humbly fall;
   crown Him, crown Him Lord of all.

2 Who is He, in yonder cot,
   bending to His toilsome lot?
   'Tis the Lord . . .

3 Who is He, in deep distress,
   fasting in the wilderness?
   'Tis the Lord . . .

4 Who is He, that stands and weeps
   at the grave where Lazarus sleeps?
   'Tis the Lord . . .

5 Lo, at midnight, who is He
   prays in dark Gethsemane?
   'Tis the Lord . . .

6 Who is He, in Calvary's throes,
   asks for blessings on His foes?
   'Tis the Lord . . .

7 Who is He that from the grave
   comes to heal and help and save?
   'Tis the Lord . . .

8 Who is He that from His throne
   rules through all the worlds alone?
   'Tis the Lord . . .

768
Judy Horner Montemayor
© 1975 Integrity Music/Kingsway's Thankyou Music

Who is like unto Thee,
O Lord among gods?
Who is like unto Thee?
Glorious in holiness,
fearful in praises,
doing wonders;
who is like unto Thee?

769
Frances Ridley Havergal (1836–79)

1 **Who is on the Lord's side?**
Who will serve the King?
Who will be His helpers
other lives to bring?
Who will leave the world's side?
Who will face the foe?
Who is on the Lord's side?
Who for Him will go?
By Thy call of mercy,
by Thy grace divine,
we are on the Lord's side;
Saviour, we are Thine.

2 Not for weight of glory,
not for crown or palm,
enter we the army,
raise the warrior-psalm;
but for love that claimeth
lives for whom He died:
he whom Jesus nameth
must be on His side.
By Thy love constraining,
by Thy grace divine,
we are on the Lord's side;
Saviour, we are Thine.

3 Fierce may be the conflict,
strong may be the foe,
but the King's own army
none can overthrow.

Round His standard ranging,
victory is secure,
for His truth unchanging
makes the triumph sure.
Joyfully enlisting,
by Thy grace divine,
we are on the Lord's side;
Saviour, we are Thine.

4 Chosen to be soldiers
in an alien land,
chosen, called, and faithful,
for our captain's band;
in the service royal
let us not grow cold;
let us be right loyal,
noble, true and bold.
Master, Thou wilt keep us,
by Thy grace divine,
always on the Lord's side,
Saviour, always Thine.

770
Priscilla Jane Owens (1829–99)

1 **Will your anchor hold**
in the storms of life,
when the clouds unfold
their wings of strife?
When the strong tides lift,
and the cables strain,
will your anchor drift, or firm remain?
We have an anchor that keeps the soul
steadfast and sure while the billows roll;
fastened to the rock which cannot move,
grounded firm and deep
in the Saviour's love!

2 Will your anchor hold
in the straits of fear,
when the breakers roar
and the reef is near?

While the surges rage,
 and the wild winds blow,
shall the angry waves
 then your bark o'erflow?
We have an anchor that keeps the soul
steadfast and sure while the billows roll;
fastened to the rock which cannot move,
grounded firm and deep
 in the Saviour's love!

3 Will your anchor hold
 in the floods of death,
when the waters cold
 chill your latest breath?
On the rising tide you can never fail,
while your anchor holds within the veil.
 We have an anchor . . .

4 Will your eyes behold
 through the morning light,
the city of gold and the harbour bright?
Will you anchor safe
 by the heavenly shore,
when life's storms are past
 for evermore?
 We have an anchor . . .

771 Jane and Betsy Clowe
© 1974 Celebration/
Kingsway's Thankyou Music

Wind, wind blow on me;
wind, wind set me free!
Wind, wind my Father sent,
the blessèd Holy Spirit.

1 Jesus told us all about You,
how we could not live without You;
with His blood the power bought
to help us live the life He taught.
 Wind, wind . . .

2 When we're weary You console us,
when we're lonely You enfold us,
when in danger You uphold us,
blessèd Holy Spirit.
 Wind, wind . . .

3 When into the Church You came,
it was not in Your own but Jesus' name:
Jesus Christ is still the same –
He sends the Holy Spirit.
 Wind, wind . . .

4 Set us free to love our brothers,
set us free to live for others,
that the world the Son might see,
and Jesus' name exalted be.
 Wind, wind . . .

772 Paul Field
© 1987 Kingsway's Thankyou Music

1 **With all my heart**
 I thank You, Lord.
With all my heart I thank You, Lord.
For this bread and wine we break,
for this sacrament we take,
for the forgiveness that You make,
I thank You, Lord.

2 With all my soul I thank You, Lord.
With all my soul I thank You, Lord.
For this victory that You've won,
for this taste of things to come,
for this love that makes us one,
I thank You, Lord.

3 With all my voice I thank You, Lord.
With all my voice I thank You, Lord.
For the sacrifice of pain,
for the Spirit and the flame,
for the power of Your name,
I thank You, Lord.

773 Arthur Tappan Pierson (1837–1911)

1 **With harps and with viols**
 there stand a great throng
in the presence of Jesus,
 and sing this new song:

Unto Him who has loved us
and washed us from sin,
unto Him be the glory
for ever! Amen.

2 All these once were sinners,
   defiled in His sight,
now arrayed in pure garments
   in praise they unite:
   Unto Him who has ...

3 He's made of the rebel
   a priest and a king,
He has bought us, and taught us
   this new song to sing:
   Unto Him who has ...

4 How helpless and hopeless
   we sinners had been,
if He never had loved us
   till cleansed from our sin!
   Unto Him who has ...

5 Aloud in His praises
   our voices shall ring,
so that others, believing,
   this new song shall sing:
   Unto Him who has ...

774   Isaac Watts (1614–1748) altd.

1 **With joy we meditate the grace**
   of our High Priest above;
His heart is made of tenderness,
   it overflows with love.

2 Touched with a sympathy within,
   He knows our feeble frame;
He knows what sore temptations mean,
   for He has felt the same.

3 He, in the days of feeble flesh,
   poured out His cries and tears;
and now exalted feels afresh
   what every member bears.

4 He'll never quench the smoking flax,
   but raise it to a flame;
the bruisèd reed He never breaks,
   nor scorns the meanest name.

5 Then let our humble faith address
   His mercy and His power;
we shall obtain delivering grace
   in the distressing hour.

775   © 1980 Norman Warren/Jubilate Hymns

With my heart
   I worship You, Jesus, Jesus;
with my heart I worship You, Jesus, Jesus:
You gave all in love for me,
saved me for eternity;
with my heart I worship You.

ALTERNATIVE VERSES:

With my lips I praise You ...

With my life I serve You ...

776   Paul Armstrong
© 1980 Word's Spirit of Praise Music/
CopyCare

Wonderful counsellor,
the mighty God,
the everlasting Father,
the Prince of peace,
the Prince of peace,
the everlasting Father,
the mighty God.

Wonderful counsellor,
wonderful counsellor,
wonderful is the name of Jesus,
wonderful counsellor,
wonderful counsellor,
wonderful is the name of Jesus.

777
Bill Yarger
© 1982 Maranatha! Music/
CopyCare

1 **Wonderful counsellor, Jesus:**
search me, know me, Jesus;
lead me, guide me, Jesus –
Wonderful counsellor, Jesus.

2 Mighty God, Son of God, Jesus;
name above all other names, Jesus:
glorify, magnify Jesus –
mighty God, Son of God, Jesus.

3 Everlasting Father, Jesus;
Holy and unchangeable, Jesus:
fill me with Your presence, Jesus –
everlasting Father, Jesus.

4 Prince of peace, rule my heart, Jesus;
know my every anxious thought, Jesus;
calm my fears, dry my tears, Jesus –
Prince of peace, rule my heart, Jesus.

5 Wonderful counsellor, Jesus;
mighty God, Son of God, Jesus;
everlasting Father, Jesus –
Prince of peace, rule my heart, Jesus.

778
Ruth Dryden
© 1978 Genesis Music/
Kingsway's Thankyou Music

Within the veil I now would come,
into the holy place to look upon Thy face.
I see such beauty there,
    no other can compare,
I worship Thee, my Lord, within the veil.

779
Dave Richards
© 1979 Kingsway's Thankyou Music

Worthy art Thou, O Lord, our God,
    of honour and power,
for You are reigning now on high,
    hallelujah.
Jesus is Lord of all the earth,
hallelujah, hallelujah, hallelujah.

780
Anon
Copyright control

1 **Worthy is the Lamb;**
worthy is the Lamb;
worthy is the Lamb;
worthy is the Lamb.

2 Holy is the Lamb . . .

3 Precious is the Lamb . . .

4 Praises to the Lamb . . .

5 Glory to the Lamb . . .

6 Jesus is our Lamb . . .

781
David Hadden
© 1983 Restoration Music Ltd/
Sovereign Music UK

Worthy is the Lamb
    seated on the throne,
worthy is the Lamb who was slain,
to receive power and riches,
and wisdom and strength,
honour and glory,
glory and praise,
for ever and evermore.

782
Mark S Kinzer
© 1976 Word of God/
CopyCare

Worthy, O worthy are You, Lord,
worthy to be thanked and praised
and worshipped and adored;
worthy, O worthy are You, Lord,
worthy to be thanked and praised
and worshipped and adored.

Singing, 'Hallelujah!
Lamb upon the throne,
we worship and adore You,
make Your glory known.
Hallelujah,
glory to the King:
You're more than a conqueror,
You're Lord of everything!'

4 My soul, bear thou thy part,
   triumph in God above:
   and with a well-tuned heart
   sing thou the songs of love!
     Let all thy days
     till life shall end,
     whate'er He send,
     be filled with praise.

783 Richard Baxter (1615–91)
         and others

1 **Ye holy angels bright,**
   who wait at God's right hand,
   or through the realms of light
   fly at your Lord's command,
     assist our song,
     or else the theme
     too high doth seem
     for mortal tongue.

2 Ye blessèd souls at rest,
   who see your Saviour's face,
   whose glory, e'en the least
   is far above our grace,
     God's praises sound,
     as in His sight
     with sweet delight
     ye do abound.

3 Ye saints, who toil below,
   adore your heavenly King,
   and onward as ye go
   some joyful anthem sing;
     take what He gives
     and praise Him still,
     through good and ill,
     who ever lives!

784 Charles Wesley (1707–88)

1 **Ye servants of God,**
   your Master proclaim,
   and publish abroad
   His wonderful name;
   the name all-victorious
   of Jesus extol;
   His kingdom is glorious,
   and rules over all.

2 God ruleth on high,
   almighty to save;
   and still He is nigh,
   His presence we have;
   the great congregation
   His triumph shall sing,
   ascribing salvation
   to Jesus our King.

3 'Salvation to God
   who sits on the throne',
   let all cry aloud,
   and honour the Son:
   the praises of Jesus
   the angels proclaim,
   fall down on their faces,
   and worship the Lamb.

4 Then let us adore,
   and give Him His right –
   all glory and power,
   all wisdom and might:
   all honour and blessing,
   with angels above;
   and thanks never-ceasing,
   and infinite love.

785 © 1984 Colin Preston

Yes, power belongs to You,
*   O Lord,*
in You we put our trust;
You are sovereign over all,
great are You.
Great in Your mercy, Lord,
great in Your love,
a mighty warrior in whom we trust.
Glorify Your name,
glorify Your name,
glorify Your name.

1 Don't worry about the opposition,
   for I stand with the few;
   the proud, the violent godless man
   will know I stand with you.
   Yes, power belongs . . .

2 Do not fear nor be dismayed,
   the battle is not yours;
   you shall not need to fight, but stand
   and see salvation of the Lord.
   Yes, power belongs . . .

3 Be still and know that I am God,
   and wait upon My word,
   responding to My Spirit's voice,
   with your breath and praise do war.
   Yes, power belongs . . .

786 John Hampden Gurney (1802–62)

1 **Yes, God is good – in earth and sky,**
   from ocean depths
       and spreading wood,
   ten thousand voices seem to cry:
   'God made us all, and God is good!'

2 The sun that keeps his trackless way,
   and downward pours his golden flood,
   night's sparkling hosts, all seem to say
   in accents clear that God is good.

3 The joyful birds prolong the strain,
   their song with every spring renewed;
   the air we breathe, and falling rain,
   each softly whispers: 'God is good!'

4 I hear it in the rushing breeze;
   the hills that have for ages stood,
   the echoing sky and roaring seas,
   all swell the chorus: 'God is good!'

5 Yes, God is good, all nature says,
   by God's own hand
       with speech endued;
   and man, in louder notes of praise,
   should sing for joy that God is good.

6 For all Your gifts we bless You, Lord,
   but chiefly for our heavenly food,
   Your pardoning grace,
       Your quickening word,
   these prompt our song,
       that God is good.

787 Albert B Simpson (1843–1919)

Yesterday, today, for ever,
Jesus is the same;
all may change, but Jesus never,
glory to His name!
Glory to His name!
Glory to His name!
All may change, but Jesus never,
glory to His name!

788
Mark Altrogge
© 1986 People of Destiny International/CopyCare

You are beautiful beyond description,
too marvellous for words,
too wonderful for comprehension,
like nothing ever seen or heard.
Who can grasp Your infinite wisdom?
Who can fathom the depth of Your love?
You are beautiful beyond description,
Majesty, enthroned above.
And I stand, I stand in awe of You;
I stand, I stand in awe of You.
Holy God, to whom all praise is due,
I stand in awe of You.

3 O the joy to see You reigning,
   You, my own belovèd Lord!
   Every tongue Your name confessing,
   worship, honour, glory, blessing
   brought to You with glad accord –
   You, my Master and my friend,
   vindicated and enthroned,
   unto earth's remotest end
   glorified, adored, and owned!

790
Mavis Ford
© 1978 Word's Spirit of Praise Music/
CopyCare

You are the King of glory,
You are the Prince of peace,
You are the Lord of heaven and earth,
You're the Son of righteousness.
Angels bow down before You,
worship and adore,
for You have the words of eternal life,
You are Jesus Christ the Lord.
Hosanna to the Son of David!
Hosanna to the King of kings!
Glory in the highest heaven,
for Jesus the Messiah reigns!

789
Frances Ridley Havergal (1836–79)
altered © 1986 Horrobin/Leavers

1 **You are coming, O my Saviour,**
   You are coming, O my King,
   in Your beauty all-resplendent,
   in Your glory all-transcendent –
   well may we rejoice and sing:
   coming soon, my living Lord,
   heralds sing Your glorious praise;
   coming! now on earth adored,
   songs of triumph we shall raise.

2 You are coming, You are coming,
   we shall meet You on Your way,
   we shall see You, we shall see You,
   we shall bless You, we shall show You
   all our hearts could never say.
   What an anthem that will be,
   ringing out eternally,
   earth's and heaven's praises meet,
   at Your own all-glorious feet!

791
Eddie Espinosa
© 1982 Mercy/Vineyard Publishing/
CopyCare

1 **You are the mighty King,**
   the living Word;
   Master of everything –
   You are the Lord.
      And I praise Your name,
      and I praise Your name.

2 You are almighty God,
   Saviour and Lord;
   wonderful counsellor,
   You are the Lord.
      And I praise Your name,
      and I praise Your name.

3   You are the Prince of peace,
    Emmanuel;
    everlasting Father,
    You are the Lord.
       And I love Your name,
       and I love Your name.

4   You are the mighty King,
    the living Word;
    Master of everything,
    You are the Lord.

792
Danny Daniels and Randy Rigby
© 1982 Mercy/Vineyard Publishing/
CopyCare

You are the vine,
we are the branches,
keep us abiding in You.
You are the vine,
we are the branches,
keep us abiding in You.

Then we'll grow in Your love,
then we'll go in Your name,
that the world will surely know
that You have power to heal and to save.

You are the vine,
we are the branches,
keep us abiding in You.

793
Michael Ledner
© 1981 Maranatha! Music/
CopyCare

You are my hiding-place,
You always fill my heart
with songs of deliverance
whenever I am afraid.
I will trust in You,
I will trust in You,
let the weak say:
'I am strong in the strength of my God.'

794
John Daniel Lawtum
© 1982 Millennium Dawn Music/
Sovereign Music UK

You are worthy, Lord,
You are worthy, so I lift my heart,
I lift my voice and cry, 'Holy'.
You have saved me, and I love You,
Jesus, evermore
I live to praise Your name.

795
Noel Richards
© 1985 Kingsway's Thankyou Music

You laid aside Your majesty,
gave up everything for me,
suffered at the hands
    of those You had created;
You took all my guilt and shame,
when You died and rose again;
now today You reign
    in heaven and earth exalted.

I really want to worship You, my Lord,
You have won my heart and I am Yours.
For ever and ever I will love You.
You are the only one who died for me,
gave Your life to set me free,
so I lift my voice to You in adoration.

796
Stuart Dauermann and Steffi Geiser Rubin
© 1975 Lillenas Publishing Co/
CopyCare

You shall go out with joy
    and be led forth with peace,
and the mountains and the hills
    shall break forth before you.
There'll be shouts of joy
    and the trees of the field
shall clap, shall clap their hands,
and the trees of the field
    shall clap their hands,

and the trees of the field
    shall clap their hands,
and the trees of the field
    shall clap their hands,
and you'll go out with joy.

797 Richard Taylor
© 1982 Word's Spirit of Praise Music/
CopyCare

**Your love is to me
    like an ever-flowing stream,**
Your love is to me
    like an ever-flowing stream,
Your love is to me
    like an ever-flowing stream
reaching out, Lord.

Lord, we need Your love,
yes, we need Your love,
we need Your love to make it through;
Lord, we need Your love,
yes, we need Your love,
we need Your love to make it through.

798 Helen Thomas
© 1984 Kingsway's Thankyou Music

    Yours, Lord, is the greatness,
    the power, the glory;
    Yours, Lord, is the greatness,
    the victory, the majesty.

1 For everything in heaven and earth
    is Yours,
   You are the King, supreme over all.
   Yours, Lord . . .

2 All riches and honour come from You;
   You are our God, You make us strong.
   Yours, Lord . . .

3 And now, our God,
    we give You thanks,
   we praise Your glorious name.
   Yours, Lord . . .

799 Graham Kendrick
© 1993 Make Way Music

1 **All I once held dear,**
   built my life upon,
   all this world reveres,
   and wars to own,
   all I once thought gain
   I have counted loss;
   spent and worthless now,
   compared to this:
    Knowing You, Jesus,
    knowing You,
    there is no greater thing.
    You're my all,
    You're the best,
    You're my joy, my righteousness,
    and I love You, Lord.

2 Now my heart's desire
   is to know You more,
   to be found in You
   and known as Yours,
   to possess by faith
   what I could not earn,
   all-surpassing gift
   of righteousness.
    Knowing You . . .

3 Oh, to know the power
   of Your risen life,
   and to know You in
   Your sufferings,
   to become like You
   in Your death, my Lord,
   so with You to live
   and never die.
    Knowing You . . .

800 Chris Bowater
© 1993 Sovereign Lifestyle Music

All-consuming, all-embracing,
fervent God of love, enthral me.
All-consuming, all-embracing,
fervent God of love, enthral me,
'til all that I am and I desire
is wholly, only owned, controlled by You.

801

Claire Cloninger and Don Moen
© 1994 Juniper Landing Music/Word Music/
CopyCare and Integrity's Hosanna! Music/
Kingsway's Thankyou Music

1 **All that I am, all that I have,**
   I lay them down before You, O Lord;
   all my regrets, all my acclaim,
   the joy and the pain,
   I'm making them Yours.
   Lord, I offer my life to You,
   everything I've been through –
   use it for Your glory.
   Lord, I offer my days to You,
   lifting my praise to You
   as a pleasing sacrifice:
   Lord, I offer You my life.

2 Things in the past, things yet unseen,
   wishes and dreams
         that are yet to come true;
   all of my hopes, all of my plans,
   my heart and my hands
   are lifted to You.
   Lord, I offer my life to You . . .

   What can we give that You
         have not given,
   and what do we have
         that is not already Yours?
   All we possess are these lives
         we're living,
   and that's what we give to You, Lord.
   Lord, I offer my life to You . . .

802

Graham Kendrick
© 1991 Make Way Music

   And He shall reign for ever,
   His throne and crown shall ever endure;
   and He shall reign for ever,
   and we shall reign with Him.

1 What a vision filled my eyes –
   one like a son of man!
   Coming with the clouds of Heaven,
   He approached an awesome throne.

2 He was given sovereign power,
   glory and authority;
   every nation, tribe and tongue
   worshipped Him on bended knee.
   And He shall reign . . .

3 On the throne for ever,
   see the Lamb who once was slain:
   wounds of sacrificial love
   for ever shall remain.
   And He shall reign . . .

803

© Timothy Dudley-Smith

1 **As water to the thirsty,**
   as beauty to the eyes,
   as strength that follows weakness,
   as truth instead of lies,
   as songtime and springtime
   and summertime to be,
   so is my Lord,
   my living Lord,
   so is my Lord to me.

2 Like calm in place of clamour,
   like peace that follows pain,
   like meeting after parting,
   like sunshine after rain,
   like moonlight and starlight
   and sunlight on the sea,
   so is my Lord,
   my living Lord,
   so is my Lord to me.

3 As sleep that follows fever,
   as gold instead of grey,
   as freedom after bondage,
   as sunrise to the day;
   as home to the traveller
   and all we long to see,
   so is my Lord,
   my living Lord,
   so is my Lord to me.

804 Thomas Ken (1637–1711)

PART I

1 **Awake, my soul, and with the sun**
thy daily stage of duty run;
shake off dull sloth, and joyful rise
to pay thy morning sacrifice.

2 Redeem thy mis-spent time that's past
and live this day as if thy last;
improve thy talent with due care;
for the great day thyself prepare.

3 Let all thy converse be sincere,
thy conscience as the noon-day clear;
think how all-seeing God thy ways
and all thy secret thoughts surveys.

4 Wake, and lift up thyself, my heart,
and with the angels bear thy part,
who all night long unwearied sing
high praise to the eternal King.

PART II

5 Glory to thee, who safe hast kept
and hast refreshed me whilst I slept;
grant, Lord, when I
        from death shall wake,
I may of endless light partake.

6 Lord, I my vows to thee renew;
disperse my sins as morning dew;
guard my first springs
        of thought and will,
and with Thyself my spirit fill.

7 Direct, control, suggest, this day,
all I design or do or say;
that all my powers, with all their might,
in Thy sole glory may unite.

DOXOLOGY
(may be sung after either part)

Praise God, from whom
        all blessings flow,
praise Him, all creatures here below,
praise Him above, angelic host,
praise Father, Son and Holy Ghost.

805 Derek Bond
© 1992 Sovereign Music UK

At the foot of the cross –
I can hardly take it in
that the King of all creation
was dying for my sin.
Oh, the pain and agony
and the thorns that pierced Your head,
and the hardness of my sinful heart
that left You there for dead!

And oh, what mercy I have found
at the cross of Calvary!
I will never know Your loneliness,
all on account of me.
And I will bow my knee
        before Your throne,
for Your love has set me free;
and I will give my life to You, dear Lord,
and praise Your majesty,
and praise Your majesty,
and praise Your majesty.

806 Graham Kendrick
© 1993 Make Way Music

1 **Beauty for brokenness,**
hope for despair,
Lord, in Your suffering world
this is our prayer.
Bread for the children,
justice, joy, peace,
sunrise to sunset,
Your kingdom increase!

2 Shelter for fragile lives,
cures for their ills,
work for the craftsmen,
trade for their skills;
land for the dispossessed,
rights for the weak,
voices to plead the cause
of those who can't speak.

God of the poor,
friend of the weak,
give us compassion we pray:
melt our cold hearts,
let tears fall like rain;
come, change our love
from a spark to a flame.

3 Refuge from cruel wars,
havens from fear,
cities for sanctuary,
freedoms to share.
Peace to the killing-fields,
scorched earth to green,
Christ for the bitterness,
His cross for the pain.

4 Rest for the ravaged earth,
oceans and streams
plundered and poisoned –
our future, our dreams.
Lord, end our madness,
carelessness, greed;
make us content with
the things that we need.
God of the poor . . .

5 Lighten our darkness,
breathe on this flame
until Your justice
burns brightly again;
until the nations
learn of Your ways,
seek Your salvation
and bring You their praise.
God of the poor . . .

807 From Revelation 4
Gerald Coates and Noel Richards
© 1991 Kingsway's Thankyou Music

1 **Behold the Lord upon His throne:**
His face is shining like the sun.
With eyes blazing fire,
and feet glowing bronze,
His voice like mighty water roars.
Holy, holy, Lord God almighty:
holy, holy! We stand in awe of You.

2 The First, the Last, the living One,
laid down His life for all the world.
Behold He now lives for evermore,
and holds the keys of death and hell!
Holy, holy, Lord God almighty:
holy, holy! We bow before
Your throne.

3 So let our praises ever ring,
to Jesus Christ, our glorious King.
All Heaven and earth resound as we
cry,
'Worthy is the Son of God!'
Holy, holy, Lord God almighty:
holy, holy! We fall down at Your feet.

808 From Psalm 18
Danny Daniels and Kevin Prosch
© 1989 Mercy/Vineyard Publishing/CopyCare

1 **Blessèd be the name of the Lord,**
blessèd be the name of the Lord.
Blessèd be the name of the Lord,
blessèd be the name of the Lord.
For He is our rock, for He is our rock,
He is the Lord.
For He is our rock, for He is our rock,
He is the Lord.

2 Jesus reigns on high in all the earth,
Jesus reigns on high in all the earth.
Jesus reigns on high in all the earth,
Jesus reigns on high in all the earth.
The universe is in the hands
of the Lord.
The universe is in the hands
of the Lord.

809

From Proverbs 18
Clinton Utterbach
© 1989 Utterbach Music Incorporated/
PolyGram International Publishing Corporation

1 **Blessèd be the name of the Lord,**
blessèd be the name of the Lord,
blessèd be the name of the Lord
most high!
Blessèd be the name of the Lord,
blessèd be the name of the Lord,
blessèd be the name of the Lord
most high!
The name of the Lord is a strong
tower –
the righteous run into it,
and they are saved;
the name of the Lord is a strong tower –
the righteous run into it,
and they are saved.

2 Glory to the name of the Lord,
glory to the name of the Lord,
glory to the name of the Lord
most high!
Glory to the name of the Lord,
glory to the name of the Lord,
glory to the name of the Lord
most high!
The name of the Lord . . .

3 Holy is the name of the Lord,
holy is the name of the Lord,
holy is the name of the Lord most high!
Holy is the name of the Lord,
holy is the name of the Lord,
holy is the name of the Lord most high!
The name of the Lord . . .

810

Noel and Tricia Richards
© 1989 Kingsway's Thankyou Music

By Your side I would stay,
in Your arms I would lay.
Jesus, lover of my soul,
nothing from You I withhold.
Lord, I love You
and adore You.
What more can I say?
You cause my love
to grow stronger
with every passing day.

Lord, I love You . . .

811

Noel and Tricia Richards
© 1992 Kingsway's Thankyou Music

1 **Called to a battle,**
heavenly war.
Though we may struggle,
victory is sure.
Death will not triumph,
though we may die.
Jesus has promised
our eternal life.
By the blood of the Lamb
we shall overcome,
see the accuser thrown down.
By the word of the Lord
we shall overcome.
Raise a victory cry
like thunder in the skies,
thunder in the skies.

2 Standing together,
moving as one,
we are God's army
called to overcome.
We are commissioned:
Jesus says 'Go!'
In every nation
let His love be known.
By the blood of the Lamb . . .

812

Chris Rolinson
© 1989 Kingsway's Thankyou Music

Christ is risen –
alleluia, alleluia!
Christ is risen –
risen indeed, alleluia!

1 Love's work is done,
the battle is won.
Where now, O death, is your sting?
He rose again
to rule and to reign,
Jesus our conquering King.
Christ is risen . . .

2 Lord over sin,
Lord over death,
at His feet Satan must fall!
Every knee bow!
All will confess
Jesus is Lord over all!
Christ is risen . . .

3 Tell it abroad,
'Jesus is Lord!'
Shout it and let your praise ring!
Gladly we raise
our songs of praise –
worship is our offering.
Christ is risen . . .

2 Christ is the One who seeks,
to whom our souls are known.
The word of love He speaks
can wake a heart of stone;
for at that sound
the blind can see,
the slave is free,
the lost are found.

3 Christ is the One who died,
forsaken and betrayed;
who, mocked and crucified,
the price of pardon paid.
Our dying Lord,
what grief and loss,
what bitter cross
our souls restored!

4 Christ is the One who rose
in glory from the grave,
to share His life with those
whom once He died to save.
He drew death's sting
and broke its chains,
who lives and reigns
our risen King.

5 Christ is the One who sends,
His story to declare;
who calls His servants friends
and gives them news to share.
His truth proclaim
in all the earth,
His matchless worth
and saving name.

813

© 1992 Timothy Dudley-Smith

1 **Christ is the One who calls,**
the One who loved and came,
to whom by right it falls
to bear the highest name:
and still today
our hearts are stirred
to hear His word
and walk His way.

814

Samuel Johnson (1822–82)

1 **City of God, how broad and far**
outspread thy walls sublime!
The true thy chartered freemen are
of every age and clime.

2 One holy Church, one army strong,
one steadfast, high intent;
one working band, one harvest-song,
one King omnipotent.

3 How purely hath thy speech come
      down
from man's primeval youth!
How grandly hath thine empire grown
of freedom, love and truth!

4 How gleam thy watch-fires
      through the night
with never-fainting ray!
How rise thy towers, serene and bright,
to meet the dawning day!

5 In vain the surge's angry shock,
in vain the drifting sands:
unharmed upon the eternal Rock
the eternal city stands.

2 Lavish our heart's affection,
deepest love and highest praise,
voice, race and language blending,
all the world amazed.
  Jesus, King of the nations,
  Jesus, Lord of all.
  Jesus, King of the nations,
  Lord of all!

3 Bring tributes from the nations,
come in joyful cavalcades.
One thunderous acclamation,
one banner raised.

4 Come, Lord and fill Your temple,
glorify Your dwelling-place,
'til nations see Your splendour,
and seek Your face.
  Jesus, King of the nations . . .

5 Fear God and give Him glory,
for His hour of judgement comes.
Creator, Lord almighty,
worship Him alone.

815 Trish Morgan
© 1991 Kingsway's Thankyou Music

Closer to You, Lord, and closer still,
'til I am wholly in Your will,
Closer to hear Your beating heart,
and understand what You impart.
O Breath of life, come purify
this heart of mine, and satisfy;
my deep desire is to worship You –
Lord of my life, come closer still.

817 Chris Bowater
© 1994 Sovereign Lifestyle Music

Confidence, we have confidence
to come, to ask for mercy.
Confidence, we have confidence
to come, to ask for mercy.
Merciful God, we cry, 'Don't pass us by.'
Merciful God, we pray, 'Don't turn away';
in Your love remember mercy,
in Your love remember mercy.

816 Graham Kendrick
© 1992 Make Way Music

1 **Come, let us worship Jesus,**
King of nations, Lord of all,
magnificent and glorious,
just and merciful.

818 John L Bell and Graham Maule
© 1992, 1995 WGRG The Iona Community

ALL
Come, Holy Spirit,
descend on us,
descend on us;
we gather here in Jesus' name.

SOLO
(Come, Holy Spirit . . .)
(Come, Breath of Heaven . . .)
(Come, Word of Mercy . . .)

3 Whence to me this waste of love?
Ask my advocate above;
see the cause in Jesus' face,
now before the throne of grace,
now before the throne of grace.

4 There for me the Saviour stands,
shows His wounds and
spreads His hands.
God is love, I know, I feel,
Jesus lives and loves me still,
Jesus lives and loves me still.

819
John Wimber
© 1982 Mercy/Vineyard Publishing/CopyCare

1 **Consider how He loves you,**
His arms of love enfold you
like a sweet, sweet perfume.
He left His word to guide us;
His presence lives inside us,
like a sweet, sweet perfume.
Don't ever think that you're worthless –
you have His life within;
you are a sweet, wholesome fragrance,
so valuable to Him.

2 He'll light up all your darkness
and fill you with His Spirit
like a sweet, sweet perfume.
Don't ever think that you're worthless . . .

3 Your prayers are very precious –
they reach the heart of Jesus
like a sweet, sweet perfume;
consider how He loves you!

821
Andy Park
© 1994 Mercy/Vineyard Publishing/CopyCare

1 **Down the mountain the river flows,**
and it brings refreshing wherever it
goes.
Through the valleys and over the fields,
the river is rushing and the river is
here.
The river of God sets our feet a-dancing,
the river of God fills our hearts
with cheer,
the river of God fills our mouths
with laughter,
and we rejoice, for the river is here!

2 The river of God is teeming with life,
and all who touch it can be revived,
and those who linger
on this river's shore
will come back thirsting
for more of the Lord.
The river of God . . .

820
Charles Wesley (1707–88)

1 **Depth of mercy! Can there be**
mercy still reserved for me?
Can my God His wrath forbear,
me, the chief of sinners spare,
me, the chief of sinners spare?

2 I have long withstood His grace,
long provoked Him to His face,
would not hearken to His calls,
grieved Him by a thousand falls,
grieved Him by a thousand falls.

3 Up to the mountain we love to go,
to find the presence of the Lord.
Along the banks of the river we run –
we dance with laughter,
giving praise to the Son.
The river of God . . .

822
Alan Gaunt
© 1991 Stainer & Bell Ltd

1 **Eternal God,**
   Your love's tremendous glory
cascades through life in
   overflowing grace,
to tell creation's meaning in the story
of love evolving love
   from time and space.

2 Eternal Son of God, uniquely precious,
in You, deserted, scorned and
   crucified,
God's love has fathomed sin
   and death's deep darkness,
and flawed humanity is glorified.

3 Eternal Spirit, with us like a mother,
embracing us in love serene and pure:
You nurture strength to follow
   Christ our brother,
as full-grown children,
   confident and sure.

4 Love's trinity, self-perfect,
   self-sustaining;
love which commands,
   enables and obeys:
You give Yourself,
   in boundless joy, creating
one vast increasing harmony of praise.

5 We ask You now,
   complete Your image in us;
this love of Yours,
   our source and guide and goal.
May love in us, seek love
   and serve love's purpose,
till we ascend with Christ
   and find love whole.

823
tr. Lilian Stevenson (1870–1960)
By permission of Oxford University Press

1 **Fairest Lord Jesus,**
   Lord of all creation,
Jesus, of God and man the Son;
You will I cherish, You will I honour,
You are my soul's delight and crown.

2 Fair are the rivers, meadows and forests
clothed in the fresh
   green robes of spring;
Jesus is fairer, Jesus is purer,
He makes the saddest heart to sing.

3 Fair is the sunrise;
   starlight and moonlight
spreading their glory across the sky;
Jesus shines brighter, Jesus shines
   clearer
than all the heavenly host on high.

4 All fairest beauty, heavenly and earthly,
Jesus, my Lord, in You I see;
none can be nearer, fairer or dearer
than You, my Saviour, are to me.

824
Chris Bowater
© 1990 Sovereign Lifestyle Music

Faithful God, faithful God,
all-sufficient One, I worship You.
Shalom my peace,
my strong Deliverer,
I lift You up,
faithful God.

825
Brian Doerksen
© 1989 Mercy/Vineyard Publishing/CopyCare

Faithful One, so unchanging;
ageless One, You're my rock of peace.
Lord of all, I depend on You,
I call out to You again and again,
I call out to You again and again.
You are my rock in times of trouble,
You lift me up when I fall down;
all through the storm
   Your love is the anchor –
my hope is in You alone.

826 David Ruis
© 1992 Mercy/Vineyard Publishing/CopyCare

1 **Father of creation,**
unfold Your sovereign plan.
Raise up a chosen generation
that will march through the land.
All of creation is longing
for Your unveiling of power –
would You release Your anointing?
O God, let this be the hour!
Let Your glory fall in this room,
let it go forth from here to the nations;
let Your fragrance rest in this place
as we gather to seek Your face.

2 Ruler of the nations,
the world has yet to see
the full release of Your promise –
the church in victory.
Turn to us, Lord, and touch us,
make us strong in Your might;
overcome our weakness
that we may stand up and fight!
Let Your glory . . .

MEN   Let Your kingdom come,
WOMEN   let Your kingdom come,
MEN   let Your will be done,
WOMEN   let Your will be done,
MEN   let us see on earth,
WOMEN   let us see on earth,
ALL   the glory of Your Son.

Let Your glory fall in this
    place,
let Your glory fall in this
    place,
let Your glory fall in this
    place,
let Your glory fall in this
    place.

Let Your glory . . .

827 E Cooper (1770–1833)

1 **Father of heaven,**
    whose love profound
a ransom for our souls hath found,
before Thy throne we sinners bend –
to us Thy pardoning love extend.

2 Almighty Son, incarnate Word,
our prophet, priest, Redeemer, Lord,
before Thy throne we sinners bend –
to us Thy saving grace extend.

3 Eternal Spirit, by whose breath
the soul is raised from sin and death,
before Thy throne we sinners bend –
to us Thy quickening power extend.

4 Thrice holy! Father, Spirit, Son;
mysterious Godhead, Three-in-One,
before Thy throne we sinners bend –
grace, pardon, life to us extend.

828 Noel and Tricia Richards
© 1994 Kingsway's Thankyou Music

1 **Filled with compassion**
    for all creation,
Jesus came into a world that was lost.
There was but one way
    that He could save us,
only through suffering death on a cross.
God, You are waiting –
Your heart is breaking
for all the people who live on the earth.
Stir us to action,
filled with Your passion
for all the people who live on the earth.
God, You are waiting . . .

2 Great is Your passion for all the people
living and dying without knowing You.
Having no saviour, they're lost for ever
if we don't speak out
    and lead them to You.
God, You are waiting . . .

3 From every nation we shall be
    gathered,
millions redeemed
    shall be Jesus' reward.
Then He will turn
    and say to His Father:
'Truly my suffering was worth it all!'
God, You are waiting . . .

829 Graham Kendrick
© 1994 Make Way Music

1 **For the joys and for the sorrows,**
the best and worst of times,
for this moment, for tomorrow,
for all that lies behind;
fears that crowd around me,
for the failure of my plans,
for the dreams of all I hope to be,
the truth of what I am:
    For this I have Jesus,
    for this I have Jesus,
    for this I have Jesus,
    I have Jesus.
    For this I have Jesus . . .

2 For the tears that flow in secret,
in the broken times,
for the moments of elation,
or the troubled mind;
for all the disappointments,
or the sting of old regrets,
all my prayers and longings
that seem unanswered yet:
    For this I have Jesus . . .

3 For the weakness of my body,
the burdens of each day,
for the nights of doubt and worry,
when sleep has fled away;
needing reassurance,
and the will to start again,
a steely-eyed endurance,
the strength to fight and win:
    For this I have Jesus . . .

830 From Luke 4
© 1990 Bernadette Farrell/OCP Publications

1 **God has chosen me,**
    God has chosen me
to bring good news to the poor;
God has chosen me,
    God has chosen me
to bring new sight
    to those searching for light:
God has chosen me, chosen me.
    And to tell the world
        that God's kingdom is near,
    to remove oppression
        and break down fear,
    yes, God's time is near,
        God's time is near,
    God's time is near, God's time is near.

2 God has chosen me,
    God has chosen me
to set alight a new fire;
God has chosen me,
    God has chosen me
to bring to birth
    a new kingdom on earth:
God has chosen me, chosen me.
    And to tell the world . . .

3 God is calling me, God is calling me
in all whose cry is unheard;
God is calling me, God is calling me
to raise up the voice
    with no power or choice,
God is calling me, calling me.
    And to tell the world . . .

831 George W Briggs
© 1952 Hope Publishing/CopyCare

1 **God has spoken – by His prophets,**
spoken His unchanging word;
each from age to age proclaiming
God the One, the righteous Lord;
in the world's despair and turmoil
one firm anchor still holds fast:
God is King, His throne eternal,
God the First and God the Last.

2   God has spoken – by Christ Jesus,
    Christ, the everlasting Son;
    brightness of the Father's glory,
    with the Father ever one:
    spoken by the Word incarnate,
    Life, before all time began,
    Light of light to earth descending,
    God, revealed as Son of Man.

3   God is speaking – by His Spirit
    speaking to our hearts again;
    in the age-long word expounding
    God's own message, now as then.
    Through the rise and fall of nations
    one sure faith is standing fast:
    God abides, His word unchanging,
    God the First and God the Last.

3   Long have our human wars
      ruined its harvest;
    long has earth bowed
      to the terror of force;
    long have we wasted
      what others have need of,
    poisoned the fountain of life
      at its source.

4   Earth is the Lord's:
      it is ours to enjoy it,
    ours, as His stewards,
      to farm and defend.
    From its pollution,
      misuse and destruction,
    good Lord deliver us,
      world without end!

832   Fred Pratt Green
       © 1973 Stainer & Bell Ltd

1   **God in His love for us**
    lent us this planet,
    gave it a purpose
    in time and in space:
    small as a spark
    from the fire of creation,
    cradle of life
    and the home of our race.

2   Thanks be to God
    for its bounty and beauty,
    life that sustains
    us in body and mind:
    plenty for all, if we learn how to share
    it,
    riches undreamed-of
    to fathom and find.

833   Chris Bowater
       © 1990 Sovereign Lifestyle Music

1   **God of grace, I turn my face**
    to You – I cannot hide;
    my nakedness, my shame, my guilt,
    are all before Your eyes.

2   Strivings and all anguished dreams
    in rags lie at my feet,
    and only grace provides the way
    for me to stand complete.

    And Your grace clothes me
      in righteousness,
    and Your mercy covers me in love;
    Your life adorns and beautifies –
    I stand complete in You.

834 © 1994 Stuart Haynes

**Great is God
whose mercy has found us,**
cast away the chains that have bound us.
We can go forth in liberty,
praising the name of the Lord!
We are free, let heaven declare it,
lift your voice, let all people share it!
We are no more in slavery –
sing with your heart aflame,
worship His holy name,
come, praise the name of the Lord!

835 Gerald Coates and Noel Richards
© 1992 Kingsway's Thankyou Music

1 **Great is the darkness
that covers the earth,**
oppression, injustice and pain.
Nations are slipping in hopeless
despair,
though many have come in Your name,
watching while sanity dies,
touched by the madness and lies.
*Come, Lord Jesus,
come, Lord Jesus,
pour out Your Spirit, we pray.
Come, Lord Jesus,
come, Lord Jesus,
pour out Your Spirit on us today.*

2 May now Your Church rise
with power and love,
this glorious gospel proclaim.
In every nation salvation will come
to those who believe in Your name.
Help us bring light to the world,
that we might speed Your return.
Come, Lord Jesus . . .

3 Great celebrations on that final day,
when out of the heavens You come.
Darkness will vanish, all sorrow will
end,
and rulers will bow at Your throne.
Our great commission complete,
then face to face we shall meet.
Come, Lord Jesus . . .

836 Graham Kendrick and Steve Thompson
© 1993 Make Way Music

*God is great, amazing!
Come, let His praises ring.
God is great, astounding!
The whole creation sings.*

1 His clothing is splendour
and majesty bright,
for He wraps Himself
in a garment of light.
He spreads out the heavens –
His palace of stars,
and rides on the wings of the wind.
God is great . . .

2 What marvellous wisdom
the Maker displays,
the sea vast and spacious,
the dolphins and whales,
the earth full of creatures,
the great and the small,
He watches and cares for them all.
God is great . . .

3 The rain forest canopies
darken the skies,
cathedrals of mist that resound
with the choirs
of creatures discordant,
outrageous, ablaze
in colourful pageants of praise.
God is great . . .

4 Above His creation the Father presides:
the pulse of the planets,
    the rhythm of tides,
the moon makes the seasons,
    the day follows night,
yet He knows every beat of my heart.
God is great, amazing!
Come, let His praises ring.
God is great, astounding!
The whole creation sings.

5 Let cannons of thunder
    salute their acclaim,
the sunsets fly glorious banners of
    flame,
the angels shout 'holy' again and again
as they soar in the arch of the heavens.
God is great . . .

837 Kevin Prosch
© 1991 Mercy/Vineyard Publishing/CopyCare

MEN **He brought me to**
        His banqueting table,

WOMEN He brought me to
        His banqueting table,

MEN He brought me to
        His banqueting table,

WOMEN He brought me to
        His banqueting table,

ALL and His banner over me is love.

MEN I am my beloved's
        and He is mine,

WOMEN I am my beloved's
        and He is mine,

MEN I am my beloved's
        and He is mine,

WOMEN I am my beloved's
        and He is mine,

ALL and His banner over me is love,
        yes, His banner over me is love.

ALL And we can feel the love
        of God in this place,
we believe Your goodness,
        we receive Your grace.
We delight ourselves
        at Your table, O God,
You do all things well,
        just look at our lives.

MEN He brought me to His
        banqueting table . . .

838 David Fellingham
© 1992 Kingsway's Thankyou Music

He has been given
a name above all names
in earth and Heaven,
let all creation claim
that Jesus Christ is King and Lord of all.
He is the victor
over Satan's reign,
His blood has triumphed
over sin and shame –
Jesus Christ is King and Lord of all.

He is the likeness of Jehovah,
through whom the world was made.
By His word the universe is sustained,
every power is subject to His name.

The name of Jesus
in victory will resound,
in every nation
let the good news sound:
Jesus Christ is King and Lord of all.

839 Gerald Coates, Noel and Tricia Richards
© 1993 Kingsway's Thankyou Music

He has risen, He has risen,
He has risen, Jesus is alive!

1 When the life flowed from His body,
seemed like Jesus' mission failed;
but His sacrifice accomplished
victory over sin and hell.
  He has risen ...

2 In the grave God did not leave Him
for His body to decay;
raised to life – the great awakening –
Satan's power He overcame.
  He has risen ...

3 If there were no resurrection
we ourselves could not be raised,
but the Son of God is living,
so our hope is not in vain.
  He has risen ...

4 When the Lord rides out of Heaven,
mighty angels at His side,
they will sound the final trumpet,
from the grave we shall arise.
  He has risen ...

5 He has given life immortal –
we shall see Him face to face;
through eternity we'll praise Him,
Christ the champion of our faith.
  He has risen ...

840 © 1994 Timothy Dudley-Smith

1 **Heaven's throne ascending,**
death's dominion ending,
Christ the strong to save!
Now in glory seated,
work on earth completed,
risen from the grave!
Join to praise through all our days
Christ the Lord of love who sought us,
and in dying bought us.

2 Powers of darkness broken,
earth from sleep awoken,
and to life reborn!
From our nature's prison
we with Christ are risen
by that Easter morn.
Join to sing our glorious King,
risen, reigning, high ascending,
Lord of life unending!

841 © 1995 Greg Leavers

1 **Here in Your presence, Lord,**
Your love is so strong, so sure.
Safe in Your presence, Lord,
I rest in You so secure.
  I worship, I worship,
  Jesus, I worship You.

2 Here in Your presence, Lord,
Your power and love break through.
Safe in Your presence, Lord,
I'm fixing my eyes on You.
  I worship ...

3 Here in Your presence, Lord,
I kneel before Your throne.
Safe in Your presence, Lord,
You tell me that I'm Your own.
  I worship ...
  I worship ...
  I worship ...

842 Graham Kendrick
© 1991 Make Way Music

1 **Here is bread, here is wine,**
Christ is with us – He is with us;
break the bread, drink the wine –
Christ is with us here.

2 Here is grace, here is peace,
  Christ is with us – He is with us;
  know His grace, find His peace –
  feast on Jesus here.
  In this bread there is healing,
  in this cup there's life for ever;
  in this moment, by the Spirit
  Christ is with us here.

3 Here we are, joined in one,
  Christ is with us – He is with us;
  We'll proclaim, 'til He comes –
  Jesus crucified.
  In this bread . . .

843 Kevin Prosch
© 1991 Mercy/Vineyard Publishing/CopyCare

1 **He is the Lord**
  and He reigns on high;
  He is the Lord,
  spoke into the darkness,
     created the light;
  He is the Lord.
  Who is like unto Him,
     never ending in days?
  He is the Lord,
  and He comes in power
     when we call on His name;
  He is the Lord.
  Show Your power, O Lord our God,
  show Your power, O Lord our God,
  our God.

2 Your gospel, O Lord,
     is the hope for our nation;
  You are the Lord.
  It's the power of God for our salvation;
  You are the Lord.
  We ask not for riches
     but look to the cross;
  You are the Lord,
  and for our inheritance give us the lost;
  You are the Lord.

Send Your power, O Lord our God,
send Your power, O Lord our God.
our God.

844 Brian Doerksen
© 1990 Mercy/Vineyard Publishing/CopyCare

Holiness is Your life in me,
making me clean through Your blood;
holiness is Your fire in me,
purging my heart like a flood.
I know You are perfect in holiness;
Your life in me, setting me free,
making me holy:
  Only the blood of Jesus
  covers all of my sin;
  only the life of Jesus
  renews me from within.
  Your blood is enough –
  Your mercy complete;
  Your work of atonement
     paid for my debts,
  making me holy:
  only the blood of Jesus.

845 Julian Perkins
© 1994 The Tehillah Trust

1 **Holy and majestic,**
  awesome God of power,
  my heart will always praise You.
  Your holy name I honour.
  Bowing down before You,
  I really do adore You –
  what can I do but love You,
  holy Lord, worthy Lord?

2 Because You are my Father,
  You beckon me to enter,
  to come into Your presence
  and gaze upon Your glory.
  Bowing down before You . . .

3 Your wondrous grace protects me;
   Your perfect love surrounds me;
   You clothe me in Your beauty;
   I know Your depths of mercy.
   Bowing down before You . . .

846 Graham Kendrick and Steve Thompson
       © 1991 Make Way Music

1 **How can I be free from sin –**
      lead me to the cross of Jesus –
   from the guilt, the power, the pain?
      Lead me to the cross of Jesus.
   There's no other way,
   no price that I could pay;
   simply to the cross I cling.
   This is all I need,
   this is all I plead,
   that His blood was shed for me.

2 How can I know peace within?
      Lead me to the cross of Jesus.
   Sing a song of joy again!
      Lead me to the cross of Jesus.
   Flowing from above,
   all-forgiving love
   from the Father's heart to me!
   What a gift of grace –
   His own righteousness
   clothing me in purity!

3 How can I live day by day –
      Lead me to the cross of Jesus,
   following His narrow way?
      Lead me to the cross of Jesus.

847 © 1992 Chris Rolinson/Jubilate Hymns

1 **How do we start to touch
      the broken hearts,**
   the barren lives,
      the lonely and bereaved?
   Lord, in Your name we shall go forth:
   Your healing power for ever is the
      same!

*That the world may believe,
that the world may believe,
that the world may believe in You!*

2 We shall proclaim
      the love of Jesus Christ –
   a man of sorrows, yet a man divine;
   His worthiness, His loveliness,
   His faithfulness for ever we will sing!
   That the world may believe . . .

3 And so we go into a lonely world
   where fear reigns and sorrow fills the
      air;
   yet, as we go Your Spirit comes –
   Your cleansing power
      You give to us to share!
   That the world may believe . . .

848 From Psalm 13
       © Barbara Woollett/Jubilate Hymns

1 **How long, O Lord, will You forget**
   an answer to my prayer?
   No tokens of Your love I see,
   Your face is turned away from me;
      I wrestle with despair.

2 How long, O Lord, will You forsake
   and leave me in this way?
   When will You come to my relief?
   My heart is overwhelmed with grief,
      by evil night and day.

3 How long, O Lord – but You forgive,
   with mercy from above.
   I find that all Your ways are just,
   I learn to praise You and to trust
   in Your unfailing love.

849 Dave Bilbrough
       © 1994 Kingsway's Thankyou Music

   How wonderful, how glorious
   is the love of God,
   bringing healing, forgiveness,
   wonderful love.

1 Let celebration echo through this land;
  we bring reconciliation,
  we bring hope to every man.
  How wonderful, how glorious
  is the love of God,
  bringing healing, forgiveness,
  wonderful love.

2 We proclaim the kingdom
    of our God is here.
  Come and join the heavenly anthem
  ringing loud and ringing clear.
  How wonderful ...

3 Listen to the music as His
    praises fill the air;
  with joy and with gladness
  tell the people everywhere.
  How wonderful ...

850 David Hadden
© 1983 Restoration Music Ltd/Sovereign Music UK

1 **I am persuaded**
    that neither death, nor life,
  nor angels, principalities, nor powers,
  nor things that are now,
    nor things that are to come,
  can separate us from the love of Christ.
  We are more than conquerors,
  we are more than conquerors,
  we are more than conquerors
  through Christ, through Christ.

2 We know that all things
    work together for our good,
  for good to those who love the Lord.
  For God has called us
    to be just like His Son,
  to live and walk according to His word.
  We are more than conquerors ...

3 If God is for us,
    who against us can prevail?
  No-one can bring a charge
    against His chosen ones.
  And there will be no separation
    from our Lord –
  He has justified us
    through His precious blood.
  We are more than conquerors ...

851 Randy and Terry Butler
© 1993 Mercy/Vineyard Publishing/CopyCare

ALL
I know a place,
a wonderful place,
where accused and condemned
find mercy and grace;
where the wrongs we have done
and the wrongs done to us
were nailed there with Him,
there on the cross.

MEN	*At the cross,*
WOMEN	*at the cross,*
ALL	*He died for our sin.*
MEN	*At the cross,*
WOMEN	*at the cross,*
ALL	*He gave us life again.*

852 © 1993 Geoff Twigg/Jubilate Hymns

1 **I know it was Your love for me**
  that led You, Lord, to Calvary;
    I know it was the sin,
    the state that I was in,
  that caused You suffering and pain.
  Lord Jesus, through Your broken heart
  You've given me a brand new start;
    O, help me to be true –
    and in eternity with You
  I'll never break Your heart again.

2 And while I live upon this earth,
I want to show the world Your worth –
this love was meant to share,
to comfort and to care
for those who thought themselves
    alone.
You gave Your life at endless cost
to serve the world and save the lost;
and Your Spirit, ever-living,
is continually giving
from the riches of Your throne.

853 E H Miller (1833–1913)

1 **I love to hear the story**
which angel voices tell,
how once the King of glory
came down on earth to dwell.
I am both weak and sinful,
but this I surely know,
the Lord came down to save me
because He loved me so.

2 I'm glad my blessèd Saviour
was once a child like me,
to show how pure and holy
His little ones might be;
and if I try to follow
His footsteps here below,
He never will forget me
because He loves me so.

3 To tell His love and mercy
my sweetest songs I'll raise;
and though I cannot see Him,
I know He hears my praise;
for He Himself has promised
that even I may go
to sing among His angels,
because He loves me so.

854 © 1993 Geoff Twigg/Jubilee Hymns

1 **I should be getting to know You:**
You're my Father, I'm Your child –
I should be getting to know You,
the touch of Your hand,
the warmth of Your smile.
Help me to listen to Your word
and then to act on what I've heard;
help me to know
    that Your love for me is sure –
O draw me closer,
    my Father and my Lord.

2 I should be getting to know You:
for, despite the wrong I do,
Lord, You still want me to know You.
You know in my heart I mean to be
    true:
teach me to love Your holy ways
and walk within them all my days,
remaining loyal to You,
    my faithful Friend,
because I know that
    Your love will never end.

855 Craig Musseau © 1991 Mercy/Vineyard Publishing/CopyCare

I sing a simple song of love
to my Saviour, to my Jesus.
I'm grateful for the things You've done,
my loving Saviour, O precious Jesus.
My heart is glad
    that You've called me Your own,
there's no place I'd rather be
than in Your arms of love,
in Your arms of love,
holding me still, holding me near
in Your arms of love.

I sing a simple song of love . . .

My heart is glad . . .
(*last time*)
holding me still, holding me near,
holding me still, holding me near
in Your arms of love.

856 Ed Pirie
© 1994 E D Pirie

MEN **I sing this song**
    as a simple act
        of worship to my Lord,
WOMEN I sing this song
    as a simple act
        of worship to my Lord.
MEN I sing this song
    as a simple act
        of worship to my Lord,
WOMEN I sing this song
    as a simple act
        of worship to my Lord.
MEN For He is holy,
WOMEN holy,
MEN holy,
WOMEN holy,
ALL holy is the Lord.
MEN He is holy,
WOMEN holy,
ALL holy is the Lord.

857 From Isaiah 6
Daniel Schutte
© 1981 Daniel L Schutte and New Dawn Music

1 **I, the Lord of sea and sky,**
I have heard My people cry;
all who dwell in dark and sin
My hand will save.
I who made the stars of night,
I will make their darkness bright.
Who will bear My light to them?
Whom shall I send?

Here I am, Lord.
Is it I, Lord?
I have heard You calling in the night.
I will go, Lord,
if You lead me;
I will hold Your people in my heart.

2 I, the Lord of snow and rain,
I have borne My people's pain;
I have wept for love of them –
they turn away.
I will break their hearts of stone,
give them hearts for love alone;
I will speak My word to them.
Whom shall I send?
Here I am, Lord . . .

3 I, the Lord of wind and flame,
I will tend the poor and lame,
I will set a feast for them –
My hand will save.
Finest bread I will provide
till their hearts are satisfied;
I will give My life to them.
Whom shall I send?
Here I am, Lord . . .

858 Brian Doerksen and Cindy Rethmeier
© 1990 Mercy/Vineyard Publishing/CopyCare

I want to know You,
Lord, I must know You.
I want to be found in You,
I want to be clothed in Your truth.
So I fix my eyes on You,
Lord, I must see You.
I put my faith in You,
I spend my life on You.
I want to know You,
I want to love You,
I want to know You more,
Jesus, Jesus.

I want to know You . . .

I want to know You . . .

859
Mark Altrogge
© 1982 People of Destiny International/
CopyCare

1 **I want to serve the purpose of God
in my generation.**
I want to serve the purpose of God
while I am alive.
I want to give my life
for something that'll last for ever:
Oh, I delight, I delight to do Your will.
What is on Your heart?
Show me what to do.
Let me know Your will,
and I will follow You.
What is on Your heart . . .

2 I want to build with silver and gold
in my generation.
I want to build with silver and gold
while I am alive.
I want to give my life
for something that'll last for ever:
Oh, I delight, I delight to do Your will.
What is on Your heart . . .

3 I want to see the kingdom of God
in my generation.
I want to see the kingdom of God
while I am alive.
I want to give my life
for something that'll last for ever:
Oh, I delight, I delight to do Your will.
What is on Your heart . . .

4 I want to see the Lord come again
in my generation.
I want to see the Lord come again
while I am alive.
I want to give my life
for something that'll last for ever.
Oh, I delight, I delight to do Your will.
What is on Your heart . . .

860
Steve Bassett and Sue Rinaldi
© 1994 Kingsway's Thankyou Music

I will cry mercy, I will cry mercy
for this land, O God.
I will cry justice, I will cry justice
for this land, O God,
for this land, O God.

Let Your tears flow from my eyes;
let Your passion melt my heart of stone.
Let Your beauty be seen in my life;
let Your heartbeat be my own.

So I'll cry mercy for this nation,
let us see healing for the people,
and I'll cry justice for this nation, O God.

861
Graham Kendrick
© 1993 Make Way Music

1 **If you are encouraged
in your union with Christ,**
finding consolation in His love,
compassion, warmth and friendship
in the Spirit's flow of life;
this is how you make my joy complete:
By being of the same mind,
and loving with the same love,
united in the Spirit,
with the same goal in sight,
by being of the same mind,
and loving with the same love,
united in the Spirit,
to the glory of Christ.

2 Be sure you do nothing
out of selfishness or pride,
never seeing past your own concerns,
but humbly keep the interests
of each other in your hearts,
seeing them as better than yourselves:
By being of the same mind . . .

862
Edward Turney
© 1983 Salvationist Publishing and Supplies/
CopyCare

1 **I'll go in the strength of the Lord,**
in paths He has marked for my feet;
I'll follow the light of His word,
nor shrink from the dangers I meet.
His presence my steps shall attend,
His fulness my wants shall supply;
on Him, 'til my journey shall end,
my unwavering faith will rely.
I'll go, (I'll go,) I'll go in the strength,
I'll go in the strength of the Lord
(I'll go).
I'll go, (I'll go,) I'll go in the strength,
I'll go in the strength of the Lord.

2 I'll go in the strength of the Lord,
to work He appoints me to do;
in joy which His smile doth afford
my soul shall its vigour renew.
His wisdom shall guard me from harm,
His power my sufficiency prove;
I'll trust His omnipotent arm,
and prove His unchangeable love.
I'll go . . .

3 I'll go in the strength of the Lord,
to conflicts which faith will require;
His grace as my shield and reward,
my courage and zeal shall inspire.
Since He gives the word of command
to meet and encounter the foe,
with His sword of truth in my hand
to suffer and triumph I'll go.
I'll go . . .
I'll go in the strength of the Lord.

863
Keith Banks
© Salvationist Publishing and Supplies/
CopyCare

I'm living my life for Jesus –
His love and His grace I've seen;
and now that I live for Jesus,
life has a new-found theme.

My life has a new-found intention,
I follow a purposeful aim,
and life has a new-found dimension –
I witness that I'm born again.

I'm living my life for Jesus –
His love and His grace I've seen;
and now that I live for Jesus,
life has a new-found theme.

864
Sondra Corbett
© 1983 Integrity's Hosanna! Music/
Kingsway's Thankyou Music

I worship You, almighty God,
there is none like You.
I worship You, O Prince of Peace,
that is what I love to do.
I give You praise,
for You are my righteousness.
I worship You, almighty God,
there is none like You.

865
Taizé Community
© Ateliers et Presses de Taizé

In the Lord I'll be ever thankful,
in the Lord I will rejoice.
Trust in God,
do not be afraid.
Our hearts untroubled,
the Lord is near,
our hearts untroubled,
the Lord is near.

866
Michael Perry (1942–96)
© Mrs B Perry/Jubilate Hymns

1 **In the streets of every city,**
bringing hope and healing strife,
living out the Saviour's pity,
caring for each precious life.

2 Through the world, in every nation,
serving Christ, with lives made whole;
in His name we speak salvation
grace for every seeking soul;
  Where it matters, there you'll find us,
  where it matters, there you'll find us
  serving Jesus;
  where it matters, there you'll find us
  in the service of our Lord.

3 In our daily time of praying,
thanking God for sins forgiven,
hearing what His voice is saying,
tasting now the joys of Heaven.

4 At His table, there you'll find us
pouring wine and sharing bread;
'Christ has died' these gifts remind us,
'Christ is risen from the dead'.
  Where it matters . . .

5 God of city, and of nation,
Lord ascended, coming King;
with resounding exultation
of Your faithfulness we sing.
  Where it matters . . .

Oh, let the living waters flow,
oh, let the living waters flow,
let the river of Your Spirit
  flow through me;
oh, let the living waters flow,
oh, let the living waters flow,
let the river of Your Spirit
  flow through me.
Flow through me, flow through me,
flow through me, flow through me.

Let the living waters flow,
let the living waters flow,
let the living waters flow,
let the living waters flow.
  Oh, let the living waters flow . . .

867 Graham Kendrick
© 1994 Make Way Music

Is anyone thirsty – anyone?
Is anyone thirsty?
Is anyone thirsty – anyone?
Is anyone thirsty?
Jesus said:
'Let them come to me and drink,
let them come to me.'

868 Terry Butler
© 1991 Mercy/Vineyard Publishing/CopyCare

It is the cry of my heart
  to follow You,
it is the cry of my heart to be close to
  You;
it is the cry of my heart to follow
all of the days of my life.
It is the cry of my heart . . .

1 Teach me Your holy ways, O Lord,
so I can walk in Your truth;
teach me Your holy ways, O Lord,
and make me wholly devoted to You.
Oh, oh, oh.
  It is the cry of my heart . . .

2 Open my eyes so I can see
the wonderful things that You do;
open my heart up more and more
and make it wholly devoted to You.
Oh, oh, oh.
  It is the cry of my heart . . .
  all of the days of my life,
  all of the days of my life,
  all of the days of my life.

869 © 1992 Chris Rolinson/Jubilate Hymns

1 **In Your arms of love so tender,**
we would our whole lives surrender:
captured by Your precious love,
we worship You.

2 Standing on this ground so holy,
gazing on the King so mighty –
crucified yet robed in glory:
Jesus Christ.

3 Holy Lord, we bow before You;
humbly we would seek to know You:
Lord, reveal Yourself so we might
worship You.

870 Phil Lawson Johnston
© 1991 Kingsway's Thankyou Music

1 **Jesus is the name we honour;**
Jesus is the name we praise.
Majestic name above all other names,
the highest heaven and earth proclaim
that Jesus is our God.
We will glorify,
we will lift Him high,
we will give Him honour and praise.
We will glorify . . .

2 Jesus is the name we worship;
Jesus is the name we trust.
He is the King above all other kings,
let all creation stand and sing
that Jesus is our God.
We will glorify . . .

3 Jesus is the Father's splendour;
Jesus is the Father's joy.
He will return to reign in majesty,
and every eye at last will see
that Jesus is our God.
We will glorify . . .

871 Gerrit Gustafson and Steve Israel
© 1988 Integrity's Hosanna! Music/
Kingsway's Thankyou Music

Jesus Christ is the Lord of all,
Lord of all the earth,
Jesus Christ is the Lord of all,
Lord of all the earth.
Jesus Christ is the Lord of all . . .

Only one God over the nations,
only one Lord of all;
in no other name is there salvation,
Jesus is Lord of all.
Jesus Christ is Lord of all,
Jesus Christ is Lord of all;
Jesus Christ is Lord of all,
Jesus Christ is Lord of all.

Jesus Christ is the Lord of all . . .

Only one God . . .

872 John Barnett
© 1988 Mercy/Vineyard Publishing/CopyCare

Jesus, Jesus,
holy and anointed One, Jesus;
Jesus, Jesus,
risen and exalted One, Jesus:
Your name is like honey on my lips,
Your Spirit like water to my soul;
Your word is a lamp unto my feet –
Jesus, I love You, I love You.

Jesus, Jesus . . .

873 Graham Kendrick
© 1992 Make Way Music

1 **Jesus, restore to us again**
the gospel of Your holy name,
that comes with power, not words
alone,
owned, signed and sealed
from Heaven's throne.
Spirit and word in one agreed;
the promise to the power wed.

The word is near, here in our mouths
and in our hearts, the word of faith –
proclaim it on the Spirit's breath:
'Jesus!'

2 Your word, O Lord, eternal stands,
   fixed and unchanging in the heavens.
   The Word made flesh
      to earth came down
   to heal our world
      with nail-pierced hands.
   Among us here You lived and breathed,
   You are the message we received.
   The word is near . . .

3 Spirit of truth, lead us, we pray,
   into all truth as we obey,
   and as God's will we gladly choose,
   Your ancient power again will prove
   Christ's teaching
      truly comes from God –
   He is indeed the living Word.
   The word is near . . .

4 Upon the heights of this dark land
   with Moses and Elijah stand:
   reveal Your glory once again,
   show us Your face, declare Your
      name –
   prophets and laws in You complete
   where promises and power meet.
   The word is near . . .

5 Grant us in this decisive hour
   to know the Scriptures and the power;
   the knowledge in experience prove,
   the power that moves and works by
      love.
   May word and work join hands as one,
   the word go forth, the Spirit come.
   The word is near . . .
   The word is near . . .
   'Jesus!'

874
Alun Leppitt
© 1993 Sound Impression

1 **Jesus, there's no-one like You.**
   Jesus, there's no-one like You.
   You are the Saviour, You are the King,
   You are the answer to everything.
   Jesus, there's no-one like You.
   All You have made
   will praise Your name,
   the glory of the Father is Yours.

2 Jesus, there's no-one like You.
   Jesus, there's no-one like You.
   You give us life, You give us peace,
   Your precious blood has set us free.
   Jesus, there's no-one like You.
   All You have made . . .

3 Jesus, there's no-one like You.
   Jesus, there's no-one like You.
   You bring healing and release,
   so mighty are Your deeds.
   Jesus, there's no-one like You.
   All You have made . . .

   Jesus, (O Jesus,)
   We praise Jesus (only Jesus).

875
Karen David
© 1990 Karen David/Ellel Ministries Ltd

1 **Jesus, take Your rightful place**
   in my life.
   I give You complete control.
   As I lay my life afresh before You,
   cleanse me and make me whole.

2 Jesus, take Your rightful place
      in my heart.
   Be seated on the throne.
   As I lift my voice in adoration,
   I worship You alone.

876

S G Stock (1838–98)

1 **Let the song go round the earth,**
   Jesus Christ is Lord!
   Sound His praises, tell His worth,
   be His name adored;
   every clime and every tongue
   join the grand, the glorious song!

2 Let the song go round the earth!
   From the eastern sea,
   where the daylight has its birth,
   glad and bright and free;
   China's millions join the strains,
   waft them onto India's plains.

3 Let the song go round the earth!
   Lands where evil's sway
   darkly broods o'er home and hearth,
   cast their bonds away!
   Let His praise from Afric's shore
   rise and swell her wide lands o'er!

4 Let the song go round the earth!
   Where the summer smiles,
   let the notes of holy mirth
   break from distant isles!
   Inland forests dark and dim,
   snow-bound coasts, give back the
       hymn.

5 Let the song go round the earth!
   Jesus Christ is King!
   With the story of His worth
   let the whole world ring!
   Him creation all adore,
   evermore and evermore.

877

David Fellingham
© 1992 Kingsway's Thankyou Music

Let us draw near to God
in full assurance of faith,
knowing that as we draw near to Him,
He will draw near to us.

In the Holy Place
we stand in confidence,
knowing our lives are cleansed
in the blood of the Lamb,
we will worship and adore.

878

From the General Thanksgiving
© 1993 Timothy Dudley-Smith

1 **Lord God almighty,**
       Father of all mercies,
   well-spring of goodness,
       fount of all things living,
   we now Your children,
       blessed by loving kindness,
   come with thanksgiving.

2 Hear us who praise You,
       first for our creation,
   formed in Your likeness,
       breath and being gaining;
   then for our keeping,
       life in all its fulness
   daily sustaining.

3 But above all things,
       for the gift of Jesus,
   love past comparing,
       source of our salvation;
   humbly we bring You,
       for a world's redeeming,
   our adoration.

4 So in thanksgiving
       for the hope of glory,
   love, grace and mercy
   all our days attending,
   more than our lips, Lord,
       let our living praise You,
   ages unending.

879

© 1993 Geoff Twigg/Jubilee Hymns

1 **Lord, help me to know Your presence**
in all I do today,
Lord, help me declare Your praises
in everything I say;
   live in my heart
   and fill every part
with Your Holy Spirit's flame –
O let the world see Jesus in me,
and glorify Your name!

2 Lord, may I become like Jesus
in everything I do:
then, if any action pleases,
glory will come to You.
   Lord, may my mind
   and will be refined
by Your Holy Spirit's flame –
O let the world see Jesus in me
and glorify Your name!

880

Geoff Bullock
© 1992 Word Music/Maranatha! Music/
CopyCare

1 **Lord, I come to You,**
let my heart be changed, renewed,
flowing from the grace
   that I've found in You.
And, Lord, I've come to know
the weaknesses I see in me
will be stripped away
by the power of Your love.
   Hold me close,
   let Your love surround me;
   bring me near,
   draw me to Your side.
   And as I wait,
   I'll rise up like the eagle,
   and I will soar with You,
   Your Spirit leads me on
   in the power of Your love.

2 Lord, unveil my eyes,
let me see You face to face,
the knowledge of Your love
   as You live in me.
Lord, renew my mind,
as Your will unfolds in my life
in living every day
in the power of Your love.
   Hold me close . . .

881

Rick Founds
© 1989 Maranatha! Music/CopyCare

Lord, I lift Your name on high,
Lord, I love to sing Your praises;
I'm so glad You're in my life,
I'm so glad You came to save us.
   You came from Heaven to earth
   to show the way,
   from the earth to the cross
   my debt to pay;
   from the cross to the grave,
   from the grave to the sky,
   Lord, I lift Your name on high.

882

Jan Struther (1901–53)
By permission of Oxford University Press

1 **Lord of all hopefulness,**
   Lord of all joy,
whose trust, ever child-like,
   no cares could destroy,
be there at our waking,
   and give us, we pray,
Your bliss in our hearts, Lord,
   at the break of the day.

2 Lord of all eagerness, Lord of all faith,
whose strong hands were skilled
   at the plane and the lathe,
be there at our labours,
   and give us, we pray,
Your strength in our hearts, Lord,
   at the noon of the day.

3 Lord of all kindliness, Lord of all
grace,
Your hands swift to welcome,
Your arms to embrace,
be there at our homing,
and give us, we pray,
Your love in our hearts, Lord,
at the eve of the day.

4 Lord of all gentleness, Lord of all calm,
whose voice is contentment,
whose presence is balm,
be there at our sleeping,
and give us, we pray,
Your peace in our hearts, Lord,
at the end of the day.

883 Jessy Dixon, Randy Scruggs and John W Thompson
© 1983 Windswept Pacific Music Ltd

1 **Lord of lords, King of kings,**
Maker of Heaven and earth
and all good things,
we give You glory.
Lord Jehovah, Son of Man,
precious Prince of Peace
and the great 'I AM',
we give You glory.
Glory to God,
glory to God,
glory to God almighty
in the highest.

2 Lord, You're righteous in all Your ways,
we bless Your holy name
and we give You praise,
we give You glory.
You reign for ever in majesty,
we praise and lift You up for eternity,
we give You glory.
Glory to God . . .

884 © 1993 Geoff Twigg/Jubilate Hymns

1 **Lord, teach us to pray;**
let us know Your will every day.
Give us the grace
to go on seeking Your face,
in obedience to all that You say,
in obedience to all that You say.

2 Lord, help us to see
with the eyes of faith, and believe.
Give us Your heart to care
for the world in our prayer,
and a vision of what it should be,
and a vision of what it should be.

885 Dave Bilbrough
© 1993 Kingsway's Thankyou Music

1 **Lord, we come in adoration,**
lay our lives before You now,
we are here to reach the nations,
to tell the world of Jesus' power.
We would seek Your awesome glory,
all the gifts that You endow.
Called to reach this generation,
and now is the appointed hour to:
Go in Your name,
go and proclaim Your kingdom.
Go in Your name,
for we have been chosen
to tell all creation
that Jesus is King of all kings.

2 We believe that You have spoken
through Your Son to all the earth,
given us this great commission
to spread the news of all Your worth.
Set apart to serve You only,
let our lives display Your love;
Hearts infused that tell the story
of God come down from Heaven
above.
Go in Your name . . .

3 Grant to us a fresh anointing,
   Holy Spirit, be our guide;
   satisfy our deepest longing –
   Jesus Christ, be glorified.
   Every tribe and every people
   hear the message that we bring;
   Christ has triumphed over evil,
   bow the knee and worship Him.
   Go in Your name . . .

887 Martin Smith
         © 1992 Kingsway's Thankyou Music

Lord, You have my heart,
and I will search for Yours;
Jesus, take my life and lead me on.
Lord, You have my heart,
and I will search for Yours;
let me be to You a sacrifice.

MEN	And I will praise You, Lord,
WOMEN	I will praise You, Lord,
MEN	and I will sing
	of love come down,
WOMEN	I will sing of love come down,
MEN	and as You show Your face,
WOMEN	show Your face,
ALL	we'll see Your glory here.

886 From Psalm 16
         © 1992 Timothy Dudley-Smith

1 **Lord, when the storms of life arise,**
   be near to keep me yet,
   my chosen portion and my prize
   in whom alone my refuge lies,
   on whom my hope is set,
   on whom my hope is set.

2 In God alone securely stand
   His saints for ever blessed,
   who shelter safe beneath His hand
   as in a fair and pleasant land,
   and in His presence rest,
   and in His presence rest.

3 Lord of our life, our strength and stay,
   whom yet unseen we love,
   uphold us in the narrow way
   and guide our footsteps night and day
   with wisdom from above,
   with wisdom from above.

4 So shall the path of life be shown,
   the prayers of faith ascend;
   until we know as we are known,
   and sing before the Father's throne
   the songs that never end,
   the songs that never end.

888 J E Leeson (1807–82)

1 **Loving shepherd of Thy sheep,**
   keep Thy lamb, in safety keep;
   nothing can Thy power withstand,
   none can pluck me from Thy hand.

2 Loving Saviour, thou didst give
   Thine own life that we might live;
   and the hands outstretched to bless
   bear the cruel nails' impress.

3 I would bless Thee every day,
   gladly all Thy will obey,
   like Thy blessed ones above,
   happy in Thy precious love.

4 Loving shepherd, ever near,
   teach Thy lamb Thy voice to hear;
   suffer not my steps to stray
   from the straight and narrow way.

5 Where Thou leadest I would go,
   walking in Thy steps below,
   'til before my Father's throne
   I shall know as I am known.

889

E E Hewitt (1851–1920)

1 **More about Jesus would I know;**
   more of His grace to others show,
   more of His saving fulness see,
   more of His love, who died for me.
   More, more about Jesus,
   more, more about Jesus;
   more of His saving fulness see,
   more of His love, who died for me.

2 More about Jesus let me learn,
   more of His holy will discern;
   Spirit of God, my teacher be,
   showing the things of Christ to me.
   More, more about Jesus . . .

3 More about Jesus, in His word
   holding communion with my Lord;
   hearing His voice in every line,
   making each faithful saying mine.
   More, more about Jesus . . .

4 More about Jesus, on His throne,
   riches in glory all His own;
   more of His kingdom's sure increase;
   more of His coming, Prince of Peace.
   More, more about Jesus . . .

890

From Psalm 93
Karen David
© 1993 Karen David / Ellel Ministries Ltd

MEN **Mighty God,**
       we give You praise,
WOMEN mighty God, we give You praise,
MEN mighty God, we give You praise,
WOMEN mighty God, we give You praise.
MEN You are robed in majesty,
WOMEN You are robed in majesty,
ALL You are robed in majesty.

ALL Mightier than the thunder
       of great waters,
   mightier than the breakers
       of the sea.
   Your throne was established
       long ago,
   You are from all eternity.

891

Mark and Helen Johnson, Chris Bowater
© 1991 Sovereign Lifestyle Music

Mighty God, everlasting Father,
wonderful counsellor,
You're the Prince of Peace.
Mighty God . . .

1 You are Lord of heaven,
   You are called Emmanuel;
   God is now with us,
   ever present to deliver.
   You are God eternal,
   You are Lord of all the earth;
   love has come to us,
   bringing us new birth.
   Mighty God . . .

2 A light to those in darkness,
   and a guide to paths of peace;
   love and mercy dawns,
   grace, forgiveness and salvation.
   Light for revelation,
   glory to Your people;
   Son of the Most High,
   God's love gift to all.

892

Jude del Hierro
© 1978 Mercy/Vineyard Publishing/CopyCare

MEN **More love,**
WOMEN more love,
MEN more power,
WOMEN more power,
ALL more of You in my life.
MEN More love . . .

ALL   And I will worship You
with all of my heart,
and I will worship You
with all of my mind,
and I will worship You
with all of my strength,
for You are my Lord.

MEN   More love . . .
MEN   More love . . .

ALL   And I will seek Your face
with all of my heart,
and I will seek Your face
with all of my mind,
and I will seek Your face
with all of my strength,
for You are my Lord,
for You are my Lord,
You are my Lord.

893 From Psalm 45
Graham Kendrick
© 1991 Make Way Music

1   **My heart is full of admiration**
for You, my Lord, my God and King;
Your excellence my inspiration,
Your words of grace
    have made my spirit sing.

2   You love what's right and hate all evil,
therefore Your God sets You on high;
and on Your head pours oil of gladness,
while fragrance fills Your royal palaces.
    All the glory, honour and power
    belong to You, belong to You.
    Jesus, Saviour, anointed One,
    I worship You, I worship You.

3   Your throne, O God, will last for ever;
justice will be Your royal decree:
in majesty, ride out victorious
for righteousness, truth and humility.
    All the glory . . .
    All the glory . . .
    I worship You, I worship You.

894 W R Featherstone (1846–73)

1   **My Jesus, I love Thee,**
    I know Thou art mine,
for Thee all the pleasures of sin I
    resign;
my gracious Redeemer,
    my Saviour art Thou,
if ever I loved Thee, my Jesus, 'tis now.

2   I love Thee because Thou
    hast first lovèd me,
and purchased my pardon
    on Calvary's tree;
I love Thee for wearing the thorns
    on Thy brow,
if ever I loved Thee, my Jesus, 'tis now.

3   I'll love Thee in life,
    I will love Thee in death,
and praise Thee as long
    as Thou lendest me breath;
and say, when the death-dew
    lies cold on my brow:
if ever I loved Thee, my Jesus, 'tis now.

4   In mansions of glory
    and endless delight,
I'll ever adore Thee
    and dwell in Thy sight;
I'll sing with the glittering crown
    on my brow:
if ever I loved Thee, my Jesus, 'tis now.

895 Daniel Gardner
© 1986 Integrity's Hosanna! Music/
Kingsway's Thankyou Music

My life is in You, Lord,
my strength is in You, Lord,
my hope is in You, Lord,
in You, it's You.
My life is in You, Lord,
my strength is in You, Lord,
my hope is in You, Lord,
in You, it's in You.
My life is in You, Lord . . .

I will praise You with all of my life,
I will praise You with all of my strength,
with all of my life,
with all of my strength.
All of my hope is in You.
My life is in You, Lord,
my strength is in You, Lord,
my hope is in You, Lord,
in You, it's in You.
My life is in You, Lord,
my strength is in You, Lord,
my hope is in You, Lord,
in You, it's in You.
My life is in You, Lord . . .

I will praise You . . .
My life is in You . . .
in You.

896 Noel and Tricia Richards
© 1991 Kingsway's Thankyou Music

My lips shall praise You,
my great Redeemer;
my heart will worship,
almighty Saviour.

1 You take all my guilt away,
turn the darkest night to brightest day;
You are the Restorer of my soul.
My lips . . .

2 Love that conquers every fear!
In the midst of trouble You draw near,
You are the Restorer of my soul.
My lips . . .

3 You're the source of happiness,
bringing peace when I am in distress;
You are the Restorer of my soul.
My lips . . .
Almighty Saviour,
almighty Saviour,
almighty Saviour.

897 Brian Thomas
© Oxford University Press

1 **'My peace I leave with you',**
    this is His promise;
'My peace I give to you',
    this is His word.
Let not our hearts be sad,
    troubled or uncertain;
'My peace I leave with you.'

2 Lord Jesus, grant to us
    that peace enduring,
not as the world imparts –
    unsure, untrue;
but inward happiness
    past our understanding –
'My peace I leave with you.'

3 O may this peace be known
    throughout all nations,
that strife and enmity
    on earth may cease,
and ways of peace replace
    weapons of destruction –
'My peace I leave with you.'

4 O happy prophecy! O blessèd promise!
O may we always strive to make it true;
and may we never lose
    our dear Master's message –
'My peace I leave with you.'

898 Robert Gay
© 1988 Integrity's Hosanna! Music/
Kingsway's Thankyou Music

No other name
    but the name of Jesus,
no other name but the name of the Lord;
no other name but the name of Jesus
is worthy of glory,
and worthy of honour,
and worthy of power and all praise.
No other name . . .

His name is exalted far above the earth,
His name is high above the heavens;
His name is exalted far above the earth –
give glory and honour and praises
    to His name.
  No other name . . .

899 Andy Park
© 1988 Mercy/Vineyard Publishing/CopyCare

1 **No-one but You, Lord,**
  can satisfy the longing in my heart.
  Nothing I do, Lord,
  can take the place of drawing
    near to You.
    Only You can fill my deepest longing,
    only You can breathe in me new life;
    only You can fill my heart with
     laughter,
    only You can answer my heart's cry.

2 Father, I love You,
  come, satisfy the longing in my heart.
  Fill me, overwhelm me,
  until I know Your love deep in my
    heart.
    Only You . . .

900 Noel and Tricia Richards
© 1989 Kingsway's Thankyou Music

  Nothing shall separate us
  from the love of God.
  Nothing shall separate us
  from the love of God.

1 God did not spare His only Son,
  gave Him to save us all.
  Sin's price was met by Jesus' death
  and Heaven's mercy falls.
    Nothing shall separate us . . .

2 Up from the grave Jesus was raised
  to sit at God's right hand;
  pleading our cause in Heaven's courts –
  forgiven we can stand.
    Nothing shall separate us . . .

3 Now by God's grace we have embraced
  a life set free from sin;
  we shall deny all that destroys
  our union with Him.
    Nothing shall separate us . . .

901 © 1992 Timothy Dudley-Smith

1 **Now is Christ risen from the dead,**
  now are the powers of darkness fled,
  Alleluia, alleluia!
  Gone is the night of sin and gloom,
  Jesus is risen from the tomb.
  Alleluia, alleluia,
  alleluia, alleluia,
  alleluia!

2 Now is Christ risen from the dead,
  empty there lies His narrow bed,
  Alleluia, alleluia!
  Christ and His cross have won the day,
  come, see the grave in which He lay.
  Alleluia, alleluia,
  alleluia, alleluia,
  alleluia!

3 Now is Christ risen from the dead,
  He who His blood for sinners shed,
  Alleluia, alleluia!
  In Him who died to bear our sins
  our resurrection-life begins.
  Alleluia, alleluia,
  alleluia, alleluia,
  alleluia!

4 Now is Christ risen from the dead,
   risen and reigning as He said,
   Alleluia, alleluia!
   Praise Him who light and life restored,
   praise Him, our ever-living Lord!
   Alleluia, alleluia,
   alleluia, alleluia,
   alleluia!

902 Graham Kendrick
© 1991 Make Way Music

1 **Now in reverence and awe**
   we gather round Your word;
   in wonder we draw near
   to mysteries that angels strain to hear,
   that prophets dimly saw:
   so let Your Spirit shine upon the page
   and teach me;
      open up my eyes, with truth to free me,
      light to chase the lies.
      Lord Jesus, let me meet You in Your
      word;
      Lord Jesus, let me meet You in Your
      word.

2 Lord, Your truth cannot be chained;
   it searches everything –
   my secrets, my desires.
   Your word is like a hammer and a fire –
   it breaks, it purifies:
   so let Your Spirit shine into my heart
   and teach me;
      open up my eyes . . .

903 John Larsson
© Salvationist Publishing and Supplies/
CopyCare

Now the fruit of the Spirit is patience,
and the fruit of the Spirit is peace,
the fruit of the Spirit is gentleness,
and joy that will never cease.
The gift of the Spirit is healing,
and hope for the darkest hour,
the gift of the Spirit is love, yes, love,
and power, and power.

904 From Psalm 63
Andy Park
© 1991 Andy Park/Kingsway's Thankyou Music

1 **O Lord, I want to sing Your praises,**
   I want to praise Your name every day;
   O Lord, I want to sing Your praises,
   I want to praise Your name every day.
      Alleluia, allelu-, alleluia, allelu-!

2 O Lord, I want to sing Your praises,
   I want to praise Your name every day;
   O Lord, I want to sing Your praises,
   I want to praise Your name every day.
      Alleluia, allelu-, alleluia, allelu-!
      Alleluia!

3 God, You are my God,
   and I will seek You;
   I am satisfied when I find Your love.
   God, You are my God,
   and I will seek You;
   I am satisfied when I find Your love.

4 And I will praise You as long as I live,
   for Your love is better than life;
   in Your name I will lift up my hands,
   for Your love is better than life.
      Alleluia, allelu-, alleluia, allelu-!

5 O Lord, I want to sing Your praises,
   I want to praise Your name every day;
   O Lord, I want to sing Your praises,
   I want to praise Your name every day.
      Alleluia, allelu-, alleluia, allelu-!
      Alleluia!

905 From 1 Peter 1
© 1992 Timothy Dudley-Smith

1 **O Christ the King of glory,**
   who chose the way of loss
   to share our human story,
   to bear that bitter cross;
   by loving self-surrender,
   by all the pains You bore,
   You won for us the splendour
   of life for evermore.

2 May God, whose care unsleeping
holds all beneath His hand,
enfold within His keeping
the Church in every land.
Through doubtings and denials,
through grief to glory come,
through all their fiery trials
He leads His children home.

3 O Lord of life, ascended
to glory from the grave,
Your grace be still extended
to help and heal and save.
O Captain of salvation,
in mercy bring to birth
Your new redeemed creation
from all the pains of earth.

4 To God alone be blessing
and heartfelt ceaseless praise,
a love beyond expressing,
to everlasting days.
Proclaim salvation's story,
dominions, thrones and powers!
By cross and grave and glory
a living hope is ours.

906 Graham Kendrick
© 1992 Make Way Music

1 **O Father of the fatherless**
in whom all families are blessed,
I love the way You father me.
You gave me life, forgave the past;
now in Your arms I'm safe at last –
I love the way You father me.
Father me, for ever You'll father me;
and in Your embrace I'll be
for ever secure.
I love the way You father me,
I love the way You father me.

2 When bruised and broken I draw near,
You hold me close and dry my tears,
I love the way You father me.
At last my fearful heart is still,
surrendered to Your perfect will –
I love the way You father me.
Father me . . .

3 If in my foolishness I stray,
returning empty and ashamed,
I love the way You father me.
Exchanging for my wretchedness
Your radiant robes of righteousness –
I love the way You father me.
Father me . . .

4 And when I look into Your eyes,
from deep within my spirit cries:
I love the way You father me.
Before such love I stand amazed,
and ever will through endless days –
I love the way You father me.
Father me . . .

907 P Doddridge (1702–51) and J Logan (1748–88)

1 **O God of Bethel, by whose hand**
Thy people still are fed,
who through this weary pilgrimage
hast all our fathers led.

2 Our vows, our prayers, we now present
before Thy throne of grace;
God of our fathers, be the God
of their succeeding race.

3 Through each perplexing path of life
our wandering footsteps guide;
give us each day our daily bread,
and raiment fit provide.

4 O spread Thy covering wings around,
'til all our wanderings cease,
and at our Father's loved abode
our souls arrive in peace.

908
From Psalm 130
Jacques Berthier
© 1982, 1983 Ateliers et Presses de Taizé

O Lord, hear my prayer;
O Lord, hear my prayer:
when I call, answer me –
O Lord, hear my prayer;
O Lord, hear my prayer;
come and listen to me.

O Lord . . .

4 Time rushes on:
 give us a heart of wisdom
that seeks Your will
 and follows Your commands;
show us Your deeds,
 Your glory to our children,
work out Your timeless purpose
 through our hands.

909
From Psalm 90
© Basil E Bridge

1 **O Lord, the refuge
 of each generation,**
 You reigned before the universe began;
we bear Your stamp,
 the marks of Your creation,
and yet how frail we are,
 how brief life's span.

2 One thousand years
 like yesterday in passing,
our fleeting lives
 like half-remembered dreams,
or weeds that flower at noon
 but die by evening –
so, Lord, to You our transient
 glory seems.

3 O Holy Lord, forgive our
 self-deceiving –
our secret sins are clear
 before Your face:
grant us release,
 the joy of those believing
they are restored by Your eternal grace.

910
© 1992 Timothy Dudley-Smith

1 **O Lord, whose saving name**
is life and health and rest,
to whom the children came
and in Your arms were blessed,
we seek Your face;
Your love be shown,
Your presence known
within this place.

2 That love be ours to share
with tenderness and skill,
with science, faith and prayer
to work Your sovereign will;
we praise You, Lord,
for banished pain,
for strength again,
for health restored.

3 When deepest shadows fall
to quench life's fading spark,
be near us when we call,
walk with us through the dark,
our Light and Way,
by grief and loss,
and bitter cross,
to endless day.

4 In God our hope is set,
beneath whose rule alone
is peace from fear and fret
and strength beyond our own.
His kingdom stands,
and those this day
for whom we pray
are in His hands.

5 Join every heart to bring
our praise to God above,
whom children's voices sing
and whom unseen we love.
O God of grace,
for evermore
Your blessings pour
upon this place.

3 O boundless love divine!
How shall this tongue of mine
to wondering mortals tell
the matchless grace divine –
that I, a child of hell,
should in His image shine!
The Comforter has come!
The Comforter has come . . .

4 Sing, 'til the echoes fly
above the vaulted sky,
and all the saints above
to all below reply,
in strains of endless love,
the song that ne'er will die:
The Comforter has come!
The Comforter has come . . .

911 F Bottome (1823–94)

1 **O spread the tidings round**
wherever man is found,
wherever human hearts
and human woes abound;
let every Christian tongue
proclaim the joyful sound:
the Comforter has come!
The Comforter has come,
the Comforter has come,
the Holy Ghost from Heaven,
the Father's promise given,
O spread the tidings round
wherever man is found:
the Comforter has come!

2 Lo, the great King of kings
with healing in His wings
to every captive soul
a full deliverance brings;
and through the vacant cells
the song of triumph rings:
the Comforter has come!
The Comforter has come . . .

912 Graham Kendrick © 1995 Make Way Music

1 **Oh, I was made for this:**
to know Your tender kiss,
to know a love divine,
to know this love is mine.
And I was made to laugh,
and I was made to sing,
given the gift of life:
You gave me everything.

2 My feet were made to dance,
my spirit made to soar,
my life is not by chance,
You give me more and more.
For I was made for You,
and I have made my choice,
and all that stole my joy,
I left it at the cross.
So I will celebrate
and drink Your cup of joy,
I will give thanks each day and sing.
My joy is found in You
and You are all my joy,
oh, I was made for this.

3 When I was far away
You ran to welcome me,
I felt Your warm embrace;
I saw Your smiling face.
And when You rescued me
I saw my destiny:
to worship You, my Lord,
to be a friend of God.
So I will celebrate
and drink Your cup of joy,
I will give thanks each day and sing.
My joy is found in You
and You are all my joy,
oh, I was made for this.

I was made to love You, Jesus,
I was made for this.
I was made to love You, Jesus,
I was made for this.
So I will celebrate . . .

914 Gerrit Gustafson
© 1990 Integrity's Hosanna! Music/
Kingsway's Thankyou Music

Only by grace can we enter,
only by grace can we stand;
not by our human endeavour,
but by the blood of the Lamb.
Into Your presence You call us,
You call us to come;
into Your presence You draw us,
and now by Your grace we come,
now by Your grace we come.

Lord, if You mark our transgressions
who would stand?
Thanks to Your grace we are cleansed
by the blood of the Lamb.
Lord, if You mark . . .

Only by grace . . .

913 From Psalm 84
Andy Park
© 1989 Mercy/Vineyard Publishing/CopyCare

1 **One thing I ask, one thing I seek,**
that I may dwell in Your house, O
Lord,
all of my days, all of my life –
that I may see You, Lord.

2 Hear me, O Lord, hear me when I cry;
Lord, do not hide Your face from me:
You have been my strength,
You have been my shield,
and You will lift me up.
One thing I ask,
one thing I desire
is to see You,
is to see You.

915 From Psalm 119
© 1993 Timothy Dudley-Smith

1 **Open our eyes, O Lord, we pray,**
enlighten heart and mind;
that as we read Your word today
we may its treasures find.

2 Open our ears, that, small and still,
Your voice be clearly heard,
to guide our steps and cleanse our will
according to Your word.

3 Open our lives to love's embrace,
our dear redeeming Lord:
Your word of life and truth and grace
within our souls be stored.

4 Open our lips, O Lord, in praise
to tell what love imparts:
the work of grace about our ways,
your word within our hearts.

916
Phil Thomson
© 1994 Ragstar/Serious Music UK

1 **Out of a heart of love**
You gave creation birth;
with grace and power and might,
You formed a perfect earth.
Such a mighty God,
in majesty arrayed,
and yet You know each step I take
from day to day.
Heavenly King,
reaching out to me,
You have turned my heart and soul
towards eternity.
Your touch upon my life
is grace and power enough;
oh, all-embracing love.

2 You move in signs and wonders,
fill heaven with Your praise,
and in Your mercy hold
all things within Your gaze.
I am amazed, O Father,
You gave the stars their plan;
yet, with such tender patience,
You hold me in Your hand.
Heavenly King . . .
all-embracing love.

917
From Matthew 6

Our dear Father who art in Heaven,
hallowèd be Your name,
Your kingdom come,
Your will be done
on earth as it is in Heaven.
Give us this day our daily bread,
and forgive our debts
        as we forgive our debtors,
and lead us not into temptation
but deliver us from the evil one,
for Yours is the kingdom,
Yours is the power,
Yours is the glory
for ever. Amen.

918
Noel Richards
© 1994 Kingsway's Thankyou Music

1 **Overwhelmed by love,**
deeper than oceans,
high as the heavens;
ever-living God,
Your love has rescued me.

2 All my sin was laid
on Your dear Son,
Your precious one.
All my debt He paid –
great is Your love for me.
No-one could ever earn Your love,
Your grace and mercy is free.
Lord, these words are true –
so is my love for You.

919
Rick Cole
© 1992 Mercy/Vineyard Publishing/CopyCare

Part the waters that surround me,
may the wind and waves be still.
Pierce the soul of my confusion,
clear the mist and rend the veil.
See the longing in my spirit,
know that I choose to be Yours.
Lord, I'm hungry and I'm thirsting
to be filled and to be used.
You're the holy Lord almighty
and I come to seek Your face,
You're my light, my hope, my mercy,
and Jesus is Your name.

Part the waters . . .
You're the holy Lord almighty . . .
You're the holy Lord almighty . . .
and Jesus is Your name.

920
From Psalm 148
vv. 1–2 *Foundling Hospital Collection* (1796)
v.3 E Osler (1798–1863)

1 **Praise the Lord,**
        you heavens, adore Him –
praise Him, angels in the height!
Sun and moon, rejoice before Him;
praise Him, all you stars and light!

Praise the Lord, for He has spoken:
worlds His mighty voice obeyed;
laws, which never shall be broken,
for their guidance He has made.

2   Praise the Lord, for He is glorious!
Never shall His promise fail.
God has made His saints victorious,
sin and death shall not prevail.
Praise the God of our salvation!
Hosts on high, his power proclaim;
Heaven and earth and all creation,
laud and magnify His name!

3   Worship, honour, glory, blessing,
Lord, we offer to Your name.
Young and old, Your praise expressing,
join their Saviour to proclaim.
As the saints in Heaven adore You,
we would bow before Your throne,
As Your angels serve before You,
so on earth Your will be done.

921   Brian Doerksen
© 1990 Mercy/Vineyard Publishing/CopyCare

1   **Purify my heart,**
let me be as gold and precious silver;
purify my heart,
let me be as gold, pure gold.
    Refiner's fire, my heart's one desire
    is to be holy,
    set apart for You, Lord;
    I choose to be holy,
    set apart for You, my Master,
    ready to do Your will.

2   Purify my heart,
cleanse me from within
        and make me holy;
purify my heart,
cleanse me from my sin, deep within.
    Refiner's fire . . .

922   Graham Kendrick
© 1994 Make Way Music

1   **Rumours of angels,**
visions of light,
new star appearing,
piercing the night.
Town full of strangers
sleeps in the gloom.
God comes among us;
there is no room.

2   Rumours of angels,
songs in the night,
deep in the danger,
unquenchable light.
World full of strangers
sleeps in the gloom.
God comes among us;
there is no room.
    And the years of our sorrow
    have rolled on and on,
    and the wars of our pride never cease.
    We have ravaged the earth
    with our envy and greed –
    tell me, when will we welcome His
        peace?
    When will we welcome His peace?

3 Hearts full of longing,
   eyes filled with tears,
   nations are waiting
   at the end of the years.
   Empires are falling,
   judgements appear.
   God comes among us;
   His kingdom is near.
       And the years of our sorrow ...

       And the years of our sorrow ...
       Oh, when will we welcome
           the Prince of Peace?

923 Howard Davies
         © 1991 Salvationist Publishing and Supplies/
         CopyCare

1 WOMEN **See how the world groans**
              beneath sin's spell!
          Lord, who will go?
          Lord, who will go?
   ALL   Someone must care
              for them, someone tell,
          tell of Christ, tell of
              His power to set men free!
          Here am I, my Lord!
          Send me, send me!
          I am wanting to be
              what You want me to be!
          Use me when and wherever
              and how You best see;
          Here am I, my Lord, send me!

2 MEN   How can I go
              with my sin and shame?
          Great God on high!
              Lord, who am I?
   ALL   Cleanse now my heart
              with the living flame!
          Make me pure, O make me
              strong – Lord, I will go.
          Here am I, my Lord ...

3 ALL   Make me a servant
              to serve just You –
          Lord, I'll obey, use me, I pray!
          Teach me to speak –
              may my life ring true!
          All my words and all my
              actions pleasing You!
          Here am I, my Lord ...
          Here am I, my Lord ...
          Here am I, my Lord, send me!

924 Adrian Howard and Pat Turner
         © 1985 Restoration Music/Sovereign Music UK

1 **Salvation belongs to our God,**
   who sits on the throne,
   and unto the Lamb.
   Praise and glory,
   wisdom and thanks,
   honour and power and strength
       be to our God for ever and ever,
       be to our God for ever and ever,
       be to our God for ever and ever,
       amen.

2 And we, the redeemed, shall be strong
   in purpose and unity,
   declaring aloud:
   praise and glory,
   wisdom and thanks,
   honour and power and strength
       be to our God ...

925 Chris Bowater
         © 1986 Sovereign Lifestyle Music

See His glory, see His glory,
see His glory now appear.
See His glory, see His glory,
see His glory now appear.
God of light, holiness and truth,
power and might –
see His glory, see it now appear.
Now we declare our God is good,
and His mercies endure for ever.
Now we declare our God is good,
and His mercies endure for ever.

926

Elaine Davis
© HarperCollins*Religious*/CopyCare

Shalom, shalom,
peace to His people;
shalom, shalom,
the grace of God be with you,
now and for ever!

1 The love of God be with you,
a boundless love without measure:
a love you daily must treasure,
now and for ever.
Shalom, shalom . . .

2 The grace of God be with you,
a boundless grace without measure:
His grace and favour we treasure,
now and for ever.
Shalom, shalom . . .

3 The peace of God be with you,
a quiet calm without measure:
God's loving peace you must treasure,
now and for ever.
Shalom, shalom . . .

927

David Fellingham
© 1988 Kingsway's Thankyou Music

Shout for joy and sing
      your praises to the King;
lift your voice and let your hallelujahs ring.
Come before His throne
      to worship and adore;
enter joyfully now
      the presence of the Lord.

You are my Creator,
You are my deliverer,
You are my Redeemer, you are Lord;
and you are my healer.
You are my provider,
You are now my shepherd
      and my guide:
Jesus, Lord and King, I worship You.

928

Graham Kendrick
© 1994 Make Way Music

1 **Since the day the angel came**
it seemed that everything had changed.
The only certain thing
was the child that moved within
on the road that would not end,
winding down to Bethlehem,
so far away from home.

2 Just a blanket on the floor
of a vacant cattle-stall,
but there the child was born.
She held Him in her arms
and as she laid Him down to sleep,
she wondered, 'Will it always be
so bitter and so sweet?'
      And did she see there in the straw
      by His head a thorn,
      and did she smell myrrh in the air
      on that starry night?
      And did she hear angels sing
      not so far away,
      'til at last the sun rose blood-red
      in the morning sky?

3 Then the words of ancient seers
tumbled down the centuries –
a virgin shall conceive,
God with us, Prince of Peace.
Man of sorrows – strangest name.
Oh Joseph, there it comes again,
so bitter, yet so sweet.
      And did she see . . .

4 And as she watched Him
      through the years,
her joy was mingled with her tears,
and she'd feel it all again,
the glory and the shame.
And when the miracles began,
she wondered, 'Who is this man,
and where will this all end?'

5 'Til, against a darkening sky,
the one she loved was lifted high,
and with His dying breath
she heard Him say, 'Father, forgive!'
and to the criminal beside,
'Today – with me, in Paradise.'
So bitter, yet so sweet.
And did she see . . .

929   William Smallwood (1831–97)

1 **Sing to the Lord a joyful song,**
lift up your hearts, your voices raise;
to us His gracious gifts belong,
to Him our songs of love and praise.

2 For life and love, for rest and food,
for daily help and nightly care,
sing to the Lord, for He is good,
and praise His name, for it is fair.

3 For strength to those who on Him wait
His truth to prove, His will to do,
praise ye our God, for He is great,
trust in His name, for it is true.

4 For joys untold, that from above
cheer those who love His sweet employ,
sing to our God, for He is love,
exalt His name, for it is joy.

5 Sing to the Lord of Heaven and earth,
whom angels serve and saints adore,
the Father, Son and Holy Ghost,
to whom be praise for evermore.

930   David Ruis
© 1992 Mercy/Vineyard Publishing/CopyCare

1 **Sing a song of celebration,**
lift up a shout of praise,
for the Bridegroom will come,
the glorious One,
and oh, we will look on His face –
we'll go to a much better place.

2 Dance with all your might,
lift up your hands and clap for joy;
the time's drawing near
when He will appear,
and oh, we will stand by His side,
a strong, pure, spotless bride.
*Oh, we will dance on the streets
  that are golden,
the glorious bride and
  the great Son of man,
for every tongue and tribe and nation
will join in the song of the Lamb.*

Sing a song of celebration . . .

Dance with all your might . . .
Oh, we will dance . . .

Sing aloud for the time
  of rejoicing is near.
The risen King, our groom,
  is soon to appear.
The wedding feast to come
  is now near at hand.
Lift up your voice,
  proclaim the coming Lamb.
Oh, we will dance . . .

931   Graham Kendrick
© 1994 Make Way Music

1 **So many centuries
of watching and waiting,**
but when the moment came,
  well, nobody saw,
traders and travellers hurried by,
and life went on just like before,
  just like before.

2 In all the clamour
  just a new baby crying,
one more poor family
  shut out in the cold.
Nothing unusual, sad to say –
hasn't it always been this way?

But nothing will ever be the same
  again –
this night has changed everything.
Nothing will ever be the same again
since the night He came.

3 So rare we recognize
    our history in the making,
  meet angels unawares
    and pass on our way,
  blind to the moment of destiny,
  while precious years
    just slip away, just slip away.

4 And now a door is standing open
    before you,
  casting its light into
    the darkness around;
  stop for a moment, step inside,
  tonight could be your Bethlehem.
    And nothing will ever
    be the same again –
    this night could change everything.
    Nothing will ever be the same again
    since the night He came.

A child is born, a Son is given,
and His kingdom of peace
    will never end.
A child is born . . .
never end, no!

    And nothing will ever
    be the same again . . .

    And nothing will ever
    be the same again . . .

Standing, standing,
standing on the promises
  of God my Saviour,
standing, standing,
I'm standing on the promises of God.

2 Standing on the promises
    that cannot fail,
  when the howling storms
    of doubt and fear assail
  by the living word of God I shall
    prevail,
  standing on the promises of God.
    Standing, standing . . .

3 Standing on the promises I now can
    see
  perfect, present cleansing
    in the blood for me;
  standing in the liberty
    where Christ makes free,
  standing on the promises of God.
    Standing, standing . . .

4 Standing on the promises
    of Christ the Lord,
  bound to Him eternally
    by love's strong cord,
  overcoming daily with the Spirit's
    sword,
  standing on the promises of God.
    Standing, standing . . .

5 Standing on the promises I cannot fall,
  listening every moment
    to the Spirit's call,
  resting in my Saviour as my all in all,
  standing on the promises of God.
    Standing, standing . . .

932 R K Carter (1849–1928)

1 **Standing on the promises
    of Christ my King,**
  through eternal ages let His praises
    ring:
  'Glory in the highest!'
    I will shout and sing,
  standing on the promises of God.

933

Sue Rinaldi and Steve Bassett
© 1988 Word's Spirit of Praise Music/
CopyCare

Stir my heart, O Lord,
let Your holy fire burn;
spark a flame within me,
strengthen my desire:
may my heart, O Lord,
be so tender in Your hand;
breathe Your life within me,
stir my heart, O Lord.

934

E Denny (1796–1889)

1 **Sweet feast of love divine!**
'Tis grace that makes us free
to feed upon this bread and wine
in memory, Lord, of Thee.

2 Here every welcome guest
waits, Lord, from Thee to learn
the secrets of Thy Father's breast,
and all Thy grace discern.

3 Here conscience ends its strife,
and faith delights to prove
the sweetness of the bread of life,
the fulness of Thy love.

4 Thy blood that flowed for sin,
in symbol here we see,
and feel the blessed pledge within,
that we are loved of Thee.

5 But if this glimpse of love
is so divinely sweet,
what will it be, O Lord, above,
Thy gladdening smile to meet;

6 To see Thee face to face,
Thy perfect likeness wear,
and all Thy ways of wondrous grace
Through endless years declare!

935

From Mark 8
C W Everest (1814–77)

1 **'Take up your cross!'
the Saviour said,**
'if you would my disciple be;
deny yourself, the world forsake
and humbly follow after me.'

2 Take up your cross – let not its weight
fill your weak spirit with alarm:
His strength shall bear your spirit up,
and brace your heart,
and nerve your arm.

3 Take up your cross, nor heed the
shame,
nor let your foolish pride rebel:
your Lord for you the cross endured
to save your soul from death and hell.

4 Take up your cross,
then, in His strength,
and calmly every danger brave;
'twill guide you to a better home,
and lead to victory o'er the grave.

5 Take up your cross, and follow Christ,
nor think 'til death to lay it down;
for only he who bears the cross
may hope to wear the glorious crown.

6 To You, great Lord, the One-in-three,
all praise for evermore ascend:
O grant us in our home to see
the heavenly life that knows no end.

936 Graham Kendrick and Steve Thompson
© 1993 Make Way Music

Teach me to dance
to the beat of Your heart,
teach me to move
in the power of Your Spirit,
teach me to walk
in the light of Your presence,
teach me to dance
to the beat of Your heart.
Teach me to love
with Your heart of compassion,
teach me to trust
in the word of Your promise,
teach me to hope
in the day of Your coming,
teach me to dance
to the beat of Your heart.

1 You wrote the rhythm of life,
created Heaven and earth;
in You is joy without measure.
So like a child in Your sight,
I dance to see Your delight
for I was made for Your pleasure,
pleasure.
Teach me to dance . . .

2 Let all my movements express
a heart that loves to say 'yes',
a will that leaps to obey You.
Let all my energy blaze
to see the joy in Your face,
let my whole being praise You,
praise You.
Teach me to dance . . .
Teach me to dance
to the beat of Your heart.

937 Martin Smith
© 1993 Curious? Music UK/
Kingsway's Thankyou Music

1 **Thank You for saving me;**
what can I say?
You are my everything,
I will sing Your praise.
You shed Your blood for me;
what can I say?
You took my sin and shame,
a sinner called by name.
Great is the Lord,
great is the Lord.
For we know Your truth has set us free,
You've set Your hope in me.

2 Mercy and grace are mine –
forgiven is my sin.
Jesus, my only hope,
the Saviour of the world.
'Great is the Lord', we cry,
'God, let Your kingdom come!'
Your word has let me see,
thank You for saving me.
Great is the Lord . . .

Thank You for saving me –
what can I say?

938 Martin Smith
© 1993 Kingsway's Thankyou Music

1 **The crucible for silver**
and the furnace for gold,
but the Lord tests the heart of this
child.
Standing in all purity,
God, our passion is for holiness;
lead us to the secret place of praise.
Jesus, Holy One,
You are my heart's desire.
King of kings, my everything,
You've set this heart on fire.
Jesus, Holy One . . .

2 Father, take our offering,
   with our song we humbly praise You.
   You have brought Your holy fire
      to our lips.
   Standing in Your beauty, Lord,
   Your gift to us is holiness;
   lead us to the place where we can sing:
    Jesus, Holy One . . .

939
Steve Chua and Ed Pirie
© 1995 Ellel Ministries Ltd

1 **The Lord is exalted
    at God's right hand,**
His banner unfurling across the land.
All power and dominion
    shall kneel at His throne,
for high in the heavens
    stands Jesus alone.
   *Let us rejoice at the coming of the King,
   let us rejoice for the victory He brings,
   lift up our heads, and let us be willing
   in the day of His power.*

2 He's raised up an army,
    the weak and the lost.
He's called us to follow,
    accepting the cost,
and if we are faithful
    and trust His commands,
He'll pour out His Spirit,
    together we'll stand.
   Let us rejoice . . .

940
John L Bell and Graham Maule
© 1988, 1997 WGRG The Iona Community

1 **The love of God comes close
    where stands an open door**
to let the stranger in,
    to mingle rich and poor.
The love of God is here to stay;
embracing those who walk His way,
the love of God is here to stay.

2 The peace of God comes close
    to those caught in the storm,
forgoing lives of ease
    to ease the lives forlorn.
The peace of God is here to stay;
embracing those who walk His way,
the peace of God is here to stay.

3 The joy of God comes close
    where faith encounters fears,
where heights and depths of life
    are found through smiles and
    tears.
The joy of God is here to stay;
embracing those who walk His way,
the joy of God is here to stay.

4 The grace of God comes close
    to those whose grace is spent,
when hearts are tired or sore
    and hope is bruised and bent.
The grace of God is here to stay;
embracing those who walk His way,
the grace of God is here to stay.

5 The Son of God comes close
    where people praise His name,
where bread and wine are blessed
    and shared as when He came.
The Son of God is here to stay;
embracing those who walk His way,
the Son of God is here to stay.

941
John Barnett
© 1994 Mercy/Vineyard Publishing/CopyCare

The precious blood of Jesus,
the only cleansing power –
my guilt and shame are washed away
beneath its crimson flood.
The precious name of Jesus,
the name by which we're saved.
He bore the cross I should have had,
a ransom for my sin.

And I'm for ever grateful,
and I will always trust
  the precious blood of Jesus,
the sacrifice of love,
the sacrifice of love.

The precious blood of Jesus . . .

And I'm for ever grateful . . .

Your mercy flows like a river wide,
and healing comes from Your hands.
Suffering children are safe in Your arms;
there is none like You.
  There is none like You . . .

942 Cleland B McAfee (1866–1944)
© Dimension Music/CopyCare

1   **There is a place of quiet rest,**
    near to the heart of God,
    a place where sin cannot molest,
    near to the heart of God.
      O Jesus, blest Redeemer,
      sent from the heart of God,
      hold us who wait before Thee
      near to the heart of God.

2   There is a place of comfort sweet,
    near to the heart of God,
    a place where we our Saviour meet,
    near to the heart of God.
      O Jesus . . .

3   There is a place of full release,
    near to the heart of God,
    a place where all is joy and peace,
    near to the heart of God.
      O Jesus . . .

944 Noel Richards
© 1989 Kingsway's Thankyou Music

1   **There is power in the name of**
      Jesus;
    we believe in His name.
    We have called on the name of Jesus;
    we are saved, we are saved!
    At His name the demons flee,
    at His name captives are freed;
    for there is no other name that is higher
      than 'Jesus'!

2   There is power in the name of Jesus,
    like a sword in our hands.
    We declare, in the name of Jesus,
    we shall stand, we shall stand.
    At His name, God's enemies
    shall be crushed beneath our feet,
    for there is no other name that is higher
      than 'Jesus'!

945 El Nathan (1840–1901)

1   **'There shall be showers of**
      blessing':
    this is the promise of love;
    there shall be seasons refreshing,
    sent from the Saviour above.
      Showers of blessing,
      showers of blessing we need,
      mercy drops round us are falling,
      but for the showers we plead.

943 Lenny LeBlanc
© 1991 Integrity's Hosanna! Music/
Kingsway's Thankyou Music

There is none like You –
no-one else can touch
  my heart like You do;
I could search for all eternity long
and find there is none like You.

2 'There shall be showers of blessing':
precious reviving again;
over the seas and the valleys,
sound of abundance of rain.
Showers of blessing . . .

3 'There shall be showers of blessing':
send them upon us, O Lord!
Grant to us now a refreshing;
come, and now honour Thy word.
Showers of blessing . . .

4 'There shall be showers of blessing':
Oh, that today they might fall,
now, as to God we're confessing,
now, as to Jesus we call.
Showers of blessing . . .

5 'There shall be showers of blessing':
if we but trust and obey;
there shall be seasons refreshing,
if we let God have His way.
Showers of blessing . . .

2 They shall come from the east,
they shall come from the west,
and sit down in the kingdom of God,
to be met by their Father
and welcomed and blessed,
and sit down in the kingdom of God.
The black, the white,
    the dark, the fair –
your colour will not matter there –
they shall come from the east,
they shall come from the west,
and sit down in the kingdom of God.

3 They shall come from the east,
they shall come from the west,
and sit down in the kingdom of God.
Out of great tribulation
to triumph and rest,
they'll sit down in the kingdom of God.
From every tribe and every race,
all men as brothers shall embrace;
they shall come from the east,
they shall come from the west,
and sit down in the kingdom of God.

946

John Gowans
© 1978 Salvationist Publishing and Supplies/
CopyCare

1 **They shall come from the east,**
they shall come from the west,
and sit down in the kingdom of God.
Both the rich and the poor,
the despised, the distressed,
they'll sit down in the kingdom of God.
And none will ask what they have been
provided that their robes are clean.
They shall come from the east,
they shall come from the west,
and sit down in the kingdom of God.

947

Phil Lawson Johnston and Chris Bowater
© 1992 Sovereign Lifestyle Music

1 **This is the mystery,**
that Christ has chosen you and me
to be the revelation of His glory;
a chosen, royal, holy people,
set apart and loved,
a bride preparing for her King.
Let the bride say, 'Come!',
let the bride say, 'Come!',
let the bride of the Lamb say,
'Come, Lord Jesus!'
Let the bride say, 'Come!',
let the bride say, 'Come!',
let the bride of the Lamb say,
'Come, Lord Jesus, come!'

2 She's crowned in splendour
and a royal diadem;
the King is enthralled by her beauty.
Adorned in righteousness,
arrayed in glorious light,
the bride in waiting for her King.
Let the bride say, 'Come!',
let the bride say, 'Come!',
let the bride of the Lamb say,
'Come, Lord Jesus!'
Let the bride say, 'Come!',
let the bride say, 'Come!',
let the bride of the Lamb say,
'Come, Lord Jesus, come!'

3 Now hear the Bridegroom call,
'Beloved, come aside;
the time of betrothal is at hand.
Lift up your eyes and see
the dawning of the day
when as King, I'll return
to claim My bride.'
Let the bride say . . .

948 Bernhardt S Ingemann (1789–1862)
tr. Sabine Baring-Gould (1834–1924)

1 **Through the night**
of doubt and sorrow
onward goes the pilgrim band,
singing songs of expectation,
marching to the promised land.

2 Clear before us through the darkness
gleams and burns the guiding light;
brother clasps the hand of brother,
stepping fearless through the night.

3 One the light of God's own presence
o'er His ransomed people shed,
chasing far the gloom and terror,
brightening all the path we tread.

4 One the object of our journey,
one the faith which never tires,
one the earnest looking forward,
one the hope our God inspires.

5 One the strain that lips of thousands
lift as from the heart of one:
one the conflict, one the peril,
one the march in God begun.

6 One the gladness of rejoicing
on the far eternal shore,
where the one almighty Father
reigns in love for evermore.

7 Onward, therefore, pilgrim brothers,
onward with the cross our aid;
bear its shame, and fight its battles,
'til we rest beneath its shade.

8 Soon shall come the great awaking,
soon the rending of the tomb;
then the scattering of the shadows,
and the end of toil and gloom.

949 L Hensley (1824–1905)

1 **Thy kingdom come, O God,**
Thy rule, O Christ, begin;
break with Thine iron rod
the tyrannies of sin.

2 Where is Thy reign of peace
and purity and love?
When shall all hatred cease,
as in the realms above?

3 When comes the promised time
that war shall be no more,
and lust, oppression, crime
shall flee Thy face before?

4 We pray Thee, Lord, arise,
and come in Thy great might;
revive our longing eyes,
which languish for Thy sight.

5 Men scorn Thy sacred name,
and wolves devour Thy fold;
by many deeds of shame
we learn that love grows cold.

6 O'er heathen lands afar
  thick darkness broodeth yet:
  arise, O Morning Star.
  Arise and never set.

950 Horatius Bonar (1808–89)

1 **Thy way, not mine, O Lord,**
  however dark it be;
  lead me by Thine own hand,
  choose out the path for me.

2 Smooth let it be or rough,
  it will be still the best;
  winding or straight, it leads
  right onward to Thy rest.

3 I dare not choose my lot;
  I would not if I might:
  choose Thou for me, my God,
  so shall I walk aright.

4 The kingdom that I seek
  is Thine; so let the way
  that leads to it be Thine,
  else I must surely stray.

5 Take Thou my cup, and it
  with joy or sorrow fill,
  as best to Thee may seem;
  choose Thou my good and ill.

6 Choose Thou for me my friends,
  my sickness or my health;
  choose Thou my cares for me,
  my poverty or wealth.

7 Not mine, not mine, the choice
  in things or great or small;
  be Thou my guide, my strength,
  my wisdom, and my all.

951 Noel Richards
© 1991 Kingsway's Thankyou Music

1 **To be in Your presence,**
  to sit at Your feet,
  where Your love surrounds me,
  and makes me complete:
  this is my desire, O Lord,
  this is my desire.
  This is my desire, O Lord,
  this is my desire.

2 To rest in Your presence,
  not rushing away,
  to cherish each moment –
  here I would stay:
  this is my desire . . .

952 Derek Bond
© 1994 Daybreak Music Ltd

1 **Touch my life, O Lord my God;**
  holy fire, come.
  Touch my lips that I might speak
  of the wonders of Your Son.

2 Touch my heart, O Lord my God,
  cleanse me with Your blood.
  Fill me with Your Spirit, Lord,
  flow through me like a flood.
  Your Spirit's anointing I desire:
  the power of God.
  To demonstrate justice, Lord, I need
  the power of God.
  To tell of Your healing and release,
  the power of God.

953 Sue Rinaldi and Steve Bassett
© 1988 Word's Spirit of Praise Music/
CopyCare

To Your majesty
        and Your beauty I surrender,
to Your holiness and Your love I surrender,
for You are an awesome God
        who is mighty,
You deserve my deepest praise:
with all of my heart,
        with all of my life, I surrender.

954

Xhosa text: South African traditional
English text verse 1: Anders Nyberg
© 1990 Wild Goose Publications/
The Iona Community

1 **We are marching in the light of
God,**
we are marching in the light of God,
we are marching in the light of God,
we are marching in the light of God
(the light of God)!
We are marching (marching,
we are marching, marching,) – Oh,
we are marching in the light of God
(the light of God)!
We are marching (marching,
we are marching, marching,) – Oh,
we are marching in the light of God!

2 We are living in the love of God . . .

3 We are moving in the power of God . . .

955

Graham Kendrick
© 1990 Make Way Music

1 **We are His children,
the fruit of His suffering,**
saved and redeemed by His blood;
called to be holy, a light to the nations:
clothed with His power,
    filled with His love.
*Go forth in His name,
proclaiming 'Jesus reigns!'
Now is the time for the Church to arise
and proclaim Him, 'Jesus,
Saviour, Redeemer and Lord.'
Go forth in His name . . .*

2 Countless the souls
    that are stumbling in darkness:
why do we sleep in the light?
Jesus commands us
    to go, make disciples –
this is our cause, this is our fight.
Go forth in His name . . .

3 Listen, the wind of the Spirit
    is blowing,
the end of the age is so near;
powers in the earth and the heavens
    are shaking,
Jesus our Lord soon shall appear!
Go forth in His name . . .

956

© 1994 Timothy Dudley-Smith

1 **We turn to Christ alone,**
the Son of God divine,
to bow the knee before His throne,
to bear His name and sign;
to bear His name and sign
and walk the narrow way,
to make His love and glory known,
His word and will obey.

2 We turn from self and sin
in penitence and shame;
we trust, to make us clean within,
the power of Jesus' name;
the power of Jesus' name,
whose cross is strong to save,
who gave His life our life to win
from sin and death and grave.

3 We turn from every wrong,
from every evil way,
who in the Spirit's strength are strong,
as children of the day;
as children of the day
from dark to light we turn,
disciples who to Christ belong,
His way of life to learn.

4 We turn to Christ as Lord
who died and rose again,
as those whose hearts receive His word,
as subjects of His reign;
as subjects of His reign,
who calls His servants friends,
our King of love to life restored,
whose kingdom never ends.

957   Doug Horley
© 1993 Kingsway's Thankyou Music

We want to see Jesus lifted high,
a banner that flies across this land,
that all men might see the truth and know
He is the way to Heaven.
We want to see Jesus lifted high . . .

We want to see,
we want to see,
we want to see Jesus lifted high,
we want to see,
we want to see,
we want to see Jesus lifted high.

Step by step we're moving forward,
little by little taking ground,
every prayer a powerful weapon,
strongholds come tumbling down
          and down and down and down.

We want to see Jesus lifted high . . .

We're gonna see,
we're gonna see,
we're gonna see Jesus lifted high,
we're gonna see,
we're gonna see
we're gonna see Jesus lifted high.

958   Noel Richards
© 1991 Kingsway's Thankyou Music

Welcome, King of kings!
How great is Your name!
You come in majesty
for ever to reign.

1   You rule the nations,
    they shake at the sound of Your name –
    to You is given all power,
    and You shall reign.
        Welcome, King of kings . . .

2   Let all creation bow down
    at the sound of Your name.
    Let every tongue now confess
    the Lord God reigns.
        Welcome, King of kings . . .

959   Graham Kendrick
© 1994 Make Way Music

1   **What kind of greatness can this be,**
    that chose to be made small,
    exchanging untold majesty
    for a world so pitiful?
    That God should come as one of us
    I'll never understand –
    the more I hear the story told,
    the more amazed I am.
        Oh, what else can I do
        but kneel and worship You,
        and come just as I am,
        my whole life an offering.

2   The One in whom we live and move
    in swaddling clothes lies bound.
    The voice that cried 'Let there be
            light!',
    asleep without a sound.
    The One who strode among the stars,
    and called each one by name,
    lies helpless in a mother's arms
    and must learn to walk again.
        Oh, what else can I do . . .

3   What greater love could He have shown
    to shamed humanity?
    Yet human pride hates to believe
    in such deep humility.
    But nations now may see His grace
    and know that He is near,
    when His meek heart,
            His words, His works
    are incarnate in us here.
        Oh, what else can I do . . .

960

Brian Doerksen and Craig Musseau
© 1991 Mercy/Vineyard Publishing/CopyCare

Whatever is true, whatever is right,
whatever is pure, whatever is lovely,
we will fix our thoughts on these things.
Jesus, You're true, Jesus, You're right,
Jesus, You're pure, You are lovely.
We will fix our thoughts on You.

MEN	Jesus,
WOMEN	Jesus,
MEN	who is like You,
WOMEN	who is like You?
MEN	Jesus,
WOMEN	Jesus,
MEN	who is like You,
WOMEN	who is like You?
MEN	Jesus . . .
ALL	who is like You?

961

From Psalm 142
Michael Perry (1942–96)
© Mrs B Perry/Jubilate Hymns

1   **When I lift up my voice,**
and I cry to the Lord,
and I pour out my troubles before
     Him;
when I see no-one cares,
and I walk all alone,
and my spirit grows weary within me,
then I sing:
   'You are my refuge,
   I will praise Your name;
   You are so good to me, O Lord!'
Then I sing . . .
   'You are so good to me,
   You are so good to me,
   You are so good to me, O Lord!'

2   Then He'll come to my side
and He'll answer my prayers,
and He'll set my soul free
     from its prison;
then the righteous will see
and they'll gather around
all because of His goodness towards
     me.
Then they'll sing:
   'You are our refuge,
   we will praise Your name;
   You are so good to us, O Lord!'
Then they'll sing . . .
   'You are so good to us,
   You are so good to us,
   You are so good to us, O Lord!'

962

From Psalm 69
Michael Perry (1942–96)
© Mrs B Perry/Jubilate Hymns

1   **When my sorrows cover me,**
    save me, O God;
when my friends abandon me,
when I seek what cannot be,
when I look and cannot see,
     save me, O God,
     save me, O God.

2   You know all my guilty fears,
     thank You, O God.
You have heard with open ears,
You have seen my contrite tears,
You will bless my future years,
     thank You, O God,
     thank You, O God,
     thank You, O God.

963
From Psalm 138
© 1993 Timothy Dudley-Smith

1 **With undivided heart**
   and ceaseless songs
   give thanks to God.
   To Him all majesty and praise belongs:
   give thanks to God.
   His love and truth proclaim,
   His mercy still the same;
   and for His holy name
   give thanks to God.

2 Exalt His name and His eternal word,
   He is our God.
   Before His throne
      our every prayer is heard,
   He is our God.
   Let kings declare His praise,
   sing of His words and ways,
   for through eternal days
   He is our God.

3 He reigns in glory
      from His throne above,
   He is the Lord:
   and in our weakness
      meets us with His love:
   He is the Lord.
   His purpose cannot fail,
   though fears and foes assail,
   His love shall still prevail,
   He is the Lord.

964
© 1992 Roger Mayor/Jubilate Hymns

With all my heart
I'll sing praises to You my King,
with all my being,
exalt Your name!
Words never can express
my heartfelt thankfulness,
but this I now confess,
'I love You, Lord.'

With all my heart . . .
'I'll serve You, Lord.'

965
Chick Yuill
© Salvationist Publishing and Supplies/
CopyCare

1 **Wonderful counsellor,**
   mighty God among us,
   everlasting Father,
      Prince who rules in peace.
   To us a child is born,
      to us a son is given,
   to those who walked in darkness
      the light has come.

2 Son of God, Son of Man,
      Word of God incarnate,
   suffering Saviour, glorious risen Lord.
   For God so loved the world
      He gave His only son;
   no more we walk in darkness,
      the light has come.

3 King of kings, Lord of lords,
      Son of God exalted;
   name above every name,
      Lamb upon the throne.
   This king will come again,
      the Father's only son;
   no more a world in darkness,
      the light will come.

966
John Pantry
© HarperCollins*Religious*/CopyCare

1 **Wonderful grace**
   that gives what I don't deserve,
   pays me what Christ has earned,
   then lets me go free.
   Wonderful grace
   that gives me the time to change,
   washes away the stains
   that once covered me.
      And all that I have
      I lay at the feet
      of the wonderful Saviour
      who loves me.

2 Wonderful love
that held in the face of death,
breathed in its latest breath
forgiveness for me.
Wonderful love,
whose power can break every chain,
giving us life again
and setting us free.
And all that I have
I lay at the feet
of the wonderful Saviour
who loves me.

967 William Reed Newell (1868–1956)
Copyright control

1 **Years I spent in vanity and pride,**
caring not my Lord was crucified,
knowing not it was for me He died
on Calvary.
Mercy there was great
and grace was free,
pardon there was multiplied to me,
there my burdened soul found liberty,
at Calvary.

2 By God's word at last my sin I learned,
then I trembled at the law I'd spurned,
'til my guilty soul imploring turned
to Calvary.
Mercy there was great . . .

3 Now I've given to Jesus everything,
now I gladly own Him as my King,
now my raptured soul can only sing
of Calvary.
Mercy there was great . . .

4 Oh, the love that drew salvation's plan!
Oh, the grace that brought it down to
man!
Oh, the mighty gulf
that God did span at Calvary!
Mercy there was great . . .

968 Steve Chua
© 1993 Steve Chua/Ellel Ministries Ltd

1 **You are the rock on which we stand,**
we place our lives into Your hands,
at the foot of the cross
we acknowledge You as Lord,
Jesus, victorious King of kings.
We give glory and praises to Your name,
we will lift You high above the earth
in the triumph of Your grace.
We give glory . . .

2 Secure and steadfast in Your love,
we stand in the power of Your blood,
with Your Spirit of truth
anointing our desire
to fight against the powers of this age.
We give glory . . .

3 Not fashioned by the pattern
of this world,
we take our cross and Jesus
we will serve,
as we offer our lives as a holy sacrifice,
refine us, Lord,
and set Your Church ablaze.
We give glory . . .
in the triumph of Your grace.

969 Mark Altrogge
© 1986 People of Destiny International/CopyCare

You did not wait for me
to draw near to You,
but You clothed Yourself in frail humanity.
You did not wait for me to cry out to You,
but You let me hear Your voice calling me,
and I'm for ever grateful to You,
I'm for ever grateful for the cross,
I'm for ever grateful to You,
that You came to seek and save the lost.

970 Trish Morgan and Sue Rinaldi
© 1990 Kingsway's Thankyou Music

You make my heart feel glad,
You make my heart feel glad,
Jesus, You bring me joy,
You make my heart feel glad.

1 Lord, Your love brings healing
   and a peace into my heart,
   I want to give myself in praise to You.
   Though I've been through heartache
   You have understood my tears.
   O Lord, I will give thanks to You.
   You make my heart feel glad . . .

2 When I look around me,
   and I see the life You made,
   all creation shouts aloud in praise.
   I realize Your greatness,
   how majestic is Your name,
   O Lord, I love You more each day.
   You make my heart feel glad . . .

971 Bob Kauflin
© 1988 People of Destiny International/CopyCare

1 **You have been given the name**
   above all names,
   and we worship You,
      yes, we worship You.
   You have been given the name
      above all names,
   and we worship You,
      yes, we worship You.

2 We are Your people,
      made for Your glory,
   and we worship You,
      yes, we worship You.
   We are Your people,
      made for Your glory,
   and we worship You,
      yes, we worship You.

3 You have redeemed us from every
      nation
   and we worship You,
      yes, we worship You.
   You have redeemed us from every
      nation
   and we worship You,
      yes, we worship You.

972 M F Maude (1819–1913)

1 **Yours for ever! God of love,**
   hear us from Your throne above;
   Yours for ever may we be,
   here and in eternity.

2 Yours for ever! Lord of life,
   shield us through our earthly strife;
   You the life, the truth, the way,
   guide us to the realms of day.

3 Yours for ever! O how blessed
   they who find in You their rest!
   Saviour, guardian, heavenly friend,
   O defend us to the end.

4 Yours for ever! Shepherd, keep
   us Your frail and trembling sheep;
   safe alone beneath Your care,
   let us all Your goodness share.

5 Yours for ever! You our guide,
   all our wants by You supplied,
   all our sins by You forgiven,
   lead us, Lord, from earth to Heaven.

973 James Wright
© 1994 Kingsway's Thankyou Music

All that I am I lay before You;
all I possess, Lord, I confess
is nothing without You.
Saviour and King, I now enthrone You;
take my life, my living sacrifice to You.

1 Lord, be the strength
      within my weakness;
   be the supply in every need,
   that I may prove Your promises to me,
   faithful and true in word and deed.
      All that I am I lay before You;
      all I possess, Lord, I confess
      is nothing without You.
      Saviour and King, I now enthrone You;
      take my life, my living sacrifice to You.

2 Into Your hands I place the future;
   the past is nailed to Calvary,
   that I may live in resurrection power,
   no longer I, but Christ in me.
      All that I am . . .

974

Dave Billington
© 1992 Integrity's Hosanna! Music/
Kingsway's Thankyou Music

As I come into Your presence,
past the gates of praise,
into Your sanctuary
till we're standing face to face;
I look upon Your countenance,
I see the fullness of Your grace,
and I can only bow down and say:
   You are awesome in this place,
      mighty God.
   You are awesome in this place,
      Abba Father.
   You are worthy of all praise,
   to You our hands we raise.
   You are awesome in this place,
      mighty God.

975

Charitie L Bancroft (1841–92)

1 **Before the throne of God above**
   I have a strong, a perfect plea,
   a great High Priest
      whose name is Love,
   who ever lives and pleads for me.
   My name is graven on His hands,
   my name is written on His heart;
   I know that while in heaven He stands
   no tongue can bid me thence depart,
   no tongue can bid me thence depart.

2 When Satan tempts me to despair,
   and tells me of the guilt within,
   upward I look and see Him there
   who made an end to all my sin.
   Because the sinless Saviour died,
   my sinful soul is counted free;
   for God the just is satisfied
   to look on Him and pardon me,
   to look on Him and pardon me.

3 Behold Him there! The risen lamb,
   my perfect, spotless righteousness;
   the great unchangeable I AM,
   the King of glory and of grace!
   One with Himself I cannot die,
   my soul is purchased with His blood;
   my life is hid with Christ on high,
   with Christ my Saviour and my God,
   with Christ my Saviour and my God.

976

Gary Sadler and Jamie Harvill
© 1992 Integrity's Praise! Music/
Kingsway's Thankyou Music

Blessing and honour, glory and power
be unto the Ancient of Days;
from every nation, all of creation
bow before the Ancient of Days.

Every tongue in heaven and earth
shall declare Your glory,
every knee shall bow at Your throne
in worship;
You will be exalted, O God,
and Your kingdom will not pass away.
O Ancient of Days.

Your kingdom shall reign
      over all the earth:
sing unto the Ancient of Days.
For none shall compare
      to Your matchless worth:
sing unto the Ancient of Days.
   Every tongue in heaven and earth . . .

977
Matt Redman
© 1996 Kingsway's Thankyou Music

1 **Can a nation be changed?**
   Can a nation be saved?
   Can a nation be turned back to You?
   (repeat)
      We're on our knees,
      we're on our knees again.
      We're on our knees,
      we're on our knees again.

2 Let this nation be changed.
   Let this nation be saved.
   Let this nation be turned back to You.
   (repeat)
      We're on our knees . . .

978
Brian Doerksen
© 1994 Mercy/Vineyard Publishing/CopyCare

Don't let my love grow cold,
I'm calling out, light the fire again.
Don't let my vision die,
I'm calling out, light the fire again.
You know my heart, my deeds,
I'm calling out, light the fire again.
I need Your discipline,
I'm calling out, light the fire again.

I am here to buy gold, refined in the fire:
naked and poor,
      wretched and blind, I come.
Clothe me in white,
      so I won't be ashamed:
Lord, light the fire again.

Don't let my love grow cold . . .

979
Geoff and Judith Roberts
© 1996 Kingsway's Thankyou Music

Draw me close to the cross,
to the place of Your love,
to the place where
      You poured out Your mercy;
where the river of life
that flows from Your wounded side
brings refreshing to those who draw near.

Draw me close to Your throne
where Your majesty is shown,
where the crown of my life I lay down.
Draw me close to Your side,
where my heart is satisfied,
draw me close to You, Lord,
      draw me close.

980
Kelly Carpenter
© 1994 Mercy/Vineyard Publishing/CopyCare

Draw me close to You,
never let me go.
I lay it all down again,
to hear You say that I'm Your friend.
You are my desire,
no-one else will do,
'cause nothing else could take Your place,
to feel the warmth of Your embrace.
Help me find the way,
bring me back to You.

You're all I want,
You're all I've ever needed.
You're all I want,
Help me know You are near.

981

David Fellingham
© 1997 Kingsway's Thankyou Music

1 **Far above all other loves,**
far beyond all other joys,
heaven's blessings poured on me,
by the Holy Spirit's power.
Love's compelling power
draws my heart into Yours;
Jesus, how I love You,
You're my friend and my Lord.
You have died and risen,
so what else can I say?
How I love You, Lord, love You, Lord.

2 All ambition now has gone,
pleasing You my only goal;
motivated by Your grace,
living for eternity.
Love's compelling power . . .

3 Looking with the eye of faith
for the day of Your return;
in that day I want to stand
unashamed before Your throne.
Love's compelling power . . .

982

Graham Kendrick
© 1996 Make Way Music

1 **Far and near, hear the call,**
worship Him, Lord of all;
families of nations, come,
celebrate what God has done.

2 Deep and wide is the love,
heaven sent from above;
God's own Son for sinners died,
rose again, He is alive.

Say it loud, say it strong,
tell the world what God has done;
say it loud, praise His name,
let the earth rejoice for the Lord reigns.

3 At His name let praise begin,
oceans roar, nature sing,
for He comes to judge the earth
in righteousness and in His truth.
Say it loud, say it strong,
tell the world what God has done;
say it loud, praise His name,
let the earth rejoice for the Lord reigns,
the Lord reigns.

983

Darlene Zschech
© 1995 Darlene Zschech/Hillsongs Australia/
Kingsway's Thankyou Music

1 **Father of life, draw me closer,**
Lord, my heart is set on You:
let me run the race of time
with Your life enfolding mine,
and let the peace of God, let it reign.
(repeat)
O Lord, I hunger for more of You;
rise up within me,
let me know Your truth.
O Holy Spirit, saturate my soul,
and let the life of God fill me now,
let Your healing power breathe life
and make me whole,
and let the peace of God, let it reign.

2 O Holy Spirit, Lord, my comfort;
strengthen me, hold my head up high:
and I stand upon Your truth,
bringing glory unto You,
and let the peace of God, let it reign.
(repeat)
O Lord, I hunger . . .

984
Don Moen and Paul Overstreet
© 1995 Integrity's Hosanna! Music/
Kingsway's Thankyou Music

God is good all the time!
He put a song of praise
in this heart of mine;
God is good all the time!
Through the darkest night
His light will shine:
God is good, God is good all the time!

1 If you're walking through the valley
and there are shadows all around,
do not fear, He will guide you,
He will keep you safe and sound,
'cause He has promised
to never leave you
nor forsake you, and His word is true.
God is good ...

2 We were sinners, so unworthy,
still for us He chose to die:
filled us with His Holy Spirit,
now we can stand and testify
that His love is everlasting
and His mercies, they will never end.
God is good ...

Though I may not understand
all the plans You have for me,
my life is in Your hands,
and through the eyes of faith
I can clearly see:
God is good all the time!
He put a song of praise
in this heart of mine;
God is good all the time!
Through the darkest night
His light will shine:
God is good, God is good,
God is good, He's so good,
God is good, He's so good all the time!

985
Carol Owen
© 1997 Kingsway's Thankyou Music

1 **He is the mighty God,**
He is the risen King,
He is the Lord of lords.
He is the first and last,
He is holy, He is true,
He is the Lord of lords.
And we know He's coming back again
in power and glory.
He is coming back again
to claim His people.
He is coming back again
to bring His children home with Him,
home with Him.

2 He is the one who gave
His life for all the world,
He is the Lord of lords,
who rose up from the grave,
defeated death and hell;
He is the Lord of lords.
And we know ...

3 He's coming in the clouds
and every eye shall see
He is the Lord of lords;
then every knee shall bow
and every tongue proclaim
He is the Lord of lords.
And we know ...

986
David Hadden
© 1994 Restoration Music Ltd/
Sovereign Music UK

He's given me a garment of praise
instead of a spirit of despair,
He's given me a garment of praise
instead of a spirit of despair.
(repeat)

A crown of beauty instead of ashes,
the oil of gladness instead of mourning,
my soul rejoices as I delight myself in God.
He's given me a garment of praise
instead of a spirit of despair.
He's given me a garment of praise
instead of a spirit of despair,
He's given me a garment of praise
instead of a spirit of despair.

987 after William Rees

1 **Here is love vast as the ocean,**
loving kindness as the flood,
when the Prince of life, our ransom,
shed for us His precious blood.
Who His love will not remember;
who can cease to sing His praise?
He can never be forgotten
throughout heaven's eternal days.

2 On the mount of crucifixion
fountains opened deep and wide;
through the floodgates of God's mercy
flowed a vast and gracious tide.
Grace and love, like mighty rivers
poured incessant from above;
and heaven's peace and perfect justice
kissed a guilty world in love.

988 Stuart Townend
© 1995 Kingsway's Thankyou Music

1 **How deep the Father's love for us,**
how vast beyond all measure,
that He should give His only Son
to make a wretch His treasure.
How great the pain of searing loss –
the Father turns His face away,
as wounds which mar the chosen one
bring many sons to glory.

2 Behold the man upon a cross,
my sin upon His shoulders;
ashamed, I hear my mocking voice
call out among the scoffers.
It was my sin that held Him there
until it was accomplished;
His dying breath has brought me life –
I know that it is finished.

3 I will not boast in anything,
no gifts, no power, no wisdom;
but I will boast in Jesus Christ,
His death and resurrection.
Why should I gain from His reward?
I cannot give an answer,
but this I know with all my heart,
His wounds have paid my ransom.

989 Lindell Cooley and Bruce Haynes
© 1996 Integrity's Hosanna! Music/
Kingsway's Thankyou Music

I need You more,
more than yesterday,
I need You more, more than words can say.
I need You more than ever before,
I need You, Lord, I need You, Lord.

More than the air I breathe,
more than the song I sing,
more than the next heartbeat,
more than anything.
And, Lord, as time goes by,
I'll be by Your side,
'cause I never want to go back
to my old life.
I need You more . . .

Right here in Your presence
is where I belong;
This old broken heart
has finally found a home,
and I'll never be alone.
I need You more . . .

990
Matt Redman
© 1993 Kingsway's Thankyou Music

1 **I will offer up my life**
   in spirit and truth
   pouring out the oil of love
   as my worship to You.
   In surrender I must give
   my every part;
   Lord, receive the sacrifice
   of a broken heart.

   Jesus, what can I give,
   what can I bring
   to so faithful a friend,
   to so loving a king?
   Saviour, what can be said?
   What can be sung
   as a praise of Your name
   for the things You have done?
   Oh, my words could not tell,
   not even in part,
   of the debt of love that is owed
   by this thankful heart.

2 You deserve my every breath,
   for You've paid the great cost;
   giving up Your life to death,
   even death on a cross.
   You took all my shame away,
   there defeated my sin,
   opened up the gates of heaven
   and have beckoned me in.

   Jesus, what can I give . . .

991
David Ruis
© 1993 Mercy/Vineyard Publishing/CopyCare

1 **I will worship (I will worship)**
   with all of my heart
        (with all of my heart),
   I will praise You (I will praise You)
   with all of my strength
        (all my strength).
   I will seek You (I will seek You)
   all of my days (all of my days),
   I will follow (I will follow)
   all of Your ways (all Your ways).

   I will give You all my worship,
   I will give You all my praise.
   You alone I long to worship,
   You alone are worthy of my praise.

2 I will bow down (I will bow down),
   hail You as King (hail You as King),
   I will serve You (I will serve You),
   give You everything
        (give You everything).
   I will lift up (I will lift up)
   my eyes to Your throne
        (my eyes to Your throne),
   I will trust You (I will trust You),
   I will trust You alone (trust You alone).

   I will give You all my worship . . .

992
Isaac Watts (1674–1748)
adapted Jonathan LeTocq
Words adaptation: © 1998 Kingsway's Thankyou Music

1 **I'm not ashamed to own my Lord,**
   or to defend His cause;
   uphold the honour of His word,
   the glory of His cross.
   Jesus my God, I know Your name,
   Your name is all I trust;
   You will not put my soul to shame,
   nor let my hope be lost.

2 Firm as His throne His promise stands,
   and He can well secure
   all I've committed to His hands
   till that decisive hour.
   Then, Lord, You'll own
        my worthless name
   before the Father's face,
   and in the new Jerusalem
   appoint my soul a place.

   I'm not ashamed to own my Lord,
   or to defend His cause;
   uphold the honour of His word,
   the glory of His cross.

993 Duke Kerr
© Duke Kerr and Remission Music UK

It is to You I give the glory,
it is to You I give the praise,
because You have done so much for me,
I will magnify Your name.
It is to You, Holy Father,
no-one else but You,
and I will praise Your name,
praise Your name,
and I will praise Your name for evermore.

994 Matt Redman and Martin Smith
© 1995 Kingsway's Thankyou Music

1 **It's rising up from coast to coast,**
from north to south and east to west;
the cry of hearts that love Your name,
which with one voice we will proclaim.

2 The former things have taken place;
can this be the new day of praise?
A heavenly song that comes to birth
and reaches out to all the earth.
Oh, let the cry to nations ring,
that all may come and all may sing:
'Holy is the Lord.'
(Every heart sing:)
'Holy is the Lord.'
(With one voice sing:)
'Holy is the Lord.'
(Every heart sing:)
'Holy is the Lord.'

3 And we have heard the lion's roar
that speaks of heaven's love and power.
Is this the time, is this the call
that ushers in Your kingdom rule?
Oh, let the cry to nations ring,
that all may come and all may sing:
'Jesus is alive!' (Every heart sing:)
'Jesus is alive!' (With one voice sing:)
'Jesus is alive!' (All the earth sing:)
'Jesus is alive!'

995 Matt Redman
© 1995 Kingsway's Thankyou Music

1 **Jesus Christ,**
I think upon Your sacrifice;
You became nothing,
poured out to death.
Many times I've wondered
at Your gift of life,
and I'm in that place once again,
I'm in that place once again.
And once again I look upon
the cross where You died,
I'm humbled by Your mercy
and I'm broken inside.
Once again I thank You,
once again I pour out my life.

2 Now You are exalted
to the highest place,
King of the heavens,
where one day I'll bow,
but for now,
I marvel at this saving grace
and I'm full of praise once again,
I'm full of praise once again.
And once again . . .

Thank You for the cross,
thank You for the cross,
thank You for the cross, my friend.
(repeat)
And once again . . .

996 Geoff Bullock
© 1995 Word Music/CopyCare

1 **Jesus,**
God's righteousness revealed,
the Son of Man, the Son of God,
His kingdom comes.
Jesus, redemption's sacrifice,
now glorified, now justified,
His kingdom comes.

And His kingdom will know no end,
and its glory shall know no bounds,
for the majesty and power
of this kingdom's King has come,
and this kingdom's reign,
and this kingdom's rule,
and this kingdom's power
and authority,
Jesus, God's righteousness revealed.

2 Jesus, the expression of God's love,
   the grace of God, the word of God,
   revealed to us.
   Jesus, God's holiness displayed,
   now glorifed, now justified,
   His kingdom comes.
   And His kingdom will know no end . . .

997
Paul Oakley
© 1995 Kingsway's Thankyou Music

Jesus, lover of my soul,
all-consuming fire is in Your gaze.
Jesus, I want You to know
I will follow You all my days.
For no-one else in history is like You,
and history itself belongs to You.
Alpha and Omega, You have loved me,
and I will share eternity with You.
   It's all about You, Jesus,
   and all this is for You,
   for Your glory and Your fame.
   It's not about me,
   as if You should do things my way;
   You alone are God,
   and I surrender to Your ways.

998
Tanya Riches
© 1995 Tanya Riches/Hillsongs Australia/
Kingsway's Thankyou Music

1 **Jesus, what a beautiful name.**
   Son of God, Son of Man,
   Lamb that was slain.
   Joy and peace, strength and hope,
   grace that blows all fear away.
   Jesus, what a beautiful name.

2 Jesus, what a beautiful name.
   Truth revealed, my future sealed,
   healed my pain.
   Love and freedom, life and warmth,
   grace that blows all fear away.
   Jesus, what a beautiful name.

3 Jesus, what a beautiful name.
   Rescued my soul, my stronghold,
   lifts me from shame.
   Forgiveness, security, power and love,
   grace that blows all fear away.
   Jesus, what a beautiful name.

999
Nancy Gordon and Jamie Harvill
© 1994 Integrity's Hosanna! Music/
Kingsway's Thankyou Music

Jesus, You're my firm foundation,
I know I can stand secure;
Jesus, You're my firm foundation,
I put my hope in Your holy word,
I put my hope in Your holy word.

1 I have a living hope,
        (I have a living hope,)
   I have a future; (I have a future;)
   God has a plan for me,
        (God has a plan for me,)
   of this I'm sure,
   of this I'm sure.
        Jesus, You're my firm foundation . . .

2 Your word is faithful,
        (Your word is faithful,)
   mighty in power, (mighty in power,)
   God will deliver me,
        (God will deliver me,)
   of this I'm sure,
   of this I'm sure.
        Jesus, You're my firm foundation . . .

1000

Jarrod Cooper
© 1996 Sovereign Lifestyle Music

1 **King of kings, majesty,**
God of heaven living in me,
gentle Saviour, closest friend,
strong deliverer, beginning and end,
all within me falls at Your throne.
   Your majesty, I can but bow.
   I lay my all before You now.
   In royal robes I don't deserve
   I live to serve Your majesty.

2 Earth and heaven worship You,
love eternal, faithful and true,
who bought the nations,
   ransomed souls,
brought this sinner
   near to Your throne;
all within me cries out in praise.
   Your majesty, I can but bow.
   I lay my all before You now.
   In royal robes I don't deserve
   I live to serve Your majesty,
   I live to serve Your majesty.

1 Praise You in the morning,
praise You in the evening,
praise You when I'm young
   and when I'm old.
Praise You when I'm laughing,
praise You when I'm grieving,
praise You every season of the soul.
If we could see how much You're
      worth,
Your power, Your might,
   Your endless love,
then surely we would never cease
   to praise.
   Let everything that . . .

2 Praise You in the heavens,
joining with the angels,
praising You for ever and a day.
Praise You on the earth now,
joining with creation,
calling all the nations to Your praise.
If they could see how much You're
      worth,
Your power, Your might,
   Your endless love,
then surely they would never cease
   to praise.
   Let everything that . . .

1001

Matt Redman
© 1997 Kingsway's Thankyou Music

   Let everything that,
      everything that,
   everything that has breath
      praise the Lord,
   let everything that, everything that,
   everything that has breath
      praise the Lord.

1002

Noel and Tricia Richards
© 1996 Kingsway's Thankyou Music

1 **Love songs from heaven**
   are filling the earth,
bringing great hope to all nations.
Evil has prospered, but truth is alive;
in this dark world the light still shines.

2 Nothing has silenced
      this gospel of Christ;
it echoes down through the ages.
Blood of the martyrs
      has made Your church strong;
in this dark world the light still shines.

For You we live,
*   and for You we may die;*
through us may Jesus be seen.
For You alone we will offer our lives;
in this dark world our light will shine.

3 Let every nation
        be filled with Your song:
    this is the cry of Your people.
    We will not settle for anything less,
    in this dark world our light must shine.
    For You we live . . .

1003 Darlene Zschech
© 1993 Darlene Zschech/Hillsongs Australia/
Kingsway's Thankyou Music

My Jesus, my Saviour,
Lord, there is none like You.
All of my days I want to praise
the wonders of Your mighty love.
My comfort, my shelter,
tower of refuge and strength,
let every breath, all that I am,
never cease to worship You.
    Shout to the Lord all the earth, let us sing,
    power and majesty, praise to the King.
    Mountains bow down
        and the seas will roar
    at the sound of Your name.
    I sing for joy at the work of Your hands,
    for ever I'll love You, for ever I'll stand.
    Nothing compares to the promise
        I have in You.

1004 William Booth (1829–1912)
adapted Lex Loizides
© 1994 Kingsway's Thankyou Music

1 **O God of burning,**
        cleansing flame, send the fire!
    Your blood-bought gift today we claim:
        send the fire today!
    Look down and see this waiting host,
    and send the promised Holy Ghost;
    we need another Pentecost!
    Send the fire today,
    send the fire today!

2 God of Elijah, hear our cry:
        send the fire!
    And make us fit to live or die:
        send the fire today!
    To burn up every trace of sin,
    to bring the light and glory in,
    the revolution now begin!
    Send the fire today,
    send the fire today!

3 It's fire we want, for fire we plead:
        send the fire!
    The fire will meet our every need:
        send the fire today!
    For strength to always do what's right,
    for grace to conquer in the fight,
    for power to walk the world in white:
    send the fire today,
    send the fire today!

4 To make our weak heart strong
        and brave, send the fire!
    To live, a dying world to save:
        send the fire today!
    O see us on Your altar lay,
    we give our lives to You today,
    so crown the offering now, we pray:
    send the fire today,
    send the fire today,
    send the fire today!

1005 Rich Mullins
© 1988 Edward Grant Inc.

Our God is an awesome God,
He reigns from heaven above,
with wisdom, power and love,
our God is an awesome God.
(repeat)

1006

Martin Smith
© 1994 Curious? Music UK/
Kingsway's Thankyou Music

Over the mountains and the sea
Your river runs with love for me,
and I will open up my heart
and let the Healer set me free.
I'm happy to be in the truth
and I will daily lift my hands
for I will always sing
of when Your love came down, yeah.
I could sing of Your love for ever,
I could sing of Your love for ever,
I could sing of Your love for ever,
I could sing of Your love for ever.

Oh, I feel like dancing; it's foolishness,
    I know,
but when the world has seen the light,
they will dance for joy
        like we're dancing now.
I could sing of Your love ...

1007

Dan C Stradwick
© 1980 Scripture in Song/Integrity Music/
Kingsway's Thankyou Music

The Lord reigns, the Lord reigns,
the Lord reigns, let the earth rejoice,
let the earth rejoice, let the earth rejoice!
Let the people be glad
    that our God reigns.
(repeat)

1 A fire goes before Him
  and burns up all His enemies,
  the hills melt like wax
        at the presence of the Lord,
  at the presence of the Lord.
  The Lord reigns ...

2 The heavens declare His righteousness,
  the peoples see His glory;
  for You, O Lord are exalted
        over all the earth,
  over all the earth.

The Lord reigns, the Lord reigns,
the Lord reigns, let the earth rejoice,
let the earth rejoice, let the earth rejoice!
Let the people be glad
    that our God reigns.
our God reigns, our God reigns.

1008

Psalm 23
adapted Stuart Townend
© 1996 Kingsway's Thankyou Music

1 **The Lord's my shepherd,**
  I'll not want.
  He makes me lie in pastures green.
  He leads me by the still, still waters,
  His goodness restores my soul.
    And I will trust in You alone,
    and I will trust in You alone,
    for Your endless mercy follows me,
    Your goodness will lead me home.

  DESCANT
  I will trust, I will trust in You.
  I will trust, I will trust in You.
  Endless mercy follows me,
  goodness will lead me home.

2 He guides my ways in righteousness,
  and He anoints my head with oil,
  and my cup, it overflows with joy,
  I feast on His pure delights.
    And I will trust ...

3 And though I walk the darkest path,
  I will not fear the evil one,
  for You are with me,
        and Your rod and staff
  are the comfort I need to know.
    And I will trust ...

1009

Stuart Townend and Kevin Jamieson
© 1997 Kingsway's Thankyou Music

1 **The King of love is my delight,**
His eyes are fire, His face is light,
the First and Last, the Living One,
His name is Jesus.
And from His mouth
    there comes a sound
that shakes the earth
    and splits the ground,
and yet this voice is life to me,
the voice of Jesus.
And I will sing my songs of love,
calling out across the earth;
the King has come,
    the King of love has come.
And troubled minds
    can know His peace,
captive hearts can be released,
the King has come,
    the King of love has come.

2 My Lover's breath is sweetest wine,
I am His prize and He is mine;
how can a sinner know such joy?
Because of Jesus.
The wounds of love are in His hands,
the price is paid for sinful man;
accepted child, forgiven son,
because of Jesus.
And I will sing my songs of love . . .

And my desire is to have You near,
Lord, You know that You are welcome
    here.
Before such love, before such grace
I will let the walls come down.
And I will sing my songs of love . . .

1010

Andy Park
© 1994 Andy Park/Kingsway's Thankyou Music

1 **The Spirit of the sovereign Lord**
    is upon you,
because He has anointed you
    to preach good news.
The Spirit of the sovereign Lord
    is upon you,
because He has anointed you
    to preach good news.
He has sent you to the poor
    (this is the year),
to bind up the broken-hearted
    (this is the day),
to bring freedom to the captives
    (this is the year),
and to release the ones in darkness.
This is the year
    of the favour of the Lord,
this is the day
    of the vengeance of our God,
this is the year of the favour of the Lord,
this is the day
    of the vengeance of our God.

2 The Spirit of the sovereign Lord
    is upon us,
because He has anointed us
    to preach good news.
The Spirit of the sovereign Lord
    is upon us,
because He has anointed us
    to preach good news.
He will comfort all who mourn
    (this is the year),
He will provide for those who grieve
    (this is the day),
He will pour out the oil of gladness
    (this is the year),
instead of mourning you will praise.
This is the year . . .

1011
Paul Oakley
© 1995 Kingsway's Thankyou Music

1 **There's a place
where the streets shine**
with the glory of the Lamb.
There's a way we can go there,
we can live there beyond time.
*Because of You,
because of You,
because of Your love,
because of Your blood.*

2 No more pain, no more sadness,
no more suffering, no more tears.
No more sin, no more sickness,
no injustice, no more death.
*Because of You,
because of You,
because of Your love,
because of Your blood.
All our sins are washed away,
and we can live for ever,
now we have this hope
because of You.
Oh, we'll see You face to face,
and we will dance together
in the city of our God
because of You.*

3 There is joy everlasting,
there is gladness, there is peace.
There is wine everflowing,
there's a wedding, there's a feast.
Because of You . . .

1012
Robin Mark
© 1997 Daybreak Music Ltd

1 **These are the days of Elijah,**
declaring the word of the Lord:
and these are the days
of Your servant Moses,
righteousness being restored.
And though these are days
of great trial,
of famine and darkness and sword,
still we are a voice in the desert crying,
'Prepare ye the way of the Lord.'

*Behold He comes riding on the clouds,
shining like the sun at the trumpet call;
lift your voice, it's the year of jubilee,
out of Zion's hill salvation comes.*

2 These are the days of Ezekiel,
the dry bones becoming as flesh;
and these are the days
of Your servant David,
rebuilding the temple of praise.
These are the days of the harvest,
the fields are as white as the world,
and we are the labourers
in the vineyard,
declaring the word of the Lord.
Behold He comes . . .

1013
Reuben Morgan
© 1995 Reuben Morgan/Hillsongs Australia/
Kingsway's Thankyou Music

This is my desire, to honour You:
Lord, with all my heart I worship You.
All I have within me, I give You praise:
all that I adore is in You.
*Lord, I give You my heart,
I give You my soul;
I live for You alone.
Every breath that I take,
every moment I'm awake;
Lord, have Your way in me.*

1014
Stuart Townend
© 1997 Kingsway's Thankyou Music

1 **We have sung our songs of victory,**
we have prayed to You for rain;
we have cried for Your compassion
to renew the land again.
Now we're standing in Your presence
more hungry than before;
now we're on Your steps of mercy,
and we're knocking at Your door.

How long before You drench
the barren land?
How long before we see
Your righteous hand?
How long before Your name
is lifted high?
How long before the weeping
turns to songs of joy?

2 Lord, we know Your heart is broken
by the evil that You see,
and You've stayed
    Your hand of judgement
for You plan to set men free.
But the land is still in darkness,
and we've fled from what is right;
we have failed the silent children
who will never see the light.
    How long . . .

3 But I know a day is coming
when the deaf will hear His voice,
when the blind will see their Saviour,
and the lame will leap for joy,
when the widow finds a husband
who will always love His bride,
and the orphan finds a father
who will never leave her side.
    How long before Your glory
    lights the skies?
    How long before Your radiance
    lifts our eyes?
    How long before Your fragrance
    fills the air?
    How long before the earth resounds
    with songs of joy?

1015
Mark Altrogge
© 1997 People of Destiny International/
CopyCare

We sing Your mercies,
we sing Your endless praises,
we sing Your everlasting love.
We sing Your mercies,
we sing Your endless praise,
Sovereign One who died,
Sovereign One who died for us.

1 Should He who made the stars
be hung upon a tree?
And should the hands that healed
be driven through for me?
Should He who gave us bread
be made to swallow gall?
Should He who gave us breath and life
be slaughtered for us all?
    We sing Your mercies . . .

2 Should He who is the light
be cast into the dark?
and should the Lord of love
be pierced through His own heart?
Should He who called us friends
be deserted by us all?
Should He who lived a sinless life
be punished for our fall?
    We sing Your mercies . . .

1016
Matt Redman
© 1994 Kingsway's Thankyou Music

1 **When the music fades,**
all is stripped away
and I simply come;
longing just to bring
something that's of worth,
that will bless Your heart.
I'll bring You more than a song,
for a song in itself
is not what You have required.
You search much deeper within
through the way things appear,
You're looking into my heart.
    I'm coming back to the heart of worship,
    and it's all about You,
    all about You, Jesus.
    I'm sorry, Lord,
    for the thing I've made it,
    when it's all about You,
    all about You, Jesus.

2 King of endless worth,
no-one could express
how much You deserve.
Though I'm weak and poor,
all I have is Yours,
every single breath.
I'll bring You more than a song,
for a song in itself
is not what You have required.
You search much deeper within
through the way things appear,
You're looking into my heart.

I'm coming back to the heart of worship,
and it's all about You,
all about You, Jesus.
I'm sorry, Lord,
for the thing I've made it,
when it's all about You,
all about You, Jesus.

1018
Ian White
© 1997 Little Misty Music/
Kingsway's Thankyou Music

You are merciful to me,
You are merciful to me,
You are merciful to me, my Lord.
(repeat)

Every day my disobedience
grieves Your loving heart,
but then redeeming love breaks through,
and causes me to worship You.
Redeemer, (Redeemer,)
Saviour, (Saviour,)
healer, (healer,)
and friend, (and friend.)
Every day, (every day,)
renew my ways, (renew my ways,)
fill me with love, (fill me with love,)
that never ends, (that never ends.)
You are merciful to me . . .

1017
Paul Oakley
© 1996 Kingsway's Thankyou Music

Who is there like You,
and who else would give their life for me,
even suffering in my place?
And who could repay You?
All of creation looks to You,
and You provide for all You have made.

So I'm lifting up my hands,
lifting up my voice,
lifting up Your name,
and in Your grace I rest,
for Your love has come to me
and set me free.
And I'm trusting in Your word,
trusting in Your cross,
trusting in Your blood
and all Your faithfulness,
for Your power at work in me
is changing me.

1019
Dennis Jernigan
© 1981 Shepherd's Heart Music/
Sovereign Lifestyle Music

1 **You are my strength**
when I am weak,
You are the treasure that I seek,
You are my all in all;
seeking You as a precious jewel,
Lord, to give up I'd be a fool,
You are my all in all.
Jesus, Lamb of God,
worthy is Your name;
Jesus, Lamb of God,
worthy is Your name.

2 Taking my sin, my cross, my shame,
rising again, I bless Your name,
You are my all in all;
when I fall down You pick me up,
when I am dry You fill my cup,
You are my all in all.
Jesus, Lamb of God . . .

1020
Geoff Bullock
© 1992 Word Music/CopyCare

You rescued me, and picked me up,
a living hope of grace revealed,
a life transformed in righteousness,
O Lord, You have rescued me.
Forgiving me, You healed my heart,
and set me free from sin and death.
You brought me life, You made me whole,
O Lord, You have rescued me.

And You loved me before I knew You,
and You knew me for all time.
I've been created in Your image, O Lord.
And You bought me, and You sought me,
Your blood poured out for me;
a new creation in Your image, O Lord.
You rescued me,
You rescued me.

2 There's a shield in our hand
  and a sword at our side,
there's a fire in our spirit
  that cannot be denied;
as the Father has told us,
  for these You have died,
for the nations that gather before You.
And the ears of all men
need to hear of the Lamb
who was crucified,
who descended to hell
yet was raised up to reign
at the Father's side.
And the angels will cry . . .

1021
Robin Mark
© 1993 Daybreak Music Ltd

1 **You're the Lion of Judah,**
  the Lamb that was slain,
You ascended to heaven
  and evermore will reign;
at the end of the age
  when the earth You reclaim,
You will gather the nations before You.
And the eyes of all men
will be fixed on the Lamb
who was crucified,
for with wisdom and mercy
and justice You'll reign
at Your Father's side.
And the angels will cry: 'Hail the Lamb
who was slain for the world,
* rule in power.'*
And the earth will reply:
* 'You shall reign,*
King of all kings
* and the Lord of all Lords.'*

COPYRIGHT ADDRESSES

A & C Black (Publishers) Ltd, Howard Road, Eaton Socon, Huntingdon, Cambs PE19 3EZ

Alexander Copyright Trust, c/o S W Grant, 12 Lawrie Park Crescent, Sydenham, London SE26 6HD

Allen, F R, Barton Cottage, Station Road, Blockley, Glos GL56 9DT

American Catholic Press, 16160 South State Street, South Holland, IL 60473 USA

Archbishops' Council, the, Church House, Great Smith Street, London SW1P 3NZ

Ateliers et Presses de Taizé, F 71250 Taizé Community, France

Austin, M C and M M, 4 Burkes Close, Beaconsfield, Bucks HP9 1ES

Baptist Union of Great Britain, Baptist House, PO Box 44, 129 Broadway, Didcot, Oxon OX11 8RT

Barnes, J M, 15 South Canterbury Road, Canterbury, Kent CT1 3LH

Barrows, Cliff, 5000 Old Buncombe Road, Suite N, Greenville, SC 29609 USA

Bible Society, Stonehill Green, Westlea Down, Swindon SN5 7DG

Boosey and Hawkes, 295 Regent Street, London W1R 8JH

Brattle, David, 22 Thornhill Drive, Belfast BT5 7AW

Breitkopf und Härtel, Walkmuhlstrasse 52, D–65195, Wiesbaden, Germany

Bridge, Basil E, 124 Linacre Avenue, Sprowston, Norwich, Norfolk NR7 8JS

Browne, C M, 5 Avondale Road, Trowbridge, Wilts BA14 8QS

Burns, Edward J, Christ Church Vicarage, 19 Vicarage Close, Fulwood, Preston, Lancs PR2 8EG

Burt, Phil, 5 Gardner Road, Warton, Carnforth, Lancs LA5 9NY

Cassell Plc, Wellington House, 125 The Strand, London WC2R 0BB

Chance, K, GlaubenZentrum, Dr Heinrich Jasper-strasse 20, D–37581 Bad Gandersheim, Germany

Chatto and Windus, c/o Random House UK Ltd, 20 Vauxhall Bridge Road, London SW1V 2SA

Christian Fellowship of Columbia, 4600 Christian Fellowship Road, Columbia, MS 65203 USA

CopyCare, PO Box 77, Hailsham, East Sussex BN27 3EF

Crabtree, Roy, 7 St Anne's Court, St Anne's Gardens, Llandudno, Gwynedd LL30 1SD

Curwen & Sons Ltd, 8/9 Frith Street, London W1V 5TZ

Daybreak Music Ltd, Silverdale Road, Eastbourne, East Sussex BN20 7AB

Downs, Elinor, 44 Allandale Street, Boston, Massachusetts 02130 USA

Dudley-Smith, Timothy, 9 Ashlands, Ford, Salisbury, Wilts SP4 6DY

Dunkerley, Desmond, 23 Haslemere Road, Southsea, Portsmouth, Hants PO8 8BB

Dyke, Rev Elizabeth M, 29 Chalfont Close, Bedworth, Warks CV12 8PB

Ellel Ministries Ltd, Ellel Grange, Ellel, Lancaster LA2 0HN

Evans, Dilys, Tan-y-Coed, Uxbridge Square, Caernarfon, Gwynedd LL55 2RE

Fudge, Roland, High Grain, Austwick, Lancaster LA2 8AN

Gabriel Music Inc., PO Box 40999, Houston, TX 77284–0999 USA

GIA Publications Inc, 7404 S. Mason Avenue, Chicago, IL 60638 USA

Gould, D R, 34 Pollard Avenue, Horsham, West Sussex RH13 5HH

Harper, Jeanne, 16 Pightle Close, Harston, Cambridge CB2 5NN

Haynes, Stuart, 26 Fiveways Close, Cheddar, Somerset BS27 3DS

David Higham Associates, 5–8 Lower John Street, Golden Square, London W1R 4HA

High-Fye Music, Campbell Connelly & Co Ltd, 8/9 Frith Street, London W1V 5TZ

Hooke, Ruth, 10 Bridgeway, Lostock Hall, Preston, Lancs PR5 5YJ

Horrobin, Peter, Ellel Grange, Ellel, Carnforth, Lancs LA2 OHN

Hutchinson, G M E, 158 Lansdowne Road, Worcester, Worcs WR3 8JA

Hymns Ancient & Modern, St Mary's Works, St Mary's Plain, Norwich, Norfolk NR3 3BH

International Music Publications, Griffin House, 161 Hammersmith Road, London W6 8BS

InterVarsity Christian Fellowship, 5206 Main Street, PO Box 1400, Downers End, IL 60515 USA

Iona Community, Pearce Institute, 840 Govan Road, Glasgow G51 3UU

John Ireland Trust, 35 St Mary's Mansions, St Mary's Terrace, London W2 1SQ

Jackson, Francis, Nether Garth, Acklam, Moulton, Yorks YR7 9RG

Jones, R McCurdy, 22 Wentworth Road, Chilwell, Nottingham NG9 4FP

Jones, Ron, 2 Dean Avenue, Wallasey Village, Cheshire

Jubilate Hymns, c/o Mrs Merrilyn Williams, Southwick House, 4 Thorne Park Road, Chelston, Torquay TQ2 6RX

Kerr, B K M, Wayside Cottage, East Dean, Eastbourne, East Sussex BN20 0BP

Kingsway's Thankyou Music, PO Box 75, Eastbourne, East Sussex BN23 6NW

Leavers, Greg, 1 Haws Hill, Carnforth, Lancs LA5 9DD

Leosong Copyright Services Ltd, 7–8 Greenland Place, London NW1 OAP

Make Way Music Ltd, PO Box 263, Croydon, Surrey CR9 5AP

Kevin Mayhew Ltd, Buxhall, Stowmarket, Suffolk IP14 3DJ

Marsh, Dr John, 19 Clarence Park, Blackburn, Lancs BB2 7FA

Methodist Church Purposes, the Trustees for, Methodist Publishing House, 20 Ivatt Way, Peterborough, Cambs PE5 7PG

Meredith, Canon Roland, 1 Deanery Court, Broad Street, Bampton, Oxon OX18 2LY

National Christian Education Council, 1020 Bristol Road, Selly Oak, Birmingham B29 6LB

National Young Life Campaign, Spring Cottage, Spring Road, Leeds, West Yorks LF6 1AD

Novello Music Publishers, 8/9 Frith Street, London W1V 5TZ

OCP Publications, 5536 NE Hassolo, Portland, OR 97213, USA

OMF International, 2 Cluny Road, Singapore 1025, Republic of Singapore

Oxford University Press, Hymn Copyright Department, 70 Baker Street, London W1M 1DJ

Patch Music, c/o Peer Music, 8–14 Verulam Street, London WC1X 8LS

Pirie, Ed, Emmanuel Evangelical Church Office, 9–23 Marsham Street, London SW1P 3DW

PolyGram International Music Publishing Ltd, Bond House, 347–353 Chiswick High Road, Chiswick, London W4 4HS

Preston, Colin, 81 Howth Drive, Woodley, Reading, Berks

Restoration Music Ltd, PO Box 356, Leighton Buzzard, Beds LU7 8WP

Remission Music, 50 Parkview Crescent, Bentley, Walsall WS5 8TY

Richards, John, Renewal Servicing, PO Box 17, Shepperton, Middlesex TW17 8NU

Robinson, Joan, 47 Woodlands Road, Beaumont, Lancaster LA1 2EH

Sanchez Jr, Pete, 4723 Hickory Downs, Houston, TX 77084 USA

Scott, Alexander, 4 Anthony Close, Colchester, Essex CO4 4LD

Scripture Union, 207–9 Queensway, Bletchley, Bucks MK2 2EB

Serious Music UK, PO Box 31, 3360 AA, Sliedrecht, The Netherlands

SGM International, Radstock House, 3 Eccleston Street, London SW1W 9LZ

Silver, Andy, Bell House Farm, Dalton, Burton-in-Kendal, Lancs LA6 1NN

SIM–UK, Wetheringsett Manor, Wetheringsett, Stowmarket, Suffolk IP14 5QX

Simmonds, Clive, School House, 81 Clapham Road, Bedford MK41 7RB

Sound Impression, 44 Adelaide Road, Chichester, West Sussex PO19 4NF

Sovereign Lifestyle Music Ltd, PO Box 356, Leighton Buzzard, Beds LU7 8WP

Sovereign Music UK, PO Box 356, Leighton Buzzard, Beds LU7 8WP

SPCK, Holy Trinity Church, Marylebone Road, London NW1 4DU

Stainer & Bell Ltd, PO Box 110, Victoria House, 23 Gruneisen Road, London N3 1DZ

Taylor, Glyn, 59 Baldwin Avenue, Eastbourne, East Sussex

Tehillah Trust, 49 St Mary's Park, Nailsea, Bristol BS19 2RP

Trustees of the late Dr Basil Harwood Settlement Trust, Public Trust Office, Stewart House, 24 Kingsway, London WC2B 6JX

Tyrrell, J, 41 Minster Road, Godalming, Surrey GU7 1SR

Waif Productions Ltd, 1 North Worple Way, Mortlake, London SW14 8QG

Josef Weinberger Ltd, 12–14 Mortimer Street, London W1N 7RD

Windswept Pacific Music Ltd, Orchard House, Tylers Green, Cuckfield, West Sussex RH17 5DZ

INDEX OF FIRST LINES

Titles which differ from first lines are shown in italics.

I will wait upon the Lord – 317
I will worship – 991
I worship You, almighty God – 864
I'd rather have Jesus – 319
I'll go in the strength of the Lord – 862
I'll praise my maker – 320
I'm accepted, I'm forgiven – 321
I'm confident of this very thing – 322
I'm for ever grateful – 969
I'm forgiven – 270
I'm living my life for Jesus – 863
I'm not ashamed to own my Lord – 323
I'm not ashamed to own my Lord – 992
I'm redeemed, yes I am – 324
I'm special – 325
I've found a friend – 352
I've got peace like a river – 353
If My people who bear My name – 318
If you are encouraged – 861
Immanuel, O Immanuel – 326
Immortal, invisible – 327
Immortal Love – 328
In Christ there is no east or west – 329
In full and glad surrender – 330
In heavenly armour – 639
In heavenly love abiding – 331
In Him we live and move – 332
In loving-kindness Jesus came – 333
In moments like these – 334
In my generation – 859
In my life, Lord, be glorified – 335
In my need Jesus found me – 336
In the bleak mid-winter – 337
In the cross of Christ I glory – 338
In the Lord I'll be ever thankful – 865
In the name of Jesus – 339
In the presence of Your people – 341
In the streets of every city – 866
In the tomb so cold – 340
In Your arms of love – 869
Infant holy – 342
Is anyone thirsty? – 867
Is this the Church of our God? – 343
Isn't He beautiful – 344
It came upon the midnight clear – 345
It is a thing most wonderful – 346
It is no longer I that liveth – 350

It is the cry of my heart – 868
It is to You – 993
It may be at morn – 347
It only takes a spark – 348
It passeth knowledge – 349
It's rising up – 994
It's Your blood – 351

Jehovah Jireh – 354
Jesus, at Your name – 355
Jesus calls us – 359
Jesus Christ – 995
Jesus Christ is alive today – 358
Jesus Christ is risen today – 357
Jesus Christ is the Lord of all – 871
Jesus Christ, our great Redeemer – 356
Jesus, God's righteousness revealed – 996
Jesus has sat down – 360
Jesus, how lovely You are – 361
Jesus, I am resting, resting – 362
Jesus, I love You – 363
Jesus, I worship You – 364
Jesus is King – 366
Jesus is Lord – 367
Jesus is Lord of all – 365
Jesus is our God – 870
Jesus is the Lord – 368
Jesus is the name we honour – 870
Jesus, Jesus, holy and anointed One – 872
Jesus, Jesus, Jesus – 370
Jesus, Jesus, You are my Lord – 369
Jesus, Lamb of God – 371
Jesus, let me meet You in Your word – 902
Jesus lives – 373
Jesus, lover of my soul – 372
Jesus, lover of my soul – 997
Jesus my Lord – 374
Jesus, name above all names – 375
Jesus, Prince and Saviour – 377
Jesus put this song into our hearts – 376
Jesus, restore to us again – 873
Jesus shall reign – 379
Jesus shall take the highest honour – 378
Jesus, stand among us – 380
Jesus, stand among us – 381
Jesus, take me as I am – 382
Jesus, take Your rightful place – 875